SELLING YOUR FATHER'S BONES

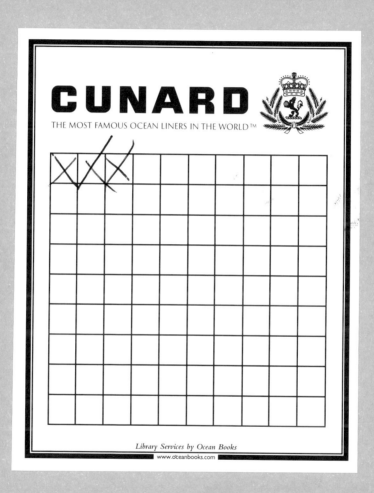

SELLING YOUR FATHER'S BONES

The Epic Fate of the American West

BRIAN SCHOFIELD

Harper
Press

Harper*Press*
An imprint of HarperCollins*Publishers*
77–85 Fulham Palace Road,
Hammersmith, London W6 8JB

www.harpercollins.co.uk

Published by Harper*Press* in 2008

Brian Schofield asserts the moral right to
be identified as the author of this work

A catalogue record for this book
is available from the British Library

ISBN 978-0-00-724292-4

Maps drawn by HL Studios
Illustration © Geoff Westby

Set in Minion

Printed and bound in Great Britain by Clays Ltd, St Ives plc

For my grandfather

CONTENTS

LIST OF ILLUSTRATIONS

'*I believe …that sooner or later … somewhere … somehow …
we must settle with the world and make payment for what we
have taken*'

The Lone Ranger's Creed

PROLOGUE

AS THE SUN glowed red across the grassland, a group of children headed away from the village, through the willow trees, to squeeze a few more games from the fading daylight. The boys, mimicking their fathers, played with sticks and bones along the banks of the winding creek, their shrieks fading into the great expanse of the valley – until a chill cut through the air, and it was time to light a fire. The gang gathered wood and huddled close to the flames. Then, as an unfamiliar presence entered the circle of light, they fell to frozen silence. 'Two men came there wrapped in grey blankets. They stood close, and we saw they were white men.'

The youngsters bolted towards the village in a panic, but when they looked back, the men in the grey blankets had disappeared – and they were soon forgotten as the games began again. Bed-time came, and the children lay down without sharing this unsettling sight with their elders.

That night, the village held a celebration, to mark a day of rest and calm, and good hunting amongst the dense herds of the grasslands. The seven hundred Nez Perce were many miles from home, they'd been travelling for almost two months to reach this riverbank, and they had still further yet to travel – but today, at least, they were at peace, and for that they gave thanks. The warriors paraded through the encampment, singing and drumming in the firelight, their blustering leader encouraging all to relax and enjoy the respite. Elsewhere, a younger chief tended to his own responsibilities, for the young and the old of the camp, the frail and the enfeebled. It was past midnight when the carousing ended, and the valley fell silent.

One hundred and eighty-three United States infantrymen crouched in the darkness and waited. The sleeping village was but a few hundred yards away, the embers of its fires still glowing, while the army shivered on the sloping meadow above, their discipline holding in the bleak, thin night – no cigarettes lit, no rifles dropped, not a sound. Hours passed. The dew soaked easily through the troopers' threadbare uniforms, tightening the vice of cold. One man struck a match, and was slapped and shushed back into darkness by the soldiers around him.

The sounds of dogs barking and babies crying drifted over the willows and rushes from the dozing village. Just before dawn, a few women emerged from their tepees to refuel the campfires, enjoy a brief gossip and head back to their warm beds. And still the soldiers watched and waited.

At the very first greying of the sky, the troops began to move through the scrubland that lay between the high meadow and the riverbank, crawling and crouching forward, hiding behind the shallow rolls in the earth. A single line of men crept over the sodden ground – then stopped dead. Across the creek, an elderly man had emerged yawning from his lodge, cheerfully accepting that his sleep was complete. Mounting his waiting horse, the elder set off slowly towards the sloping meadow, to check on the village's grazing herd. His eyes were beginning to wear with time, and he peered into the half-light as his horse forded the creek and strolled through the morning mist – heading straight towards the waiting army.

Fear coursed through the troops as the lone rider wandered closer to their ranks, a hundred yards distance shading to fifty, then thirty, twenty – and still the old man, blessed with a morning to himself, saw no sign of the long, thin line of rifles trained upon him. Ahead, lost in the mist, hearts raced and nerves strained. A cluster of untrained men, callow volunteers, were wound tightest of all – the old man was riding straight for the cleft in the earth where the five lay. He was just ten yards away now. Still he rode on, humming into the lifting gloom. Huddled against the soil, the volunteers heard each footstep approach, battling to summon their courage and keep their senses. The gap closed, and closed, barely five yards now.

The young men, breathless with panic, snapped. Leaping to their feet, they raised their rifles. Across the glistening valley, the deer and the antelope, the buffalo and the coyotes scattered into the distance, away from the echoing crack of gunfire.

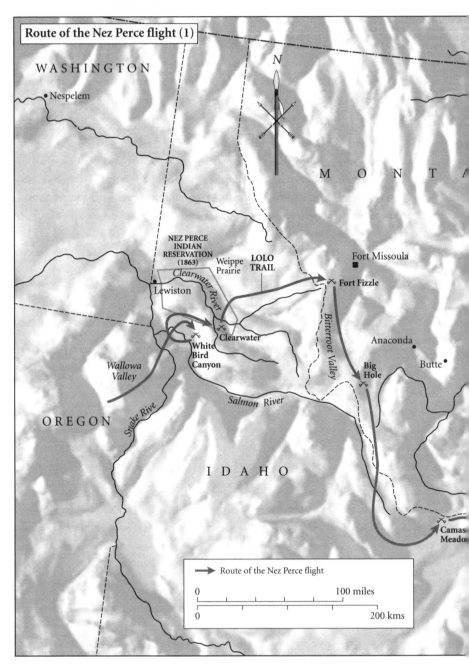

Route of the Nez Perce flight (1)

WASHINGTON

Nespelem

N

M O N T A

NEZ PERCE
INDIAN
RESERVATION
(1863)

Weippe
Prairie

LOLO
TRAIL

Fort Missoula

Clearwater River

Lewiston

Fort Fizzle

White
Bird
Canyon

Clearwater

Bitterroot Valley

Anaconda

Butte

Wallowa
Valley

Big
Hole

OREGON

Snake River

Salmon River

I D A H O

Camas
Meado

Route of the Nez Perce flight

0   100 miles

0   200 kms

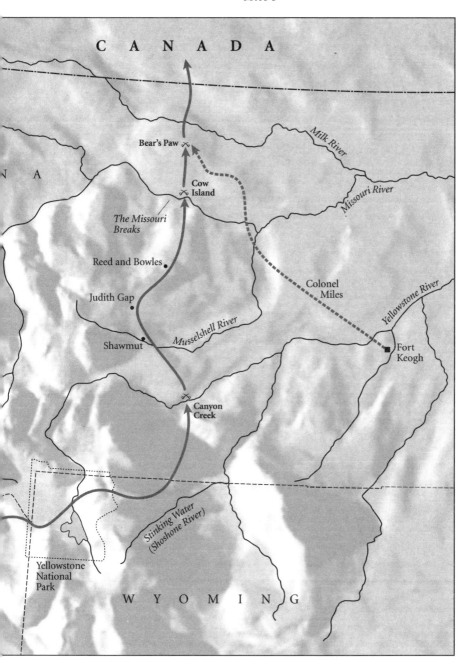

CANADA

Milk River

Bear's Paw

Cow
Island

The Missouri
Breaks

Missouri River

Reed and Bowles

Colonel
Miles

Judith Gap

Yellowstone River

Musselshell River

Shawmut

Fort
Keogh

Canyon
Creek

Stinking Water
(Shoshone River)

Yellowstone
National
Park

WYOMING

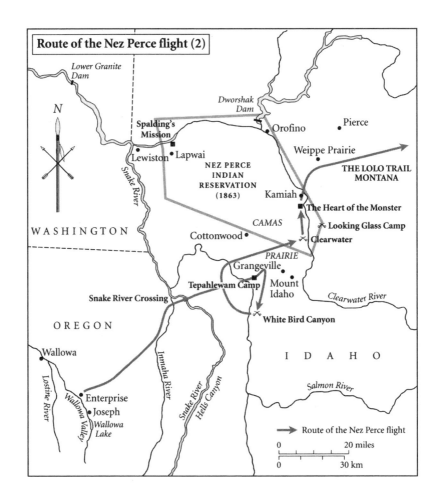

Route of the Nez Perce flight (2)

Lower Granite Dam

N

Dworshak Dam

Pierce

Spalding's Mission

Orofino

Weippe Prairie

Lewiston • Lapwai

NEZ PERCE INDIAN RESERVATION (1863)

THE LOLO TRAIL MONTANA

Snake River

Kamiah

The Heart of the Monster

WASHINGTON

CAMAS

Looking Glass Camp

Cottonwood

Clearwater

PRAIRIE

Grangeville

Snake River Crossing

Tepahlewam Camp

Mount Idaho

Clearwater River

OREGON

White Bird Canyon

Wallowa

Imnaha River

I D A H O

Lostine River

Enterprise

Joseph

Wallowa Lake

Wallowa Valley

Snake River Hells Canyon

Salmon River

Route of the Nez Perce flight

0   20 miles

0   30 km

CHAPTER ONE

HOMELAND

'These persons inculcate a sanctimonious reverence for the customs of their ancestors; that whatsoever they did, must be done through all time; that reason is a false guide'

THOMAS JEFFERSON, third President of the United States

'I belong to the earth out of which I came'

TOOHOOLHOOLZOTE, Nez Perce leader

THIS IS HOW the people came to be.

Coyote was helping the salmon swim up the Columbia River, to ensure everyone would have plenty of fish to eat, when he first heard the shouts:

'Why are you bothering with that? Everyone's gone, the monster has them.'

The meadowlark told Coyote that everyone had been swallowed by the giant monster, to which he replied, 'That is where I must go, too.' He bathed his fur, to ensure he was as tasty as possible, and tied himself to three mountains with long ropes. On his back he put a

1

pack containing five stone knives, some pitch and a fire-making kit. He then walked over the ridge to see the vast body of the monster stretching into the distance, and shouted his challenge: 'Oh Monster, we are going to inhale each other!'

'You go first,' replied the monster, and Coyote breathed in with all his power, trying to swallow the monster, but could only make the beast quiver and shake a little. Next came the monster's turn, and he breathed in like a roaring wind, lifting Coyote through the air towards him. As he flew, Coyote left camas roots and serviceberry bushes in the ground, saying, 'We are near the time when the human beings will come, and they will be glad of these.'

Coyote flew into the monster's mouth, and began walking through its body, past the bones of fallen friends, asking the living for directions to the fiend's heart. From the shadows, Bear rushed at him, but Coyote shouted, 'So! You're only aggressive to me?' and kicked him on the nose. Then, as he went deeper, Rattlesnake bristled at him: 'So you are only vicious to me?' said Coyote, stamping on the snake's head, flattening it for good.

When he reached the heart, he started a fire with his flint, and smoke began to pour from all the monster's orifices. 'Coyote, let me cast you out!' begged the agonized monster, but the tricky Coyote reminded the fiend that he'd just swallowed a pillar of the local community, with serious responsibilities, who couldn't be seen to be covered in vomit or phlegm: 'Oh yes, and let it be said that he who was cast out is officiating in the distribution of salmon!'

'Well, then leave through my nose.'

'And will they not say the same?'

'My ears?'

'Ha! "Here is earwax officiating in the distribution of food!"'

'By the back door?'

'Not a chance.'

By now the monster was writhing in pain. Coyote began to cut away at his heart, breaking first one stone knife on the flesh, then another, then three, four, five. Finally he leapt on the heart and tore it away with his bare hands, killing the beast. In its death throes, the monster opened all its orifices, and everyone ran out, kicking the bones of their dead neighbours ahead of them. The muskrat, unwisely, chose to use the rear exit, and it closed tight on his tail, stripping it of hair forever.

Once everyone was out, Coyote sprinkled the blood of the monster on the bones of the dead, bringing them back to life, then he began to carve up the monster's flesh, spreading it across the distant lands, towards the sunrise and sunset, the warmth and cold. And wherever the flesh came to rest, there arose the destiny of a people – the Coeur d'Alêne to the north, Cayuse to the west, Crow to the east, the Pend d'Oreille, Salish, Blackfoot, Sioux, until people were destined to cover the wide lands, and nothing more remained of the monster.

Then Coyote's oldest friend, Fox, pointed out the beautiful, bountiful land where they were standing, and said: 'But you have given nothing to this place!'

'Why did you not tell me earlier?' snorted Coyote. 'Bring me some water.'

He washed his hands, and sprinkled the bloody water around where he was standing, sealing the destined arrival of one last people: 'You may be small, because I neglected you, but you will be powerful. Now, only a short time away, will be the coming of the human race.'

It seems we'll never know the precise moment when man first reached North America. The most mainstream pre-historical consensus, though, is that the first arrivals poured over the Bering land bridge from northern Asia around 13,000 years ago, chasing the mammoths, mastodons and giant bison to extinction as they went.

The local archaeological evidence, of arrowheads, rock art and cooked animal bones, points to the earliest population of the Columbia Plateau, the inland mountain and forest watershed of the great Pacific-bound river, as dating back at least 11–12,000 years. As tribal memory tells it, one of the earliest names for the first people of the plateau was Cupnitpelu, The Emerging or Walking Out People. One story recalls that the animals met to discuss the impending arrival of man; those that decided to help him, such as the salmon and the buffalo, stayed, but those that chose not to help, such as the woolly mammoth and short-nosed bear, left for good.

Once in situ, the Columbia Plateau's residents certainly played their part in what was probably the most remarkable cultural explosion in human history, as the North American continent began to throw up a wildly diverse wave of new civilizations, each forged by the demands of their surroundings and rendered unique by this capacious land. From the proto-socialism of the Pueblos to the senatorial politics of the New York Iroquois, from the conspicuous, slave-based wealth of some Pacific coast communities to the eternal fires of the Mississippian temple-mound faith, the range, fluidity and distinctiveness of these cultures would fill several lifetimes' study. It's estimated that more than six hundred distinct and autonomous societies were in place in Canada and North America by the fifteenth century, speaking a range of at least 250 mutually unintelligible tongues, subdivided many times by dialect.

In the eastern Columbia plateau, in the land surrounding the Snake River, one language group formed around the Sahaptin dialect – and at the centre of the linguistic region lay a loose community of families and bands, dominating the area where the wide Snake, Salmon and Clearwater rivers converge. They came to call themselves Nimiipuu – meaning We, The People.

The Nimiipuu way of life was never trapped in aspic, but was, rather, in constant development and amendment; nevertheless, a snapshot of that lifestyle in the centuries prior to the first approaches of the white man can illuminate a vital, enviable culture. Semi-

*Nimiipuu petroglyphs on the banks of the Snake River,
thought to be 9–11,000 years old.*

nomadic, the Nimiipuu moved about their varied homeland in a
seasonal round trip, each village band – only loosely connected to
one another, in a friendship recognized as neither tribal nor national
– moving to their favoured camping spot to perform each task in the
annual natural cycle. There were as many as seventy of these village
groups scattered across the homeland, very rarely reaching three
hundred members and often much smaller, each with a recognized
home base and other seasonal outposts. A leader controlled each
band, but with very conditional authority – individual freedom was
highly valued and the right to do your own thing was well protected.

That annual natural cycle, essential for the survival of a hunter-
gatherer culture, was revered in ceremony and song, providing the
basis for all endeavour. With the first melt of spring it was time to
head to the alpine meadows and harvest the freshly exposed edible
root plants; as June approached the salmon spawn beckoned, and

fishing platforms and trapping weirs, known as wallowas, needed building at the most bountiful rapids along the homeland's rivers; in the height of summer the camas, a kind of wild garlic, bulged beneath lush, wide-open prairies, and the Nimiipuu gathered on the grasslands for weeks of socializing and harvesting; in fall the deer and elk were at their most active and the hunters would disappear into the high country for days in pursuit, while closer to home the serviceberries and huckleberries needed picking and drying. But the long, fierce winter was perhaps the most remarkable season; having dried and stored food in preparation, the Nimiipuu would gather at the base of the lowest, mildest valleys in extended A-framed matting lodges, known as longhouses (sometimes over thirty metres long) to see the snows out together, the families sleeping along the edge of the lodge, with fires burning in the middle. It was a time to make and repair clothes and tools, teach children crafts, and for the elders to tell the young people stories – stories of an earlier time, when people and animals conversed, when the lessons and rules of inhabiting the earth were learned, and the mischievous, capricious Coyote ruled the roost.

It was most certainly not a life of ease, but the Nimiipuu were blessed with a bountiful and ceaselessly beautiful territory, of clean, well-stocked rivers, forests dense with game and plentiful meadows, and their comparative natural wealth and subsequent inclination towards openness, friendliness and, where possible, peace was well captured by one of their earliest non-Indian friends, the historian L. V. McWhorter, in 1952: 'They were the wilderness gentry of the Pacific Northwest.'

One of the most oft-repeated assertions when modern Nimiipuu discuss their ancestors is that they had no religion in the compartmentalized, Sunday Service meaning; instead they possessed an all-encompassing way of life, in which devotional acts and the actions required for living were inseparable. Spirituality was recognized in everyday moments, such as greeting dawn in prayer or song; in celebrations of the various significant events in the natural calendar, such as the arrival of the salmon or the ripening of the camas roots; and a child's developing capacity to participate in the life of the band was also sanctified in a series of rites, such as a girl's first outing to gather roots or a boy's first hunting expedition.

The most significant and revealing of these rites was the spirit quest, the search for a *wyakin*, or protective spirit. After several years of preparatory conversations with the elders, each Nimiipuu child (when aged from around nine to fifteen) would head away from the lodges and into the wilderness, without food or water, to begin a lonely, cold vigil for the arrival of their personal *wyakin*. Sitting alone on a mountain-top or outcrop sometimes for days on end, they would seek the revelation of a source of spiritual strength, an image, sometimes real, sometimes coming in a dream or hunger-induced hallucination, that filled their consciousness and left them certain that protection was being offered – an eagle soaring above them, a bear crossing the horizon, a passing hummingbird, rain falling in the distance. Blessed with this vision, they stumbled back home, now in personal and private possession of a supernatural guardian, to whom they could appeal in times of tribulation, effort and, for some, war.

The *wyakin* quest offers us today a powerfully illuminating vision: of a Nimiipuu world view in which everything within their lands possessed a spiritual centre. Protection was not the preserve of angels or divinities, because spirits resided in creatures, rivers, land forms, weather patterns, all of creation. And to be connected to that natural order, partly revealed in a knowledge of the patterns and foibles of the local environment on which survival depended, partly in your respect for your spiritual kinship with all nature, was to be a Nimiipuu. The band leader whose eloquence would earn him unwelcome fame, Young Joseph, expressed this state of permanent communion best:

As the Nez Perce man wandered through the forest the moving trees whispered to him and his heart swelled with the song of the swaying pine. He looked through the green branches and saw white clouds drifting across the blue dome, and he felt the song of the clouds. Each bird twittering in the branches, each water-fowl among the reeds or on the surface of the lake, spoke its intelligible message to his heart; and as he looked into the sky and saw the high-flying birds of passage, he knew their flight was made strong by the uplifted voices of ten thousand birds of the meadow, forest and lake, and his heart, fairly in tune with all this, vibrated with the songs of its fullness.

In a time of great stress, he reduced this sentiment to its essence: 'The earth and myself are of one mind.'

This affiliation to the earth was redoubled by the prominent position that ancestors held in Nimiipuu culture. Referred to often in ceremony and conversation, commemorated in careful genealogy and in the passing on of names, possessions and skills, the ancestors were a constant presence in the villages, with those who have passed on serving both as an example in life and a familiar face in death. Nez Perce spiritual leader Horace Axtell received this explanation from an elder: 'He said, "This is what we do. We look at these tracks laid by our ancestors and we follow them to where they are now. These tracks lead us to the Good Land, The Good Place, where all Indians go after they have spent their time on this earth."'

The spiritual power of songs, prayers, dances – and of everyday actions such as berry picking or salmon fishing – thus sprang from two sources, the affiliation to the spirit forces of creation and also the connection, by repetition of their actions, words, names and tunes, with the past Nimiipuu – as Axtell observes, 'the reason our spirituality is so strong is because it comes from our old people, our old ancestors'.

This tradition contributed greatly to the Nimiipuu's most historically significant shared characteristic: their attachment to their homelands, to the sparkling landscapes of the Wallowa, Snake, Clearwater and Salmon valleys. If your route to the Good Place is in your father's footsteps, where else can you live but in his home? And, if the spirits of your ancestors are constantly among you, how much more sacred are the lands in which they are buried – land not demarked by a cluster of wooden crosses and a picket fence, but by the entire area in which your ancestors are part of the spiritual community, a community of which you are also a member? Persuading non-Indian visitors to comprehend this unbreakable bond with a specific area of land and water has always been difficult. Chief Seattle, from another Pacific Northwest tribe, the Dwamish, said the following to a white interloper in 1855:

> You must teach your children that the ground beneath their feet is the ashes of our grandparents. So that they will respect the land, tell your children what we have taught our children, that the earth is our mother. Whatever befalls the earth befalls the children of the earth. If you spit upon the ground you spit upon yourselves. Our dead never forget the beautiful world that gave them being.

The Crow chief Curley was forced to make a similar point when trying to preserve the remnants of his people's homelands in 1912, telling white people who wanted the land for cultivation and enrichment: 'You will have to dig down through the surface before you can find nature's earth, as the upper portion is Crow. The land, as it is, is my blood and my dead.'

The homeland was inseparable from both individual growth and community life. Personal wisdom was acquired not only through the ancestors' stories and skills, but through direct experience of the landscape, the seasonal whims and the interrelations of the flora and fauna, that both dictated survival and taught the young Nimiipuu their inseparable link to what modern Native American thinker Donald L. Fixico calls 'the Natural Democracy' of the home landscape – 'This democracy is based on respect. In this belief, all things are equally important. Where a native person grows up is relevant to how one understands all things around him or her … and this set of surroundings becomes fixed in the mind like reference points for later in life.' From a community perspective, the homeland conferred humility: its encapsulation of the past, present and future of the Nimiipuu serving as a reminder from dawn to dusk that individual fulfilment took second place to the continuation of a narrative of which your life was a small but integral part.

It's important not to romanticize excessively the Nimiipuu's relationship with the natural world, as many sympathetic chroniclers of Native America have. The image of the American Indian as the irreproachable steward of an unsullied continent is a powerful and popular one – and one that has also been ferociously challenged in recent years. The Nimiipuu, of course, were human beings, inclined towards improving their lives and capable of changing their surroundings, and they affected their landscape through hunting, harvest, burning and grazing. But what seems certain is that not just their spirituality but their survival *did* depend on a cautious management of the naturally occurring flora and fauna around them. As numerous tribal oral histories testify, if you didn't let enough salmon escape the fish traps, there'd be nothing in those traps in three years' time. Hunt elk while they were carrying or caring for foals and there would be fewer elk the following year.

But it also seems clear that in this independent era there was little conflict between the tribe's stated values and their material ambitions, thanks to a luxury of space – in the years just prior to the arrival of the white man the Nimiipuu are estimated to have numbered from four to six thousand people, enjoying near-exclusive occupation of around thirteen million acres of land. The defining characteristic of the Nimiipuu, in terms of their environmental impact, was simple lack of numbers – they were at a point on the curve where their actions, though crucial to their immediate locality and their own survival, were not likely to shatter entire ecosystems. As a local anthropologist put it to me: 'It doesn't really matter if you run a few hundred buffalo off a cliff, if you only do it once a year.'

Then, of course, everything would change. And to question the sincerity of a culture's core values because they were not too severely tested until you came along seems churlish, at best – particularly as you arrived uninvited.

For the Nimiipuu the first impact of the European invasion of the Americas was largely a benign one – the reintroduction of the horse. Despite their prominence in the mythical West, horses had in fact disappeared from the continent at the same time the first spear point had swept through it, the attractions of protein outweighing load-bearing capacity in those early hunters' estimation.

Columbus then brought horses to Hispaniola on his second Atlantic crossing, the Spanish left many behind on their subsequent murderous ramblings through Mexico, and by the early eighteenth century the burgeoning mustang herds, and European concepts of domesticating and riding horses, had reached the Columbia Plateau. The ever-adaptable Nimiipuu rapidly became expert riders and breeders, developing a herd numbered in thousands, greatly expand-ing the range of their endeavours. Larger groups could now travel further afield in search of game and trade, over the rough crossing routes of the Bitterroot Mountains into modern-day Montana, onwards to the wide open Big Hole Valley, still further east to the eerie, steaming landscapes of Yellowstone, north into the great plains of the buffalo tribes. New skills were learned, such as covering lodges in buffalo hides, friendships and intermarrying relationships were strengthened, for example with the Salish people to the east, and military rivalries sprang up with once-distant enemies, now rivals for the bounty of the hunting grounds. The arrival of the horse, the rifle and the East Coast Pilgrims had greatly destabilized Native America's already fractious territorial arrangements, with many tribes dominoing west, while others expanded rapidly with their new tools of war, and as the Nimiipuu fought their share of conflicts with raiders and land-grabbers the tribe's warrior culture developed rapidly. Bravery in battle had been a rich source of male identity in pedestrian times, but now that the Nimiipuu were a horse people, the ceremonies of war grew more regular, the traditions of scalp-taking and counting coups (getting close enough to an opponent to touch him, then retreating unharmed) became more ingrained across the Northwest and the prestige of conflict grew ever more alluring to the young and the fearless. The Nimiipuu became proud of their reputation as one of the toughest and smartest martial opponents in the region, sharpening the tactics of warfare and horsemanship that they would later rely on for their very survival.

Around the end of the eighteenth century, during an otherwise unremarkable skirmish in the eastern buffalo fields, a Nimiipuu woman was captured by a raiding tribe and taken north to Canada, where she encountered proof of a long-rumoured apparition – white faces, thick beards and strong medicine. She was well cared for by the trappers and fur traders she encountered, and, fatefully, returned to her village by 1805. Without her elderly recollection that white people were kind and harmless, the seven half-starved men who stumbled into a Nimiipuu camas-gathering camp in the autumn of that year might well have met the fate that many of the village leaders prescribed for them – a swift dispatch. The Nez Perce are not the only tribe in the American West to recall, with bleak humour, that life might have been a great deal simpler if they'd only decided to fatally hinder the Lewis and Clark expedition, rather than graciously help it.

William Clark and Meriwether Lewis had been challenged by President Thomas Jefferson to find a route from the Mississippi to the Pacific Ocean, ostensibly to uncover the geographical and biological wonders of the continent but, in reality, to open up territory to the fur trade and establish nautical links with Asia. Twenty-eight years after achieving independence from Britain, the United States was now engaged in an old-fashioned mercantile struggle with the mother country for control of its hinterland's resources, and packing the West with fur trappers who had an easy sales route to the Orient seemed the best way to squeeze the giant British trading enterprise the Hudson's Bay Company (an enemy larger and better resourced than the juvenile US government) up into Canada, or even into the sea. Jefferson had struck a mighty blow against the British in 1803 when Napoleon had sold him 800,000 square miles of land between the Mississippi and the Rockies for $15 million. When Lewis and Clark's Corps of Discovery expedition set off west in May 1804 it had thus become a much grander, nation-building enterprise – the United States had just more than doubled in size, without a clue what resources, or peoples, most of its new hinterland possessed.

The Corps of Discovery's stumbling progress towards the Pacific has, in many conflicting ways, become a defining image in the creation of America. The heroism, fortitude and sheer bloody-mindedness of the party are beyond dispute, as they paddled against the current of the Missouri for five months, saw out a blinding sub-Arctic winter on its banks, crossed the armour-plated spine of the Rocky Mountains, coped with rattlesnake bites, grizzly bear attacks, dysentery, malaria, starvation and more. Equally certain is that the western wilderness would have eaten them alive and spat out the bones without the help, sustenance and advice of the many Native peoples they encountered on the way, including the Mandan, Dakota, Oto and Shoshone, a fact Lewis and Clark often acknowledged in their famous travel journals. But the exchange of gifts with these peoples, the smoking of pipes, the borrowing of guides and horses, the cheerful demonstrations of such European innovations as the magnet and the magnifying glass, obscured the plain truth – Lewis and Clark were casing the joint.

By 1804 Jefferson had persuaded America's leaders that the salvation of their new country would be space. A generous excess of land would be capable of dissipating the increasingly crowded and industrialized eastern seaboard into a simple, spread out and morally upstanding agrarian culture, preventing the decline into European-style fan-fluttering dilettantism with a national backbone of honest, hard-working farming families. 'The small land holders are the most precious part of the state,' he declared, and the greater the area these people could occupy, the greater their bracing influence on America's character. The wealth of evidence that Lewis and Clark would secure, that the lands both within and beyond the new American territories were performing precisely that role already – but for someone else – was never going to act as a deterrent to expansion.

His outriders were themselves on the brink of death (not for the first time) when they reached the Nimiipuu. William Clark and six other men had gone ahead of the main expedition party to search for the Lolo Trail, an ancient route over the sprawling massif of the Bitterroot Mountains that would hopefully lead them onto the Columbia River and a downstream drift to the coast. The expedition's previous babysitters, the Shoshone people, had warned them that the path was rough, obscured by tree fall and landslides, and sorely lacking in edible game, but Clark was undeterred. Eleven days later his men were eating their dogs, horses, even candles; they were ravaged by sickness, cold and exhaustion, and facing defeat at the hands of what one member described as 'the most terrible mountains I ever beheld'. As they fell out of the forest and onto the camas grounds of the Wieppe Prairie, it is perhaps understandable that the Nimiipuu who found them and took them into camp concluded, from their unkempt beards, ravenous appetites and pungent lack of hygiene, that these visitors were half man, half dog.

This camp was under the guidance of Twisted Hair, an elderly leader who resisted suggestions of slaughtering the Corps of Discovery in their sleep, and instead fed them up, helped them dig out five canoes from felled trees, guided them to a safe put-in for the Columbia River and even offered to care for their horses while they glided towards the Pacific, and triumph. On their return journey,

Lewis and Clark stayed several weeks with the Nimiipuu (who had cared for their horses well), tending to villagers' ailments from their medicine bag, giving demonstrations of their magical technologies and conversing at length with Twisted Hair, explaining to him the number and power of the white man's country, the significance of the Great Father (an explanatory title for the president which Jefferson, among others, enjoyed far too much) and the impending arrival of fur trappers and trading posts in the Nimiipuu's lands.

When they parted, Lewis wrote, 'I think we can justly say, to the honor of this people, that they are the most hospitable, honest and sincere that we have met with on our voyage.' Twisted Hair, for his part, made a solemn promise that the Nimiipuu would never spill the white man's blood. Lewis and Clark, for theirs, promised the Nimiipuu 'peace and friendship'.

The first efforts by fur trappers and traders to follow in the Corps' footsteps were underwhelming, at best. American mercantile adventurers, supposedly the next wave of the Jeffersonian expansion, failed to persuade the Nimiipuu and other Columbia Plateau tribes to abandon their crucial sustenance activities and stand in freezing rivers trapping beaver for them instead, while the Nimiipuu proved discouragingly astute in spotting a seller's market for their healthy, well-fed horses, and set their prices accordingly. The Bostons, as the Indians came to call the Americans, soon skulked off.

British and French Canadian trappers were more resilient, though (in the early nineteenth century the Oregon Territory, the vast sweep of land that took in the north-west USA and Alaska, was still 'up for grabs' in the great geopolitical board game), finding villages which would accept dependence on the fur economy, establishing permanent trading posts in the Columbia region and gradually inveigling their way into local life. The Nimiipuu became involved in the trading culture, if not immersed in it: the tools and trinkets such as knives, kettles, fish-hooks and blankets were worth swapping the occasional fur for, and, in times of conflict with the Blackfoot and Shoshone tribes, bullets had become an absolute necessity. But geographical isolation and an impenetrable sense of superiority towards the white man's antics kept the Nimiipuu at arm's length. As one trader complained in 1824, the Plateau Indians were still 'very independent of us, requiring but few of our supplies'.

One thing had changed, though – the Nimiipuu had accepted, from the outside world at least, a new name. French Canadian trappers, noting that some men of the tribe had adopted the coastal practice of piercing their noses (often with shells), had started calling the villagers Nez Percé, which was soon democratized to Nez Perce (rhyming with 'fez verse'). As was often the case, the name proved much more resilient than the fashion, and 'Nez Perce' stuck.

Around 1824 the Bostons returned to the plateau with a vengeance, muscling in on the British market with all the vigour of an invasive coffee-shop chain. Introductory special offers of over-the-top payments for furs and horses lured away loyal customers, and the Americans' more informal treatment of the Indians forged stronger friendships than the well-practised colonial disengagement of the British. A less honourable marketing device also began to flood the plateau – whiskey. While the British Empire could scarcely be described as a temperate endeavour, the New Republic was lubricated to a quite unprecedented degree: by one 1830 estimate, the average American adult was knocking back seven gallons of alcohol a year, and while the disastrous impact of this free-flowing intoxicant on Indian cultures was well known by the 1820s, the federal ban on trading whiskey with the tribes was of marginal significance several thousand miles from Washington. In 1831 the dominant American trader in the Oregon Territory, William Sublette, hauled 450 gallons of whiskey into his premises on the plateau, claiming every drop was needed to sustain his staff of boatmen. As he did not, in fact, employ a single boatman, the destiny of the drink is unarguable – the highly profitable degradation of people and communities that were socially and, many claim, physiologically, unprepared for the ravages of the wicked water. Once again, geographical protection and a natural aloofness allowed the Nez Perce to protect their culture better than many other tribes, a fact reflected, paradoxically, in the many observations by trappers of the time that the dignity and integrity of the Nez Perce marked them out as the *least* Indian of the Indians – but they were being drawn ever closer to the ever more numerous Americans. From 1827, many Nez Perce men became regular attendees at Rendezvous, the notorious annual trade conference of fur trappers which one historian, writing in 1918, recalled as a carnival of 'carousal and dissipation'. The trappers, fiercely independent adventurers in mythology, overworked salarymen in reality, would come in from their travails in the forests and icy streams to spend a few days blowing a year's wages in the luxury of human company: 'Men with impassive faces gambled at cards; flat liquor-kegs and whiskey bottles were opened and emptied; and scenes of wildest revelry followed. The Indians, not to be outdone by the white men, joined in the gambling, horse-racing and drunken quarrels.'

And as the British retreated from this unfamiliar new colonialism with their usual good grace – adopting a scorched-earth policy of overhunting to ensure they weren't followed north – it became increasingly likely that the Oregon Territory would, before long, become part of the ever-expanding 'alcoholic republic' of the United States.

In this fur-trading era, the white arrivals were measured in the hundreds at most, their numbers insufficient fundamentally to disrupt Nez Perce life – but these visitors did bring with them the first barrages of what is now seen as the most effective, murderous weapon in the diminution of indigenous America. There are no records of wilful efforts to introduce disease to the people of the Northwest – it was 'Back East' that the British military commander,

17

Lord Amherst, had ordered the mass-murderous delivery of smallpox-infected blankets to the Delaware people in 1763 – but the unwitting impact was no less disastrous. Once again, the Nez Perce were spared the worst – for now – but as smallpox, cholera and measles devastated the Blackfoot to their north-east, Columbia tribes to their west and Snake River tribes to their south, the sense of encroaching doom grew, as did the divisions among the tribe, with those who coveted the material benefits of trade with the Bostons increasingly at odds with those who were fast concluding that nothing good could be gained from engaging with the white man. In epidemiological terms, at the very least, the isolationists couldn't have been more right – the wave of disease that swept ahead of the white settlement of the Americas is among humankind's greatest catastrophes: the population of North, Central and South America fell by as much as two-thirds in the century following Columbus' arrival, a loss of up to forty million souls. Some North American tribes buried three-quarters of their people within a couple of months of their first white visitor. As the geographer Jared Diamond made clear in 1988, there's little contest between 'guns, germs and steel' when civilizations fight for survival, the microscopic proving the most potent of the three by far. Diamond did, however, neglect to list the most cancerous and tenacious of all the implements of territorial conquest – gods.

Precisely why four Nez Perce men travelled to St Louis in the summer of 1831 and asked for a copy of the Bible is still fiercely contested. Some historians suggest they encountered this seemingly desirable source of the white man's power at Rendezvous; others believe they were jealous of the two young male members of the nearby Kootenai and Salish tribes, who had been rented from their families by the Hudson's Bay Company and sent to boarding school, whence they'd returned in collars and ties, speaking English, reciting the Ten Commandments and humming 'Amazing Grace'. Yet others suggest that a local prophet had foreseen the arrival of the white man and his great book as heralding the end of this world and the start of a better one, while some modern Nez Perce are keen to revise the spiritual motivation altogether: 'They didn't go there for the Bible,' contends tribal historian Allen Pinkham. 'They went to learn how to communicate with written words. They wanted the technology of writing, not the Christian faith. We already knew about the Creator. We had our own faith.'

Whatever they wanted, they didn't get. Two of the men died in St Louis, the other two on the journey home, all unable to resist a city of unfamiliar illnesses. But their mission did cause a sensation – they met their old friend William Clark (perhaps taking the time to let him know that, as a result of his relationship-building endeavours back in 1806, a red-haired Nez Perce was now entering his twenty-fifth year) and visited a Catholic church, while newspapers and Christian societies all the way to the East Coast marvelled at the thought of four 'Red Men' wandering through St Louis in full regalia, displaying their manifest hunger for the word of God. A call for missionaries to answer their plea rang out, with this letter to the New York *Christian Advocate* typically understated: 'How deeply touching is the circumstance of the four natives travelling on foot 3,000 miles through thick forests and extensive prairies, sincere searchers after truth! ... Let the Church awake from her slumbers and go forth in her strength to the salvation of these wandering sons of our native forests.' For the Nez Perce, this salvation would come in the less than beatific form of the Reverend Henry Spalding.

Photographs of Henry Harmon Spalding are incomplete without a scowl. He was a man of fierce and unforgiving temper, his character a primal soup of vanity and spite, arrogance and churlishness. He may well have fancied that the greasy comb-over dominating the top half of his head and the rampant beard obscuring the bottom half lent him the appearance of a Sistine god; in fact he looks almost precisely as unappealing as his historical legacy. Not surprisingly, this old-fashioned bastard, born of an uncaring mother and an indeterminate father, was unlucky in love, and his routinely black mood can scarcely have been lightened by the companionship, on his 1836 mission to minister to the Nez Perce, of the woman who had broken his heart. Narcissa, travelling with her husband Marcus Whitman, had once rejected Spalding's hand in marriage but by 1836 he had recovered somewhat and acquired a match, Eliza, who made up the westward-bound foursome, all forced to share a single tent for the entire trip. After two earlier attempts to open a mission in Nez Perce country failed, this unlikely double date was heading to Rendezvous in the hope of meeting the tribes which had sent their emissaries to St Louis, then following them home to establish ministries within their villages. On reaching Rendezvous, the two white women caused a sensation among the attendant natives, most, perhaps even all, of whom had never seen a female Boston, and competition erupted as to which tribe would take these dainty and prestigious visitors home. Ultimately, it was decided that the Whitmans would go and live with the Cayuse in the Walla Walla Valley, while the Spaldings would follow the Nez Perce home, the good reverend demanding, in a sign of things to come, that the Nez Perce clear a path through the forest for his wagon, rather than force his wife into the indignity of riding on a horse.

'What is done for the poor Indians of this western world must be done soon. The only thing that can save them from annihilation is the introduction of civilisation.' With that self-proclaimed motto, Spalding launched into the agricultural and technological salvation of the Nez Perce with as much vim as he devoted to his spiritual duties. He dug irrigation trenches, ploughed fields and used the power of the Clearwater River to run a wood saw and flour mill, encouraging the Nez Perce to adopt these new skills, becoming farmers and cattlemen rather than hunters and gatherers. He built a

The Reverend Henry H. Spalding.

substantial loghouse – or, rather, made the Nez Perce build it for him, then made them take it apart and rebuild it on a spot with a cooler breeze – and set up a schoolroom in which Eliza taught English. The initial response was enthusiastic, with the promise of the secrets of the Good Book and the revelation of labour-saving innovations drawing villages from around the homeland to make camp near Spalding's settlement at Lapwai on the Clearwater. One of the most influential village leaders, Tuekakas, brought his people to winter at Lapwai each year, returning during summer to their favoured lands in the isolated Wallowa Valley on the western fringe of the Nez Perce territory. He studied the Bible as deeply as the language barrier with Spalding allowed, and was baptized with a Christian name, Joseph. Later, his son would also take the same name. But Tuekakas' loyalty to Spalding and the Bible were soon tested, as the man and his mission began to disturb and divide the Nez Perce.

Spalding's insistence on using a horsewhip to encourage his hosts to labour was one of his earliest transgressions – a humiliation for people raised in a culture that emphasized human dignity – but there were many more. He began to insist that converted Nez Perce should cut their hair, take to western dress and abandon all their traditional faiths and rites, including their *wyakin*. He began to reveal dark and confusing inconsistencies in his preaching, drawing diagrams of the Presbyterian path to Heaven and the Catholic path to Hell. Strangest of all, when a government agent arrived at the mission in 1843, he and Spalding drew up a list of laws for the Nez Perce to live by, and Spalding hung a metal hoop from a tree to facilitate whippings for the new 'crimes', many of which the Nez Perce had been committing for centuries, such as borrowing one another's food. Spalding and the agent also trampled over Nez Perce concepts of freedom and community by naming a 'head chief' of the tribe, an insubstantial young man called Ellis (Tuekakas and other more senior village leaders were initially bemused and irritated by this seemingly point-less gesture, but within years its capacity for devastation would become clear).

Thus the voices of dissent towards Spalding's way grew ever stronger. Elder spiritual leaders questioned the wisdom of scarring Mother Earth with a plough, forcing her to work rather than simply accepting her gifts; stories abounded that the great diseases which had destroyed neighbouring tribes had arrived as a punishment for similar violence towards the soil. They also questioned Spalding's new devices, the mills and the saws, as insults to the way of life that the Creator had specifically given to the Nez Perce to preserve. In their support was the swirl of rumours brought back from buffalo hunts to the east, of what had happened to other tribes who had wel-comed the missionaries – invasion, settlement, displacement, des-titution.

For the many Nez Perce who had settled into the new regime, though, this was backwardness and heresy. Spalding's way offered less strenuous and time-consuming sources of food, the possibility of wealth through trade and, most importantly, the guaranteed avoidance of eternal suffering in the fiery netherworld of which the reverend spoke so often. Learning English, cutting their hair, keeping pigs, reciting chapter and verse, the Christian Nez Perce were a roaring success – but by an entirely different measure to their traditional clansmen.

By the measure of the ignoble history of colonial missionary work, Henry Spalding was certainly a success. By 1843, profound and insoluble conflicts were beginning to appear in the Nez Perce community, scuppering their response to the next, decisive, wave of white arrivals. In June 1843 around a thousand people set off from the town of Independence on the banks of the Missouri, to make the 1900-mile wagon journey in search of free land and new lives in the Oregon Territory. After division, comes conquest.

Dancers at the Tamkaliks Celebration, Wallowa Valley, Oregon.

CHAPTER TWO

SETTLEMENT

'All hail, thou western world! by heaven design'd
Th' example bright, to renovate mankind'
'Greenfield Hill', by TIMOTHY BRIGHT, 1794

'Annuit coeptis – *He has approved this undertaking'*
The Great Seal of the United States

THE OREGON PRAIRIE dozed in the scalding midsummer heat, the only movement the irrigation machines hopelessly spritzing the Columbia River into the gasping dry air. The miles passed as the truckers, farmers and loggers showed the way eastwards and inwards through the crisp, lifeless wheatfields. The highway started to rise, weaving over the Blue Mountains then sliding down into another frying pan, the valley of the Grande Ronde, a river scarcely worth the name crawling through the drought-stricken farmland, dotted with the dog-eared little towns of Alice, Imbler ('We're too blessed to be depressed' proclaimed the church sign defiantly), Summerville and Elgin.

Finally, the road began to curve upwards again, a merciful breeze rolled in, the tan grass was dotted, then clustered, then shaded with pine trees, and the angles of the land tightened from lowland curves to alpine edges. The road was struggling to find a way now, clambering towards the high country, over the barricade of Minam Summit, the fading, clunking camper van beginning to strain and steam at the incline. The hill topped out at last to a broad-shouldered summit, revealing the treasures it protected, a view that had raised the spirits of homecomers, newcomers, guests and transgressors for millennia. This was Nez Perce country.

Steepling pine-covered slopes folded away to the horizon, falling swathes of meadowland breaking the deep green wash, and, below, the fast-running Minam River caught the last of the afternoon sun as it carved out its canyon walls. The road careered down to meet the river, where fishermen were chasing salmon and a family of deer was hunting out the shade within the riverbank willows. Soon, the Minam poured into the main event, the Wallowa River, and the canyon's sides began to release their grip, widening and slackening until it was time for them to fall away entirely, and let the softening light flood across the full sweep of the Wallowa Valley. And then, the wonder of the place strikes in an instant, and it's a dull heart that doesn't echo the thoughts of Joseph F. Johnson, one of the very first white men to drive their stakes into this land and claim it as their own: 'As soon as I looked out into the valley I said to myself, "*This is where I want to live.*"'

You could find nowhere better. The heart of the valley is the river basin, corralled into farmland and pasture, speckled with lonely red barns and white ranch houses, with the Wallowa and Lostine rivers winding lazily through the greenery. Serving guard on one flank of the valley lies a bank of rolling, sun-dried grassland hills, while on the other the Wallowa Mountains shoot skywards in a precipitous flurry of forests, cliff faces and snowfields, suggesting adventure and isolation away from the homely calm of the lowlands.

The town of Wallowa itself, the first in the valley, is little more than a picturesque bend in the road, a few shops and a diner clustered between the gas station and the espresso shack, the kind of place where the teenagers do laps through the evening shade in their pick-up trucks, in search of something to do. It was only a short drive to the north edge of town, where the tepees were clustered against the edge of an irrigation ditch, mosquitoes plundering in the darkness, the craggy mass of Tick Hill looming over the encampment meadow like an unfriendly giant. Someone had lit a fire, and the lawn chairs were gathered for a chat.

The next day we busied ourselves with preparations for the annual gathering that would rouse this field to life, Tamkaliks: 'From where you can see the mountains'. I joined the local youth conservation volunteers, gradually and messily mastering the art of turning a lodgepole pine tree into a working lodgepole, stripping off the bark with double-handled sickles, covering ourselves in pungent, tenacious sap. A circular wooden arbour lay in the centre of the meadow, with bleachers and hay bales stacked in the shade for the spectators. We worked all day, and, as the afternoon came to an end, a crowd gathered from their jobs in the valley to help in the raising of the arbour's roof – an old army tank parachute, a billowing mass of military-green fabric that hung from a central pole to fill the centre of the circle, and shade tomorrow's dancers from the fierce peak of summer. The men were enjoying the banter and sweat, but a woman, Sarah Lynne, was quietly running the show, allocating tasks, keeping an eye on the youth volunteers and hauling the hay in her pick-up. Her great-grandfather had come into this valley as one of the first white squatters, she said: 'My grandfather said one of his earliest childhood memories was the sparks of the cavalry's hooves when they rode into the valley, in 1877, the shoes hitting against the rocks in the dark. Because my great-grandfather could speak some Nez Perce, he helped interpret for Young Joseph when the cavalry came. Joseph even came down to my great-grandfather's house before everything started and said, "Take your wife and your papoose, and leave – there's going to be trouble." My family were never all that happy with what happened to the Nez Perce – but governments do what governments do. They wanted to mine and log and pursue the so-called progress of the West – so there you are.'

Saturday bustled in the heat, the vendors on their summer pow-wow trail gathering their stalls around the arbour, selling jewellery, art, fabrics, ice cream, Indian tacos and countless gallons of lemon-ade to the growing, sweltering crowd, a mix of locals enjoying a chance to chat, flirt and gossip, plus pilgrims from across the western states, a group of greying military veterans in their pressed white shirts and, away from the stalls, enjoying the calm of 'Tepee Alley', the drummers and the dancers, dozing, sewing, unpacking, preparing.

I killed time at the taco stall with Fred Minthorn, a Wallowa Nez Perce, grinning widely beneath a capacious baseball cap and wrap-around shades.

'I look forward to Tamkaliks all year. I love it here, I can bring my grandkids, let them run free, let them be kids, you know? Not like back on the reservation, you have to look out for them all the time there, with all the drugs and the alcohol. We had a guy die last week on the reservation – OD'd.'

Fred worked as a maintenance man at the tribal casino, but his real passion was his horses and the journey they offered away from a present he had little time for and back to his ancestral past: 'My great-great-aunt used to tell stories of how this valley was filled with our horses, so many of them, thousands. She was one of the last remaining survivors of the great retreat, when we were pushed out of here; she was raised here in this valley, and she was descended from Young Joseph's father-in-law, and she helped raise us. So that's our connection, that's what makes us descendants, me and Brian, my cousin. We're going to be buried up on that hill,' he smiled wide again, pointing up to the craggy edge of Tick Hill.

As the ten-minute call for the Grand Entry was delivered over the tannoy, the bleachers filled with spectators – but this was not a show, and there would be no hurrying. At the five-minute call, the elders took to their lawn chairs in the front row, at showtime the drummers took their seats (four or five men circled around each hide drum, young boys peering over their shoulders for lessons), then the absolutely last call came through, the drummers started to play – and only then was the floor filled with dancers, from toddlers to patriarchs, following the Stars and Stripes and the tribal staff into the arena, porcupine quills, eagle feathers, buffalo horns, neon shawls, bell-strewn jingle dresses, pristine fans, buckskin waistcoats, fur-trim boots, beaded bags and bracelets all in perfect order. From the crowd-melting Tiny Tots to the cold-eyed competitiveness of the Golden Age Men, the evening passed through the age brackets and dance styles, each rigid to a dress code and etiquette of movement, sometimes reflecting the wings of a butterfly, others the posturing of a prairie chicken, the action of warriors ducking cannon balls or flattening the long grass for a camp, while the drum groups took it in turns to control the floor like puppeteers, beating rhythm and straining for their stratospheric harmonies.

As night fell the crowd in the bleachers grew larger, the dancing more expressive, the darkness adding theatre and concentrating our minds on this unlikely circle of light. Brian Conner, Fred's cousin, was serving as emcee and announced that the central moment of the weekend was due – the veterans' honour dance. 'This is a time for us to heal, a time for us to come together – and that's what this ceremony is all about.'

Any veterans of military service, Indian and non-Indian, were invited to take to the floor and follow the flags of the armed forces in a circle dance (forty-eight men and women stepped up, many of whom, it transpired, had travelled hundreds of miles just for this moment), then the whole crowd, maybe three hundred of us, walked the circle shaking each hand and offering our thanks for their sacrifices, to starch-pressed veterans of Omaha Beach and Korea, bearded and Hawaiian-shirted baby boomers with Vietnam tours to recall, eerily fresh-faced returnees from the War on Terror. 'The warriors are home,' declared Brian as we circled, reminding us that

Native Americans contribute a greater proportion of military servants than any other ethnic group in the US, that more than four hundred Nez Perce have served in the past century: 'These people fought for the freedom to sing our songs, and tonight we pay tribute.'

The microphone was passed around, each veteran asked in turn to describe their service, each lengthily applauded, many unable to hold back the tears as they spoke of fallen friends and stolen youths. Steve Reuben, a Nez Perce, recalled, 'I never met a single Native American in Vietnam – then I came home and went to a clinic for post-traumatic stress disorder, and it was all Indians – from twenty-two tribes!* And it's all hard to forget, and we cry now, but these are tears of happiness, because we're here with you all today, in a circle.'

The last man to take the microphone wore a Purple Heart on his white short-sleeved shirt, his flawless ponytail falling beneath a US Marines cap: 'I just want to thank you all; this is a heartwarming experience for me, and a healing …' He began to weep deeply, quietly. 'I was in Vietnam, and … I've still got the stress disorder, the dreams. When I think about some of the things I've seen … and when I think about some of the things I've done …' Most of us are crying now … 'Well, this is the most healing I've done in a long time, and, just, thank you all.'

The dancing went on late into the night.

On Sunday Tamkaliks wound to a close, with a traditional Nez Perce religious ceremony in the morning, a friendship feast of buffalo, elk and salmon, then there was a final round of dances, a closing prayer, and that was that. The tepees started to come down, the vendors shut up their vans. As the heat of the day passed, I

---

* Native Americans were indeed more than twice as likely as white soldiers to suffer PTSD after Vietnam, with almost two out of three Native soldiers affected. The official studies blamed dislocation from community, institutional racism, high exposure to combat and a 'condition' labelled, quite remarkably, as 'gook identification syndrome': an inability to dehumanize Charlie, and to shake the nagging sense that what was happening to the Vietnamese and Cambodians had happened somewhere else before.

climbed Tick Hill, reaching the low summit and overlooking the meadow from beneath a hackberry tree that had forced its way through the rock face. Below, the arbour was still glowing at the centre of the emptying meadow, as a few sparks of dry lightning fled from the blood-red clouds to the east, and the local patrol of Canada geese cruised soundlessly over the river on their daily route home. The Wallowa band of the Nez Perce were packing their cars, facing the long drive home to Idaho, Washington, the Oregon Prairie and elsewhere, leaving the valley to its placid routine of yard sales, baseball games, fundraising breakfasts and coffee-morning gossip.

'We ask the children to dance first,' Brian Conner had said, 'then the women and then the men. We do this to honour first those children, then those women and those men, who took part in that long retreat, when we left this valley, one hundred and thirty years ago. Because, as we all know, one hundred and thirty years is not a very long time.'

The wagon train was trapped in the Rocky Mountains when the blizzard struck, scattering the horses, enfeebling the children and obscuring the onward path. The emigrants had been travelling since spring, and for many this was the final straw. They had overcome the sapping monotony of the prairies, driven their creaking, oxen-hauled wagons through mud, marshlands and boulder fields, crossed the swollen Snake River, lost friends and family to sickness and accidents, and faced down the constant terror of Indian attack for the past five months. Some of the tribes they'd met had been friendly, and the settlers had followed the orders of their leader, the legendary scout and mountain man Breck Coleman, to ease their path through Indian Country – 'They'll probably bring their families to beg, so feed them well and feed them right.' But other bands had been implacable, staging daring raids that had forced the wagons into a defensive circle, arrows and bullets filling the air. And now winter was approaching, the snow was falling ever thicker, and spirits were sagging – the heads of each family took a vote on turning back, and the decision to accept defeat was made. Dreams of a new life in the lush, unsettled valleys of the Oregon Territory were set aside.

Breck Coleman was having none of it. Knee-deep in the drifting whiteness, seemingly impervious to the cold, he urged the travellers not to lose heart:

'We can't turn back! We're blazing a trail that started in England! Not even the storms of the sea could turn back those first settlers. And then they carried it on further, they blazed it on through the wilderness of Kentucky – famine, hunger, not even massacres could stop them. And now we've picked up the trail again – and nothing can stop us, not even the snows of winter nor the peaks of the highest mountains. We're building a nation! But we've got to suffer – no great trail was ever blazed without hardship. And you gotta fight, that's life, and when you stop fighting, that's death. So whaddya gonna do, lie down and die? Not in a thousand years – you're going on with me!'

With a mighty cheer the emigrants hitched their wagons and rolled on, finally coming to rest and building their new lives in the fertile, unpopulated valley of their fantasies. As for young Breck Coleman, his towering, lopsided figure would later be seen defending the Alamo, taking the sands of Iwo Jima, riding the Rio Grande and shooting Liberty Valance, in a fifty-year career for which *The Big Trail* (Fox Films, 1930, directed by Raoul Walsh and starring John Wayne and Marguerite Churchill) would prove a mere canapé.

Tuekakas' favourite summer camp lay at the junction of the Wallowa and Lostine rivers, just a few miles south-east of Tick Hill. There was plentiful grazing for his people's horses, the two rivers ran red with

'This is where I want to live' – the Wallowa Valley, Oregon.

trout and salmon, and the narrow Lostine Valley led away from the flat-bottomed plain and up into the forested mountains where deer and elk abounded. In his time, when only the unreliable rains brought growth, the valley floor was a semi-desert of sagebrush and hardy, tawny grasses, mingled with pine groves and, where the rivers fled their banks, the odd patch of floodland, thick with migrating fowl. Now, however, the relentless tsk-tsk-tsk of the irrigation machines shared the rivers' flow across a confected delta, turning the ceaseless pasture and hayfields an unlikely luscious green under the fierce sun. The pine groves were long gone, while the rivers had been straightened in places, dredged and divided up between each farmstead.

The sprays were working overtime as the heatwave had yet to lift; the radio warned that Oregon was under a state of emergency, and the haze beginning to fill the valley was evidence that the lightning on the last night of Tamkaliks had found the forests kindling-dry. At the site of the old camp, a family of deer was foraging in the shade of a grain store, and water was trickling over the edge of the narrow

33

country lane – an enlightened rancher was trying to rebuild a portion of the long-drained wetlands, to help restore the salmon runs and secure a home for the valley's sentinel geese.

The road streaked on to the town of Enterprise, a low-slung and likeable place with an air of hard luck about it that wasn't significantly alleviated by the decision to pipe the local radio station through tinny loudspeakers along the length of Main Street. Like the rest of the valley, Enterprise was still battling to recover from a sucker punch delivered in the 1980s, when all but one of the local lumber yards shut down, shedding more than four hundred family wage jobs in the process, and the country music echoing thinly around the deserted, sun-bleached streets did little to raise the mood. Today, though, a feeble festivity was in the air – discount offers, special menus, live bands and more were being heralded throughout town, as everyone sought to capture a slice of the passing trade drawn in by the main event about to start a few miles down the road – Chief Joseph Days.

Out here, every town has its Days – an annual commemorative weekend when the chamber of commerce crams the calendar with tourist-enticing parades, barbecue cook-offs, fun runs and fundraisers, all hung on a local historical hook. And the town of Joseph, Oregon, at the far end of the Wallowa Valley, has its own fine example – the day before Chief Joseph Days was due to spring into action, the pavements and parking spots of this studiously cute little place were already filling up with gaggles of ambling, half-lost out-of-towners.

At first sight, Joseph seemed to be a town that had cheerfully accepted its fate. The Outlaw Bar, the Stubborn Mule Steakhouse, the Indian Lodge Motel, the spotless parquet pavements and the bronze municipal sculptures of noble chieftains, bucking cowboys and soaring eagles all colluded in the tourist-friendly Western tableau. Pleasantness washed over the place, and had clearly not gone unnoticed – the power-walkers, micro-breweries and cookie-cutter coffee/book/gift/chintz shops were but a hint of the influence of the last decade's new arrivals in town, a wave of affluent retirees, downsizers and summer-home shoppers. (The only disreputable, properly intimidating bar in town, the Hydrant, was up for sale.) Main Street ran in a steady incline from the cattle pastures on the edge of town towards the great bowl of Wallowa Lake, its waters, dotted with fishing craft and scored by jet skis, held in place between a featureless, grass-covered glacial moraine and the alpine silhouette of the Wallowa Mountains. To complete the familiar scene, many of the tourists were disappearing into a reverie of an alternative life, ice creams in hand, at the garrison of estate agents' windows.

A marginally less cheery cameo was being played out at the registration table for the upcoming children's parade. From a peak of three hundred entrants a few years earlier, the parade was now down to two hundred, accurate testimony to the Wallowa Valley's altered demographics – the population had been stable for the last ten years, but the number of school-age children had fallen by almost a third, as all those Cornetto-dripping summer-home snatchers had priced the working (or not working) local families out of their home towns. 'I remember when it took two buses to get the kids to school up this valley,' one bustling grandmother muttered; 'now you could do it in a van.'

Still, two hundred kids is enough for a mighty good parade. Effort was variable – tying a handkerchief around your dog's neck and dragging it down the baking tarmac was never going to bring home the rosette – and the organization slipped on occasion: during the ten-minute delay while a young gentleman resolutely refused to abandon his mission to pogo-stick the length of town, the crowd lining the street in their lawn chairs grew slightly restless in the heat, but the mood was generally as sunny as the day. We applauded pirates, crusaders, hula-girls, cowboys, a young man in desert fatigues steering a cardboard tank – and, of course, plenty of pint-sized pioneers, driving balsa-wood oxen from beneath the canopy of their covered wagons, rolling west down Main Street.

Dr Daniel Drake may have got his wish. Writing in 1815, in contemplation of the possibilities offered up by the wide open spaces of the freshly purchased West, this Cincinnati doctor dreamed of the civic fibre that the future inhabitants of such a spacious, separated province would be bound to possess:

> Debarred by their locality, from an inordinate participation in foreign luxuries, and consequently secured from the greatest corruption introduced by commerce – secluded from foreign intercourse, and thereby rendered patriotic ... the inhabitants of this region are obviously destined to an unrivalled excellence ... in public virtue, and in national strength.

The idea that the American interior could serve as a kind of national health service for the United States was as old as the republic, and by the time that first wagon train set off for Oregon, it was a political commonplace that only the morality and patriotism of fresh rural communities in the West could keep this young country's unique enthusiasm for itself alive.

The wagon trains were also seen as invigorating America's nation-building in another way – as the winning move in that great nineteenth-century territorial board game. As Lucas Alaman, the Mexican secretary of state, ruefully observed in 1842: 'Where others send invading armies, [the Americans] send their colonists.'

The settlers proved a roaring success in the expansion of America. More than twenty thousand farmers and ranchers had poured into Texas in the early 1830s, while it was still under Mexican control, their presence ultimately securing independence for the Lone Star Republic in 1836. The Mexicans were similarly overwhelmed by a wave of arrivals in California, leading to their retreat south to Baja in 1848. And as for the British in the Northwest, with their famous affectation of imperial absent-mindedness, they often told themselves that the territory was abandoned as a result of reports that the local salmon offered substandard fly-fishing, but the reality was that from the first caravan of families into Oregon, the land was lost. The Hudson's Bay Company would read the runes and retreat north of the 49th parallel in 1846. America was nearing completion.

But such territorial endeavours cannot flourish if their mundane mechanics are on show; they need romance, poetry, narrative, a mission that can be evoked to justify the required investments, the compromises and, particularly, the crimes. And the expansionists possessed such a dogma, a creed of American chosen-ness, special-ness and divinely ordained progress that would be remembered by history as 'Manifest Destiny'.

A cocktail of Puritan fervour, geographical predestination and, predominantly, political cynicism, Manifest Destiny proclaimed, in essence, that the American continent had been created by God for a single, obvious purpose – to host the greatest Christian nation in history.

The phrase itself was first coined by John O'Sullivan, a scholarly cheerleader to Andrew Jackson – a president whose principles amounted to a kind of territorial *laissez-faire*, with a deliberately inactive government simply holding the doors open to conquest by settlers. O'Sullivan wholly approved, citing in 1845, 'our manifest destiny to overspread and to possess the whole continent which providence has given us for the development of the great experiment of liberty and federated government'.

Just how much more was at stake was emphasized by the writer and orator William Gilpin the following year, as he gave full vent to the possibilities that God had laid before the Americans and, by extension, the burden of their duty:

The untransacted destiny of the American people is to subdue the continent – to rush over this vast field to the Pacific Ocean … to establish a new order in human affairs … to teach old nations a new civilization – to confirm the destiny of the human race – to carry the career of mankind to its culminating point … to perfect science – to emblazon history with the conquest of peace – to shed a new and resplendent glory upon mankind – to unite the world in one social family … to absolve the curse that weighs down humanity, and to shed blessings round the world!

Gilpin's 'culminating point' for humankind, of course, was Revelation, the divine return. As the planet's final unconquered continent revealed itself in its entirety, and the calls to create from it a single, earth-shaking nation grew ever louder, apocalypse was often evoked. As Ralph Waldo Emerson wrote, one simply had to conclude that continental America was 'a last effort of the Divine Providence on behalf of the human race'.

With so much to gain and so much to lose, the troublesome fact of the prior occupation of the land could be dismissed as mere detail. One either felt sympathy for the fact that divine ordination seemed to have marked the Native Americans out to be steamrollered, or, more widely, one pointed to their failure to grasp the opportunity themselves. It was declared from the pulpits that the Indians had forfeited their claim to the land by failing to tame and exploit it, in breach of God's very first commandment – 'Be fruitful and increase in number; till the earth and subdue it. Rule over the fish of the sea and the birds of the air and over every living creature that moves on the ground.' President John Quincy Adams delivered a resonant sermon on this theme in 1839: 'Shall the lordly savage not only disdain the virtues and enjoyments of civilization himself, but shall he control the civilization of the world? Shall he forbid the wilderness to blossom like a rose? Shall he forbid the oaks of the forest to fall before the axe of industry?'

The settlers on that Missouri riverbank were thus armed with a sense of both national and divine purpose, a sacred mission on behalf of humanity itself – which added gravitas and grandeur to their more prosaic concerns. All they really wanted was land.

When people spoke in the slums of New York, London and Naples of the 'land of opportunity' of inland America, it was the first word that counted. In its formation, the US had elevated the sanctity of private property, almost to the level of a faith: 'liberty' referred chiefly to the freedom to own and use land; democracy manifested itself in equitable access to land; 'no taxation without representation' was a proclamation of property rights, not human rights. This gospel, combined with the realities of a literally immeasurable quantity of seemingly unoccupied territory, generated an unimaginably enticing possibility for the poor and dispossessed of Europe and the American East – if you headed out West, staked out a quarter-mile of land, built a home and worked the soil, then that property was forever yours.

And to achieve this fantasy, the men, women and children who left their homes and rode the Oregon Trail in search of free land took on a mission no less fearsome or uncertain than any of those flag-planting endeavours whose leaders still decorate the bank notes and piazzas of old Europe. They surely deserved at least some of the avalanche of praise that would soon be heaped upon them, typified by this eulogy in a 1918 history of the pioneer days: 'The early settlers were as noble, patriotic, industrious, unselfish, intelligent, good, generous, kind and moral people as ever were assembled together in like number.' The trail was, to a degree, mapped out – the adventurer and self-publicist John C. Fremont had tapped his father-in-law, the expansionist congressman Thomas Hart Benton, for government funds for a settlers' route-finding mission in 1842 – but the families who gathered their wagons on the banks of the Missouri in the spring of 1843 had no idea what lay ahead of them. The gap between expectation and reality is well illustrated by the recollection of the diarist Francis Parkman midway through the 1900-mile journey:

> It is worth noticing, that on the Platte one may sometimes see the shattered wrecks of ancient claw-footed tables, well waxed and rubbed, or massive bureaus of carved oak. These, many of them no doubt the relics of ancestral prosperity in the colonial time, must have encountered strange vicissitudes. Imported, perhaps, originally from England; then, with the declining fortunes of their owners, borne across the Alleghenies to the remote wilderness of Ohio or Kentucky; then to Illinois or Missouri; and now at last fondly stowed away in the family wagon for the interminable journey to Oregon. But the stern privations of the way are little anticipated. The cherished relic is soon flung out to scorch and crack upon the hot prairie.

The challenges of the five- or six-month journey were indeed impossible to anticipate, a situation not helped by Fremont, whose best-selling trail notes pitched the expedition as exactly the kind of jolly family house move for which one would pack a walnut dresser. The privations of the prairie were specific: thirst, starvation, boredom and murderous Indian attack, the seemingly endless days of westward travel across the waterless grasslands permanently undercut with fear that a band of plains Indians would descend on a horse-stealing raid, or to deliver fatal punishment for trespassing on their hunting grounds. Watches were posted every night, the wagons circled for scant protection. Once into the mountains, river crossings brought the threat of drowning and precipitous trails crumbled, hurling oxen, wagon and driver over the edge. Illness, finally, was the greatest scourge, with precious few trail parties bearing medicine of any note. It's estimated that one out of every ten Oregon Trail pioneers died on the route – one diarist recalled seeing 'a grave every 80 yards' on the way. The mythology of the West would almost instantly memorialize the optimism and stoicism of the Oregon Trail immigrants, but Parkman's diaries speak more of melancholy suffering, of 'men, with sour, sullen faces' dragging their families through unimagined hardship, more refugees than empire-builders: 'It was easy to see that fear and dissension prevailed among them ... Many were murmuring against the leader they had chosen, and wished to depose him ... The women were divided between regrets for the homes they had left and apprehension of the deserts and the savages before them.'

The struggle proved no deterrent, however; the year after the first wagon train, almost twice as many immigrants gathered at the Missouri, to set off as soon as the snows had melted and the prairies had turned green. By 1850 more than 13,000 non-Indian people had taken up residence in Oregon, with many more forking south from the trail into the California gold fields, and by the time the railways had fully overspread the West, at the turn of the century, fully 300,000 people had rolled their wagons along the Oregon Trail.

Route-finding soon ceased to be a challenge: by the late 1840s the trail was an unmistakable swathe of overgrazed grass and churned-up mud, several hundred metres wide in places. Bent on survival and 'just passing through', the emigrants thought little of housekeeping. Every tree within miles of the trail had been chopped down and burned, waterholes were fouled by rubbish and the swollen carcasses of cattle and horses, 'trail trash' littered the ground, and every creature that came into rifle range was felled. One emigrant, Esther Macmillan Hanna, took the long ride in 1852, and recalled: 'I do not think I shall ever forget the sight of so many dead animals seen along the trail. It was like something from Dante's Inferno.' The Shoshone chief Washakie described the experience of an Indian whose homeland was on the route: 'Before the emigrants passed through his country, buffalo, elk and antelope could be seen upon all the hills; now, when he looked for game, he saw only wagons with white tops and men riding upon their horses.'

From the vantage point of Minam Summit, on the western edge of their homelands, the Nez Perce watched the wagons roll past, more numerous each summer. The Oregon Trail didn't trespass on their central territories, but it did head straight up the outlying Grande Ronde Valley, through traditional Indian meeting and trading grounds. Some Nez Perce profited from the desperation of the pilgrims for supplies and horses, but others urged caution, particularly when increasing numbers of settlers chose not to push on north-west to the famously fertile Willamette Valley, but elected instead to stay and cultivate the Grande Ronde. But it was one hundred or so miles further up the trail that the most fateful impacts would be felt – in the Walla Walla Valley, home of the Cayuse and, for the past ten years, of the Whitman mission.

Almost as charming as Henry Spalding, his rival in love and salvation, but considerably less ingenious or industrious, Marcus Whitman had singularly failed to convert the Cayuse people to the good word, and was considered little more than an irritant and an ingrate by his hosts. Much of this was in fact due to the fickle hand of romance. Eliza Spalding had turned out to be a natural carer and teacher, who had learned the Nez Perce language, while Narcissa Whitman was a prude and a fusspot, who had barred the Cayuse from her house for fear of parasitic infestation. As soon as the first white settlers began to pass by their house, the Whitmans rewrote their mission statement, concluding that life in a parish vicarage would far exceed the isolation and stress of continuing as an outpost for the Lord. 'I have no doubt,' Whitman wrote in a report to his paymasters, 'our greatest work is to be to aid the white settlement of this country.' The missionaries offered food and prayer to the families that passed by, even taking in seven children who had been orphaned on the route, and encouraged travellers to unhitch their wagons and build a life in the growing white community that surrounded their mission. As for the Cayuse, they were no longer a potential fresh harvest of Christian souls, Marcus rationalized, but the heathen casualties of destiny: 'I am fully convinced that when a people refuse or neglect to fill the designs of Providence, they ought not to complain at the results; and so it is equally useless for Christians to be anxious on their account. The Indians have in no case obeyed the command to multiply and replenish the earth, and they cannot stand in the way of others doing so.'

Ignored and encroached upon, the Cayuse simmered with resentment until, in 1847, the wagons brought an outbreak of measles to their homeland. Whitman tried his best to administer care but could do little, and more than half the tribe died – while the evidence of precious few white fatalities spread rumours that Whitman's doctoring was actually spreading the disease. On 29 November of that year rough justice was applied: Marcus Whitman was shot then hacked to bits on his front porch, and Narcissa met the same fate on the living-room settee. Eleven more settlers died in the subsequent bloodletting. Oregon's tiny white population flew into a panic (among them Spalding, who quit Nez Perce territory) and demanded military protection, an army of four hundred arriving on a punitive mission against the Cayuse. The Nez Perce were instrumental in defusing the situation (especially Tuekakas, who had Cayuse blood) but while the Whitman massacre didn't spark a full 'Indian war', it did set the Columbia Plateau, and the Nez Perce, on a very familiar course. As the settlers began to return to the Oregon Territory, they were now burnishing one of the most potent myths of American expansion – the conquerors as victims. The pioneer yeoman farmers, fulfilling the demands of faith and history and carrying the soul of the nation, were forever on the brink of being massacred, kidnapped and (for complex psycho-sexual reasons that need not detain us) getting 'ravaged' by Indians. This image, immortalized in numerous newspaper accounts of attacks and hostage takings, insisted upon two conclusions: first, that the settlers' mission warranted military protection, a demand served by the growing number of army forts dotting the West's immigrant trails; secondly, that the white and red man were as oil and water, incapable of safely sharing a landscape. As Oregon's valleys began to fill more rapidly with settlers in the early 1850s, drawn by rumours that the California gold fields might have a northern outcrop, and by a law passed in 1850 clarifying the offer of 320 acres of free Oregon land to any family who could till it, the Northwest became the last corner of America to develop its own 'Indian problem'. Savagery and civilization needed to be separated, and the solution was one that had long been established on the continent: the Columbia Plateau tribes belonged on a reservation.

The Walla Walla grand council of May 1855 must have been a sight to scorch the memory. The Nez Perce arrived first, more than five hundred warriors parading the treaty grounds in full regalia before establishing camp, followed two days later by more than four hundred Cayuse men, dressed for war, beating their drums and firing their rifles in the air. The Yakama came next, then the Umatilla and Palouse – around five thousand Indians were present at the opening of the council, their tepees clustered across the grassland in temporary townships. Representing the United States of America was a young man called Isaac Stevens, whose prodigious energies and ambitions as a soldier and administrator had secured him the governorship of the Washington Territory of the far Northwest at just thirty-seven. Under pressure to guarantee the safety of the settlers, and eager to secure the land for his grand plan of a north-western rail route, Stevens had set off on a whirlwind treaty tour of the territories in late 1854. His negotiating tactics were simple – he would offer almost anything that came to mind – from free education to free healthcare, cash, farming equipment, fishing boats, apprenticeships, a blacksmith's shop, a carpenter – until the tribes of the Northwest agreed to limit themselves to reserved lands, leaving the remainder open to settlement. The Walla Walla council was Stevens' sixth in five months, and the mission was going well – at his first meeting the coastal tribes of Puget Sound had handed him more than two and a half million acres of homeland, limiting themselves to less than 4000 acres, and only a handful of tribes had refused similar deals since. Now he and his right-hand man, Superintendent Joel Palmer, spread out the map and told the Nez Perce and their neighbours where they were being asked to live.

In the context of nineteenth-century Indian-American treaties, the Nez Perce were offered a reasonable deal. Their reservation would at least be within their traditional territories, covering an area of 7.5 million acres, just over half of the aboriginal homelands, and it contained many of their most treasured areas, such as the Wallowa Valley, the Camas Prairie and the junction of the Clearwater and Snake rivers. Stevens promised financial compensation for the ceded land, government protection from trespassing settlers in the form of a federal Agent, and the freedom to leave the reservation to hunt, fish and gather in the tribe's 'usual and accustomed places'. There were a few voices of dissent, particularly from the still-fractious Cayuse, led by Young Chief: 'I wonder if the ground is listening to what is said? I hear what the ground says. The Great Spirit appointed the roots to feed the Indians on. The water says the same thing. Neither Indians nor the whites have the right to change these names. The ground says "it is from me man was made".'

But the Nez Perce leaders were eventually united in the belief that this treaty held the best hope of a secure future. In fact, just as it had been for tribes stretching across the continent, this was the beginning of the end.

The US government's treaties with the peoples of Native America rested on the flyweight foundation of two huge misunderstandings and one bald lie – and the Nez Perce had just placed their future on such a footing. Firstly, by exchanging land for money and gifts, they had accepted the white man's ideas of property – Mother Earth could be owned, and sold, and what had been negotiated for money once could be negotiated again, regardless of any promises of permanence. Secondly, they had been driven into the white concept of

A sketch of Tuekakas drawn by Gustavus Sohon during the
Walla Walla Treaty Council of 1855.

representative leadership – fifty-six chiefs had signed the treaty, the
Christian 'head chief' Lawyer first on the list, and under the white
man's law the whole tribe was now bound, whether or not they
agreed. The freedom to walk your own path had been signed away,
and the Nez Perce had just become a nation.

Finally, they had been deceived. Stevens knew the government had
neither the reach nor the desire to control the movement of settlers,
who would take what land they wished as they struggled for survival
in the unfamiliar, inhospitable Northwest. The settlers had been sold
the West as a sacred national mission, a haven of individual freedom,
inviolable property rights and determined progress, and the government was irretrievably committed to serving as their protector and
facilitator. To frustrate their dreams – particularly in order to protect
a reservation whose inhabitants still enjoyed more than 1000 acres of
land per person – was unthinkable. The nearby Yakama tribe learned
this lesson sharply: within six months of signing their version of the

Walla Walla treaty their new reservation had become overrun with settlers. When the Yakama violently affirmed their property rights, Stevens crushed them in a punitive war.

Tuekakas saw the future. After signing the 1855 treaty he returned to the quiet of the Wallowa Valley, and resolved to have as little contact with the white man as possible, to raise his sons, Joseph and Ollokot, according to the traditional Nimiipuu beliefs, and to encourage his people to follow the ways of their ancestors. For a few more years, the Wallowa Nez Perce could live in peace.

The advertisement took up most of a page in the local paper, promising a huckleberry bake-off, a Dutch-oven cooking contest, a softball tournament, a parade, a firewood auction and more. The town of Pierce, just across the border from Oregon into Idaho, tucked away in the north-east corner of the 1855 Nez Perce reservation, was throwing its own Days the following weekend. This time, the historical hook to draw the punters was the event that brought the state of Idaho into being, and that ultimately brought the Nez Perce nation to its knees. 'Come and Join the Fun at the Pierce 1860 Days!' – from noon to 7.00 p.m. on Saturday, in the parking lot of the Cedar Inn Bar and Grill, you could even try your hand at panning for gold.

CHAPTER THREE

FEVER

'Let him who writes sneering remarks about the conduct of the people in the early days of the settling of Idaho remember that it was these brave, good old pioneer men and women that braved all the dangers incident to the reclaiming and planting of civilisation here. It would seem that they might turn their brilliant talent to some more onward and progressive movement, rather than attempt to reach away back to write sneeringly about the society of old times of which they knew but little, if anything'

JOHN HAILEY, Idaho State Librarian, 1910

CHIEF LOOKING GLASS: *Will you mark the piece of country that I have marked and say the Agent shall keep the whites out?*
SUPERINTENDENT PALMER: *None will be permitted to go there but the Agent and the persons employed, without your consent.*

Walla Walla treaty negotiations of 1855

'WELCOME TO IDAHO – *Now Go Home!'* Much of the public discourse in the town of Pierce seemed to take place through the medium of bumper stickers: 'Forest products built America'; 'This family supported by timber dollars'; 'Earth Firsters Suck!'; and the eloquent image of a small boy leaning back to urinate expansively on the word 'Environmentalists'. Though infused with the traditions of Western hospitality – the first hint of a foreign accent drew the calorific welcome of a free pancake breakfast from the local Lions Club – Pierce was clearly a community that knew its mind. The town council had recently built a shelter for public events in the district park, choosing to represent the establishing pillars of its community with four carved icons – a pickaxe, a fishing rod, a saw and a rifle. Just across the road, a local home-owner had endeavoured to embellish the tone by placing his own municipal trinity prominently on the front lawn: a twelve-foot-high crucifix, a flag of the Confederacy and a large orange No Trespassing sign.

Pierce was a one-street town hidden in the high pine forests north of the Clearwater River, just five miles from the grassland clearing where Lewis and Clark had first stumbled into Nez Perce territory. The town's sloping main street ran from a couple of bars at the top of the hill to a couple of bars at the bottom, with little more than an old courthouse and a Laundromat between them. The prominence of the watering holes was fitting – Pierce had been proud possessor of a hard-drinking, hard-punching reputation for decades, a weekend-gathering and paycheck-blowing haven for the lumberjacks and millworkers labouring in the surrounding woods. The resolutely unpretentious programme of events for 1860 Days confirmed that local feet were still firmly on the ground.

The biggest draw by far was the ATV ride, a sociable convoy of four-wheeled motorbikes roaring and puffing their way into the forest for a morning of dirt-grinding and dust clouds, but the soft-ball tournament, at which tolerance for the sickly liqueur Jaeger-meister was being as rigorously examined as any ball skills, was also proving a hit. The pie-eating contest was less well attended, however, perhaps because there was only ever going to be one winner, a young man with a technique for obliterating a chocolate cake reminiscent of a wolf inside a buffalo's guts.

As the morning wore on, a thin crowd gathered on Main Street for the parade. Fundraising stalls had been laid out for browsers (the local Drug Free Youth Club had baked its own cookies and brownies, but for those with bigger budgets they were offering a range of hunting knives) and a scattering of lawn chairs filled the sidewalk. The parade itself was, sadly, some way short of Rio (or, indeed, of Joseph, Oregon) – a few candidates for the upcoming local elections threw sweets from poster-covered convertibles, the high school's cheerleaders waved languidly from the back of a pick-up and a truckload of lumber was parked up and sold to the highest bidder. One local young lady walked alone down the street, grinning and waving, dressed up as a Nez Perce maiden. Though well applauded, her smiling presence was perhaps a less than adequate acknowledgement that this entire pocket calypso – just as any other day in the history of Pierce, Idaho – was taking place on someone else's land.

In the summer of 1860 what is now Main Street was covered with forest, with just a small, seasonal stream at the base of a shallow, shaded valley to entice the deer and elk. They in turn drew predators – wolves, cougars and bears, and Nez Perce hunting parties from their villages at the base of the escarpment. Within twelve months, however, this whole high-country valley had changed beyond all recognition, or redemption.

A Captain E. D. Pierce had heard rumours from the Nez Perce wife of an old brother in arms that the streams above the Clearwater glittered with the same soft rocks that had drawn the white men to California. He trespassed onto the reservation in September 1860 and, as promised, found gold in the riverbeds. The captain's efforts to conceal the strike failed spectacularly when one of his party left the mountains carrying $800 in gold in his saddlebags, and within a year more than eight thousand miners had descended on the site, chartering every steamer in the Northwest to head up the Columbia, driving their pack mules through the spring snows, in some cases simply downing tools in California and walking north – and the flood of arrivals set Idaho's first boom town in full swing. Pierce's miners were making as much as Wall Street bankers, initially not even bothering to pan for gold dust because there were enough lumps of treasure, known as 'lunkers', to go round. Many miners employed Chinese salarymen to do the hard labour, to speed the rush to empty the mountain of its bounty; the unending flurry of gossip told of one prospector, known as 'Baboon', earning $500 from a single pan of gravel, and eventually riding off the mountain carrying half his weight in gold.

Speed was of the essence as miners raced to get their share before the strike played out. Every tree for miles around was cut down for firewood, shelter, or for the mining necessity of transporting water. Streams were diverted, divided, water was dropped through hoses from great heights to generate pressure and blast hillsides away, the rivers were silted up and drained to the point, as one miner recalled, where they were 'too thick to flow and too thin to drink'.

Everyone was too busy mining to grow food, so supplying the camp became a lucrative business (and one from which several of the Christian Nez Perce, with their large cattle herds and well-run farms, profited handsomely) as pack trains arrived daily to deliver whiskey, meat and potatoes to the hungry cash economy. As another miner, W. A. Goulder, recalled, Pierce was no centre of culinary excellence: 'uncooked potatoes sliced up and soaked in vinegar were far from affording an appetizing dish, but it proved a sovereign remedy for the scurvy.' Soon, a supply town sprang up to serve Pierce and the handful of other mining camps that dotted the mountains; named after one half of America's famous pioneering pair, Lewiston was a rowdy and lawless tent city of seven thousand profiteers and prostitutes squatting on Nez Perce land at the convergence of the Snake and Clearwater rivers, as far upstream as a paddle steamer could navigate.

In its heyday, Pierce was no less salubrious than its supply chain.

A myth has built up around America's early miners that has proved almost as tenacious as the historical glow which surrounds the pioneer settlers, a eulogistic mood perfectly captured by C. J. Brosnan, describing the men of Pierce in his history of the state of Idaho, published in 1918:

> In addition to representing the vigorous young manhood of the nation, these argonauts were a singularly courageous and adventurous body of men … The pioneer miner was a genuine friend … A partner was affectionately known as 'pard', and the bond of friendship between cabin associates was something sacred … Their humour was sometimes grim, sometimes irreverent, but always picturesque and rollicking … Many a learned discussion on history, religion, philosophy or the classics was waged around the camp-fires.

An accurate picture, perhaps, but certainly an incomplete one. Pioneer mining was a youngster's game – with over half of the great California gold rush consisting of men in their twenties, for example – and a robust one. Panning was a popular career for those on the run from the law, and in the early 1860s Idaho was a favoured destination for deserters from the Civil War; when the editor of the first newspaper in Lewiston attempted to raise the flag of the northern Union over his office in 1863, it was promptly riddled with bullets. Whiskey served as both an alternative currency in Pierce and as the only safe thing to drink, so fouled were the rivers, ensuring that quarrels and gambling debts were often settled violently, and indeed fatally. Until the courthouse was built, mob justice ruled, with the regular vigilante hangings accompanied by the miners' favourite motto, relishing Pierce's mildly infernal reputation: 'If a man ain't good enough to live here, he ain't good enough to live anywhere.' Considering the obliterated landscape, the mass alcoholism and the ceaseless violence, the *Portland Oregonian* was kind enough to describe Pierce in May 1861 as 'the most disagreeable hole to be imagined'.

A darker streak also ran through the pioneer mining story – brutal racism. The Californian rush had been an international affair, with French, Mexicans, South Americans and tens of thousands of Chinese prospectors joining the great migration of 1849, but the white Americans had used a mixture of punitive taxes, violent intimidation and, ultimately, legal banishment to bully the other nationalities out of the mountains. The Chinese were particularly hard done by; initially exploited as cheap labour by both miners and railway companies, their work ethic generated resentment, particularly as they would often find gold where whites had given up looking, and they were considered fair game for sabotage, theft and intimidation. (In the end, anti-Chinese sentiment became a Western political movement, successfully persuading Congress to rewrite the country's immigration laws in 1882, specifically to exclude China's poor and huddled masses from Lady Liberty's embrace.)

But it was the Native inhabitants of the gold fields who paid the heaviest price. Most of the tribes of the California mountains – such as the Pomo, the Yana and the Yuki – were simply obliterated in a frenzy of greed and loathing. Death squads of volunteer miners were organized to butcher unhelpfully located families. Children, perhaps as many as ten thousand, were abducted and sold for labour. Entire bands were enslaved to work the mines, then were starved or driven to death. The upstanding citizens of settler towns held collections to pay bounties on Native scalps. If any Indians retaliated, they were branded murderous savages, and the army would be sent in to teach them a terminal lesson. In a competitive field, the treatment of California's indigenous peoples is probably the worst crime of the North American expansion; in the twenty years following the gold rush of 1849, the state's Native population of around 100,000 was reduced to little more than 30,000.

Not surprisingly, the miners of the Idaho rush, many of whom were veterans of the California fields, did not bring with them an enlightened vision of Anglo-Indian relations. Despite the commonplace that the Nez Perce were the most 'civilized' and respectable of the West's tribes, many miners had little compunction about stealing their produce or livestock, reneging on agreements and resorting to violence. In the decade following the gold strike, more than twenty Nez Perce were murdered by whites, often in cold blood – one elderly woman had a pickaxe driven through her back when she confronted a pair of young drunks, another tribe member was persuaded to help float timber down the Clearwater River to Lewiston, then was bound and thrown into the water to save paying his wages. The tribe suffered in other ways – the miners brought disease, they chased away game, they disrupted family life by taking and abandoning wives, and they turned the river of whiskey flowing through the Nez Perce villages into a catastrophic flood. When tribal leaders complained to the rare representatives of the government – about whiskey peddlers on their land, about unpunished murders, about the fact that many of the miners seemed to be ignoring the Nez Perce's generous permission to camp temporarily on their territory, and were shaping to settle permanently – they received short shrift. The revenues from Idaho's gold were helping Lincoln win the Civil War, the miners could do as they pleased – and in any event, the pattern of the West was set, and Idaho was just falling into line. Mining camps didn't last forever, but their impact on Native peoples almost always did. In 1862 there were around 3500 Nez Perce living on their reservation, land legally protected for their sole use by the US government. They had been joined by almost 19,000 uninvited guests.

Sure enough, Pierce's gold didn't last forever. By 1870 the town's population had plummeted to barely more than six hundred, over three-quarters Chinese, sifting through the dust in claims the white prospectors considered worked out. The town slipped into hibernation until, at the turn of the century, another bull market developed in these mountains – for white pine. As timber culture historian Ralph Space recalled: 'In 1900 the rush to get Idaho white pine timberlands became a mad scramble. There was a race to locate and file on choice parcels of timberlands and long lines, sometimes two blocks long, formed at the land office in Lewiston.' Another flurry of entrepreneurial spirit surrounded Pierce, with the woodlands besieged with saws and axes.

But the pioneer lumberjacks were soon ousted by corporate adventurers from the East, and Pierce was transformed once again, this time into a company town, surrounded by 700,000 acres of prime timber owned by Potlatch Forests Inc., the giant company that the great Minnesota capitalist Frederick Weyerhaeuser had formed. Now the wild times reminiscent of the gold rush rolled down Main Street again – work for any man who wanted it, either at the local plywood plant or out in the woods, wages on which to raise a family, and on Saturday nights the loggers would come in from the forest and tear the place apart. Folklore has it that there was so much money swirling around that those loggers who died unmarried left their savings to the brothel-keeper at the bottom of the mountain – who became one of the richest women in Idaho. In 1960 the *Lewiston Morning Tribune* sighed cheerfully, 'Pierce has been one of the West's few lucky boom towns. Its wealth, in one form or another, has never petered out.'

In the year 2000, with the forests nearing exhaustion, Potlatch closed the plywood plant, with the loss of 1200 jobs. By then, most of the loggers had already been outsourced, downshifted and mechanized into redundancy. A lot of people in Pierce didn't even bother to sell their homes; they just boarded them up and left them to the debt collector. Unemployment in Clearwater County hit 22 per cent. It has fallen slightly since – but chiefly because more people have moved out. The area's average age climbed five years in a decade, the surest sign that family-raising wages were as rare as lunkers. Even some of the bars had closed down.

On the Saturday night of 1860 Days Pierce's few surviving drinking holes were doing a brisk trade to an increasingly slow-moving clientele. The softball tournament had declined somewhat into a succession of teary, Jaegermeister-fuelled marital tiffs, and the young man who'd ridden his ATV off the edge of a cliff had finally been pulled, bruised and embarrassed, from his ravine, so it was time for relaxation, with an option on melancholy oblivion. A few souls were sitting on the creaking balcony of a run-down bar, enjoying plastic cups of Coors and soaking up the last light of the day – a teenage boy who wasn't allowed inside, but was bored with sitting in the car, waiting for his mother and her boyfriend to finish drinking; an unsteady fisherman venting his spleen on an out-of-town couple who'd been debating, perhaps unwisely, the ecological impacts of illegal sewage dumping within his earshot: 'Screw Nature! Screw F— Nature! Do you hear me? Nature adapts! Do you have a problem with that point of view? Do you?'; and a couple of ATV riders from Colorado who'd misread Pierce's hard-partying reputation as a guarantee of glorious carnal conquest, and were now drinking through the disillusion: 'Seriously, British dude, do not go back in there, it's a f—ing hog pen! I think maybe *one* of 'em's still got her own teeth, but she's married.'

Hormonal off-road warriors might soon be more regular visitors to these bars. Desperate for an economic injection, the burghers of Clearwater County had spotted that ATV ownership had increased tenfold in the States in a decade, and were jealously eyeing the tourist dollars secured by neighbouring Utah's decision to turn much of its backwoods into a motorized playground. The fact that significant swathes of Utah's high country now resembled a smoggy, rutted, grassless speedway was a detail worth dismissing, and the pleas for

federal funding for the all-new Clearwater ATV Trail had been filed
– after gold and wood, Pierce badly needed to find another way to sell
its landscape, and to start another boom.

The Nez Perce's horizon was dark and uncertain in the years following
the Pierce gold strike. Miners were sprawling over the tribe's reserved
territory, their trespassing unhindered, their crimes unpunished. The
1855 treaty had been sitting in Washington in-trays for four years, and
even once it was ratified the flood of compensatory cash, housing,
school construction, farming equipment and medical care that Isaac
Stevens had promised failed to materialize, as a succession of Indian
Agents, the bureaucrats charged with fulfilling treaty obligations on
the ground, diverted the trickle of government funds into their own
pockets. By 1862 the US government had realized that the flourishing
settlements around Lewiston and Pierce, and the tension their ille-
gality was fomenting, required a touch of federal muscle, and the
leader of the Christian Nez Perce, Lawyer, was persuaded to accept the
arrival of a permanent military garrison in Lapwai. The Nez Perce
were told the soldiers were needed to ensure the integrity of their
reservation, while the settlers were reassured that such a presence
would protect them from savagery and their womenfolk from ravage;
in reality, the troops were dispatched to ensure the orderly flow of
Idaho's mineral wealth eastwards out of Idaho. Finally, the exponential development of white towns and cities right across the
Northwest had created a new and vocal political lobby, one steeped
in settler mythology, singing hymns to the foot soldiers of Manifest
Destiny, endlessly invoking the conqueror as victim, and forcefully
reminding Washington that, having sold the West to its immigrants,
it could never abandon them there. An inevitable, and very well
precedented, process had caught the Nez Perce in its undertow.

In May 1862 the pioneer Senator J. W. Nesmith of Oregon made it official, delivering one of the most notoriously nefarious speeches in the history of the great House. He spoke movingly of the raw deal the Nez Perce had been handed in recent years: their lands had been overspread, in violation of the 1855 treaty, their compensation had been late, derisory and often stolen, and should they ever breach their admirable pact of non-violence against the white man they faced immediate 'exterminating war'. The only fair solution was an obvious one – as the United States was clearly incapable of keeping its legal obligations, a new treaty must be negotiated. And, as a bonus, such a pact could generously relieve the Nez Perce of their burdensome millions of acres: 'The Indians are anxious to dispose of the reservation and remove to some point where they will not be intruded upon …'

The Senate concurred. A new treaty council was called for May 1863.

The precise details surrounding the council of 1863 remain shrouded in a fog of resentment and recrimination even to this day. What's certain is that the United States negotiators, led by Calvin H. Hale, arrived with an ambitious shopping list – they intended to secure at least 90 per cent of Nez Perce land for white settlement – and a well-worn but effective playbook. Speaking with the original forked tongue, Hale opened the council by addressing himself to 'the whole Nez Perce nation' – despite the fact that many of the tribe's more implacable bands, such as those of Tuekakas and White Bird, had yet even to reach the treaty grounds. His tactics were transparent – to drive a decisive wedge down the fault line that had been now growing in the Nez Perce community for a generation, between those who had embraced Christianity, modernity and a mercantile relationship with the whites and those who had favoured tradition and isolation.

The Nez Perce had indeed arrived in a fractured state, argument over religious orthodoxy and submission to United States' law compounded by resentment over Chief Lawyer's status as spokesman for the nation, and by perceptions of uneven generosity from the scarcely competent Indian Agents. But the tribe's capacity to talk a problem into a solution revealed itself once more, and a united front was eventually formed. The Nez Perce, still represented by Lawyer, offered to sell the gold fields and the land around Lewiston to the government, but to retain the remainder of the territory which Stevens had promised would be theirs for eternity. It was a sane and fair proposal, which received a prompt response – Hale and his cronies began tirelessly sowing division. They held private meetings with the leaders of the Christian bands, emphasizing the generous compensation on offer, often including the promise of a large chief's home and personal salary, showing them that the new shrunken reservation would displace others but in fact protect their village's homelands, and reminding them of the eternal fires that awaited the heathen hold-outs. By contrast the traditionalist tribes were insulted in public, ignored in private session, threatened with penury and oppression as the only alternatives to submission and conversion. At the forefront of this noxious campaign was a familiar face, that of Henry Spalding, recently returned to his Lapwai mission having failed in his efforts to organize a fortune-raising expedition to the gold fields, and now using all his fire and brimstone to condemn the non-Christian tribes whom he had come virulently to detest. Even his old friend Tuekakas was declared damned.

Under such pressure, the fragile consensus between the disjointed bands collapsed. The gap between those who saw the new demands as onerous but bearable and those who felt them simply inconceivable was growing ever wider. At a marathon overnight tribal council, the leaders regretfully agreed that they could no longer act in unison – those bands who wished to sign a new treaty could do so, those who wished to head home and deal with the government later (or preferably never) would not be bound by what was agreed without them. Tuekakas, White Bird and others packed up their lodges and left.

Hale acted decisively and gleefully. The treaty was drawn up, handing over just under seven million acres of Nez Perce land to the US government, reducing the reservation by 90 per cent. The nugget of retained property surrounded most of the Christian bands around Lapwai and the Clearwater River, while the government claimed ownership of Tuekakas' beloved summer and winter valleys of the Wallowa and Inmaha rivers, the White Bird band's territories around the bountiful Salmon River, the elk and deer ranges of the great valley of the Snake River, much of the wide root-harvesting fields of the Wieppe and Camas Prairies, and the Lolo forest with its routes to the buffalo grounds. Hale then cobbled together fifty-one signatories, led by Lawyer and drawn almost exclusively from the Christian bands (there were fifty-six marks on the 1855 treaty, and Hale was clearly collecting Xs to make this new document appear just as universally accepted as that one – always eager to assist, Spalding signed) and brazenly declared that the *entire* Nez Perce nation had expressed its will. The reality is cloudy in some cases – a few dissident leaders may have agreed with the treaty but refused to sign out of personal resentment towards Lawyer – but is crystal-clear in others. The White Bird and Tuekakas bands, for example, had just had their homelands sold on their behalf, without a single village member being in attendance, let alone in agreement. Not for nothing is the 1863 compact still called the Thief Treaty.

That Hale, Spalding and their crew were acting in wholly bad faith is beyond debate, but the more complex and divisive figure in this scene is Chief Lawyer. Records of the discussions show that he made no effort to explain to the Americans that he no longer spoke for the whole tribe. Why did he comply with the conceit that the unified Nez Perce were still being represented, even after the dissident bands had left the treaty grounds? The least favourable explanation is preferred by many of the descendants of the bands whose land was lawlessly sold, whose characterization of Lawyer bears comparison with that of Napoleon the pig in George Orwell's *Animal Farm*, corrupted

Chief Lawyer, seated centre, representing the Christian Nez Perce at a treaty amendment in 1868.

until he became indistinguishable from his oppressors.

Lawyer was certainly on friendly terms with many white arrivals, particularly Spalding, and as a tribal leader he was legally entitled to a salary and house from federal money, but tenacious rumours of further enrichment also persisted. Some believed he'd taken a bribe to accept the construction of a ferry and warehouse at Lewiston; another evocative story tells of a young Nez Perce, Paukalah, stumbling into the local Indian Agent's office one night to find Lawyer counting a tableful of gold coins by lamplight. Whatever his fiscal circumstances, it seems reasonable to state that Lawyer's frequent outbursts of fury at the mistreatment of his people, particularly regarding the laughable failure to fulfil all those treaty promises of schools, doctors and farm equipment, demonstrated that he hadn't sold out the Nez Perce. A complicating consideration, though, is the disintegration of his relationship with the other tribal leaders. The trust between the bands had rapidly eroded since the white arrivals, and in the years prior to the treaty Lawyer had often referred to the isolationist villagers as 'children', unwilling to accept the move to historical adulthood that modernity represented, while as a fast-improving preacher he could speak at length on the terrible fate that awaited the unconverted. It's surely no coincidence that the return to Lapwai of Lawyer's favourite Bible tutor was followed soon after by his decisive break with the intra-tribal bond.

Finally, a more sympathetic answer is on offer. Like the protection racketeers they were, the US negotiators had spoken of their desire to shield the Nez Perce from the threat of violence – while taking the sinister step of calling their troops to the treaty grounds. No one needed to explain that the tiny US Army garrison at Lapwai was the tip of a martial iceberg of a magnitude the tribe could scarcely contemplate. Military obliteration was never mentioned – Hale knew that to threaten violence, or 'show the rifle', was a scandalous breach of tribal council etiquette – but it didn't need to be. As Rebecca Miles, the chairwoman of the Nez Perce Tribal Executive Committee, said of the Thief Treaty in 2006: 'Our leaders had no choice. They were being threatened with being wiped out.'

Betrayal or not, the Christian tribes received very few pieces of silver for their troubles. The treaty set a price of just £262,500 for almost seven million acres of land, plus the usual sweeping promises of education, healthcare, farming instruction and so on. Once again, the treaty got held up in Washington, and any money that did reach Idaho rarely got past the web of government graft and waste. In 1864 the governor of Idaho, Caleb Lyon, visited Lapwai and gave this assessment of what had been done for the Nez Perce by the Indian Agents employed to serve their needs and fight their corner:

> I find no schoolhouse, church or Indians under instruction … I find
> that the farmers at the Agency have lived on the United States,
> seemingly in indolence, not raising enough for their own sustenance,
> neither devoting any time to instructing the Indians … I find the wife

of one of the employees set down on the papers as a Blacksmith and the wife of another employee to be an Assistant Teacher, who has never taught a single hour ... I find the name of a Physician on the papers at a salary of $1,200 per annum who is not at the Agency more than three hours per week ...

The only work being done was dishonest. The Agents sold timber on Nez Perce land to local lumbermen, then realized that they could actually sell it *twice* – once as standing trees, then, after buying the felled logs back with federal funds (to build all those promised tribal buildings), they could then shift it again as firewood. Agents took bribes to let settlers occupy the buildings that were constructed for tribal purposes, or to use the mill and blacksmiths intended exclusively for tribal use. Appalled, the inspecting governor accurately summarized the US government's record for keeping its treaty promises to Native America: 'I find nothing but criminal negligence and indifference to the treaty stipulations with the Indians.' His outrage, though justified, may not have been entirely sincere – Governor Lyon's later career was dogged by the allegation that he'd faked a robbery in a Washington hotel room in order personally to pilfer $40,000 of Nez Perce appropriations.

Lawyer's frustrations were far from unique. The US government would soon lose patience with negotiating with Native America, but not before reaching a grand total in excess of 370 individual treaties brokered, drawn up, and, in every single case, breached.

Just as signing the treaty garnered no immediate benefit for the Christian Nez Perce, not signing was of little instant consequence to the dissident, or non-treaty, bands. They returned to their homelands and no effort was made to evict them, nor did any flood of settlers invade – the Idaho gold was already playing out, and many adventurers were moving on. Those who stayed, however, were putting down roots, either as farmers and ranchers claiming bottomland in the Salmon and Inmaha valleys or as traders and civic leaders in Lewiston, a town now on firmer legal foundations, well situated to serve as a mercantile crossroads for the Northwest. As one local historian put it in conversation: 'Think of Lewiston as a Wal-Mart. It sold everything to everybody for miles around.'

Most vigorously, it sold Idaho, with newspapers and local politicians entering the most competitive fray in the West – boosterism. Immigration was the lifeblood of a newly founded town, and leaflets, exhibition stalls and newspaper articles eulogizing a new life in Western towns desperate for warm bodies were sprayed across the country in a Darwinian marketing brawl. An article in the *Lewiston Teller* – in response, as most such examples were, to a fictitious enquiry about the area from a potential emigrant back East – sets the tone: 'Our soil cannot be excelled ... Our climate is mild, healthy and invigorating ... [Immigrants] will prosper and become more affluent more readily than in any other locality we know of.'

Taking up the familiar theme of divine design, another local paper offered this fragrant analysis of the just purchased Camas Prairie in response to another 'letter to the editor': 'The Almighty never planned a piece of country so big as this with less waste land. Every element of prosperity lies at the doorstep of every man who has the good fortune to own a quarter section of this fertile soil. Tickle it with a plough and it will laugh you a harvest of flour.'

With luring new arrivals a prerequisite for survival, Lewiston and its farming outposts hardened towards the dissident Nez Perce – north-central Idaho had to appear placid and safe to outsiders, not a haven for, as they were now routinely called in the local press, 'outlaw Indians'. The small number of sympathetic voices faced a chorus of antagonism towards the non-treaty tribes that grew louder by the year. And anyway, as the anglicized dress, language and financial success of a handful of Christian Nez Perce headmen was taken to prove,

'Indianness' would, it was widely believed, prove an impermanent local feature.

In fact, the opposite was growing more likely. Bewildered and embittered by the Thief Treaty and harassed by settlers arriving in their valleys with fence posts and ploughshares, the dissident Nez Perce were returning to their traditional rites and belief systems with the zeal of the recently unconverted. Life had manifestly been better before the whites had arrived, so band leaders such as Tuekakas, Toohoolhoolzote and White Bird encouraged their people to replicate those times in their hunting and gathering, celebrations and prayers. The teachings of a local prophet, Smohalla, also chimed with this ambition: armed with a tale of his own resurrection, that borrowed from both a *wyakin* quest and the Easter teachings of his missionary rivals, the hunchback Smohalla preached that a return to traditional faiths and the ancient reverence for Mother Earth would rid the Northwest of the white newcomers and return to life those killed by their diseases and devil water. Considering the ubiquitous evidence that hymns and haircuts were not serving the best interest of the natives of the Northwest, Smohalla's individual influence is hard to quantify, but the widespread revival of traditional Indian rites in the 1860s and 1870s came to be associated with his 'Dreamer' movement. This association was most widely promoted by white advocates seeking to belittle the claims of any discontented tribes – the *Oregonian Telegram* suggested that any tribal leader connected to the Dreamers should be banished from the Northwest, as the 'cult' was 'teaching them to despise civilisation and ignore the authority of the United States' while the *San Francisco Chronicle* offered this eerie analysis of their public enemy number one:

> Smohalla, the Dreamer, is a sort of Indian Mohamet. His doctrine is a destroying one – to exterminate the palefaces, and to restore the whole country to the Indians. He has a most inspiring manner, and has thousands of followers. All the disaffected and renegade Indians

who refuse to go upon the reservations ... will wage war upon the whites, agreeably to the teachings of Smohalla.

Tuekakas, despairing of his efforts to make peace between competing faiths, had indeed torn up his Bible in 1863, and imposed strict rules of traditional worship, language and practice on his people. Protected by the natural isolation of their valley and the ample unclaimed land that still lay beyond their borders, the Wallowa band of the Nez Perce were now among the last Native peoples within the United States whose lifestyles remained largely unsullied by colonial influence. Tuekakas fiercely protected their independence, marking the boundaries of his homelands by building a line of cairns running over Minam Summit, refusing the offers of free government beef that were clearly intended to undercut the band's hunter-gatherer lifestyle, and destroying the equipment of any speculators or surveyors who wandered in from the increasingly populated Grande Ronde Valley in search of unclaimed grazing land. His position was clear: 'Inside is the home of my people – the white man may take the land outside. Inside this boundary all our people were born. It circles around the graves of our fathers, and we will never give up these graves to any man.'

But Tuekakas was growing frail, his sight now so weak that a Nez Perce boy was assigned to share his saddle, acting as his eyes. His sons would soon have to lead the band – the gregarious and vigorous Ollokot, revered as a hunter and warrior, and the more thoughtful Hin-mah-too-yah-lat-kekht, a name approximately anglicized to Thunder Rolling over the Mountains. Having accompanied his father to many councils and meetings, Hin-mah-too-yah-lat-kekht, just thirty-one, had developed an impressive ability to handle the eccentricities of white people, one reason why he would soon acquire nationwide fame; another, in the rapidly simplifying world of the mass media, was that he had a second, recognizable and pronounceable name. He had adopted his father's baptized title, and had come to be known as Joseph.

Tuekakas died in August 1871. His son Joseph would later eloquently describe his final moments in a famous passage that, while possibly unreliable in translation, is piercingly clear in sentiment:

Soon after this my father sent for me. I saw he was dying. I took his hand in mine. He said, 'My son, my body is returning to my mother earth, and my spirit is going to see the Great Spirit Chief. When I am gone, think of your country. You are the chief of these people. They look to you to guide them. Always remember that your father never sold his country. You must stop your ears whenever you are asked to sign a treaty selling your home. A few more years and white men will be all around you. They have their eyes on this land. My son, never forget my dying words. This country holds your father's body. Never sell the bones of your father and mother.'

I pressed my father's hand and told him that I would protect his grave with my life. My father smiled and passed away to the spirit land. I buried him in that beautiful valley of winding waters. I love that land more than all the rest of the world. A man who would not love his father's grave is worse than a wild animal.

Tuekakas was buried near his favourite summer camp at the confluence of the Wallowa and Lostine rivers. Later, in 1926, his (probable) remains were moved to the head of Wallowa Lake in a sombre and unlikely funeral procession of costumed warriors and Model-T Fords, where an obelisk was erected in his honour. (Next to the monument there is now a patch of open pasture, whose owner has been campaigning for more than a decade for the right to turn the land neighbouring the likely resting place of one of Native America's most important leaders into a subdivision of luxury homes, or, failing that, a trailer park. The memorial to a man who died proclaiming his people's right to their homeland is currently overlooked by a giant Stars and Stripes, next to a large placard bearing the slogan 'Private Property is the Foundation of Freedom'.)

Joseph's pledge to his father would be tested within weeks. The well-settled Grande Ronde Valley experienced a drought in 1871, and the failing pastures forced a handful of enterprising cattle and sheep farmers to enter the Wallowa in search of lush grazing and a harvest of hay. Finding almost unlimited forage for their herds, as well as a river stocked with mysterious but delectable red fish and nearby forests crammed with game, they resolved to settle, and in 1872 brought their wives and children. By the end of that year seventy-five settlers had laid claim to a patch of land in the Wallowa. Joseph met these settlers at a series of good-natured but inconclusive meetings, where he would patiently explain that his father had never sold the valley, while they would insist that they had been informed that it was now United States public land, to which they had a rightful claim. Under the homesteading law designed to inspire westward settlement, you simply paid $16 at a registry office, took your fence posts and marked out 160 vacant acres; once you could prove that you'd occupied and worked on the land for two years, it was yours.

The next spring, the stalemate became slightly worse. Eleven of the less congenial settlers sent a petition to the local Indian Agent claiming that Joseph had 'threatened to burn our houses etc. etc.' and demanding armed protection. This inflammatory nonsense caught something of a nerve, for on the southern border of Oregon a charismatic tribal leader known as Captain Jack was cutting a swathe through neighbouring settler communities in the opening exchanges of what would be known as the Modoc War. Perhaps wary of getting too involved in another Indian dispute on the ground – Captain Jack had responded to the peace proposals of the government's representative, General Edward Canby, by shooting him in the face, stabbing him repeatedly and stealing his coat – the responsible powers tried to impose a solution from a distance. In an office in Washington a map of the Wallowa Valley was divided in two: one end (the one with almost all the white settlements in it) was assigned to the Nez Perce, while the other (unsettled, and dominated by Indian fishing grounds and hunting trails) was handed to the whites. Back in the valley, both sides largely ignored the plan, confident that someone would eventually recognize its idiocy.

In fact, such a sane and sanguine attitude continued to characterize most white and Indian relations in the Wallowa. The Nez Perce were willing to tolerate such a small amount of settlement, provided their lifestyle remained sustainable, and the settlers, by and large, simply wanted their status confirmed one way or the other. Numerically, the settlers knew they faced only obliteration if trouble truly flared (there were fewer than 150 of them, actually only slightly less than the Wallowa band, but the Indians had access to fearsome reinforcements) and they were by no means wedded to the Wallowa – many admitted they were just hanging on for a government payout to leave the land to the Indians. One observer, Captain Whipple, noted the settlers' willingness to 'sell out at the first opportunity and move to a more promising locality. This shows how the white people who reside here regard this valley. On the other hand, the Indians love it.' In this relatively level-headed context, friendships could form – a shared love of horse-racing (and gambling on it) offered a sporting common ground, while most of the settlers were happy for their children to hero-worship the playful Joseph.

Sadly, however, beyond the valley, hysteria reigned. The petitioners' scaremongering fused with lurid newspaper reports of the Modoc War to convince the citizens of the surrounding towns of Lewiston and the Grande Ronde Valley that, in the words of one local paper, 'another Indian scare is about to transpire' in the Wallowa. In February 1873 the citizens of La Grande, the nearest large town west of the Wallowa, sent for two hundred rifles to put down the imminent uprising, while Joseph was mythologized as a kind of pirate king, certain to join forces with Captain Jack, and the settlers' funeral eulogies were written, casting them, of course, as the pristine victims of the piece. When the government's map-making folly was announced, the Union County *Mountain Sentinel* called it 'the crowning act of infamy ... actually driving earnest, honest and hardy pioneers from their homes', before the editor, unexpectedly, slipped into blank verse: 'The Wallowa Gone; Dirty, Greasy Indians to Hold the Valley; Two hundred white men and families driven from the beauty spot of Oregon ... Citizens of Wallowa! Awake and Drive Joseph and his Band from the face of the Earth.'

Such enthusiasm for another man's squabble should have aroused suspicion. In fact, this was the overture for a persistent theme – the image of the doughty, impoverished settler, keeper of the pioneer flame, was being invoked by those in less straitened circumstances, to force the hand of a government wedded to the homesteading myth. The reality was that the struggle for the Wallowa wasn't being fought on behalf of a couple of hundred settlers, but for many thousands of cattle. The prosperous stockmen of the Grande Ronde Valley were growing dependent on the summer range of the Wallowa (the number of cows that summered in the valley trebled between 1873 and 1874, while human settlement at best stagnated) and they resented the competition for grass from the Nez Perce's own herds of cattle, and particularly their thousands of horses. From early 1873 an alliance of influential stockmen, malleable local politicians and bilious newspaper editors, almost none of whom lived in the Wallowa and many of whom had never even seen it, waged a voluble campaign ostensibly upholding the rights of the valley's heroic settlers over the demands of the transient, 'roaming' Indians. They got their way, and on 16 June 1875 President Grant signed a bill abandoning all efforts to redeem the map-making farce, and simply reopened the entire valley to white settlement. Most of the young warriors in the Wallowa band, in concert with the leaders of other dissident Nez Perce bands, such as White Bird and Toohoolhoolzote, many of whom were suffering far worse encroachment and depredation from settlers on their territories, took this as the signal for war. Joseph and the Clearwater chief Looking Glass, a forthright character who had learned much of the power of the United States from his frequent travels east to the buffalo country, successfully argued that that way oblivion lay. Whatever the solution, it would be found through dialogue.

Following the reopening, more people (and cows) made their home in the Wallowa, around seventeen bi-pedal families arriving in the spring of 1876. An air of permanence began to settle – more log homes, post offices, churches, school houses, irrigation ditches, a petition for a county road. Soon, one of the more tangential products of a burgeoning settler community would appear: a marriage agency. The enterprising D. B. Reavis noted that 'old bachelors are largely in the majority' in the Wallowa, while further east 'Missouri was full of young and old maidens and blushing widows'. He took orders from the valley's lonely hearts, most of whom seemed concerned with matters other than moonlight and romance: one suitor requested 'a good woman of any age or size; one who has a natural fondness for pigs, and stock generally'; another demanded his mate 'not to be over 30 years old, weight 130lbs, be good looking, a good conversation-alist, and fond of fish', while the Tully brothers asked for a job lot of two, 'with even temper, not particular as to size, large one preferred. One to be a good cook and the other with a suitable voice for cow calling.'

Another sign of encroaching 'civilization' emerged. Citizens from the Grande Ronde began visiting the valley on hunting and fishing expeditions, and a few enterprising locals even began building a boat to take the tourists onto Wallowa Lake to maximize their catch. The valley's prodigious fauna, unscathed by the passage of an immigrant trail and well managed, both by design and circumstance, by the Nez Perce, was drawing widespread interest. As one early settler, Loren Powers, recalled:

> Large herds of deer and elk were frequently seen crossing the valley, while bear were so numerous as to be a decided menace to the stock industry. Prairie chicken, grouse, pheasants, ducks and geese were also

much in evidence. The streams also abounded with trout, salmon and red fish ... One could stand on a bridge and see schools of these fish that would darken the whole stream.

Those unfamiliar 'red fish', sockeye salmon spawning from the Pacific to Wallowa Lake in their millions in early summer, attracted comment from almost every visitor; the match-making Mr Reavis recalled 'red fish so easily caught and in such countless numbers', while a passing soldier made a diary note that he and half a dozen comrades reeled in at least seventy salmon in a day's sport: 'killed red fish in leisure'.

It would take just one generation for the leisurely application of fishing lines, shotguns, rifles and bear traps to complete their work in the Wallowa. In 1905 a correspondent to the local paper moaned that the deer, elk and bears had been practically wiped out: 'game has disappeared except to the wildest points.' And as for 'the peculiar species of Red Fish' that once darkened Wallowa Lake – 'the white settlers used them in such quantities as to destroy the species entirely'.

This efficient dispatch of the Wallowa's wildlife was far from unique; in almost every valley and prairie the opening of the American hinterland to settlement had an impact on its fauna that almost belies description. The ecological historian Tim Flannery perfectly captures the teeth-clenched mood of those who have chronicled this quasi-military assault, describing the continental conquest as 'a history of ruthless environmental exploitation, the audacity and imbecility of which leaves one gasping for breath'. In a national drama in which wilderness stood for evil and those who tamed and cultivated it doing God's work, the fauna served as fall guy. Between the arrival of the first colonists on a teeming continent and the low point of North American biodiversity, in the 1950s, it's estimated that the European settlers had reduced America's wildlife population by no less than four-fifths.

The annihilation of the animal republic passed over each portion of the continent in a series of distinct, if sometimes coincidental, waves – all of which broke over the Wallowa. First had come the fur trade, with initially French, British and Dutch trappers, then newly liberated Americans, skinning beaver, martens, raccoons, bears, wolves, minks and otters as if they were (as was often the case in flighty European society) going out of fashion. At the height of the trade single French ports reported taking in more than 100,000 beaver pelts a year; London alone was importing 50,000 wolf skins and 30,000 bear pelts per annum. The whims of couture saved the beaver on the brink of extinction, while less prodigious species, such as the sea mink, weren't so lucky.

The next wave was formed of pioneer settlers, killing for food as they faced starvation crossing and populating marginal lands. The followers of the Oregon Trail and similar routes had helped destroy the West's great herds of tule elk, mule deer, white-tailed deer, prong-horned antelope and bighorn sheep, forcing the rump of their populations deep into the mountains. Once communities became more settled, pursuing these game creatures into their high country retreats then became a sustaining sport, and they were all but wiped out. The diarist Hamlin Garland recalled the impact of a single year of settlement on the Iowa plains where his family, surrounded by other homesteaders, had driven their stakes: 'All the wild things died or hurried away, never to return … all of the swarming lives which had been native here for countless centuries were utterly destroyed.'

Next, with secure settlement, came reclassification. Any creature whose behaviour conflicted with yours, or whose numbers were inconveniently boosted by your environmental impact, could only be one thing – a 'varmint'. And pests needed controlling.

The most vigorously persecuted varmints were those that were deemed capable of killing valuable calves and, later, sheep – namely wolves, coyotes, cougars, bears, golden eagles and, incorrectly, bald eagles. Most new stock-raising communities, including the Wallowa,

organized volunteer committees for predator eradication, and bounties were placed on the ears of coyotes, cougars and, most importantly, wolves. However, the explosion of edible stock across the
Western landscape ensured the resilience of small predator populations, so around the turn of the century the fiercely independent and
self-reliant Western communities did what they were rapidly
becoming accustomed to doing – they lobbied the federal government for help. Federal predator control began in 1914, opening an
astonishing chapter of bureaucratic incompetence and insensitivity:
agents scattered strychnine pellets across prairies, set cyanide guns to
shoot into passing creatures' faces, injected hens' eggs with thallium
and left poisoned horse carcasses in open fields to slay any passing
scavengers, inadvertently intoxicating the soil *and* killing any creature which might later feed on the corpses of the intended victims.
The murder was indiscriminate, inefficient (bureaucrats privately
admitted, for example, that bobcats didn't eat stock, but someone
was getting work killing them, so they carried on) and remarkably
unrelenting. (It was Richard Nixon, a president whose environmental legislation offers a considerable rebuke to his many detractors, who finally banned the poisoning of predators on public land –
only for Ronald Reagan, a president whose environmental record
serves as Exhibit A, to repeal the law.)

On one level, the federal programme worked well. By the 1950s
there were no more than six hundred grizzlies left in the contiguous
United States (some ecological historians believe there may once
have been 1.5 million) while the grey wolf, the creature that had
taught the Nez Perce to sing, had been completely wiped out west of
the Mississippi. Only the mercurial coyote, too clever for traps and
stink bombs, could never be broken.

The final wave of attack probably accounts for the Wallowa's
mysterious red fish – industrial harvest. When the 'free wealth' of the
American continent's bountiful consumable fauna met the right
technological innovation, oblivion came swiftly. For example, to the

east, just as the Wallowa was being settled, the invention of the breech-loading shotgun was seeing off the most numerous bird on earth, the passenger pigeon. Single flocks of this elegant, fleet creature could number two billion, blocking out the sun as they passed over, their guano falling like snow. Breech-loading was invented in 1870 – and the last wild passenger pigeon fell to earth in Ohio in 1900.

Meanwhile, to the valley's west, in 1866, another invention was being rolled out, when the first salmon cannery opened on the Columbia River.

It's quite hard to fish a species to extinction, because you'll normally stop making a profit before the last cod dies (as we'll see later, there are much more effective ways of wiping out aquatic ecosystems). The salmon fishermen on the Columbia River did their best, though, their output peaking at over forty-five million pounds of canned salmon (considered, ironically, a base, working-class foodstuff) in a year at the turn of the century. For over twenty years the fishermen actually dumped tens of thousands of the red sockeye salmon belly-up into the sea, selling only the superior chinook – faced with what looked like a limitless supply, the early Pacific salmon industry allowed about half of their catch to rot – but over-fishing halved the chinook run between 1884 and 1888, so the sockeye started to go in the cans, and the species all but collapsed.

The red fish, just like the deer, elk, wolves and bears, were gone. The canneries wouldn't be the last assault on the salmon runs that had helped define the Native tribes of the Northwest – nor would this be the last time the Nez Perce crossed paths with the technology of extinction.

While the pressure on the Wallowa's wildlife was just beginning to build, the strain on the valley's pastures had already reached breaking

point. The seasonal grazing of the Nez Perce horse herd was a growing irritation to those settlers with dreams of cattle baronetcies, and
as the year-round inhabitants and 'improvers' of the valley, the immigrants' claims of rightful ownership grew more insistent by the year.
Few were more obstreperous than Wells McNall, a violent-tempered
Indian hater who was endlessly appealing for military protection for
his farmland, and who took to corralling and castrating any Nez
Perce horses that strayed into his fields. In June 1876 McNall's running feud with the tribe took a fateful turn, as he stormed into a Nez
Perce hunting camp and falsely accused a group of warriors of stealing horses. Alec Findley, McNall's peaceable and popular neighbour,
attempted to defuse the argument, but McNall and a young Nez
Perce known as Wilhautyah came to blows. As both men scrambled
for McNall's gun (the Indians were unarmed), McNall soon found
himself staring down his own barrel, and indeed at his Maker, as he
squealed to Findley: 'Shoot the son of a bitch! Shoot, you damned
fool!'

Panicking, Findley let fly, killing Wilhautyah instantly. It certainly
wasn't the first murder of a Nez Perce by a settler (more than thirty
tribal members had so far been unlawfully killed, with just one settler
convicted of any crime) but in the tinderbox of the Wallowa it was
by far the most significant.

The Nez Perce dressed for war and the settlers dug in for a siege.
Warriors took target practice in clear view of Findley's home; the
whites sent for rifles and begged for military support. At a series of
stormy meetings Joseph and Ollokot, close friends of Wilhautyah,
demanded that Findley and McNall be handed over; the distraught
Findley offered himself for surrender several times, but the other
settlers resisted such capitulation. Government agents arrived to
meet Joseph and Ollokot, and faced restrained but uncompromising
demands – the camel's back had been broken and it was time the
whites left the Wallowa for good. The unlawful spilling of Nez Perce
blood in the valley only made the land more precious, more certainly

owned. An explosion seemed likely; many settlers left, and two cavalry companies were sent from Lapwai to keep the peace. Ultimately, though, a resentful compromise was reached in September 1876: Findley stood trial for the murders in the Union County Court, but, with the Indian witnesses unwilling to participate in the white judicial system, he went free.

An uprising had been averted, but the murder of Wilhautyah had focused federal minds, and all Washington agreed that the tense uncertainty of the Wallowa was no longer acceptable – chiefly because in twenty minutes, on 25 June 1876, the rules had changed forever. That's how long the rebellious Sioux and Cheyenne warriors led by Crazy Horse, Gall and Sitting Bull are believed to have taken to cut down General George Armstrong Custer, at the time the most famous soldier in America, and more than two hundred of his men, at the Battle of Little Big Horn. It was a firestorm in which America's national faith in the inevitability of continental conquest was painfully bruised, and the mood of the government was irreparably darkened, as the West was flooded with yet more troops with orders to drive any 'renegade' Indians into exile, extermination or surrender. The history keepers of the tribe that fought at the Big Horn now acknowledge that the finest hour of their resistance also marked the moment when their subjugation became inevitable – but for many other tribes of the West, the distant battle would prove an equally gloomy turning point. (Perhaps that explains why, according to several reports, Custer died laughing.)

All were agreed – the Nez Perce problem now demanded a permanent solution, and the roaming Dreamer bands needed to be securely tied down. It was the perfect task for that most predictable of historical arrivals, 'the man from the government', a distant appointee unencumbered with any basic understanding of the situation yet burdened with an absolute faith in his own compassion, wisdom and decision. General Oliver Otis Howard was just such a man.

CHAPTER FOUR

POISON

'I never thought I'd see the day when you went to the store for a bottle of water. Water?'
HORACE AXTELL, spiritual leader, Nez Perce tribe

'Did you ever see a real rose?'
'Nope, but maybe some day, if they ever dam the river, we'll have lots of water and all kinds of flowers'
The Man Who Shot Liberty Valance,
directed by JOHN FORD, 1962

GENERAL OLIVER HOWARD had earned his spurs – but lost his right arm – in the Civil War, before going on to secure a reputation as a redoubtable Indian fighter pursuing the Apaches across the southern deserts. His widely admired career received another garland in 1874 when he was appointed Commander for the Department of Columbia, with responsibility for patrolling and pacifying America's most north-westerly corner. He actually met young Joseph very early in his tenure, a chance encounter when both men were visiting the Umatilla reservation. Joseph asked Howard if he brought news from Washington of the Wallowa Valley's legal status; the general replied that he did not, the men shook hands, and parted.

*General Oliver Otis Howard, the Commander of the
Department of Columbia.*

Howard, a devout Presbyterian who enjoyed his press nickname 'The
Christian General' and who fancied himself as a sympathetic student
of the red men's plight, read plenty into the exchange: 'I think Joseph
and I then became quite good friends.' In the winter of 1875 Howard
proclaimed himself a champion of the Wallowa band's property
rights, writing to Washington that 'it is a great mistake to take from
Joseph and his band of Indians that valley … possibly Congress can
be induced to let these really peaceable Indians have this poor valley
for their own.' A military colleague, George Crook, recalled that
Howard had ordained himself to a mission of mercy: 'He told me he
thought the Creator had placed him on earth to be the Moses of the
Negro. Having accomplished that mission, he felt satisfied his next
mission was with the Indian.'

In early 1876 Howard instructed his right-hand man, Major
Henry Clay Wood, to undertake a legal study of the status of the
Wallowa Valley. Wood returned from the treaties and textbooks

unequivocal – the Indians still owned the land, their title had not been extinguished by the Thief Treaty, and the government needed to choose between purchasing the valley properly or paying off the settlers to leave. His report to Howard also revealed an understanding of what was at stake that, though unable fully to escape the ethnocentricity of the age, probably represents the clearest insight from any government figure during the whole Nez Perce tragedy:

> I cannot refrain from adding a word to express my convictions of the real cause of the dissatisfaction existing among the Nez Perce with the treaty of '63. Nature has implanted in the human heart a strong and undying love of home – the home, with its scenes and attachments, of childhood. This sentiment pervades the heart of the child of the forest and plain – the rude child of nature – no less, perhaps with a *more* fervent glow, than the breast of the native of the city, the pampered child of enlightened and luxurious civilisation.
>
> To the parties to the treaty, it brought no loss, no change; to the non-treaties it revealed new homes, new scenes; it left behind deserted firesides; homes abandoned and desolate; casting a shadow upon their wounded and sorrowing hearts ...
>
> In this God-given sentiment – the love of home – is to be found the true cause of the Nez Perce division.

Howard began to bandy about the idea of a commission of wise Washington men that would judge the case of the Nez Perce bands which had not signed in '63 – and, once the Wilhautyah murder and Bighorn rout had focused their minds, the politicians agreed. In October 1876, Howard hand-picked three estimable easterners whom a Lapwai local would later describe as 'excellent men ... all kings of finance, but with not a speck of Indian sense, experience, or knowledge' and set off back for Idaho. The dissident Nez Perce bands converged to meet the commission at the Indian Agency in Lapwai in hopeful spirits – knowing that their self-proclaimed friends, General

Howard and Henry Clay Wood, would be the fourth and fifth wise men.

The commission performed quite startlingly badly. Stark false-hoods were accepted as fact – for example, that Tuekakas *had* been bound by the treaty of 1863 (Howard would claim his was the third signature on the paper), while some statements from the Washington magi, for example that the Wallowa was too cold for Indians to live in, bordered on the infantile. The Dreamer movement was end-lessly referred to as a cross between a blood-drinking cult and a pan-American guerrilla network, and Joseph's patient, placatory descriptions of the legal reality and moral rightness of the tribes' demands were cut short and discounted. His now famous analysis of the US government's negotiating tactics – that they took your horses, but paid your neighbour for them – cut no ice.

Realizing they were facing a stitch-up, the non-treaty bands walked out, leaving the commission to draft its recommendations alone – the non-treaty Nez Perce were to be moved out of their homelands and onto the Christian reservation under the threat of force, where each family would receive a twenty-acre plot of the worst available land; the leaders of the Dreamer 'fanaticism' were to be banished to Indian Territory in distant Oklahoma to end their pernicious influence on the Northwest; and, finally, the army was requested to occupy the Wallowa Valley immediately to usher Joseph's band permanently over the mountains and away.

To his considerable historical credit, Henry Clay Wood refused to sign the report. Howard, by contrast, had all but written it, domi-nating the commission from start to finish. His conversion, in less than a year, from Nez Perce advocate to their oppressor in chief is as instructive as it is disconcerting.

Firstly, he was demonstrating the extent to which events at the Little Big Horn had changed everything. Howard knew that, just four months after banner headlines of massacres and scalpings, his elected paymasters were in no mood to negotiate with renegades.

Traditionalist, or 'Dreamer' Nez Perce in 1876. Timlpusman, second from right, is the great-grandfather of the Nez Perce spiritual leader Horace Axtell.

Secondly, his Christianity had been challenged. In the days prior to the commission, the non-treaty bands' implacable foes (including the federal Indian Agent who was supposed to represent them, and a handful of Christian Nez Perce leaders) had bombarded Howard with testimony regarding the heathen Dreamers, persuading him that Joseph had fallen under the mind control of the hunchback sorcerer Smohalla. It was a gross misrepresentation of the Wallowa band's independent commitment to their traditional faith, but it worked: the commission reported to Washington that 'a kind of wizard' was now Joseph's spiritual string-puller, 'who is understood to have great power over him and the whole band'. Under such circumstances, the Christian General felt that legal niceties should be shelved, and the non-treaty bands needed hastily corralling as close to a pastor as possible.

Finally, after two years in the Northwest, Howard had clearly learned the realities of settler politics. Helping the Nez Perce would have been profoundly unpopular, and almost certainly impermanent. To understand why, one needs to turn to Lewiston.

The last few years had not been kind to the tent city at the confluence of the Snake and the Clearwater. None of the local gold strikes had lasted much longer than Pierce's, the estimated $50 million that had been dug from the surrounding hills in a decade had generated little permanent wealth, locally at least, and catering for the new wave of farming settlers offered steady, but certainly not spectacular, business. By 1876 many of Lewiston's traders had, in the ceaselessly mobile fortune-hunting style of the early white West, simply drifted away. The town's status as territorial capital of Idaho had also been stolen – literally, the governor making a daring over-night escape with the Territorial Seal, in response to a better offer from the city of Boise. Lewiston's sole growth industries were now prostitution and corruption – the arrival of the libidinous US Army and the supposed flow of funds to the Christian Nez Perce offering easy pickings – and the town's population had fallen well below the boom-time peak of ten thousand souls.

One reason for leaving Lewiston must have been that it was a profoundly challenging place to love. Situated at the entrance to a canyon, this was the lowest point in Idaho, a suntrap capable of sustaining fearsome summer temperatures, with little hope of the blessed intervention of rain – local lore has it that drenching thunderclouds often roll down the Clearwater Valley, divide to leave Lewiston bone dry, then re-form as they head towards the Wallowa. Nez Perce legend recalls that when this land was young, Símíinekem, the place where two rivers meet, was considered unfit for human habitation, 'because it was far too hot' (a conclusion with which this author can sympathize: in the heatwave of August 2006 the down-town temperature reached 117 degrees Fahrenheit – no time to be living in a camper van in the parking lot of the Lewiston Wal-Mart).

In 1873 a sterling remedy to Lewiston's permanently parched state was proposed, and work began on a ditch that would run precious water out of the Clearwater and into the Snake, via the centre of town. The project was blighted and ultimately bankrupted by the legal wrangling that would soon come to dominate the West – deciding who owned the water – but the ditch finally opened in 1874, conferring upon Lewiston the joys of orchards, rose gardens and the town's very own defining characteristic: a dreadful smell. The ditch immediately became the local sewer, garbage dump, pet cemetery and livestock trough, noxious at the best of times, overwhelming during the frequent water cut-offs for repairs. One reporter (actually writing in 1889, by when the town had been forced to put a lid over the open pit) described a flow of 'iron pots, oil cans, fruit cans, vegetable cuttings of all kinds, dead hens, dead cats and dogs ... the stench which arises from some portions of the covered ditch must be very offensive. There must be dead carcasses or other putrid matter lodged along its margin.'

As the ditch also served as Lewiston's main source of drinking water, the municipal baths and the best place to leave a rowdy drunk, public health was far from robust – a local doctor estimated in the mid-1870s that two-thirds of the town was sick at any one time. Those who drank from the ditch may have been the lucky ones – many of Lewiston's inhabitants sourced their water from a spring that percolated through the town's hilltop cemetery.

In the relentless, rootless search for the riches of the new West – land, gold, timber, salmon – death always walked too close to leave room for sentiment. If an enterprise wasn't raising a profit, you got out, and if a town was dying, you packed up, and it promptly died. In 1876, Lewiston's very survival remained uncertain. The craving for the lifeblood of immigration was palpable – as the *Lewiston Teller* stated in an editorial, the only future for the town lay with attracting 'the great number of robust and healthy people entirely destitute of remunerative employment' on the eastern seaboard 'to our fertile and healthy soil'. For Lewiston's press boosters, Indian uprisings such as Captain Jack's war and the Sioux and Cheyenne rebellions were an unthinkable prospect in their back yard, as 'report of it abroad would greatly check immigration to our borders'. Not surprisingly, petitions were regularly drawn up demanding the prompt subjugation of the dissident Nez Perce and (in a consistent request across the frontier West) the generous reinforcement of the local military presence.

When Henry Clay Wood's legal opinion was published, suggesting a magnanimous response to the Wallowa controversy, Lewiston laughed in his face, proclaiming him a Washington meddler who should leave such matters to the locals, 'who comprehend the situation', and suggesting, in what may be one of the earliest printed instances of the Mountain West's distaste for the nation's crucible of woolly liberal-mindedness, that Wood might be better employed 'on a fishing excursion somewhere in California'. The town was as steeped in the public commonplaces of self-reliance, independence and local volunteerism as the rest of the pioneer West, and the advice of a bookish top-down bureaucrat like Wood would never be welcome. Howard's commission was similarly derided – the *Teller* called it 'a farce' that the US government that 'has once bought this land and paid the purchase money' was renegotiating, simply, in their estimation, to appease an outlaw.

For young Joseph, viewed through the prism of Sitting Bull and Captain Jack, had been transformed into something of a hate figure in edgy Lewiston (and, indeed, across the Northwest), a violent rebel-in-waiting whose dignity and intellect, in a suitable phrase for a town densely populated with Deep Southerners, made him 'uppity'. He was characterized in the local press as 'haughty, insolent and defiant', of 'wanton and independent spirit', a man who 'manifested a degree of dignity and reserve importing more with the character of the chief of some great nation than that of a leader of a small band of outlaws'. Crowds would gather in towns that Joseph passed through, the locals fascinated by their local warrior king and possible bloody nemesis (ironically, they were often actually looking at Ollokot, who *was* a prodigious fighter, and a fearsome sight). There were even slanderous conspiracy theories that Joseph had already taken a house and salary from the government, or that the Wallowa in fact belonged to another band. So when Howard chose to call the commission rather than summarily put Joseph in his place – on the reservation – it was argued that he only increased the renegade's insolence, and thus the likelihood of a fatal conflagration. Howard's patriotism, and by extension his masculinity, were volubly called into question – one Oregon paper proclaimed that the Nez Perce felt nothing but love for the Christian General: 'just as they love their squ—s* for their inherent willingness to submit to all things the buck commands'. Successfully baited as being 'soft on defence', whatever charitable ambitions Howard had brought with him to the Northwest rapidly evaporated, the fix was in, and the Nez Perce's last chance for justice passed. The man from the government had done his worst.

It's an irony that cheers few of Lewiston's modern inhabitants that their home town's defining characteristic remains its smell. The composition of the air has changed considerably – but it still reeks. The eye-watering miasma that envelops the city daily also serves as unignorable proof that the Western settlers' folk philosophy of self-reliance, unfettered individual freedom and bitter distaste for external meddling is very much alive, though not, perhaps, alive and well.

The timber boom that enveloped Pierce at the turn of the century also re-energized Lewiston, restoring it as a trade hub for the Clearwater Forest lumber that floated downstream into giant log ponds on the edge of town. The area's corporate behemoth, Potlatch Forests Inc., opened a large sawmill in town and then, in 1950, a paper mill, efficiently converting Idaho's woodlands into everything from milk cartons to kitchen roll. Work was plentiful, the city grew fast, but paper production is a burdensome enterprise – it requires the use

---

* Now seems the best time to tackle this notorious nomenclature. To understand precisely how offensive the word sq—w is, resolve to attend work tomorrow referring to all your female colleagues exclusively by the 'c-word'. For that, sadly, is the exact etymology of the colloquial pioneer term for an Indian wife – a distasteful slur leading, understandably, to modern-day campaigns to rename the numerous Western streams, lakes and hilltops still bearing that mark. Always eager to avoid accusations of political correctness, most of the Western states have stridently resisted such changes, citing the cost of all the new maps and road signs, and raising the awful possibility of tourists getting lost.

and fouling of huge quantities of water (the paper mill used three times more water than the entire city) and generates a large quantity of airborne particles that happen to smell of raw cauliflower, possess the capacity to rot paint and metal and can make people very sick. The story goes that Potlatch's scientists spent a suitably biblical forty days divining the prevailing wind before locating the mill – and for every one of those forty days the wind blew in the opposite direction to its normal path, ensuring the smokestacks were built precisely upwind of the town centre. For the thirty years after the mill opened, as a tiny sample of the news reports from the *Lewiston Morning Tribune* amply illustrates, Lewiston served as an ailing case study of what happened when Western *laissez-faire*, a philosophy built around the plucky little farmer, met the equally plucky giant corporate polluter …

'Potlatch Corporation's main wastewater pipeline burst twice Sunday, sending more than 1.5 million gallons of effluent into two levee ponds … The coffee-coloured wastewater is the end-product of the pulp and paper process.'

'A malfunction at Potlatch Corp. pulp mill at Lewiston Monday evening and a minor temperature inversion Tuesday morning reduced visibility in the valley … A Miller Grade resident who said he was "choking to death" called the *Tribune* Monday evening for information about the pollution.'

'Failure of an air pollution control device at Potlatch Corp. may cause an increase in visible emissions for several weeks.'

'A leak of deadly chlorine gas at the Potlatch Corp. pulp mill at Lewiston forced the evacuation of hundreds of workers.'

'Bits of fuzzy, brownish fluff drifted across the Lewiston Clarkston Valley Wednesday. The culprit was the secondary treatment ponds at Potlatch Corp.'

'The big noise from the Potlatch Corp. plant will start again this afternoon.'

'Alice Swan, a Colfax nurse, testified that her doctor advised her to leave the valley. Her symptoms, including nausea and congested chest and sinuses, disappeared when she left.'

Her doctor had a point; in the 1970s Lewiston was labelled a 'non-attainment area' for consistently falling below federal healthy air-quality standards. For thirty years the town had well above average rates of allergies, respiratory illnesses and worse – 15 per cent of all lung cancer in the United States is caused by industrial particulates. Perhaps the finest gift from Potlatch to Lewiston came in Christmas 1971 when the plant shut down its effluent disposal pipe for cleaning, and simply dumped all its wastewater directly into the narrow, shallow Clearwater River. A fisherman notified the authorities that the entire river had turned a thick brown. In 1970, unsurprisingly, the Council on Economic Priorities had described Potlatch as a firm with 'records indicating no concern for environmental protection'.

But this is no cause for an exclusive hatchet job. As one local journalist with more than thirty years' experience of covering the region put it to me: 'Potlatch is not a particularly bad company. These are just the rules.' The founding principles of the West offered considerable leeway to those wishing to pollute the new continent – and this was never more true than in the last corner to be colonized.

The history of this epidemic of fouling begins when the Industrial Revolution crossed the United States at a stupefying speed – national pig iron production rose 1300 per cent in the six years from 1850, oil output rose from just two thousand barrels to 4.25 million in the decade from 1859, and from 1867 to 1897 steel output rose from just 1643 tonnes to over seven million, outstripping the supposed industrial heavyweights of Germany and Britain combined.

From 1850 to 1900, America's population trebled, but its economy multiplied *twelvefold* – an expansion unknown in human history.

With individual corporate kingdoms earning more money than the weakling federal government's entire budget, the impact of this largely unmanaged, unregulated industrial growth on the country's air and water was predictable (the easiest crystal ball would have been, of course, a visit to smog-bound industrial Britain). And by the time the economy underwent another startling boom, following the Second World War, the continent's natural elements were undeniably in a truly parlous state.

As the post-war boom proceeded a series of scandals revealed the toll that the continent's compromised air and water were taking on America's human and animal health. In 1959 a group of St Louis physicians discovered worrying levels of the radioactive contaminant strontium-90 (one of the main components of the Chernobyl disaster's fallout) in local babies' teeth, and realized that American children were being poisoned by their mothers' milk. In 1962 a group of fisheries managers were caught pouring poison into more than four hundred miles of Wyoming's Green River, purposefully exterminating all the local species prior to dropping in scores of rainbow trout, which were more fun to catch. In the same year Rachel Carson revealed that the agricultural industry's witless use of military-grade pesticides was wiping out everything from freshwater mussels to peregrine falcons, as well as filling Americans' bodies with yet more carcinogens. Soon after, Lake Erie was declared 'dead' by the national press – this wasn't quite true, but the water was so clogged with phosphates that the fish were, unnervingly, drowning. Finally, in 1969, *Time* magazine shook the nation with the news (nothing new to the long-suffering locals) that Cleveland's Cuyahoga River, reduced to a combustible soup of industrial waste, was on fire.

Deafened by protests, the federal government acted, and the early 1970s witnessed a raft of environmental laws, including the Clean Air and Clean Water Acts, that remain the legislative foundation of all efforts to clean up America. It seemed that *laissez-faire* had finally fallen to people power.

The State of Idaho ignored the Clean Water Act for twenty-two years. Irreparably in hock to the logging, farming and mining interests that were soiling their landscapes, and almost congenitally indisposed towards regulating free enterprise, the local legislators declined to perform even the preparatory act of compiling a register of polluted streams. When they were finally prosecuted into action, the tests revealed that at least 962 rivers and streams in the state were unacceptably polluted. Stung into decision, Idaho announced a clean-up programme – but one so woefully funded that it would take 150 years to complete. That, in a nutshell, is the legal – and philosophical – environment Potlatch inhabited. Those were the rules.

More than thirty years after the Clean Air and Water Acts, Americans still subsidize their economy with their health to a degree unique in the developed world. One in every six American women has levels of mercury in her blood that pose a danger to her unborn child; America's Food and Drug Administration has isolated fifty-three carcinogenic pesticides still at use in the nation's food industry; in the year 2000 half of all Americans lived in communities where the air quality fell below safe standards at least part of the year; 40 per cent of the country's rivers and lakes are considered unsafe for fishing or swimming, and forty-one states now warn fishermen to eat no more than one local catch a week; studies suggest more than a quarter of the country's underground water is also seriously polluted (this should come as no surprise as two-thirds of America's toxic waste output is injected straight into the continent). A quarter of the American population lives within a few miles of one of the country's estimated 450,000 unstable toxic waste sites.

And for the army of grassroots anti-pollution campaigners that have coalesced since the late 1960s, by far the greatest barrier to protecting the modern continent, particularly in the battle to cleanse the West, remains the pathological dislike of outside meddlers and imposed rules which has characterized towns like Lewiston since their very foundation. In 1947 the essayist and historian Bernard

DeVoto (whose columns for *Harper's Magazine* are the most dispiriting companion any writer can take into the West, as they seem to contain every worthwhile insight ever written – only sixty years ago) noted that the West's public discourse was dominated by the fear that the settler culture of 'the axe-wielding individualist' was being corrupted from Washington 'by a system of paternalism which is collectivist at base and hardly bothers to disguise its intention of delivering the United States over to communism'. Every local editorial page in the West, DeVoto contended, contained a daily 'ringing demand for the government to get out of business, to stop impeding initiative, to break the shackles of regulation with which it has fettered enterprise'. Thirty years later a former matinee cowboy would build towards an unprecedented electoral sweep of the West (followed by a concerted effort to weaken the clean air and water laws) on the back of a pledge to revive the independent pioneer spirit, encapsulated in one perfectly pitched one-liner: 'The nine most terrifying words in the English language are: "I'm from the Government, and I'm here to help."' Over two elections, just under 70 per cent of Idahoans voted for Ronald Reagan; only Utah posted higher numbers for the great apostle of flimsy government and axe-wielding individualism. The implications for the natural continent were made clear by the leader of Reaganism's Greek chorus, the eminently quotable and undeniably influential broadcaster and author Rush Limbaugh: 'The key to fixing the environment is unfettered free enterprise ... We have a right to use the earth to make our lives better.' Welcome to Idaho – now go home.

Potlatch Inc. has at least modified its local act somewhat since the darkest days of the polluted continent. In the mid-1980s it invested in a burner that could capture most of the Lewiston paper mill's particulates – enough to satisfy the local lawmakers, but not, sadly, enough to eliminate the smell of raw cauliflower. The locals call it 'the smell of money', although they're unfortunately mistaken: as the town's dilapidated Main Street, pawnshops and bail bondsmen serve to testify, those parts of the US that allow high pollution don't get prosperity in return: they actually have higher unemployment and greater poverty levels than the national average.

At least in 1994 the federal government concluded that Lewiston's air was no longer carcinogenic, a vast improvement considering that in 1990 the levels of chloroform in the air were estimated to increase the cancer risk by forty times. (In 2003, the town still had above average incidence rates for at least nine cancers.) The Snake remains on the government's list of fouled rivers: Potlatch is permitted to pump in up to forty million gallons of warm water a day, carrying sediment, alien nutrients and some carcinogenic dioxins (again, reduced in recent years, but the dioxins do collect in the local fish, giving them tumours and rendering it unwise to overeat them).

In the late 1980s the company also began to draw down its Lewiston activities, closing the sawmill and cutting staff at the paper mill, citing, in part, the cost of their new-fangled environmental practices. Now, like so many Western company towns, Lewiston waits, like a meek, abused spouse, for divorce: as several locals testified, 'We all know they're going to leave town, they'll be gone someday soon.' Those, as the people of Pierce would tell them, are also the rules.

The cause of the plucky pioneer had acquired a vigorous convert in Oliver Howard, who affected distaste for what he saw as the uncultured libertarianism of Lewiston's settlers, while deferring to their every bidding. The findings of his commission were rapidly approved in Washington, troops were prepared to occupy the entrance to the Wallowa prior to a forced evacuation and a delegation of Christian Nez Perce were dispatched to break the distressing news to Joseph and Ollokot. Sensing that the situation was being driven towards a violent conflict they couldn't hope to win, the two brothers spent the early months of 1877 in a frenzy of last-ditch diplomacy, seeking meetings with Howard, their Indian Agent, other neighbouring Agents, anyone who would listen to their pleas and counter-offers – they suggested the eighty or so Wallowa band members could move west to the traditionalist Umatilla Reservation, they wondered if the Umatilla themselves should be moved east to share the Wallowa, or perhaps the two reservations should be joined? They begged Howard not to deploy his troops, pointing out that they knew full well that any aggression on their part would cost the lives of their wives and children. Howard grew impatient – each time he met one of the brothers the local press ridiculed his indulgence afresh – and he finally drew a line in the sand. The leaders of the dissident bands – Joseph and Ollokot, plus White Bird, Looking Glass, and Toohoolhoolzote from the more easterly bands, and also the leaders of two roaming bands from the Palouse peoples, Husishusis-kute and Hahtalekin, were convened at Lapwai to talk once more, on 3 May 1877. The chiefs believed they'd been granted one last chance to plead their case; in fact, Howard intended to get down to brass tacks. Each band would be forced to choose the reservation land they would move onto, and to agree a deadline to leave their homelands forever.

The Lapwai Council was the last expression of Nez Perce freedom. Once more the bands arrived in full regalia, riding in strict formation and singing their traditional songs, and established their camps surrounding the meeting grounds. In a calculated display of unity, the leaders chose Toohoolhoolzote as their sole spokesman; a strict and militant traditionalist, he could well express the depth of their feeling.

Howard opened proceedings briskly, eager to demonstrate the balance of power and to subdue the dissidents with, in his own immodest phrase, his 'fearless sternness'. Toohoolhoolzote countered with a long and impassioned speech on the simple wrongness of what was occurring: 'I belong to the land out of which I came. The

Earth is my mother. The Great Spirit made the world as it is, and as He wanted it, and He made a part of it for us to live upon. I do not see where you get authority to say that we shall not live where He placed us.'

As the peroration continued, Howard bit his tongue, but the noises of assent from the other Nez Perce grew worryingly loud, thoughts of Captain Jack's bloody negotiating skills sprang to mind, and the council was hastily adjourned for the weekend. Come Monday morning, though, little had changed. As the warrior Yellow Wolf recalled: 'Chief Toohoolhoolzote stood up to talk for the Indians. He told how the land always belonged to the Indians, how it came down to us from our fathers. How the earth was a great law, how everything must remain as fixed by the Earth-Chief. How the land must not be sold! That we came from the earth, and our bodies must go back to the earth, our mother.'

Howard had heard enough, and cut in, a considerable breach of council etiquette: 'I don't want to offend your religion, but you must talk about practicable things; twenty times over I hear that the earth is your mother and about chieftainship from the earth. I want to hear it no more, but come to business at once.'

The details of the slanging match that followed have been obscured by time and language. It seems that Toohoolhoolzote, a chief whose remote mountain homeland had helped cultivate a generous contempt for white culture, challenged the authority of Washington and the sanity of those who would divide and parcel the earth, while Howard demanded in ever more aggressive terms whether the chief was choosing submission or rebellion. Finally, according to some reports, Toohoolhoolzote dismissed Howard's conduct as an insult to his manhood, while taking an illustrative grip on his own manhood, a gesture which drove the prudish Christian General over the edge. Incandescent, Howard ordered Toohoolhoolzote arrested and locked in the guardhouse, before bellowing to the remaining chiefs that the time for talk had ended: 'If you do not mind me, I will take my soldiers and drive you onto the reservation!'

Howard had shown the rifle. The threat of violence in a treaty council was a shattering transgression, an insult and a challenge that breached the very purpose of peaceful dialogue. For many of the young Nez Perce warriors this was the declaration of war they had long hoped for, but the chiefs knew that the satisfaction of slaughtering Howard and his tiny garrison would surely be followed by vengeful annihilation from the East. Prudence won the day, and subjugation was grudgingly accepted. The chiefs agreed to ride out with Howard the next day and choose the reservation land for their new homes.

It's an indication of the optimism and resilience of the Nez Perce leadership that the five-day search for their reservation patches took place in largely good humour. Despite the theft with menaces they were being subjected to, the chiefs joked with Howard, challenged his cavalrymen to horse races, and declared themselves satisfied with the lands they chose to rehouse their peoples, along the Clearwater and Sweetwater rivers. On his release from the stockade, it even emerged that Toohoolhoolzote had struck up an unlikely friendship with one of his fellow inmates, a gregarious young army bugler called John Jones whose intemperate enjoyment of a good drink had recently offended General Howard's piety. It seemed the Nez Perce problem was going to be solved amicably, if not fairly.

But Howard had one more insult to hurl. On the final morning of the council he announced the timetable for the Nez Perce to move permanently onto the reservation – they had just thirty days. It was an impossible demand: the bands needed more time than that to gather their horse and cattle herds from their scattered pastures, let alone make the journey, with all their possessions, to their new homes. Worst of all, late spring would mark the high point of the thunderous floods in the great Snake and Salmon rivers, ensuring treacherous crossing for the elderly, the infirm and, in Joseph's particular case, his heavily pregnant wife, Toma Alwawinmi. The chiefs begged for more time, but Howard was implacable, citing a petition he had just received from the white settlers on White Bird's tribal lands (a particularly rancorous and prejudiced bunch of pioneers) proclaiming that only the very swiftest eviction would prevent an outbreak of violence. (Some years later, Howard would claim that the chiefs never asked for more time – this was a stark lie, intended to deflect any blame for the rough justice that was about to befall those very same white inhabitants of White Bird's territory.) Howard let his 'good friend' Joseph know that the troops stationed at the entrance to the Wallowa would resort to force if the deadline was missed by a single day.

Crestfallen, Joseph and Ollokot returned to their people to organize the gathering of the herds, the collection of their band's sacred and valuable possessions, and the preparations for the final caravan away from the land of the winding waters. The son would have to break his promise to his dying father, but only to protect the lives of those who were his pastoral responsibility. Some years later, Joseph would admit that the inevitability of this moment had long weighed on his mind:

> I have carried a heavy load on my back ever since I was a boy. I learned then that we were but few, but the white men were many, and that we could not hold our own against them. We were like deer. They were like grizzly bears. We had a small country. Their country was large. We were contented to let things remain as the Great Spirit Chief made them. They were not; and would change the rivers and mountains if it did not suit them.

The band congregated at a peaceful valley floor in their winter range, camping by the confluence of the Grande Ronde River and a narrow stream now known as Joseph Creek, where herons gathered to pluck eels from the shallow riffles. The mood was far from placid, though – Joseph and Ollokot were struggling to control their young warriors, whose pride could bear no more scars. As the truth sank in – that much of the band's carefully raised livestock, its very wealth, would have to be left behind for the white settlers to appropriate – the clamour for action grew, and the arrival of Toohoolhoolzote and his followers only fuelled the rage, the old chief proclaiming his willingness to join the Wallowa's young men and die defending his homeland. Somehow, the brothers retained control, and the retreat began peacefully, but in gloomy spirits, for ahead lay some of the roughest, least forgiving terrain in the whole Northwest.

With their worldly possessions packed on their backs or loaded on horses, the Nez Perce fought their way down narrow, precipitous gullies to the river bottom of the Inmaha Canyon, driving what was left of their herds ahead of them. Almost impassable in the dry season, in the mud and loose rock of the spring thaw these exhausting descents needed every ounce of the band's animal sense and wilderness skills. Then, after grazing the herd in the relative ease of the valley bottom, it was up and over once more, slowly climbing then descending a steep flank of land to drop into Hell's Canyon – the lair of the great Snake River.

This baked, chaotic, barren gorge, the deepest in America, is not a place to tarry. The wrinkles of land fold away for a bewildering distance, obscuring the shining path of the thick, brooding river, while above the earth loses its grip on the valley's towering slopes, as if exhausted by their relentless gradient, to fall away and reveal crumbling, disorderly cliff faces. Rarely less than broiling hot, the valley floor is thick with rattlesnakes. Nearly one hundred years later, on 8 September 1974, the canyon's gruelling inhospitability would be forever fixed in America's national consciousness when Bobby 'Evel' Knievel endured one of his trademark near-death experiences during a failed rocket leap across the gorge. And now, in late May 1877, the Nez Perce scrambled down to the banks of the Snake to find that the river, just as predicted, was in full flood.

For the young men this was no challenge. Swimming swollen

The likely Nez Perce crossing point on the Snake River, before they climbed the facing wall of Hell's Canyon.

rivers had long been a means for warriors and hunters to build and prove their strength – indeed, a more dramatic display involved driving a wild horse into a torrent, swimming in after it and riding it out. But the entire band had never attempted such a crossing as this, with the elderly and children included, plus thousands of cattle and horses. Makeshift rafts were built in a well-worn piece of fieldcraft, stretching buffalo hides across a ring of wood, and the elderly clung to horses that the young dragged and drove through the current. Some people were taken by the flood, and only reached the far bank, bedraggled and exhausted, up to a mile downstream. The whole shattering, terrifying effort took two days, and it was astonishing that no lives were lost. Crucial possessions did drift away forever, though: cooking and hunting equipment, robes, hides and blankets, and, most importantly, horses and cattle in their hundreds. Those horses that had been ridden across largely made it, but many of the wider herd drowned or bolted. The cattle fared far worse – the calves stood

98

little chance, nor did the older beasts, whose calm heads were vital for making the herd manageable. Their bloated carcasses washed up and rotted in the shallows downstream.

Resilient still, the Nez Perce dried themselves off and began the awful ascent of the eastern side of Hell's Canyon, driving their depleted herd ahead of them. One of the wealthiest bands of Native Americans in the interior Northwest had been reduced not only to homelessness but to penury.

It is appropriate, in a sharp, bitter way, that such a catastrophe took place in the foaming waters of the Snake River. The story of what happened here next, of what befell this landscape after it was taken from its indigenous occupants is, more than anything, the story of the rivers – and the story of the twisted magic that wrought modern Idaho from the fragments of its Native nations is, more than anything, the story of the Snake.

The Snake River allows itself a picaresque tour of the best of the Northwest. Springing to life from the meltwaters of Wyoming's voluptuous Grand Tetons, the flow heads south into Idaho, to begin a long, westward sweep of the flat, dry scrubland that constitutes most of the southern state, before steering north into the wild lands of Hell's Canyon. Gorged there on the contributions of the Salmon, Grande Ronde and Inmaha rivers, the Snake then meets the Clearwater at Lewiston and, fatter still, takes a turn west – finally to defer to a bigger beast, the great Columbia, for the final leg to the Pacific Ocean. Depending on the season, the Snake's journey is a placid meander or a hurtling stampede; and sadly, when the Nez Perce crossed the river in the spring of 1877, the flow was faster and wider than was usual even for the great spring thaw. Such an unlikely torrent would cause suffering both immediate and deferred.

In the late 1870s the climate of the interior Northwest was going through one of its rare, and typically brief, wet phases. Precipitation was oddly plentiful, the air had lost some of its usual gasping dryness and the rich soil was springing to life. As the wave of immigrant farmers drawn by the free land of the westward expansion reached its peak, the Washington preachers of Manifest Destiny, the small-town boosters, land speculators and profiteers from the nascent railroad industry (who had almost two hundred million acres of federal land grants to sell to settlers) were thus able to lure the optimistic home-steaders further and further west, as conclusive proof emerged that the 'Great American Desert' was in fact the perfect place to raise both crops and a family.

Except that it wasn't. Across almost the entire western third of the United States (with the exception of the rainforests and damp hillsides of the Pacific Coast) in a normal year it didn't rain anything like enough to produce a decent crop on 160 acres. In a bad year, it didn't rain at all. The terrain was gloriously varied, from rolling bad-lands and semi-desert scrubland to wide-open prairies, genuine, flat-baked desert and high mountain ranges (where it rained, at least, but it also froze), but in whatever form the land had something in common – staking out a family-sized farm, tilling the earth and wait-ing for the heavens to open was never going to work.

The boosters were either unaware or unconcerned. Fiction was the medium of choice for promoting immigration – Nevada claimed never to get hot, Dakota claimed never to get cold, Nebraska pro-moted the moral improvement guaranteed by breathing its air, Idaho published an annual death rate of 0.33 per cent (a sliver off state-wide immortality), everywhere claimed they could cure tuberculosis in an instant, while official state maps were printed with hoped-for towns and roads marked as real features, and the pesky Indian reser-vations unsubtly erased – and the most widely promulgated fiction of all was bountiful rainfall. Insanely inaccurate official records of annual inches were standard fare, as was the infamous proclamation that the farmers would actually induce rain by their very presence –

'rain follows the plough'. The *Idaho County Free Press* offered a typical explanation of the theory: 'When seventy-five or ninety per cent of the land is plowed land brought under cultivation we may expect to see a change take place in the nature of the seasons ... The evaporation of moisture from the wet earth will cool the air and attract the rain clouds which will afford a fresh supply of moisture.' When you took into account the liberally promoted 'fact' that railroad engines disturbed the air enough to generate rainfall – and, most importantly, when you observed that precipitation *did* in fact increase just as westward immigration swelled (a cruel climatic coincidence) – then the future looked damp indeed.

In fact, homesteading on the Western drylands was almost insufferably hard, and most of those who had travelled West in hope faced a litany of biblical setbacks: if the grasshoppers didn't take your crops, a roaring prairie fire might, or a sharp thunderstorm onto bone-dry land might flood out the house that you'd fashioned from mud bricks, that offered little solace from summer heatwaves and winter blizzards. Desperate to survive, many farmers ruined their land claim through overgrazing or monoculture. And one crop failure, through ignorance or ill fortune, was enough to ruin most farming families, thanks to the great optimist's burden – debt. Railroads and their land agents sold parcels of land at highly profitable interest rates, and Eastern banks instructed their new Western outposts to think of a number and double it whenever farmers arrived seeking funds for equipment or seeds. Many farmers found themselves in situations distressingly similar to those they had left behind in Europe or the East – working for their creditors or, worse still, a landlord. In 1886 the *San Francisco Chronicle* lamented that a fundamental tenet of the settler dream seemed to be going awry: 'Since the formation of our Government the impression has been given at home and abroad that the farmers in this country owned the lands they tilled. We have expressed a great deal of sympathy for the poor farmers of Ireland, England, Scotland and

*As Uncle Sam headed west, from smog to paradise, the key to
selling immigration was the promise of 'irrigated land'.*

Germany, who were obliged to pay an annual rent to grasping
landlords.' In fact, the author pointed out, America, the land of
democratic property, already had more tenant farmers than Great
Britain and Ireland combined.

The only get-out clauses were water and scale. If you could get
land on a riverbank, with access to the relatively easy life of irrigation
farming, or if you could get your hands on enough acreage finally to
make the West's feeble crop yields profitable, you had a chance of
survival. Most successful settlers did both, and riverbank property
was the target of fierce speculation, consolidation and shameless
fraud, as large farms and ranches came to dominate the West's well-
lubricated valleys, despite the government's timorous pleas that the
region be dominated by small, upstanding family enterprises. As
property prices for watered land rocketed and the large farms drove
down produce prices, the West's small farmers found themselves, in
historian Patricia Nelson Limerick's words, 'being squeezed by
history'. A few communities, such as Lewiston, attempted communal
irrigation projects, but the majority came to be dominated by

profiteers who held the farmers to ransom for their water – only the Mormons, polygamous pariahs of the West but blessed with a fierce work ethic and doughty team spirit, had managed to make a success of community irrigation in their lonely Utah valleys.

Lack of rain was ruining the dream of settlement and the government that had spun the dream knew it. The year before the Nez Perce crossed the Snake, the geographer and explorer John Wesley Powell had informed Congress that the dry West was only good for two lifestyles – precisely the kind of wide-ranging, semi-nomadic herding that was currently being violently purged from the landscape, or irrigation farming on a leviathan scale, with the government throwing millions of dollars at harnessing and distributing fairly the only reliable source of water on offer – the West's great rivers – to a modest ribbon of small farms near their banks. Congress laughed him out of the room – the West was being won for an unlimited army of settlers, who were building a towering new civilization through individualism, self-reliance and an acute allergy to government handouts. (The Western politicians were by far the noisiest gainsayers: Powell was derided as just another outside meddler, and by now most of the region's democratic representatives were profiting both through personal speculation and campaign donations from the great empires of land emerging from the chaos out west.)

Then the rain stopped. In the late 1880s the climatic cycle swung back to blinding, heart-breaking drought, as crop failures, livestock die-ups and foreclosures pushed back the tide of settlement. It's estimated that 60 per cent of the one million or so families who'd tried to build lives on the Great Plains headed back east in defeat. Some south-western states lost half their population. *Now* the politicians took notice. Powell's report was dusted off, and one proposal was seized upon as the salvation of the great project of Western settlement – 'build a lot of dams'.

After a couple of false starts, the US government got into the business of dam-building with gusto in 1902, with the passage of the Newlands Act, the starting pistol for an era of central government largesse unlike any in history. Under the act, the government would build dams, storing the water of the Western rivers, then sell that water to farmers for, in the main, nothing. (The law actually demanded that the settlers' water payments funded the public works, but the majority of the farmers simply defaulted on the interest-free fees, and were never pursued.) In a yet more benevolent procedure, the government also handed vast land grants to private corporations to build dams (paid for with interest-free federal loans) before the businessmen then sold their now irrigated land to farmers and counted their cash.

Within sixteen years of the passage of the Newlands Act, the Snake River and its tributaries were irrigating an area of Idaho larger than the Nile delta, as the dusty, deathly scrubland south of Hell's Canyon was transformed into a strip of bizarrely lush farmland and rapidly growing cities. Another new feature had also appeared on Idaho's landscape – the potato millionaire. Legal provisions that all this government water should be used for *small* farms were utterly ignored, as subsidized speculators hoarded huge acreages of irrigated farmland, driving down produce prices and forcing yet more family operations to sell up and get out. But there were no regrets – the West had discovered a new mode of thought, a new mantra, that the values the settlers upheld in their role as America's vestal virgins, tending the eternal fires of individualism, self-reliance and free enterprise that embodied the nation, could only be preserved through generous government activism. The towering inconsistency was simply ignored, while the fact that many of the beneficiaries of the new subsidies were often disconcertingly rich, and often not even from the West, was dismissed as a detail – those demanding help without hindrances embodied the 'spirit of the pioneers', if not the reality. As DeVoto eternally put it, the great Western Paradox had been created, a schizophrenia that would last for generations: 'It shakes down to a platform: get out and give us more money.'

The irrigation that has created lush meadows from the scrubland of the
Wallowa Valley.

But the damming of the West had yet even to hit top gear, a nadir
reached following two events – the perfecting of the technology for
drawing electricity from falling water, and another cycle of drought,
this time striking overused land that dried up and blew away in the
continental disaster of the Dustbowl. Now dams offered multiple
benefits: reservoirs for irrigation, stifled rivers for barge transpor-
tation, unthinkable quantities of cheap, clean power, and, best of all,
jobs for victims of the Depression. From the 1930s on, bewildering
state-funded monuments to human ingenuity and ambition began
to plug some of the greatest rivers on earth – the Hoover Dam,
Grand Coulee Dam, Shasta Dam, Chief Joseph Dam, and so on. By
the time the spree ended, in the mid-1970s, the Snake had been
dammed twelve times, the Columbia River thirteen: counting all the
Columbia's tributaries, the Northwest's greatest watershed was
dammed thirty-six times. The reservoirs backed up so far behind the
Columbia and Snake dams that Lewiston, over 450 miles from the

coast, had become a thriving sea port. The USA had acquired no fewer than fifty thousand major public dams, to add to an estimated two million private ponds and plugs – by 2006, just 2 per cent of the contiguous nation's rivers still flowed freely. Considering the thousands of valleys submerged, rivers stilled and millions of acres irrigated, the chief chronicler of this mania of construction, Marc Reisner, described the damming of the West as 'the most fateful transformation that has ever been visited on any landscape, anywhere'.

The dams conferred blessings and curses on an equally grand scale. The great desert cities of Phoenix, Tucson, Reno, Denver, Las Vegas, Albuquerque and many more burst into life and began to sprawl across the landscape, their spacious suburbs fuelled by cheap electricity and what seemed to be limitless lawn-spraying water. The agricultural empires of California, Washington, Oregon, Idaho and elsewhere grew bloated on the water the government engineers were hoarding for them (causing a growth in production that, of course, drove down prices and forced yet more small farmers to sell up to the big boys). The unprecedented hydroelectric output of the Western dams was also essential in helping to liberate Europe from fascism, allowing the US to outpunch the Axis in arms and aircraft production – and without the dams' megawatts the Allies would have simply been non-starters in the race for the atomic bomb.

Most of all, though, the dams built good lives. In his magical memoir of a family life dominated by the Columbia River dams, *A River Lost*, Blaine Harden recalls that his settler grandparents had, quite typically, been ruined three times in three decades, on three different patches of the West where the promised rains never came (a struggle that had left his grandmother dead aged just forty). Then his twenty-one-year-old father left the destitute family home and hopped on a boxcar to the great river – just in time to catch the dam-building boom. There, 'my family's dismal cycle of westering dreams, dry-land failure and bankrupt flight was suddenly and permanently broken'. Steady construction work was all but guaranteed, with enough money to inhabit a suburban idyll – the spacious lake-front house, plenty of new cars and a university education for the next generation. But the memories of the bitterly tough life that had preceded the dams were never abandoned:

> Like many beneficiaries of the engineered river, my father and our family savored those hardtack memories – even as we became middle-class cheerleaders for federal subsidies. Applying a brand of logic peculiar to westerners who prosper with the help of federal money, we understood the government-planned, government-run, and government-financed damming of the Columbia as an affirmation of our rugged individualism. We incorporated the harnessed river into our mythic West.

The dams also destroyed life. Throughout the construction boom, the government's engineers showed a disconcerting inclination towards reservoirs that displaced or disrupted Native American communities. During the plugging of the main flow and tributaries of the Missouri River, for example, the engineers managed to affect reservation land belonging to the Sioux, Chippewa, Shoshone, Black-foot, Crow, Cree and Assiniboine people, while sacrificing millions of gallons of water storage to avoid inconveniencing white towns that faced inundation. The greatest crime of the Missouri's damming, though, befell the Hidatsa, Mandan and Arikara people who lived and raised cattle along the banks of the river, on the Fort Berthold Reservation in North Dakota. In 1948 the US Corps of Engineers decided to flood almost the entire reservation behind the behemoth Garrison Dam, displacing 1500 families and obliterating a centuries-old way of life. Among the many iconic images of the depredations endured by Native America, few demonstrate the astonishing longevity of their sufferance better than the famous photograph of George Gillette, tribal representative of the Fort Berthold peoples, attending the signing ceremony confirming the purchase and flooding of his people's land. As Cap Krug, the United States Secretary of the Interior, signed the order, Mr Gillette burst into tears.

Further west, another potent image was the sight of the fishermen at Celilo Falls. For over seven hundred generations, the tribes of the Northwest, including the Nez Perce, had visited these tumultuous rapids on the Columbia River to harvest the seasonal migratory battalions of salmon and steelhead trout, the bands using nets and spears, and constructing rickety wooden platforms that overhung the roaring waters. The falls defined several tribes: this was the place where they became 'salmon people', dependent on the health of the fish and their river for sustenance, wealth and identity – and once settlement began, they were not alone in drawing their living from the rapids. By the 1920s the Celilo Falls fishermen, white and Native, were the Northwest's top tourist attraction, clambering across the rocks and their flimsy constructions in daredevil pursuit of the protein-rich trophies powering their way upstream.

The Dalles hydroelectric dam closed on 10 March 1957 and Celilo Falls was submerged forever; some tribal members recalled coming home from military service overseas to find their way of life inexplicably underwater. Celilo's rocks and rapids now lie at the bottom of what's considered the finest windsurfing lake in the United States. This story has a twist, though, one which foretold the end of the West's love affair with dams – the greatest landscape gardening project in history would be driven backwards not by revelations of its human impact but by the realization of what was happening to the fish.

There was a time when somewhere between ten and sixteen million salmon and steelhead trout commuted through the Columbia River every year. To paraphrase one of the most remarkable lifestyles on the natural planet, the fish are conceived and born in the shallows, pools and lakes of the inland Northwest, drift downstream in huge numbers in their adolescent stage (pointing tail first so they'll, somehow, remember the way home) before spending a few years growing muscular and fearsome in the open sea, then charging manically back to their birthplace to spawn and, in most cases, die. Perhaps the most heroic species of all tackles the Snake itself – the Snake River sockeye faces more than nine hundred miles of upstream effort to get home to Redfish Lake, Idaho.

Within two generations of European settlement, the fish were fading fast – industrial harvest, pollution, the ruination of their spawning grounds by the lumber and cattle industries and the lowering of rivers by irrigation all took a chunk off – but the runs at least remained. Then came the dams – and the number of ways a dam can kill a salmon almost suggests that the dam was designed for the purpose.

By drastically slowing their flow, dams make rivers considerably warmer, thus cooking the fish. The reservoirs behind the dams also become predatory killing fields. If you remember to put a fish ladder in your plans (not every engineer did) then the powerful adults heading upstream have a decent shot at bludgeoning their way past the concrete wall – but the tiddlers heading downstream have next to no chance: they get chewed up in the hydroelectric turbines, or the drop kills them (the plummeting water is too rich in nitrogen and gives them the bends). If the little guys do somehow negotiate the assault course, the lengthened journey to the sea disrupts their careful physiological transition from freshwater to saltwater creatures, or they're simply exhausted and head out into the Pacific to expire. By the end of the Columbia River system's damming, the wild fish population had lost somewhere between 97 and 99 per cent of its historic levels. In 1990 not one Snake River sockeye made it back to Redfish Lake. The next year, just one straggled home – the locals called him Lonesome Larry.

Remarkably, the dam-builders knew this would happen; all the scientific evidence regarding the impact of dams on migrating fish was gathered, analysed and largely agreed upon. (Exactly the same process was taking place in the 1930s and 1940s a few hundred miles north of the Columbia, regarding Canada's Fraser River salmon runs. There, the scientists examined the facts, and didn't build the dams.) The waterworks would surely slaughter the Columbia salmon, but they could still go ahead – this, after all, was the West, built on the faith that money trumped nature every time. Particularly government money. The solution, clearly, was federal fish.

Conceived in a bucket, incubated on a tea tray and reared in a giant concrete maze, the average government salmon might expire if it only understood the weight of symbolism it bears on its shiny shoulders. Tens of millions of these creatures are brought to life every year across the Columbia watershed, and raised in over eighty sprawling riverside hatchery compounds until they're large enough to tackle the journey downstream – at which point many of them are released to try and overcome the defences of the turbines, the predator pools, the bends and so on by sheer weight of numbers, in a bloody suicide mission to rival the Red Army. Others are given a better chance, and are driven beyond the dams in milk trucks, then pumped into the lower river. Still more swim serenely downstream aboard giant barges. Once pointed out to sea they're overfished by the tiny rump of a Pacific fleet that has joined the ranks of government beneficiaries, before a minuscule proportion of the original release (often as low as 0.1 per cent) returns upstream to spawn. It depends on the species, but there are usually at least four times more federal fish in the average spawning migration than wild fish – meaning that after all the barges and buckets, the total Columbia system population, federal and wild combined, still languishes at no more than 5 per cent of its historical levels.

For decades, the federal fish programme was little more than a genial, bumbling way to spend a huge amount of money and employ a garrison of scientists, without actually making much headway in resurrecting the great salmon runs (while also negating any genuine effort to return the fishes' river system to something less than a death trap). Then, however, a pivotal development in the recent history of man and the Northwest began to make its effects felt. The demographic character of the Northwest started to change – the collective weight of the urbanites of the region's booming damp coastal cities of Seattle, Portland and Tacoma (vast conurbations brought to life, to a very significant degree, by cheap hydroelectricity) outgrew the inhabitants of the dusty, hard-scrabble interior, and the metropolitan desire for clear rivers, healthy landscapes and at least some wildlife beyond the city limits coalesced around one mute romantic hero. In 1991, just as Lonesome Larry was being stuffed and mounted by the governor of Idaho, years of environmental campaigning bore fruit when the Snake River sockeye was belatedly declared an Endangered Species (meaning, in US law, its survival was now the statutory responsibility of every public and private body currently killing it off). Legal, political and cultural battle was drawn. Two competing symbols were now heralded as the embodiment of the spirit of the West – the doughty settler, struggling to build an empire of freedom in an unforgiving land, versus the mighty salmon, rapidly transforming from the prosaic contents of a tin can into the much-eulogized embodiment of the region's hoped-for cultural and ecological sustainability. The battle, as ever, was all about the water.

Ever since the Columbia salmon were declared endangered, the beneficiaries of the dam-building boom – the farmers, the power companies, the barge operators and the 'sea port' of Lewiston – have been locked in an endless total war of lawsuits, lobbying and legislation against the alliance of ecologists, fishermen and tribal leaders (whose role is discussed at length in a later chapter) eager to resurrect the fish. Every gallon of water is now fought over in court, council session or enquiry, as the need to keep the rivers cool and swift is balanced against the kilowatts lost, the depth of the barges and, most vigorously of all, the need to keep the potato fields damp. Dams that were built to last millennia are being assailed by bouncing bombs of litigation and campaigning. That man and nature have conspired, via the dams, to generate a conflict between generously subsidized farmers and predominantly federal fish is an irony rarely dwelt upon.*

Nor is it often acknowledged that this seems to be a battle in which there are only losers. The fish, despite all the effort, appear doomed unless some of the giant dams are breached – in 2007, out of the massed ranks of government-bred Snake River sockeyes that had attempted to approximate their species' once great migration, a far from sustainable *four* made it back to spawn at Redfish Lake.

But for the small farmers in whose name the dams were built, the squeeze of history will also not relent. Man at his most ingenious and disingenuous cannot alter the reality of the West's rainfall. The demands on the available water grow every year, not just because of the protectorate of the salmon but also the relentless growth of the suburbs, all sprinkler systems, sand traps and swimming pools. The abiding image of the overallocation of the West's rivers is the mighty Colorado, winding from its home state into Utah, Arizona, Nevada and California then south into Mexico, where, during most summers in recent years, it fails to reach the sea, running dry into pebbles and sand where a thriving delta once lay. Unsurprisingly, the efforts to move water around the West have grown ever more desperate, with rivers being turned around, pumped uphill, whatever it takes to keep

---

* In this fevered atmosphere the salmon have made powerful political enemies, particularly amongst those seeking to drain the last drop of electoral mileage from the potent settler mythology. In 2005 the Idaho Senator Larry Craig learned that his generous campaign benefactors in Columbia's hydroelectric power business were having their freedom of enterprise threatened by pesky government biologists, who were proving beyond doubt that the salmon population was still endangered. Senator Craig, once named 'Legislator of the Year' by the hydro-power industry, found a simple solution – and drafted a law cutting off all funding to the blameless fish-counting scientists, attempting to render the Columbia salmon statistically invisible. In 2002 another cheerless figure, presidential *consigliere* Karl Rove, applied vigorous pressure to alter scientific documents, to ensure water that the Klamath River salmon desperately needed to live was hoarded behind the dams during a summer drought, to better serve Oregon's parched irrigation farmers. As a direct result, more than 33,000 dead fish rotted in the shallow waters, the largest recorded 'die-up' in history. A fight over water is always a fight to the death.

the desert green. And while there has always been an alternative to tapping the river – digging a well and hoping to hit groundwater – even that choice is collapsing beneath the weight of demand. The United States is currently drawing over twenty-eight trillion gallons of groundwater a year, almost all of it at a faster rate than nature can replenish it. The greatest groundwater aquifer on earth, the Ogallala, upon which the rural economies of Nebraska, Kansas and Texas depend, is currently being drained at over eight times the rate of replenishment. The Ogallala aquifer supports around 40 per cent of America's wheat, grain and cotton imports, and will be effectively dry within a few decades if current use continues. The story is the same across the West, with unregulated and largely unmeasured depletion of groundwater turning the timeless metaphor for the ruination of a shared natural resource into a literal truth – it really is a race to the bottom of the well.

Finally, there's the fact that most civilizations built on irrigation have an inescapable built-in obsolescence. Irrigation deposits salt into the soil, while reservoirs evaporate under the desert sun, turning river water ever more briny – ready to season the land further. Salination is killing thousands of acres of Western farmland a year, and the traditional application of optimism, know-how and government money through desalination plants, drainage systems and tactical flooding has yet to reverse the trend. The most remarkable solution under consideration is the planting of genetically modified crops that absorb more salt, thus cleansing the soil, raising the possibility that the American public might soon be subsidizing their farmers through their chronic hypertension.

However, while the Western weather might have long placed the region's small farmers under the care of the nation (it's estimated that federal irrigation represents a cash gift of $4.4 billion a year from the taxpayers to the West's farmers) the most significant truth is that that same affection is made equally, often more, available to their agri-businessmen neighbours. And it's the pressure from the big boys, hogging the subsidies, driving down prices and buying up land since the first days of settlement, that has always weighed heaviest on the homesteader and his descendants. Less than 3 per cent of Americans are now employed in agriculture – despite the nation producing a quarter of the world's food. The West, the heroically settled West, now has by far the lowest proportion of rural dwellers in the country. The irony that such a fate should befall land supposedly pilfered from its prior tenants on behalf of the poor and huddled masses has not, of course, gone unnoticed. Considering the modern travails of the West's dwindling rural poor, the Arizona author Dave Gowdey made this typical observation: 'Crazy Horse must be laughing himself silly.'

CHAPTER FIVE

OUTBREAK

'War is made to take something not your own'

YELLOW WOLF

A DISTINGUISHED CAST of characters began to gather at Tepahlewam, the place of the Split Rocks, in the first week of June 1877. The Wallowa band had hauled themselves out of the gorges of the Snake and Salmon River Wilderness and reached an agreed rendezvous at this traditional tribal meeting ground in the corner of the Camas Prairie. There, White Bird, a venerable medicine man in his seventies, had brought his displaced people from their nearby canyon home, the young men of this much mistreated band scarcely controllable in their rage at Howard and the ever vociferous settlers. Toohoolhoolzote was also there, the muscular outdoorsman and hunter accompanied by his small, free-spirited band of thirty or so men and their wives and children. Looking Glass, respected by all the Nez Perce as a warrior and ambassador, was in attendance, but without his whole band – they were not to be removed from their idyllic village on the banks of the Clearwater, as it fell within the Christian reservation, and Looking Glass simply wanted the other groups to take up their new residences with the minimum of fuss. In addition, the two small groups of dissident Palouse peoples had also set up their lodges. Joseph and Ollokot were not at camp themselves – a small party from the Wallowa band, including Joseph's teenage daughter Hophoponmi, was butchering cattle by the Salmon River – but the whole gathering totalled roughly six hundred. The intention was to rest, gather roots and enjoy the last few days of freedom before complying, give or take a day, with Howard's 14 June deadline for arriving safely on the reservation.

The Nez Perce's capacity for good humour in the face of tribulation was evident once more, as horse races and games were organized to divert the men while the women gathered and dried roots. But the sport was not enough to shift the growing mood of militancy as young warriors wound each other up with tales of countless white transgressions, Howard's insult and Lawyer's perceived betrayal. On 10 June, after a long night of drumming and dancing, Looking Glass read the runes and left the encampment, hoping to distance his people from any coming conflagration. A few days later, his decision was bloodily vindicated.

The spark would strike the kindling of the White Bird band. This community had a veritable encyclopaedia of grievances against the Europeans who had settled in their dry canyon land along the Salmon River, with beatings, whippings, thefts, frauds, dog maulings and more stoking their antagonism – not to mention the whites' recent petition to Howard demanding a prompt exile of the Nez Perce, spring floods or not. Among the most distressing crimes, however, was the murder of Eagle Robe. This peaceable tribal leader had granted a settler named Larry Ott permission to live on a parcel of his land, but in the spring of 1875 Eagle Robe had surprised Ott sneakily attempting to increase his holding by fencing off more property. After protesting vigorously, Eagle Robe emphasized his point by throwing a stone at Ott's head. Ott replied with his pistol. Eagle Robe took a while to die – long enough to extract a promise from his son, Wahlitits, not to avenge him violently lest it spark war. For two years, the promise held.

On 13 June, with the Nez Perce defiantly eking out their penultimate day of liberty, the young men of the encampment held a horseback war parade through the tepees, a procession in which the kudos ascribed to each position was carefully calibrated. The prized honour of riding in the rear of the column was awarded to Wahlitits, son of Eagle Robe, now grown into a prodigious athlete and hunter, who was sharing a horse with his cousin, Sarpsis Ilppilp. As the two young warriors rode through the camp, Wahlitits' horse scattered a pile of roots that had been carefully laid out on canvas to dry. Not best pleased with this treatment of his wife's hard work, Yellow Grizzly Bear hurled a regrettable jibe: 'If you're so brave, why don't you kill the white man that killed your father?'

That night Wahlitits wept bitter tears for his father and his honour but by dawn his resolve was settled. He and Sarpsis Ilppilp compelled their teenage relation Swan Necklace to join them as horse minder for a visit to Larry Ott's farm, and the party rode silently out of camp towards the White Bird territory. The next day passed in surreal fashion as the young Nez Perce rode down the Salmon River Valley exchanging pleasantries with white settlers, borrowing a knife grinder at one farm, trying to trade a horse for a rifle at another. Soon after midday they reached Ott's farm, only to find that he had gone; one account suggests he was sick in bed in a nearby mining camp, another that he'd run off and disguised himself as a Chinaman. Frustrated, the warriors picked another target, a curmudgeonly Englishman named Richard Devine who was known to have set his dogs on visiting Indians and was accused of murdering a crippled tribe member called Dakoopin. Swapping more cheery halloos with local farmers as they went, the raiding party continued up the valley, reaching Devine's home in darkness. The old reprobate never stood a chance and was shot with his own gun. Determined to administer more justice on their return journey, the men then rode to the property of another notorious Indian-baiter, a German named Henry Elfers. Elfers, his cousin and one of his hired hands (all implacable enemies of the White Bird band) were killed, then a whiskey peddler and murderer called Samuel Benedict was shot and wounded, but survived by playing dead. It was a strange kind of killing spree – the warriors were accompanied by Wahlitits' wife for much of it, and they took pains to warn off friendly settlers, even sitting down to eat with one family – but it was a momentous one. Realizing the potential impact of their conduct, Wahlitits and Sarpsis Ilppilp stayed outside the Nez Perce camp on their return, sending in Swan Necklace, astride Henry Elfers' prize racehorse, to announce their deeds.

The news fractured the camp. Several of the young warriors noisily rejoiced that their pride could at last be salved by action, and around sixteen men rode out to join the two renegades. The remainder of the camp, seized by panic, couldn't agree on how to douse this fire. Once Joseph and Ollokot had learned of the long-dreaded development, the Wallowa band counselled for staying put and waiting to meet Howard and sue for peace, but others believed revenge was inevitable and demanded that the women and children be moved to safety. Amid chaotic scenes of frantic packing, dismantling of tepees and arguing, the Wallowas were left behind as the other bands headed north to the Clearwater River, leaving just a few sentinels to ensure Joseph didn't betray them; with just one Wallowa warrior on the warpath, it seemed conceivable the Joseph band could avoid the blame and retribution.

But the conduct of the expanded raiding party punctured any hopes of peace. First Samuel Benedict then his whiskey were finished off, launching a two-day drunken riot of bloodshed, burned-out homes and looted stores that left another six settlers on the Salmon River, including one woman, dead. The lunacy spread beyond the narrow valley and onto the Camas Prairie, where more property and crops were burned, and Nez Perce outriders encountered settlers frantically rushing over the open country towards makeshift fortifications. Men, women and children died when warriors first intercepted a consignment of whiskey then drunkenly ran down a packed stagecoach of terrified pioneers. Across the prairie and the valley, wounded and traumatized people cowered in the under-growth, walking scores of miles to find shelter. Some were driven insane by the ordeal. In all up to fifteen settlers' lives were lost, plus that of one Nez Perce raider. It was a desperate situation – decades of subjugation, mistreatment, humiliation and crime had spilled over into incoherent violence, and there would be neither forgiveness nor mitigation. The tombstone of one victim, William Osborne, beneath the shade of a gnarled hackberry tree overlooking White Bird Creek, set the tone perfectly: *'In memory of WILLIAM OSBORN, born in Mass. May 9 1825. Killed by the Nez Perces Indians, June 15 1877. A devoted husband and dearly beloved father was torn from his happy family, by the rude hands of savages.'*

To add to Joseph's troubles, he now had a newborn daughter to care for, as Toma Alwawinmi had given birth at Split Rocks. The Wallowa band had waited there in isolation while the raiders terrorized the prairie and the other bands fled north. But a group of white men on horseback approached their camp at nightfall, and a bullet tore through Joseph's tepee. It was time to accept that peace was not going to be offered and the next morning the brothers told their band to break camp: they were joining the other dissident bands in the north. As Yellow Wolf of the Wallowa band remem-bered, 'From that time, the Nez Perces had no more rest. No more soft pillows for the head.' When the Wallowas rejoined the main party, all agreed to prepare for the worst; the open prairie was too exposed, and Chief Looking Glass had made it clear he didn't want this trouble being imported into his Clearwater Valley stronghold to the north. So the six hundred or so Indians veered south, towards a defensible position in the White Bird Canyon. There they could wait for the army and hope for dialogue.

The army was on its way. Once the settlers had sent out riders carrying their horror stories, prefaced with desperate pleas for arms and men, north-central Idaho was rapidly scorched with fear and loathing. Every newspaper ran graphic accounts of the depredations of the 'red devils' and 'incarnate fiends', detailing 'the sacrifice of the innocent' and 'the work of destruction'. Howard, expecting to bask in the peaceful relocation of the non-treaty bands, was furious when the couriers of bad news reached Lapwai (quite incorrectly, his rage centred on Joseph, whom he'd convinced himself was the supreme commander of the non-treaty Nez Perce). Howard hastily dispatched a force of just over one hundred men, Companies F and H of the First Cavalry, under the command of the experienced Civil War veteran Captain David Perry. The force had considerable Indian-fighting pedigree among its officers, including William Parnell at first lieutenant, an indestructible Irishman who'd so far survived the Charge of the Light Brigade, nineteen Civil War battles and Captain Jack's Modoc War. Howard allowed himself a joke with Perry as the force departed – 'You must not get whipped!' 'There is no danger of that, Sir!' – and was confident that his plan of attack, to use Perry's troops to stabilize the prairie while he collated a monstrous force for a single crushing battle with the Natives, was close to foolproof. He calmed his superiors' nerves with a telegraph: 'Think we will make short work of it.'

But Captain Perry was about to fall victim to old-fashioned Western optimism. After marching all night and all day through the smouldering prairie, his exhausted troops reached the settler town of Grangeville on the evening of 16 June, praying for a plate of beans and some sleep. But Perry was harangued by belligerent settlers who demanded more than protection – they wanted vengeance. The Indians were cowards and savages, they claimed, no match for the US Army, particularly when augmented with a volunteer force of highly motivated locals. Their leading spokesman, Arthur Chapman, told Perry that the Indians were camped on terrain that was exposed to attack, but were certain to move off and disappear into the Snake–Salmon Wilderness at any moment. He promised Perry thirty more steely-eyed fighting men; why simply deter the Nez Perce when you could defeat them?

The soldiers had barely had time to touch their supper before Perry ordered them to move out again, for an overnight march to White Bird Canyon (for which, despite his bluster, Chapman had roused just eleven volunteers, of questionable fettle). How precisely the command expected to surprise an Indian camp that was on the highest possible alert is anyone's guess. As William Parnell recalled, somewhere along the stumbling march someone lit a match: 'Almost immediately the cry of a coyote was heard on the hills above us – a long, howling cry, winding up, however, in a very peculiar way not characteristic of the coyote.'

At daybreak on the 17th the troops trotted down a steep flume of grass and rock towards an encampment that had long been expecting them but had little desire to fight them. A delegation of six Nez Perce was sent forward, waving a white flag and requesting a parley. One of the group, Wettiwetti Houlis, shouted to the soldiers: 'What do you people want?' Arthur Chapman knew what he wanted – he spurred his horse into a charge and opened fire on the white flag. Captain Perry deployed his troops for battle.

Now is perhaps the time to give brief consideration to the fighting effectiveness of the United States Regular Army in the age of the frontier West. By and large, it was pathetic.

The army had been hastily knocked together from old Civil War units, when the plains and desert tribes had vigorously refuted the declaration of nationwide peace in 1865, and for a few years the forts and outposts of the West were largely manned by battle-hardened veterans of America's great internal struggle. But by the mid-1870s most of the former Union and Confederate soldiers had gone home, leaving the rank and file awash with 'greenhorns', military beginners who'd wandered into a recruitment office straight off the immigration ships or soup-kitchen lines, in search of a regular salary and a chance to head West. The desperate recruiters paid little attention to volunteers' physical condition, mental wellbeing or shiftiness of character, and made negligible effort to explain the realities of frontier life. Those realities were, in the words of one estimable historian of the enlisted men, Don Rickey, Jr, 'isolation, boredom and monotony'. Either stranded in a lonely fort or marching around the countryside in search of something to do, the lowly American soldier endured shoddily built accommodation, scurvy-inducing food and dilapidated kit – the military-issue boots were famously so poor it didn't matter which foot you put them on. Only the rifles and pistols they were issued were beyond reproach, but as most soldiers were never trained in their upkeep a distressing proportion rusted up or jammed.

The most likely source of injury in most forts was venereal disease, followed by chronic alcoholism, testimony to the perils of using cheap whiskey and still cheaper women to combat tedium. As one cowboy diarist recalled, the lowly social status of regular soldiers, miserably paid and widely derided as state-sponsored layabouts, only added to the risk: 'a prostitute's standing in her profession depended on her clientele, and … when a woman went to the dogs, she went to the soldiers.'

Not unsurprisingly, desertion from the frontier was pandemic: between the end of the Civil War and the pacification of the West, about a third of all enlisted men absconded. Disillusion, mistreatment or a nearby gold strike would all thin the ranks, as would the announcement of impending action – understandably, many men chose to flee from the prospect of battle hardening for which they'd barely been trained.

For the Frontier Army suffered most from a familiar malaise – it was overstretched. With a vast landscape to patrol, maintaining their isolated forts with tiny numbers of men took up most of the forces' time, leaving little scope for drills, war games or the new-fangled concept of target practice. More than one memoirist recalled cavalry companies setting out on a campaign before some of the men had learned how to ride a horse, and in the rearguard action following Little Big Horn the officers had decided not to let their troops 'fire at will' because they knew none of them could hit a barn door. One company surgeon in the Seventh Cavalry gave this prognosis of the battle-readiness of the rank and file: 'cavalrymen … as a general thing are about as well fitted to travel through a hostile country as infants, and go mooning around at the mercy of any Indian who happens to catch sight.'

Companies F and H of the First Cavalry were certainly not exempt from such an analysis. Of the eighty-five privates under Captain Perry's command, fewer than ten had ever fought Indians before. Company H hadn't had target practice in six months.

The Nez Perce may not have wanted a battle, but they'd prepared for one. Their potential fighting force was depleted to fewer than seventy men following a long night drinking stolen whiskey, but they'd been wisely deployed, with some warriors protecting the village from a direct charge while two further groups prepared to sweep up the valley and counter-attack against both sides of the cavalry's stand. It looked like a tough day was in prospect – the Nez Perce were out-numbered, facing uphill, had far fewer rifles and were preoccupied with protecting their women and children. In fact, the White Bird battle would be settled within half an hour of Arthur Chapman's starting gun.

As the bugle was sounding out Captain Perry's call to battle, an elderly Nez Perce named Otstotpoo wagered that he could down the trumpeter – fully 300 yards up the valley. Remarkably, he made the shot and Bugler John Jones, the convivial new friend of

*White Bird Canyon: the US forces held this vantage point, while the
Nez Perce village lay on the valley floor.*

Toohoolhoolzote, dropped dead. Captain Perry turned to his second
trumpeter to complete the order, only to find he'd lost his bugle. Now
shorn of his primary means of controlling his troops, Perry barely
managed to set his force on a ridge overlooking the village, while the
Nez Perce riders poured up the valley like rattled hornets. Ollokot led
the men swinging around to tackle the army on their right side, while
a warrior named Two Moons led a group towards their left – three of
whom, including the cousins Wahlitits and Sarpsis Ilppilp, defiantly
wore red blankets to attract enemy gunfire. Some warriors fired from
horseback, concealing themselves from the troops by riding behind
their horse's flank, shooting beneath the creature's neck, while others
dropped to the ground, picked off an opponent then remounted
their patient, perfectly trained horses to seek a new target. Capable of
fighting in unison but free to follow their own mind, they were a
formidable and unpredictable enemy.

Captain Perry's situation first began to fall apart when it emerged that Arthur Chapman's volunteers had little stomach for this fight. Most turned tail and fled back to the prairie, while a tiny rump abandoned the crucial position Perry had unwisely assigned them, leaving his own men open to attack. The regular troops took a little longer to disintegrate, but then did so in some style. Company H had insanely attempted to stay on horseback (F, knowing their limits, had all dismounted) and the combination of skittish, inexperienced horses, a growing stampede of riderless mounts and the fact that firing from a horse was a tricky technique, far beyond the troopers' training, rendered half of Perry's force quite useless. Many of the cavalrymen had even forgotten to tighten the girths of their saddles, and slid gracelessly to earth over the side of their horses. Meanwhile, all those rusty, badly maintained guns jammed – not that it mattered much, as Two Moons later recalled: 'Soldiers seemed poor shots' – and discipline rapidly faltered in the face of greenhorn panic. As troops either perished or ran, Nez Perce women collected their guns and ammunition and hastily delivered them to their husbands, ensuring the warriors grew ever better armed.

Perry called a retreat, but most of the troops had already instigated their own, fleeing pell-mell back up the valley's walls. Some groups of men were left behind to be cut down, others rode into dead-end ravines and lasted only as long as their ammunition. Only the leadership of a few old dogs of war, William Parnell to the fore, maintained a semblance of order – at one point in the flight Perry considered making another stand and holding out until nightfall, only for Parnell to point out, presumably with a choice garnish of Irish vocabulary, that it was still only seven in the morning.

Nez Perce warriors harried the fleeing troops all the way out of the valley and across the Camas Prairie, to within sight of the settlers' barricades in the town of Mount Idaho. There, as Yellow Wolf recalled, they relented: 'Some of the chiefs commanded, "Let the soldiers go! We have done them enough! No Indian killed!"'

No Indian killed indeed. Three Nez Perce had been wounded, but all recovered. But thirty-four soldiers had died at White Bird, a third of Perry's command. Sixty-three rifles and countless cartridges were also left on the battlefield for the Nez Perce to collect. The traditional symbols of martial triumph – the scalps of the fallen – were left undisturbed, though: the Nez Perce were disconcerted by the poverty of their opponents, and saw little to celebrate in this startling victory. The young and the foolhardy aside, they'd wanted to avoid a fight, and now they would surely have to flee from crushing retribution.

The next development was cheerful, however: the day after the battle a group of Nez Perce buffalo hunters returned from the eastern plains to join the group and hear the news of exiles, outbreaks and battles. Among them were two revered fighting chiefs, Rainbow and Five Wounds, partners in scores of battles who also knew the tribe's wider terrain well. With the two leaders joining the council, a strategy for survival was forged – it was decided that General Howard's callous demand for the Nez Perce to face the spring floods would be thrown back in his face. The chiefs agreed to lead their people back into the wilderness between the Snake and Salmon rivers, hoping that their intimate knowledge of the rivers' currents and shallows could help them across the torrents, while any pursuing army would flounder in ignorance. With the troops splashing around, the tribe could then consider their next move – Joseph favoured a return to the Wallowa, but the most likely next step was a journey east, over the mountains and away from the hatred and violence of Idaho. Camp was broken and the Nez Perce crossed the foaming Salmon.

There was little in the way of measured tactical contemplation in the white American response to the White Bird battle. Newspapers across the continent picked up on the defeat, parroting fictional accounts of war dances, scalpings and mutilation of corpses, inflating the Nez Perce fighting force from seventy to three, even four hundred, and always paying tribute to the tactical genius of the warrior king Joseph (who was actually hardly involved in the battle). Across the north-west states, crowds now gathered for news at telegraph offices, volunteer forces were drawn up and collections were raised for rifles; it was widely and fearfully assumed the Nez Perce would inspire every tribe in the region to join a full-blown war of rebellion. Communities hundreds of miles from the battle abandoned their farms to huddle in stockaded towns, leaving their cattle and horses for enterprising rustlers to gather at leisure. Even *The Times* in London found space between the burning local issues – the Russo-Turkish War and the Henley Regatta – to cover this victory for 'the red skins'.

General Howard learned that he'd presided over one of the worst losses in the history of the Indian resistance in an entirely fitting way: two troopers had turned and fled at the very outset of the battle, and didn't stop riding until they got back to barracks. Howard reacted to their news like a man whose glittering career was suddenly on the line, hastily gathering an army of almost four hundred men, calling in troops from Alaska to Georgia, to launch a punitive campaign against the renegades. For the Northwest to remain peaceful, he later reasoned, there could be no chance of the dissident Nez Perce surviving as a symbol of enduring freedom: 'The campaign needed to be prolonged, persistent pursuit and final capture, to put to rest forever the vain hopes of these dreaming, superstitious nomads.' With narcissism that would get its just deserts, the general even embedded a tame journalist for the adventure, Thomas Sutherland of the *Portland Standard*.

Howard's army set off for White Bird Creek on 22 June – with their first task to bury at last the battlefield dead, now decomposed and attended to by coyotes – before moving onto the banks of the Salmon River, where the Nez Perce rearguard patrolled tantalizingly in view on the opposite shore. A distressingly ill-tempered encounter ensued – members of the leading families of the Christian Nez Perce had joined Howard, to serve as scouts (and mediators in the expected surrender talks), and now they traded insults across the water with the dissident warriors.

'You cowardly people!' yelled one scout, James Reuben. 'Come over here. We will have it – a war!'

'You call us cowards when we fight for our homes, our women, our children!' came the defiant reply. 'You are the coward! You sit on the side of the Government, strong with soldiers! Come over. We will scalp you!'

The massed ranks of Howard's troops darkened the hills behind Reuben as the abuse continued, and when the first volley of rifle fire echoed around the gorge the non-treaty warriors retreated, unhurt.

The symbolism of the cameo was impossible to ignore. The Christian Nez Perce were not acting from spite; theirs was a precarious position, with their homes, women and children certainly under threat. The panic among the settlers had blurred the distinction between rebellious and peaceable Indians, and Lewiston was enduring nightly false alarms that the Christian bands were heading to town on the warpath. The *Teller* was also fabricating a suspicious shortage of able-bodied young men on the reservation, suggesting the rebel Joseph was being secretly reinforced – 'it is more than probable that he has received large accessions to his warriors from the Agency Indians' – and in the febrile atmosphere mob beatings of Christian Nez Perce were becoming commonplace. Another persistent theme of the West's colonial history was clearly acting itself out – once frustration and subjugation finally sparked violence, it never took long for settlers' pleas for military retribution to be amended by another request, that their 'Indian problem' be solved once and for all, by breaking up the reservations, scattering the tribes and, by happy coincidence, opening their valuable land to purchase. As one correspondent wrote to the press from behind the barricades in Mount Idaho:

When! Oh when will our government be brought to see the fallacy of its Indian policy and take steps to render life and property secure on the frontier? Time, the Bible, nor civilisation has worked no change in the nature of the Indian, what he was when Columbus kissed the shores of San Salvador, he is today, and will be, so long as he is permitted to keep up his tribal relations and be governed by an independent law.

But on the other side of the river there was little sympathy for the concerns of the Christian Nez Perce, men whose family names were upon the Thief Treaty and were now assisting the government in hounding down their own relations and former allies. Yellow Wolf was among those on the bank, boiling with rage: 'Sold our country which they did not own. This stayed in our minds, and now their followers were helping soldiers take all from us.'

The next service the Nez Perce scouts offered Howard, in concert with most of his white guides, was to point out discreetly that the general was about to make a royal fool of himself. The non-treaty bands were clearly planning to use their superior knowledge of their homeland, and their remarkable capacity to travel through it at speed, to lead the army a merry dance. Howard was undeterred, though, and convinced himself that the women and the elderly would delay the Nez Perce in the unforgiving mountains ahead of them. Ordering boats to carry his artillery, he began the tedious process of getting an army across the swollen Salmon River, to chase the renegades down.

Standing on the high ridge of the Salmon River gorge, one can understand his confidence. The climb up from the riverbank is a relentless, exposed, lung-busting slog, only to be rewarded, beyond the ridgeline, with 'high plains country' ahead of you, a crinkled, irregular mass of valleys, gorges and gullies, mottled with forest and grassland.*

---

* The punishing challenges of the landscape surrounding the Salmon would be demonstrated over time by the lack of development that could conquer this terrain. So untouched by settlement was much of the Salmon's watershed that when the Wild and Scenic Rivers Act was passed in 1968, as part of the post-war environmental-legislative revolution, seeking to protect

When it was clear that Howard was committed to tackling the challenges of the wild Salmon country, the Nez Perce promptly set off north into the high plains. Young and old joined a rough, undulating march of almost two straight days, leaving behind more valuable possessions and provisions to lighten the uphill loads, somehow driving a herd of perhaps three thousand horses ahead of them. Their route cut the corner off a huge bend in the Salmon, and they reached its banks again around twenty-five miles downstream from where they'd first crossed. There, news arrived from their back-markers that Howard had finally overcome the river, and was now on their side – at which point they employed their time-worn raft-building techniques to cross back swiftly and head for easier terrain, leaving the army to enjoy the high plains alone.

Behind them, General Howard was possibly regretting his decision to invite the press. His army was making slow progress through tough country, with rain, snow and unwieldy artillery compounding the fact that no one knew their way around. Howard eventually sought help from a local settler, who amply demonstrated his affection for the landscape he'd claimed as his own: 'The only white man we met living on the west side of the Salmon was a farmer named Brown,' reported Sutherland, our man from the *Standard*, 'but so ignorant of the surrounding country that he had never ascended any of the mountains that almost encircled his little home.'

---

those rivers that 'represent vestiges of primitive America', it was inevitable that much of the Salmon would fit the bill. Sure enough, in 1980, seventy-nine miles of the Salmon were declared officially 'wild' – and thus completely off-limits to any development. The idyll was then spoilt, sadly, by the enterprising but wholly illegal construction of two fishing lodges and one hotel right along the riverbank, in the heart of the statutory wilderness. Local environmental campaigners were predictably furious, and in the year 2000 they obtained a court order which reaffirmed the owners' legal responsibility to tear down their trespassing eyesores. But progress is not so easily halted out West. The hoteliers made a few telephone calls, and in November 2004 Senator Larry Craig (Rep., Idaho) quietly sneaked a 'rider' onto a Congressional Bill, granting a special dispensation to the three interloping developments, miraculously rendering the illegal legal, and the wilderness negotiable.

Reduced to slow, uncertain progress, the army ran low on supplies, and the jaded, sodden troops took to shooting and eating any stray Nez Perce horses they could find. Howard's men finally reached the Salmon River crossing point three days behind the tribe, only to find they couldn't emulate their enemy – the river comprehensively defeated them. Howard made his men build a raft out of a nearby house, but it broke up and floated downstream; the Indian scout James Reuben gave a demonstration of how to ride a horse across a flood, but the cavalrymen couldn't match him. Not for the last time, the Nez Perce's expert handling of the challenges of the natural West left the army quite perplexed. As one sergeant recalled: 'How the whole tribe of Indians with horses, women, papooses, etc., got across was a puzzle. It is yet a puzzle. We didn't seem to have engineering skill enough to devise ways and means to cross.'

Flummoxed, Howard ordered a depressing retreat – his army marched for two days back to where they'd first forded the Salmon, floundered across and finally left the high plains behind. Only the loyal *Portland Standard* saw the bright side of the general's opening incursion into this conflict, pointing out that the army had captured some tobacco, a few horses and 'large numbers of fat cattle'. Everywhere else the Christian General, once too soft in negotiations, now too slow in pursuit, was a laughing stock. 'Does the General now think he will make short work of it?' sneered the *Lewiston Teller*.

Peace reigns on the Camas Prairie – peace and space. Here, those pastoral blessings are luxuriously conferred on the clapperboard farmhouses that lord over this open acreage, flagpoles on the front lawns, gate posts linked by rolling, gravel tracks that disappear dead straight over placid ripples of bone-dry land, between wheatfields shifting in the breeze, beneath a pristine crystal sky. The prairie is even spared the monotony of a Midwestern kitchen-table horizon –

The expanse of the Camas Prairie.

to the east lie the fearsome mountains that bar the path to Montana, to the south stands the ridgeback that leads to the Salmon Wilderness, all offering hope of plentiful high-country game to anyone with strong legs and a good eye.

At night, however, the prairie carries a slight menace – the silent, starlit air of isolation, abandonment, of a phone call to the distant police not being worth the effort should footsteps break your sleep. Out here, the gun beside the bed isn't bravado. And as if to emphasize the point, on patches of high ground and near rare gatherings of boulders and scrubby trees, a few more flags fly, cenotaphs are sculpted, memorials are stringently maintained. They recall the time when fear, and death, scorched across this open land, in the days following the Nez Perce's arrival here from the high plains country – days, one suspects, when life on the Camas Prairie never felt so lonely.

For the Nez Perce this landscape had been among the most beloved corners of their homeland. It offered pasture for their herds, a feast of root bulbs to harvest and memories of long summer gatherings, rites and games. Now, though, the prairie had become a considerable obstacle to their survival; although Howard was stranded far behind, there were surely other troops in the vicinity, and as the Indian caravan headed across the wide-open terrain their women and children would be fearfully exposed to attack.

A loose strategy was hastily improvised. Bands of warriors (many still barely under control) would range over the prairie to execute a scorched earth policy of torching farms and crops to keep the settlers cowering safely in their barricaded townships. If messengers and couriers were foolhardy enough to try and cross the prairie, then Nez Perce scouts, stationed on the roads, would fatally ensure any information about the bands' whereabouts didn't get through. Finally, any pockets of troops that Howard had stationed on the prairie needed to be harassed and pinned down, completing the distraction and confusion that would, it was hoped, allow the senior warriors to lead the women and children safely across the plain. In the next few days, the Nez Perce would amply demonstrate their understanding of the very best form of defence.

On the morning of 3 July, two days before the Nez Perce caravan would attempt its run across the prairie, an outrider known as Seeyakoon Ilppilp chanced upon two volunteer army scouts, William Foster and Charles Blewitt. Blewitt didn't survive the encounter, but Foster made it back to the small cavalry force he'd been sent from, and a rescue party was arranged, in case Blewitt had merely been wounded. Ten troopers, under the belligerent command of Lieutenant Sevier Rains, followed Foster back to the site of the skirmish at a gallop – where they promptly rode straight into a trap set by the worldly plains fighter Five Wounds. They perished to a man. The young warrior Yellow Wolf recalled that some of the soldiers had strong *wyakins* and took many bullets to die.

The Rains Massacre disheartened the small army presence on the prairie, now under the command of Captain Perry, freshly returned to the fray with a supply train for his waterlogged general. On 4 July, Perry's troops dug in on a hilltop ranch where the town of Cottonwood would soon develop, carving trenches into the hillside while Nez Perce fighters harassed and taunted them. Duly pinned down, the force of 120 men then spent the morning of the 5th exchanging sporadic fire with their besiegers while watching, in the distance, as the women, children and elderly of the Nez Perce were ushered, unmolested, across the Camas Prairie.

Captain Perry's agonies were not complete, though. That same morning a gung-ho civilian by the name of D. B. Randall decided that the pitiful US Army needed rescuing. An intemperate soul and something of a chancer, who was living illegally on reservation land, Randall rustled up sixteen more volunteers for his mercy mission and rode out from the settlers' barricades in Mount Idaho, heading for Cottonwood. Two miles from Perry's fortifications, the 'Valiant Seventeen' found their path blocked, a few hundreds yards ahead, by a Nez Perce war party, dispatched to distract any attack on the caravan. Memories grow hazy in the rush of conflict, but the Nez Perce group was numbered somewhere between sixteen fighters, according to the tribe's recollection, and more than 150, waiting in silence for half a mile along the horizon, in the volunteers' version of events. Randall, unperturbed by such an overwhelmingly superior (or slightly inferior) enemy force, gave the order: 'We are going to charge the Indians.'

The seventeen careered towards their foe – and straight through them, the warriors splitting to allow the charge to pass, before turning and giving chase. It was now a straight horse race to the trenches, a cloud of dust and bullets barrelling towards Perry's position. Within a mile, the volunteers were run down, Randall's horse was shot out from under him and the seventeen were forced to dismount and take a stand. For over three hours the warriors took potshots from protected vantage points, badly wounding Randall and one other volunteer, Ben Evans. Weesculatat became the first Nez Perce to die in battle, taking bullets in the leg and chest from which he would die that evening. The warriors slowly closed in on the survivors, tightening their circle – but one thing bemused them, as Yellow Wolf recalled: 'We did not know why the soldiers in their dugout rifle pits did not come to the fighting. We could see them where they were on higher ground. They seemed a little afraid.'

The soldiers in the rifle pits were in fact giving full voice to a hearty series of blazing rows. Understandably wary of presiding over two routs in quick succession, Perry was affecting jaded insouciance towards the shoot-out unfolding beneath his barricades, telling his second in command that the volunteers 'are being all cut to pieces' and that it was 'too late' to save a single man. The fifteen who were actually holding out on the prairie even fired a rifle volley in Perry's direction to gain his attention, but the captain remained certain that protecting his supplies trumped rescuing a lost cause. Friends of Randall's party inside the barricades were reduced to begging Perry to send out a relieving charge, and his officers joined the rapidly disintegrating shouting match, questioning their commander's courage – insults were even hurled from the rank and file, letting Perry know his prudence was tarnishing the First Cavalry's honour. Eventually, a pair of civilian volunteers disobeyed orders and galloped off into the fray, prompting a battle-hardened Sergeant Simpson to announce he could no longer stomach the shame, and that he was leading twenty-five fellow mutineers down the hill at once, whether to death by Indian rifle or firing squad. Perry relented and finally dispatched around sixty men to rescue the desperate volunteers. In no mood for a full-scale battle, and with their women and children safely disappearing into a gorge in the prairie, the Nez Perce fighters called it a day and headed back to the caravan. The volunteers, carrying the body of Ben Evans and the rapidly fading Randall, were escorted back to their families at Mount Idaho, where the recriminations began. The US Army had been humiliated four times in three weeks – at White Bird, the Salmon River wild goose chase and now twice on the

Camas Prairie – by a group of Indians who'd never even wanted a fight. Morale among north-central Idaho's European population was rock-bottom: some even discussed what life might soon be like as the slaves of the Nez Perce warrior king.

'They carried D. B. Randall over to Mount Idaho on a wagon. And you know, he carried a watch in his jacket pocket, one of those big old watches – and a bullet had hit the watch. But it had pushed the pieces of crystal deep into his chest, and that's what killed him: he bled to death on L. P. Brown's kitchen table. Anyway, that's the story my family told, and I saw that watch once, with the big dent in it. I wish I had it now, it would be a nice thing to give to the museum.'

Almon E. Randall was a jovial and time-worn bag of skin and bones, his baseball cap, thick checked shirt and jeans, rolled up over solid workman's boots, seeming to weigh more than his bantam frame could carry. A long plastic tube ran from his nostrils to the oxygen tank in the middle of his kitchen floor, tethering him frustratingly: 'Before I got the pneumonia, I could do everything you can do!' A 'shirt-tail relative' of the gung-ho volunteer, Almon and his beloved dogs shared a ramshackle, single-storey home that still looked out over the checkerboard of the Camas Prairie, perched above the route of that shell-shocked rescue party's retreat.

'His wife, Belle, well, she was my great-grandmother. My grandmother was born of Belle's second marriage, but then she grew up and married a nephew of Randall's, getting back the family name. That man, my grandfather, well, he was a kind of a lazy man, so he was bought this land – which was passed to my father, then on to me. I was born right here – we tore the old house down, and built this one up out of scraps. It keeps the sun and the rain off …'

Like everyone on the prairie, Almon had an opinion on the bloody summer of 1877: 'Howard was no Indian fighter. He just didn't savvy

Indians. He was pretty good at following them around, but he couldn't get them in one place to deal with them. And they were smart. They watched the soldiers' drills down at Fort Lapwai, and they'd learned – shoot the bugler! Shoot the bugler, you get chaos!

'Those Indians, though ...we did kind of run over them. Yep, we ran over them. It was a dreadful mistake forcing those ones out of Oregon. They weren't doing anyone any harm. And the Indians we had out here, they were civilized – they weren't savages, they weren't Apaches.

'When I was a kid, I remember the Indians used to come by here on their buggies, going up the mountains to pick huckleberries. They camped up in the hills – a lot of people were camped up there then, there were a lot of squatters on the mountain. It was a hard time then, this was in the late thirties, and lots of folks just went up into the hills and lived off what they could find up there. You ever read *The Grapes of Wrath*? Well, it was like that.'

He knew the prairie and the hills behind it like his own living room – 'I used to take a gun and a sack up into the hills, and be gone a week' – but now, like many of the area's elderly, his life was harshly confined. During the short burst of summer, he was under doctor's orders to stay at home because the ceaseless forest fires that had recently come to define the region's warmer months were ruining the air quality. Outside the farm's windows, the Camas Prairie was clogged with a thick, tea-stained haze. 'I've never seen it this bad in my life. If it would just rain it would clear it all off, but it's just getting stuck. I do think the world's warming up – the winters aren't so bad now, when I used to work on the roads, you used to get snowdrifts as high as your head. It's never like that now.'

Not surprisingly, Almon was in no rush to send off his guest, preferring to 'visit' a while, peacefully passing the time, with a dopey chocolate Labrador snoozing at his feet: 'D. B. Randall, he wasn't an exceptional man. He didn't do much – but then maybe I haven't done much more. I raised my family up pretty good, kept them all out of jail – my son lives next door, on family land. This here is a nice area, you can raise a family good round here. I mean, I've never been anywhere else, so I don't know … You married?'

'Engaged.'

'Gonna start a family?'

'Hope so.'

'You're starting the best part of your life, right now. I was married thirty-eight years, ten months and fifteen days. I worked every day of it, and I came home, gave my wife all the money, and she bought the food and all with it, and kept the rest. When she died, turns out she'd done okay, and we had a lot of money saved up! I thought it was going to be the other way round, though, that I'd go first, but she had a heart attack …'

We looked through his collections of antique pocket watches, pipes, knives and scores of old guns, and explored the small workshop where he hand-made his own bullets to fit the vintage barrels. Eventually it was time to leave, but halfway down the long road into town I had to spin the van round, realizing I'd left a bag of notebooks behind. Almon Randall was standing behind his screen door, grinning, too old and with too much sense to be ashamed of his lonely prairie life: 'I saw you put it down on the floor and I hoped you'd forget it – that way you'd have to come back …'

The Nez Perce caravan had expertly escaped their isolation and exposure on the prairie, and now made camp at a sheltered site on the valley floor of the south fork of the Clearwater River, to consider the next move in their running retreat. While they were resting and praying, another weary caravan of Indians came up the riverbank towards them – the Looking Glass band. It turned out that General Howard's troops hadn't let themselves down entirely – they'd somehow picked up the rudiments of vindictiveness and thuggery

Chief Looking Glass, who joined the fleeing Nez Perce after an unprovoked attack on his village.

and had applied them with relish to a people desperate for peace.

Just before disappearing on his Salmon River misadventure, Howard had decided that despite the Looking Glass band's transparent desire to avoid trouble – their chief had abandoned the tribal gathering at Split Rocks when he sensed the first uprising was imminent, and had refused any dissident Nez Perces' requests for shelter – they were still an unacceptable risk. Fictitious rumours reached the general that Looking Glass's warriors had secretly joined the warpath, and he resolved to respond firmly. He picked Captain Whipple to take around sixty men and arrest Looking Glass and subdue his warriors, and on the morning of 1 July, Whipple's force (accompanied by twenty volunteers under the command of D. B. Randall, making the most of the four days he had left to live) had gathered on a hillside above the Looking Glass village.

They would have looked upon an idyllic sight. The village was nestled between a tiny, shaded creek and the wider, flawless Clearwater River, the small flood plain lying in the shadow of two steep hills, creating an enclave in which the world could pass by unnoticed. The band had grown vegetables, and tended cattle and horses as well as enjoying the bounties of the fishing grounds. When Whipple's troops appeared soon after sunrise on the ridge above this bucolic home, there was no motion for war – Looking Glass paraded a white flag and sent out representatives to tell Whipple to leave his people alone. The captain was intent on snaring his man, however, and demanded Looking Glass ride out to see him in person. As the tense negotiations went on, one of Randall's men snapped, and fired into the village; this was followed by a full volley from the trigger-happy volunteers, then a terrifying free-for-all of firepower from the pent-up troops. With bullets tearing into their tepees, the men, women and children fled from the onslaught – three, perhaps four, warriors were killed, while a young woman with a baby strapped to her back tried to cross the Clearwater to safety. The current took both woman and child to their deaths.

With the camp nigh-on undefended, Whipple instigated a charge; some troops concentrated on stealing the band's horses and setting fire to their lodges, while the volunteers focused on plundering the tepees for blankets, furs and trophies. The tribe's gardens were crushed under the stampede, the cattle were driven away as spoils. Remarkably, some soldiers would later be commended for their actions – Lieutenant Sevier Rains, another young man who would soon be answering for his actions in a higher court, was garlanded for 'gallantry and daring' during the smash and grab.

The Looking Glass Raid was, however, as counter-productive as it was spiteful – no one was arrested, or confined, and all that Whipple had done, Howard grimly accepted, was 'stirred up a new hornet's nest'. Exactly one week after the attack, Looking Glass and his people joined the other Nez Perce dissidents, fresh from their adventures on the Camas Prairie, at their camp on the banks of the Clearwater. The caravan was now increased to around seven hundred in number, with (estimates vary) between 200 and 250 fighting men to defend the large protectorate of women, children and the elderly. The horse herd, without which the camp's movement and defence would be all but impossible, still numbered around three thousand. Finally, Looking Glass, one of the most influential and experienced of all the tribal leaders, was now an implacable enemy of the US Army, and General Howard in particular. His leadership would prove decisive in the coming months, for good and ill.

The union of the bands was not entirely sombre, though – the fearless warrior Yellow Wolf was reunited with his mother, who'd been staying with Looking Glass at the time of the attack; she had even remembered to rescue her boy's favourite rifle from the beleaguered village. This was a woman of whom any son would be proud: 'My mother could use the gun against soldiers if they bothered her. She could ride any wild horse and shoot straight. She could shoot the buffalo and was not afraid of the grizzly bear.'

General Howard, not the recipient of glowing praise from any quarter, was finally back in the game. His weary force had emerged from the Salmon River country and made it to the prairie town of Grangeville, from where, on 9 July, a reinforced army of some five hundred men set out to track down the Nez Perce and engage them in final battle. Though daunting in size, the command was not in the brightest of spirits – there was dissension in the ranks over the performance of the senior officers, two volunteer scouts stormed off following a row revisiting Perry's conduct during the Randall shoot-out and nerves were so frayed that during one overnight camp the nightwatchmen took to shooting at each other. Undaunted, Howard led his men, bolstered with fearsome technology in the form of Gatling guns and howitzers, onto the high tablelands that overlooked the south fork of the Clearwater. Yet more journalists were invited along for the ride this time – Howard knew that at this point only a well-publicized victory could salvage his career.

The Nez Perce, meanwhile, were tarrying at the camp where Looking Glass had joined them. There was still considerable discussion about where to head next – east out of war-torn Idaho, south-west to the defensible Wallowa, or just the few miles into the Agency at Lapwai to start discussing surrender terms? Meanwhile, Ollokot and some of the young warriors were being distracted by another group of foolhardy volunteers who'd ridden too close to the camp and were now besieged, offering the Nez Perce men some sport and the chance to reclaim many of the horses stolen from Looking Glass. No Indians or settlers died in the skirmish but a day was wasted. For the first time since the White Bird battle, nearly a month before, the Indians were allowing their grip on events to loosen.

Though not a deep river gorge by Idaho standards, the south fork of the Clearwater does cut a sharp, precipitous scar in the sweeping prairie and wooded tablelands that lie above its path. The sides of the valley are steep enough, and so regularly encrusted with outcrops and cliff faces that an entire cavalry and infantry force could easily pass along the top of the ravine, within a hundred yards of its edge, without realizing that an Indian encampment of seven hundred lay at the bottom. And that, on the mid-morning of 11 July, is very nearly what happened; as Howard's army marched along the high road in search of a battle, a lieutenant left the main party to peer over the valley's edge, only to return at a gallop with the news that they'd all but overshot the unsuspecting camp. It was a suitably stumbling start to the Clearwater battle, the strangest and most contentious of all the fights in the Nez Perce's epic retreat.

The valley's sides were too steep for a direct charge so Howard was forced to back his men up in search of a manageable slope. However, in another startling display of horsemanship, the Nez Perce warriors pointed their mounts directly up the crumbling, narrow gullies to meet the enemy as high and as far away from the village as possible. With the hardy Toohoolhoolzote to the fore, they blocked the attack on a barren, open plateau – but this time there was no rout, Howard held his men firm and the two sides engaged in a bloody firestorm of charges, counter-attacks and flanking attempts. Most of the battle's casualties were sustained during the manic early searches for a knock-out blow, but, as the afternoon wore on, a dug-in stalemate developed amid the rocks, trees and hastily created barricades. The Nez Perce even found time to converse with the Indians serving on Howard's side – the son of the fallen Weesculatat was working as an army scout, and he learned from shouts across the defences that his father had died following the Randall battle. Realizing he was on the wrong side, the young man jumped onto his horse for a suicidal sprint across no-man's-land, bullets from both sides flying past (the Nez Perce thought he was attacking, the army knew he was deserting), before stripping to his breechclout and joining battle with the renegades. There were few other bright spots for the Indians, though; with four times the men, some powerful weapons at their disposal, and under Howard's doughty, unspectacular command, the army looked unlikely to collapse as it had at White Bird Canyon, leaving the Nez Perce warriors debating, as night fell, exactly what they were fighting for. 'No use fighting when soldiers are not attacking our camp,' some reasoned, suggesting the battle should be abandoned as soon as the women and children could be moved to safety. A handful of others voted for self-preservation by quietly drifting into the darkness and heading to the Indian Agency at Lapwai, pretending they had never been part of the uprising. No strategic agreement was reached, and when battle was rejoined the next day it was little surprise that the disunited Nez Perce proceeded to defeat themselves.

The morning continued in stalemate, but in the afternoon, when the army charged the Nez Perce one more time, they encountered little resistance – too many warriors had gone down the hill to the village to check on their families (some Nez Perce memoirs suggest this excuse was a cover for cowardice – with Gatlings and howitzers on the battlefield, this was a cacophonous fight, testing even the stiffest nerves) and now the possibility of an orderly retreat was replaced by a desperate rush to abandon the camp. Joseph, who had fallen naturally into the role of guardian of the protectorate of women and children, galloped down from the battlefront to try and organize the hasty rush through the long riverside grasses and into the hills beyond, while word was hastily passed to the last few fighters that they were being left in the lurch. Leaping their horses down lunatic cliff faces, the warriors flew back to a camp in chaos, possessions and lodges abandoned, cannonballs exploding in the dirt (Howard targeted the families without compunction). Yellow Wolf was the last to leave the front, careering down the slope to meet a desperate scene – in the confusion, Joseph had believed his wife, Toma Alwawinmi, and his infant daughter had been sent on ahead of him. In fact, he'd left them behind ...

Crossing the river and reaching where the now empty camp stood, I heard a woman's voice. That voice was one of crying. I saw her on a horse she could not well manage. The animal was leaping, pawing, wanting to go. Everybody else had gone. I hurried towards her, and she called, 'Heinmot! I am troubled about my baby!'

I saw the baby wrapped in its cradleboard lying on the ground.

*Yellow Wolf, the young warrior who fought
tirelessly throughout the retreat.*

I reached down, picked up the cradleboard, and handed it to the woman. That mother laughed as she took her baby. It was the cannon shots bursting near that scared her horse.

Together they raced to catch up the rest of the caravan, and the family was reunited. Although valuable shelters and possessions had been lost, only four warriors had died in nearly two days of fighting against a far superior force (fourteen troopers were lost), the caravan was still in one piece and the priceless horse herd was intact. The situation could have been much worse – inexplicably, Howard made no real effort to chase down the retreat, preferring to let his troops scour the abandoned camp for booty while he informed the press that they'd just witnessed a comprehensive and conclusive victory, a fiction they dutifully repeated nationwide. He even made sure the president was telegraphed directly with the news (a clear breach of the chain of command) to further shore up his precarious tenure at the head of the campaign.

Oblivious to their enemy's crowing, the Nez Perce headed further up the Clearwater River – past the outcrop created when the heart of the monster had turned to stone, and Coyote had sparked their people's destiny – and rested at another waterfront camp at Kamiah, near where the south and middle forks of the Clearwater engaged.

They were now, ironically, within one of the patches of the Christian reservation that Howard had offered to Joseph for the peaceful resettlement of his people, back at the final peace council in May. There would be no settling down now, though, as the caravan reached Kamiah: all were agreed, to move was to stay alive.

'Now you've seen the New World ... GO HOME!'; 'Homeland Security – protecting our borders since 1492'; 'My heroes have always killed cowboys'; 'I'm a little bit white, but I can't prove it' – the bumper stickers and the T-shirts and the baseball caps at the Chief Looking Glass Days Pow-Wow, in Kamiah, Idaho, had plenty to say for themselves. Few here would take offence, though; this was the Friday afternoon of the celebration weekend, a time for the Nez Perce Reservation Indians to conduct their own business, and, while outsiders were welcome, they were sparse – numbering just myself, a pair of local old-timers and, in the corner of the basketball hall where we'd gathered, a young doctor offering free diabetes screenings. The hall, a blessed haven of cool air in the torpid heatwave that had engulfed this tiny, somnolent riverside town, was a scene of jovial chaos. Children were charging around and clambering everywhere, seemingly discovering a different relation to pester at every turn, while an army of organizers arranged the welcome lunch, gaggles of teenagers mooched about impassively and the new arrivals from long, straight drives sought out old friends and paid their respects to the elders, seated front and centre in their fading lawn chairs.

Once fed, the bulk of us (perhaps two hundred in all) took our seats in the grandstand while the tribe's spiritual leader, Horace Axtell, helped to open the floor with prayer and song, his stooped, octogenarian frame, mottled skin and ash-grey pigtails renounced by his spoken vigour as he offered up thanks for this day in the undulating, arrhythmic Nez Perce language. 'We pray to the Creator God, and we sing our flag song. This is a very old song, that our ancestors sang at the treaty meeting in 1855.' (Then, in 1877, Horace's great-grandfather, Timlpusmin, had passed through the land where we stood now, a warrior in the caravan of refugees.)

The afternoon's main business was a memorial gift-giving. The family of a recently departed grandmother gathered on the court, thirty-three relations in all, to offer us gifts and ask our permission to move on from their loss. And what gifts – the hall floor was covered with blankets, baskets and boxes, fruit, Tupperware, crockery, toys, clothes, perfume, towels, jewellery, cushions, baking dough, buffalo jerky, coffee-makers and more. It took forty-five minutes for the generosity to end – even I walked out the new owner of a bandana, a salt shaker, a saucepan, some earrings, several pens, a notepad and (essential after six weeks on the road) a pair of clean socks. It was a muscular display of family strength, both humbling and enviable.

The following evening, the people of the Nez Perce Reservation would show their strength in unison. The celebration had now moved outside to the grass dance circle, with more white spectators in attendance, respectfully filling up the wooden bleachers while the Native elders sat beneath ringside plastic pagodas, as the sun finally relinquished some of its furious strength. Among them, Nancy Looking Glass beamed beneath her greying ringlets and from behind bottle-top glasses, a cast on her frail wrist. She still lived on the very parcel of land the government had allotted to the great chief's family, she told me, her smile fading to earnest defiance – 'We're still here – we're still here.'

After the colours of the United States and the Nez Perce were paraded to open the floor, Horace Axtell spoke once more:

147

'I am thankful that the descendants of the great chiefs put this event on, to remind us of the good people that we were. This is our way of life, that we keep alive tonight. Our ancestors, they laid down our ways for us, how to behave, how to treat and honour each other, and the sound of the beautiful drum reminds us of that. We're not doing this to show off, we're doing this because we have a reason – and we will keep coming back here every year, until it is our time.'

Horace then shuffled over to inspect his son's drum group as they began to play an inter-tribal dance – an invitation to every one of the hundred and more costumed dancers to take to the grassy floor, circling slowly as the sunset warmed the colours of their fabrics and feathers. Steadily, as the floor filled, the plaintive tune began to build in volume and urgency, the singers' chords straining and rasping as the caravan of dancers, some carrying infants, others stomping and swirling with an energy belying their years, whooped and yipped their encouragement. Horace, whose commitment to the dance had earned him two knee replacements, one new hip and a medical request to give it a rest, could contain himself no longer, and he broke into a grin and joined the fray, an eagle-feather fan clasped ahead of him. For ten minutes the song ranged on, filling the darkening sky as the ring of colour and light, union and cheer continued to turn. This was the thirtieth year of the Chief Looking Glass Days Pow-Wow – it began in 1977, to commemorate the centenary of the great retreat, an event which many believed would surely draw down the curtain forever on Indian-ness in Idaho. Tonight was some riposte.

In a long weekend of conversation and camera toting, the realities of modern life on the Nez Perce Reservation often interjected into this tableau of ancient music, costume and dance. The reservation's health crisis could not be ignored – the Lewiston Wal-Mart had recently started stocking a new lawn chair called the 'Big Boy', as if to suggest that needing enough fabric beneath your rear end to support two moderate human figures was something of an achievement, and suffice it to say there were far too many 'Big Boys' in the spectators'

*The opening night of the Chief Looking Glass Days Pow-Wow
in Kamiah, Idaho.*

circle for comfort. There were also strains of discord and judgement
(never, one is often told, in short supply on the reservation) as some
dismissed what they saw as their neighbours' temporary affection for
their ancestral culture: 'Too many of these people want to be Indian
for just three days a year,' one gentleman muttered to me, 'but they
don't hunt, they don't fish, they don't join our ceremonies. You've got
to learn the ways and the beliefs, then learn how to apply them, first
to yourself and then to the world – and then you're ready to be
accepted. Just because you can dance doesn't make you an Indian.'
There was also some unease at the commercialization of the event –
'I don't think young people should be dancing to win envelopes of
money,' one elder shrugged. 'We danced because we loved it, and the
elders just gave gifts to young people who conducted themselves
well.' (The event was, in fact, very restrained by modern standards,
the tiny Nez Perce tribal casino at Kamiah contributing, along with
private donors, to a relatively token prize pot for each dance style; on

the same weekend, the dancers could have been over in Washington, competing for $40,000 in prize money at the 'Yakama Nation Legends Casino's 4th Annual Rodeo and Pow-Wow'.) But overall, the mood was a cheerful one of gathering and kinship, of enjoying a display of unity, tradition and shared identity that the inhabitants of many rural communities and cultures would recognize from their past – and, if they're very lucky, from their present.

After I packed up the van to leave, I wandered over to thank the organizing committee for their tolerance and welcome. One of the leader's husbands, Howard, shook my hand with a lopsided smile:

'I hope you enjoyed it. You'll notice, though, that nobody has said anything to you that exposes himself to you in any way. I know I certainly haven't.

'You see … we don't trust white people. I don't trust you. You can't win our trust just by walking around asking a few questions – we judge people by actions. So … you go home, and you write your story – and if we like what you write, the next time you come here, we'll say "Hello". But if we don't like it, then we'll just ignore you.'

For the seven hundred Nez Perce retreating through Kamiah in July 1877, the challenges and consolations of reservation life were not on offer – the options were flight, defeat or the uncertainty of surrender. Trust was scarce between the caravan and the Christian Indians whose land they were now passing through – the reservation Nez Perce were expecting punitive horse-stealing raids from their homeless erstwhile comrades, and they had moved their riverboats to ensure they offered the renegades no help in crossing the wide Clearwater. Undaunted, the non-treaty bands once again built rafts from buffalo hides and placed an early summer torrent between themselves and the pursuing army.

Not that they were being pursued with any real menace. Howard's force dawdled into Kamiah soon after the Nez Perce had crossed the Clearwater, and, following a desultory and fruitless effort at an artillery barrage towards the vanishing procession, the general inexplicably called a two-day recuperative halt. Finally, on 15 July, it seems to have dawned on him that this was not the time for washing uniforms and sewing on buttons – if the Indians were not run down in the next few days, they would surely disappear into the almost impenetrable mountain wilderness that lay immediately to their east. At daybreak, Howard led a force out to cut off this likely retreat – only to be called back to Kamiah urgently. Chief Joseph wanted to surrender.

Ecstatic, Howard surmised that the caravan was running low on provisions and ammunition, and that dissension had broken out: 'I see evidence of the band's breaking up,' he telegraphed to his superiors, and began to plan for the trial and punishment of the Joseph band, declaring magnanimously, 'He and his people will be treated with justice.' Back at Kamiah, he found a young warrior called Zya Timenna serving as Joseph's representative, offering to discuss surrender terms across the Clearwater. The conversation was long and detailed, but ended less than satisfactorily from the general's point of view, with Zya Timenna demonstrating his esteem with a timeless gesture involving his exposed buttocks and percussive hands, before disappearing into the hills. The ruse had worked perfectly, buying the Nez Perce enough time to reach the edge of the mountain wilderness unscathed. After the setback of the Clearwater battle, they had regained the initiative and were now ready, men, women and children, to tackle one of the most arduous and unforgiving high-country journeys in the entire inland Northwest – the Lolo Trail.

CHAPTER SIX

UNEQUAL WAR

'Did you know that trees talk? Well they do. They talk to each other, and they'll talk to you if you listen. Trouble is, white people don't listen. They never learned to listen to the Indians so I don't suppose they'll listen to other voices in nature'

TATANGA MANI, Nakoda First Nation

I see that you're a logger, and not a common bum
'Cos no one but a logger stirs his coffee with his thumb.
My lover was a logger, there's none like him today.
If you poured whiskey on it, he'd eat a bale of hay

ANONYMOUS

THE YOUNG BOY was lost in the mountains when he met Ha-Hats, the grizzly bear. The bear, wishing to protect his land from incursion, prepared to attack – and yet the boy showed no fear. 'I can only die,' he shrugged, 'death is part of life.' Impressed with such courage, the bear resolved to share the secrets of his mountains with the boy – he revealed where to hunt the elk, moose, deer and beaver, where to find the huckleberries and service berries. And finally he showed the boy, K'useyneísskít, the trail that ran along the backbone of the mountains, towards the buffalo country.

When he had taught the boy all he knew, the bear disappeared, and the boy returned to the Nimiipuu.

The Nez Perce refugees would leave their homeland via the same route as the Europeans had wandered in.

On 20 September 1805 the Lewis and Clark party had stumbled onto the Wieppe Prairie following their tribulations along the Lolo Trail, the first white Americans to reach this hidden, hallowed land, and had placed themselves at the mercy of its native occupants, a people whose tenure pre-dated the Pyramids of Egypt. And now, within a single lifetime, on the evening of 15 July 1877, the chiefs of the dissident bands gathered on this open pasture high above the Clearwater River for a solemn council to discuss the inconceivable – their exile from Nez Perce country. To their east lay the Bitterroot Mountains, a contorted spine of forested ridges and peaks over one hundred miles wide, offering a harsh escape route from a month of battles, retreats, burials and wounds, and a generation of betrayals, affronts and belittlements.

All were hopeful that this would be a temporary departure – once Idaho had reclaimed its sanity, discussions of reservation status could surely resume – but there was equal agreement that the improvised, hastily agreed tactics that had kept most of their people alive so far now needed knocking into shape. What *was* their survival strategy? Where were they actually heading?

Joseph and Ollokot, perhaps more aware than most of how swiftly white settlement could redefine a situation, wanted to plan a rapid return to the homelands, either by turning west immediately and heading to the Wallowa, or shaking off Howard in the mountains, then doubling straight back. The elderly White Bird knew he wasn't fit enough to take on the role of war leader, but according to some testimonies he reportedly favoured tackling the Bitterroots, then heading due north, to Canada. Following the punitive US Army campaigns that had inevitably followed Custer's defeat, the Sioux chief Sitting Bull was now in exile north of the border, currently being tolerated by the British Empire. Joining him in diplomatic stasis may have seemed like the ideal circumstance in which to wait for Idaho to cool down.

But it was Looking Glass, more senior than the two Wallowa brothers but less ancient than White Bird or Toohoolhoolzote, and with the hectoring, rallying manner of a good shop steward, who drove through his plan of action. The Nez Perce would head into the Bitter-roots, following the Lolo Trail east into Montana. Once there, Looking Glass declared he was on good terms with both the Salish Indians and the white settlers living on the eastern flank of the mountains, and, with Howard, it was hoped, disinclined to follow, the Nez Perce could then make their next move in peace – further east, to the Great Plains, and Crow country. Fearsome warriors with whom Looking Glass had fought against the Sioux a few years earlier, the Crow could be allies in fending off any further attacks, while their wide-open territory, thick with buffalo, would be the perfect place in which to elude the army until the crisis calmed down. Joseph was said to be disconsolate as this plan emerged as the consensus – Crow country was around six hundred miles from the Wallowa, perhaps double that distance along navigable terrain, and the Nez Perce hunters who had travelled to the buffalo plains usually took at least a year or two to return. The valley of the winding waters was growing ever more distant.

But Looking Glass's guarantees of a peaceful reception on the other side of the Bitterroots, of an end to the fighting and fleeing, were seductive, and Joseph grudgingly agreed to submit to the scheme, declaring that his continued contribution would be to manage the protectorate of over five hundred women, children and the elderly. That night, after the meeting, the chiefs rode around the prairie, a lush combination of marshland and meadow surrounded by pine forests, ordering the young warriors of the camp to restrain themselves as soon as they entered Montana; the fight the Nez Perce had never wanted would be left behind in Idaho.

For a few tribe members the new strategy would be impossible to abide by. They had relations in the reservation bands, and suspected this exile on the plains would last longer than Looking Glass promised. They packed up their lodges and headed down the hill towards Kamiah, to join the reservation. The largest contingent of departures was the Red Heart band, some thirty people, none of whom had been involved in the retreat up to now – they had, in fact, been trying to avoid the conflict by hiding away on the Wieppe Prairie when the caravan had chanced upon them. After meeting the other leaders, Chief Red Heart decided to lead his people down to Kamiah and explain their impeccably peaceable intentions to General Howard – who, on meeting the party of supplicants, took one look at their long hair and traditional dress and arrested them as Dreamer renegades. The blameless 'prisoners of war' – mostly women, children and the elderly – were then subjected to a sixty-mile forced march to Fort Lapwai under the July sun, before being shipped off to spend the next nine months in prison. Howard's concept of Christian morality was never easy to pin down – the very same day he had some of his mule-packers arrested for blaspheming intemperately at their animals.*

Few experiences could capture the bewildering scale of the Northwest's wild, empty places better than a venture along the Lolo

---

* It is worth acknowledging that, despite the use of the word 'war' in translations of several original Nez Perce testimonies, many contemporary Nez Perce point out that a conflict in which one side was almost always trying to avoid a fight isn't a war – it's a retreat, or a flight, but not a war. This is not pedantry – the standards of acceptable conduct fall considerably in wartime, particularly with regard to prisoners and fatalities. This is a distinction the United States government fully understood in 1877, cloaking all Frontier Army action as events in the 'Indian Wars' – and seemed to understand just as well in the twenty-first century, when it continued to engage in conflicts in which one side was recognized as legally at war, but the other wasn't.

Trail, a journey of such relentless inhospitality that to emerge on the other side alive was the very limit of human endeavour. Stretching some 250 miles north to south, the massif of pine-covered, razorback ridges, boulder-strewn summits, tenuous slopes of scree and meadow and rare respites of mountain lakes and marshland clearings barred the route from Idaho to the wide glacial valleys of Montana and the buffalo plains to their east. The crossing of the mountains, along an often indistinct route that endlessly climbed and fell with every fold of the terrain, and was perennially blocked by thick stands of timber, fallen trees and landslides, was rendered yet more challenging by the paucity of game. But for the Nez Perce the journey offered rewards that justified the suffering – trade, alliance and marriage with the Salish people on the other side, or buffalo hides and martial honour on the Great Plains. The 120-mile crossing had also developed cultural significance over the centuries – various campsites were known as meeting points for convivial discussion of the whereabouts of good game or journeying family members, travellers would leave messages at recognized clearings describing their movements or hunting successes, and, like so many other cultures, the Nez Perce had embraced the spiritual value of an unbroken mountain-top view of unblemished creation. At such uplifting sites cairns were laid, pipes were smoked, prayers and songs were offered, and sunrises welcomed. Despite some efforts at clearing a marked trail, the white settlers had so far failed to create a safe thoroughfare over Lolo, and the easily lost Indian trail was a journey very few white traders and hunters took yearly. With such a border between the two territories, it's quite understandable that the Nez Perce believed they could be at war in Idaho but at peace in Montana.

Almost nothing is recorded of the eleven-day crossing the seven hundred Nez Perce undertook in July 1877 – Chief Joseph's terse recollection 'we retreated to Bitterroot Valley' being typical of the Native witnesses' sanguine dismissal of the challenge. It's clear that with each family responsible for packing their horses and breaking camp, the caravan moved efficiently along the tortuous path, in weather that swung from parching heat to sleet and gales. As the path narrowed, the procession must have stretched for over a mile, with the priceless horse herd still being driven along, riders regularly swapping their mounts to protect the creatures' welfare – still, some of the animals were injured as they were dragged through the sharp, dense forest, while others were broken by their loads and were left for the scavengers. The people had to pick berries for their own sustenance, and also scraped away at the soft second layer of the surrounding pine bark for an energy-rich snack of sugar crystals.

They also posted back-markers to watch for Howard's next move, a decision which led to two significant encounters. On the second day of the retreat, an advance party of troops and citizen volunteers from Howard's force, led by a dozen Christian Nez Perce scouts, blundered into the waiting back-markers. Two of the scouts, Abraham Brooks and John Levi, were killed; and as an indication of the esteem in which the Christian Nez Perce were held, despite favouring the US government over their brethren, both the soldiers and the settler volunteers decided to head home rather than help carry the Indian wounded and bury their dead. Emboldened by the ambush, Looking Glass then led a daring and strategically inspired raid all the way back to Kamiah, to steal horses from the Christian Nez Perce.

The combined effect of these two incidents was to leave General Howard languishing in Idaho for two weeks. That the bulk of their local army might disappear over the mountains and into Montana was a cause of Idahoan concern, bordering on hysteria, as locals felt sure the Red Napoleon was not yet finished with them. The *Lewiston Teller* had a tip-off: 'We learn that Joseph says he will return and burn out the settlers on Camas Prairie within from four to six weeks when the weather is dry.' The isolated mountain towns near the Wieppe Prairie were solemnly awaiting oblivion at the hands of the returning hordes: Pierce, quivering behind flimsy barricades, was said to have two rifles, two revolvers and a shotgun to defend the entire town.

Surrounded by such self-pity and such certainty that the Nez Perce would double-back, Howard was unable to break away and chase down or cut off the caravan in Montana, and had to wait until sufficient reinforcements arrived to serve as a home guard. He finally led his army, now seven hundred fighting men strong, towards the Lolo on 30 July – fully two days after the Nez Perce had emerged on the other side of the mountains.

The military memoirs give a fuller picture of how hard the crossing was. The endless climbs and descents were sapping on dry days, 'slippery, sticky, muddy and filthy' on wet ones, as the army tackled mountains that one member declared 'make ordinary picnic mountains, as for instance, the Adirondacks, "appear as holes in the ground"'. Advance teams of woodcutters had to widen a path for the long pack trains of mules bearing bacon, sugar, coffee and bread (the US Frontier Army was not versed in living off uncultivated land, and only ate what it could bring, buy or shoot), but the creatures gradually broke down as a result of the tough climbs and poor foraging, or slipped to their deaths down the precipitous slopes. The whole column was stretched up to five miles along the narrow path by the end of each day's sixteen-mile march, with the cavalrymen joining the infantry on foot as their horses steadily went lame. Some nights the troops, in below-freezing conditions, had to dig a shelf into the steep hillsides to sleep on, other nights they couldn't even do that: 'According as the tents were pitched, or beds made in them, we slept almost erect or standing on our heads.'

But despite the exhaustion, the cold, and the jarring 5.00, 4.00, even 3.00 a.m. reveilles, the filthy, ragged troops were not immune to the beauty of what they were passing through. As Major Mason wrote: 'The scenery is very grand from the tops of the mounts we cross, while all day long it has been pleasant to travel through the dense woods, with the sunlight glinting through the trees.'

Today, the Lolo Trail retains its ability to dispense both wonder and discomfort in generous proportions. An old forestry road now follows the route, a narrow, crinkled and rutted ribbon of dirt, rubble and boulders that at times acquires the gradient and topography of a waterfall as it labours through the forest, often crumbling and slipping away down the worst slopes, or becoming blocked by fallen timber or exposed rocks. With the heatwave still at full blast and the forest fires smouldering, hiking the hundred-mile 'motorway' (much used in the hunting season, all but deserted the remainder of the year) was not an option. So, guided by silent prayer and white knuckles, my ageing, wheezing camper van was pointed forth to bounce and grind its way slowly to Montana.

At the start of the track, the town of Wieppe was a tiny diaspora of wooden bungalows, with just a couple of bars, a gas pump and an abandoned hardware store at its centre, the few streets rambling out into the open farmland of the small prairie. First the buildings fell away, then the meadows, surrendering to the pine forests that dominated the Wieppe tableland. The sun still glinted through the trees here, but perhaps a little brighter than it did in 1877 – the western edge of the forest is mostly Potlatch company land – and in places the pines lining the roadside were, in the deathly jargon of the lumber industry, just 'beauty strips'. A couple of metres behind the curtain of adult pines, open fields of stumps and spindly infant trees revealed the agricultural nature of modern lumber land – it is, as any local will tell you, just like growing and reaping big fields of corn. As the lumber trucks roared past fearlessly, hurling up choking phantasms of dust, the road signs left travellers in no doubt as to their debt to the trade: 'Timber Harvest Built These Roads'.

Once away from the tree farms, the road plummeted to the foot of the Lolo range, before heading agonizingly upwards to the first crest – and the first glimpse of a dozen and more ridges of pine ahead, the trail's end lying somewhere beyond an elusive horizon. For the next two days the van fought its way along the dirt, cooking the brakes and boiling the engine, as its driver (by no measure an off-road fiend) yelled and bellowed to fend off the isolation, disorientation and fear. For hours the trees would hold the parlous road in their dense grip, a dark tunnel offering no sense of place or progress, before the crests and meadows opened up to reveal a truth more intimidating than inspiring – there was no one, nothing, for many miles. The forests rolled away interminably, the only breaks in the monochrome the distant tea-coloured plumes of fresh woodsmoke. The modern desire to commune with untrammelled nature could fade fast here, faced with such leviathan, unbending emptiness.

After two days' driving the van had travelled barely fifty miles, less than half the trail. It was time to set out on foot to reach the highest point on the crossing, the Indian Post Office, sweeping the cobwebs from the rising, still narrowing road in a race against sunset to the seven-thousand-foot summit camp. The next morning, woken by a deer nuzzling around my bivouac, I took a cup of campfire coffee up to the grassy ridgeline, dotted with Indian cairns, to watch the sun rise. In the half-light the frozen ripples of the countless mountain chains ahead were still pin-sharp silhouettes, each razorback emerging from the dewy fog that enveloped the valley floors. The land turned and the clouds flared white, then mellowed to red as the sun gently emerged and the mists fizzled to nothingness, revealing the forests lost in the great glacial curves of the highlands.

It was an unfinished masterpiece, though; where the Lolo Trail wound ever downwards and onwards towards Montana, great swathes of the forest seemed to lose their oceanic monotony as the daylight improved, with harsh, perfectly delineated collapses in the colour and texture of the distant terrain suggesting the scene of a controlled catastrophe, a battleground fought within rigid borders. Dense woods switched in an instant to eroded, parched grassland, or the lush, neon green of unshaded undergrowth, then flipped straight back to brief respites of thick pine. Countless roads scored the hillsides like scars from a ragged blade.

Indian prayer site on the Lolo Trail, with the first signs of the
'Checkerboard' in the distance.

That afternoon, now approaching Lolo Pass, and the point where
the Nez Perce had passed through the ancient forest into Montana,
this patchwork wasteland came into full, jarring view. In places, the
hillsides had been bludgeoned into rough, crumbling terraces, elsewhere lone, spindly pines stood guard over sprawling acres of rotten
stumps and greying kindling, or soundless fields of tiny, sickly
saplings. In a few patches, the blackened bark of the few standing
trees showed that fire had assisted in this miserable grand design, but
the roads spreading over the hillsides like veins, now running,
laughably, to nothing worth visiting for centuries, apportioned the
bulk of the blame. A roadside sign offered a shcepish explanation:
'Welcome to the Checkerboard'. This drained landscape, it explained,
was in 'alternate ownership', divided into a grid, with all the white
squares on the board under public stewardship, and the black in the
careful hands of the Plum Creek Timber Company, the handiwork
on view offering some justification for the infamy that surrounds a

corporation once labelled 'the Darth Vader of the timber industry'.

There had been, though, previous occupants of this land, the sign conceded, the Salish and Nez Perce Indians. It went on to remind us, with an understatement only a civil servant could have composed in contemplation of such an undiluted disaster area, that 'The Native Americans had a much less visible style of land management than we have today.'

In a parade of the natural gifts which the North American continent has conferred upon the North American economy, the furs, the iron, the coal, the gold, the copper, the oil, the fish and the soil would all be vying for second place, behind the forests. When the first Pilgrims landed, the entire eastern third of this land was almost exclusively wooded, tens of thousands of square miles of uninterrupted pine, oak, cedar, sycamore, chestnut, walnut, maple, birch and more, each forest offering a seemingly inexhaustible supply of vital, centuries-old giants waiting to be felled. The discovery was serendipitous indeed – by the seventeenth century, Europe was in a wood famine, generations of clearance colliding with economic expansion to create a bull market for barrels, ships, buildings, charcoal and more. England clung tight to the new colonies predominantly for their wood – particularly the towering white pines of the great north-eastern forests, tall and strong enough to serve as the ship's masts on which modern war and trade depended. In the mid-eighteenth century the old country then strengthened its dependence on the new territories in one of the earliest examples of the outsourcing of an environmental disaster, when Parliament resolved to transfer pig-iron production, which was burning up the last of England's woods, to the forested, disposable colonies.

And those forests thus drew the early colonists deeper and deeper into the continent. There were fortunes to be made, as the lines of sawmills headed ever further inshore along the eastern riverbanks, harvesting the 'free money' that could be made in export to Europe or the equally deforested West Indies; there was land to be claimed for farming, and fuel to be collected for the New World's most enviable luxury, permanently roaring hearths. For the pilgrims of faith, the conquest of the brooding woods was also a spiritual mission; if God's Country was to be built here, one Puritan declared, the first task was to defeat the forest, 'a waste & howling wilderness where none inhabited but hellish fiends & brutish men'.

The 'brutish men' were having their ancient hunting grounds and fishing streams ruined by this invasion of axes and saws, and many of the earliest Indo-European wars were sparked by desperate efforts to stop the arboreal plunder, but to no avail. The unending bounty of timber made the enrichment and empowerment of the colonies all but inevitable – and then, when England's efforts to chain down the giant finally failed, the new nation rolled its sleeves up and really started chopping.

America's steamboats and early trains ran on wood, its ironworks, factories and bakeries burned wood, its houses were almost all made of wood – during the nineteenth century, while the country's population increased tenfold, *per capita* consumption of wood increased *eightfold*. And at the vanguard of the search for fresh timber were the pioneer settlers, roving westward through the shade; if you only found a stream to power a mill, you had enough to start a town right there, as the trees alone would provide cash crops, fuel and shelter. The average American's skill with an axe was the most widely and proudly quoted evidence of the young nation's vigorous bloodstock and tackling the forest on your patch of land was considered as much a national service as a personal achievement – as one pioneer wrote of her typical contemporary: '"Clearing" is his daily thought and nightly dream; and so literally does he act upon this guiding idea, that not one tree, not so much as a bush, or natural growth must be sufficed to cover the ground, or he fancies his work incomplete. The very notion of advancement of civilization or prosperity seems inseparably connected with the total extirpation of the forest.' When Alexis de Tocqueville was on one of his many journeys through America's backwoods, he was drawn by the sound of a swinging axe towards a typical pioneer scene:

> As we came nearer, traces of destruction marked the presence of civilized man: the road was strewn with cut boughs; trunks of trees, half consumed by fire, or mutilated by the axe, were still standing in our way. We proceeded until we reached a wood in which all the trees seemed to have been suddenly struck dead; in the middle of summer their boughs were as leafless as in winter; and upon closer examination we found that a deep circle had been cut through the bark, which, by stopping the circulation of the sap, soon kills the tree. We were informed that this is commonly the first thing a pioneer does, as he cannot, in the first year, cut down all the trees in his new domain.
>
> We suddenly came upon the cabin of its owner, situated in the centre of a plot of ground more carefully cultivated than the rest, but where man was still waging unequal warfare with the forest; there the trees were cut down, but not uprooted, and the trunks still encumbered the ground which they so recently shaded.

Unequal warfare indeed. The greatest woodsmen on earth created an empire of farmland from the great eastern forests, and an industrial behemoth from the timber that once covered them, in just a few generations. Their pace was startling – between 1811 and 1867 enough timber was harvested to deforest 300,000 square miles, or the area of France plus the United Kingdom; 40 per cent of all of America's dense forest cover was cleared in just twenty years, from 1850 to 1870. The transformation stunned those who blinked and missed it – the state of Michigan, for example, lost 96 per cent of its great white pine forests within a single lifetime of white settlement. The Americans weren't doing anything their forefathers hadn't already done to Europe's woodlands, but the scale of their ambition and endeavour was unprecedented – an 1880 federal government report estimated that America's great mid-eastern forests had been subjected to the same level of clearance in one hundred years as the timberlands of Germany and Austria had experienced in one thousand.

Something else was also different. As the economy scoured the continent's great forests, the images of the pioneer chopping lustily away and the small town emerging from a clearing in the trees remained, but the reality was that the wood industry had become the domain of corporate players, timber barons with East Coast or City of London money behind them, acquiring vast areas of forest they never even saw, hiring entire towns of lumbermen to clear the trees at breakneck speed, then moving their operations swiftly on, leaving exhausted, eroded land, clogged rivers and jobless communities as they went. As the firefighter and campaigner John Osborn wrote, 'The natural history of the timber industry is to overcut and leave behind stumps and unemployed workers.' This is what the timber trade had become by the time it followed the settlers out West.

And those settlers found more trees. On the far side of the unshaded plains and prairies, the Northwest was dominated by two great swathes of forest – in the damp patch between the Cascade Mountains and the Pacific Coast, temperate rainforest thrived, while further inland pines and firs held a more tenuous perch on the mountain slopes that surrounded the Nez Perce homeland, in the Salmon Wilderness, the Blue Mountain range (that included the Wallowa) and the Bitterroots. The elevations here caught precious rain – and, more certainly, snow – while volcanic activity had fertilized the soil just enough to keep hardy, slow-growing conifers alive. But this was no Amazonian riot of life: much of the inland forests were just a few thousand years old, tentative acts of ecological improvisation on uncertain ground. This fact would only come to be fully understood once the fragile truce of the forests was disrupted on an industrial scale.

These woods were not untouched, though – the tribes of the inland Northwest had, predominantly since the arrival of the horse, been using fire to clear undergrowth and to facilitate their hunting, a fact which has variously been heralded as proof of Native America's admirably perfect knowledge, or wilfully imperfect treatment, of the processes of nature. Once again, it's hard to pass judgement on the ecological wisdom of a practice that was violently curtailed before it might eventually have revealed unwelcome ecological consequences. There were local anecdotes, for example, of Indian burning damaging the shade cover over mountain streams, which might eventually have depleted salmon stocks – but there's no evidence that this effect was visible, because entire river systems were never destroyed, and the salmon runs remained bountifully healthy. Indian burning had certainly changed the forests of the interior Northwest, but it's hard to discern whether man and nature were set on a collision course, or had formed a mutually sustaining partnership. All we can say for certain is that when the Europeans arrived the forests were standing.

Wherever the Oregon Trail passed by timber – with its promise of cash, fuel and shelter – settlers would leave the path and set up home. The wide-open, airy nature of much of the inland forests – a feature of ponderosa pine woods that fire, both human and natural, emphasized – was particularly attractive to settlers, offering welcome shade, easy navigation, and, ironically, echoes of the great eastern forests that they remembered from their childhoods. The settlers could try and raise crops in the valley bottoms, graze livestock within the woods and build their houses from the giants that surrounded them. Many grew ambitious, and built sawmills to profit from the timber that seemed to be anyone's for the taking; you could either file a homesteading claim on a patch of forest and start chopping or just steal the trees off unclaimed public land and almost certainly never get caught. In a spirit of lawlessness and cheerful free-for-all, the settlers took the first nibbles at the fringes of the Northwestern forests – but what suits the doughty settler also suits the mighty corporation, and within just a few years of the Nez Perce finally relinquishing control of these forests, the timber barons moved in.

The scale of the land grab that followed is scarcely comprehensible. Facing falling harvests from exhausted forests back East, the timber barons dispatched their agents (accompanied by a parasitic bloom of speculators, who could smell a boom a thousand miles off) to get hold of the Northwest, by fair means or foul. Drunks, vagrants and foreigners were paid to pose as settlers at the local land office, claiming their 'homestead' and selling it straight on to the agents. Still more fictional pioneers made provisional claims, laying a tiny deposit on land they 'planned to settle' in a few years; in fact, the agents intended to strip off the trees and move on, letting the claims lapse and allowing the abandoned stumps and mud to revert to public ownership. (Using this trick, some of the largest trees on earth were purchased for just twenty cents an acre.) It wasn't all dog eat dog: speculators and timber agents also formed gentlemanly cartels, forcing down the selling price of genuine homesteaders who'd failed to make a go of their new lives. Several millions of acres were thus acquired, utterly swamping the area of the inland Northwest allocated to genuine settlers; according to a long overdue review by the Commissioner of Public Lands, 90 per cent of the private timberland ownership in the West was the fruit of a fraud.

Nothing the agents could get up to, however, would ever match the Checkerboard. In 1864, the men who said they could build a Northern Pacific Railroad persuaded President Lincoln that to fund this great engineering endeavour they needed an unprecedented land grant – in short, a gift from the public domain that they could use to finance the railway. The land they received – in return for a promise to avoid the farragoes of bad debt and financial collapse that had characterized the great rail-building adventures thus far – was no less than thirty-nine million acres, running in a checkerboard pattern, alternating public and railroad ownership, in a strip of land between

40 and 120 miles wide from Lake Michigan to the coast. It represented 2 per cent of the United States.

What followed was ... the usual farrago of bad debt and financial
collapse, but in 1883, seven years late, the Northern Pacific was finally
finished. (Sitting Bull, by then something of a celebrity, was invited
to the railroad's grand opening, and gave a short speech to the
assembled worthies in his native tongue: 'I hate you. I hate you. I hate
all the white people. You are thieves and liars,' he solemnly intoned,
while the translator relayed a different speech altogether.)

The terms of the land grant stated that once the last spike was
driven, the railroad had five years to start selling the land to settlers
at a fair price. In fact, the magnates (led by the notorious J. P.
Morgan) sold it to their dinner-party companions, the timber
barons, in vast job lots. Another 2.5 million acres of the Northwest
was eventually siphoned off this way and still more was retained by
the railroad itself, which quietly morphed into a logging company.
It's not hard to explain how Northern Pacific pulled this grand
larceny off – the railroads were instrumental in inventing
Washington's famous 'revolving door', with the politicians of the day
reliably cropping up as directors, trustees and stockholders of the
very businesses they were constitutionally required to regulate.
Presidents, vice-presidents and countless congressmen were profiting
from the Northern Pacific land grab – while the timber communities
of the mid-eastern states, being left in the jobless lurch by a wood
rush stampeding westward, were written off as losses. There was little
thought given to their passing: the lumber magnate Henry F. Chaney
offered an unsentimental estimate of abandoned sawmill towns,
claiming these communities were never anything 'but tools in the
rescuing of the timber and would be discarded just like a worn-out
hoe or plow or any other piece of equipment whose purpose had
been served'.

Once in possession of their tracts of land, around the turn of the
century, the logging firms started to cut the Northwest, and to cut

hard. Entire river systems were ruined as valleys were cleared of all their larger trees, causing soil erosion, flooding and catastrophic fires; any wood that wasn't marketable was left on the ground to dry out and catch a spark. Not content with destroying their own properties, the firms also engaged in large-scale theft, sending their lumbermen onto public property to pilfer trees.

The evidence of what was going on – entire ecosystems might soon collapse, and a nationwide timber shortage seemed an inevitability – forced the government to act: thankfully it still had the tools with which to do so. One of the defining characteristics of the West – and the one that makes it most intriguing to students of the modern, globalized management of the planet's resources – is that, despite the rush of settlers and the plundering of the speculators, the government had yet to give away the majority of its Western lands to its citizens. The West had proven far too large and too uninhabitable to support the dreamed-of civilization of small landholders, and thousands of square miles remained unclaimed, unsettled, and thus still within 'the public domain' of government-controlled territory; even today, Idaho is still 63 per cent public land. This landholding meant that as the century turned, the dynamic, transformative government of Theodore Roosevelt could act to prevent the timber carnage, and placed much of the wooded public domain into giant Forest Reserves, ultimately creating the United States Forest Service to administer them. The grand, idealized scheme was to keep both the forests and the sawmill communities alive by practising scientific, sustainable forestry – the federal foresters would determine which trees could be spared without imperilling the long-term health of either the woods or the watersheds, and would then invite the lumbermen (favouring the smaller local operations over the barons) to chop and haul the chosen few. That, at least, was the idea.

To understand where it all went dreadfully wrong, a crash course in 'sustained-yield forestry' may be of value. Essentially (if not tastefully), if human beings were farmed for meat, we'd never get

The Checkerboard still marks the Lolo forests today,
as satellite photographs show.

past our eighteenth birthdays. To keep us alive once we'd done most of our growing would be inefficient; the farmer would get a better return on his food and water by replacing us with a faster-growing youngster. This means that if you were charged with turning an ordinary, naturally occurring town into an efficient people farm, your first task would be to harvest everyone over the age of eighteen – they're old, and in the way. But *don't rush* – remove all the oldies in one go and you'll only have a tiny harvest of teenagers to depend on while you wait for your new crop to grow up. Ideally, you should take eighteen years to thin out the adults gradually, thus keeping yourself busy while you slowly transform the town into a perfectly balanced farm, where every age group from 0 to 18 has an equal cohort. You then harvest and replace the high school graduates each year, and that's your 'sustained yield' forever more.

Armed with this seemingly watertight theory, the Forest Service saw the great ancient trees of the Northwest, with a thousand rings and more, not as majestic or beautiful, but, in the official language of the day, as 'decadent', or 'overripe' – they had to be cut out, to get the forests growing quicker, to build a sustainable timber economy and stave off the impending national wood famine. But in this typically strident mood of Western optimism, that man could control nature to achieve his economic ends, everyone forgot the part about not rushing. As ever, the problem was controlling man.

Starting in the 1920s, the federal foresters of the Northwest started offering huge swathes of public trees to private fellers – with the large timber corporations muscling to the front of the queue. But the barons drove hard bargains – awash with debt, they wanted access to ever more trees, and to get them out ever more quickly. Eager to get their efficient tree farms growing, and cheered on by the local communities that were getting the timber jobs, the foresters demurred, even though they were breaking their sustained-yield rules left, right and centre. Timber historian Nancy Langstrom describes the euphoria in the small communities of the old Nez Perce territories when the public lands felling started, and every town boomed – but too much timber was being pulled out, far too fast: the sustainable tree farms the foresters promised the locals should have taken 180 years to create, but, in fact, 'The pine that was going to bring them centuries of stability and prosperity was gone in less than a decade.'

And then the trap really tightened. After the Second World War, improved demand, technology and transport allowed the private landholders to attack their own timber faster and deeper into the mountains, while demanding that the Forest Service let them do the same on public land. With sustained yield now just a fig leaf, the foresters set a new policy goal – 'stabilizing communities'. In short, the timber companies were fulfilling their stereotype to the letter, logging their property unsustainably and planning to move on. To keep them, and their jobs, in place, the federal foresters had to serve up ever more generous gifts of public trees – often at a public loss, the cost of mapping and administering the forest and building the free road to it exceeding the price of the timber. The Northwest's public woods spun out of control, with junk science scattered around to obscure the fact that the Western Forest Service had fallen into enemy hands. The foresters adopted the very worst practices of the private landholders, using 'clear-cutting' – the complete obliteration of a patch of forest (now called 'even-age management', and presented as replicating the natural effects of a fire, or a nasty storm) – and they clung to tiny ecological victories to prove there was still a semblance of a plan – such as the revival of some deer populations (a species that would have flourished almost anywhere on earth, once you'd shot all its predators). Timber harvest from public lands rose from around one billion board-feet of wood a year before the Second World War to 13 billion by 1965 – and just kept on climbing. And then, in the 1980s, came the reckoning – with the now unrecognizable homeland of the Nez Perce at its epicentre.

By now, the white communities across the mountain ranges of the old homeland, from Wallowa, Enterprise and Joseph to Pierce, Wieppe and (to a lesser degree) Lewiston had become cheerfully and totally dependent on the timber trade as their economic cornerstone. Folk memory recalls this as a golden age of stable jobs and solid communities, thriving softball leagues, rising school rolls and crowded bars – although some research suggests that timber-dependent communities were actually characterized by above average levels of poverty, divorce and poor health, and that the attritional, dangerous nature of the work meant that the image of a logging 'job for life' needed amending, to a job for, on average, less than seven years. But just as in the dam-building boom, some sort of gilded age did undeniably roll over the wood towns of the Northwest in the post-war years, another defeat of the endless struggles and disappointments of settlement.

In 1985, the *Wallowa County Chieftain* endeavoured to define the qualities of life a thriving lumber town could offer to any man willing to put in a hard day's work: 'warm homes, a couple of cars in the garage, a good selection of merchandise from local merchants, a secure job, an array of useful and interesting objects in the home ...' Psychologically, too, there was the confidence of entering a trade still eulogized as the epitome of American manhood, combining the wilderness skills of a pioneer woodsman with the blue-collar integrity of a Springsteen album – as this homily from the Potlatch corporate communications department illustrates, yet another Western myth was clearly in the making:

A logger is the voice of America's great timberlands, reaching out to inspire the imagination of a nation. He gets closer to nature than almost anyone else, every day. He likes it that way. He builds roads with bulldozers, track drills and dynamite. He is a farmer of the forest, harvesting the trees like the crop they are.

Sometimes he works so hard he feels like he has shrunk. But so important is his work, such a vital part in the life and death of his country are his efforts, so indispensable are the trees he provides, that deep inside HE KNOWS, we all know, that he has not shrunk at all. BECAUSE THE LOGGER IS A GIANT.

What Potlatch neglected to mention was that the logger was also expendable. A veteran journalist at the *Lewiston Tribune* recalls a press trip to the company's timberlands around Pierce: 'So they took us all up there and spent the day explaining how difficult it was to be profitable nowadays, how responsible they were being, all the replanting they were doing, their commitment to the local communities, and the regulations they had to cope with. But then right at the end of the day, they just couldn't resist showing us their new toy – a machine that grabbed, chopped, stripped and carried the trees all in one process. They were so pleased with it! Each one of those machines could do the work of twelve men.' Between 1978 and 1988, timber production in the Northwest actually rose, but 20 per cent of the timber jobs were lost.

Mechanization wasn't the only threat to the timber towns – many of the firms were also moving their operations on again, heading to the south-east of the continent, where milder, wetter conditions rendered their vast private tree farms much more productive than in the hardy, slow-growing West. Much of the woodland the early Europeans had first targeted was now returning, and, as one corporate spokesman put it, if you considered the American continent as one vast tree farm, 'We're on sustained yield. When we clean up the timber in the West, we'll return to New England, where the industry began.'

Foreign timber was also proving alluring: in the tropics, labour was cheaper and the authorities were often more malleable even than the US Forest Service. In 1971, for example, the 'Potlatch Story' corporate newsletter pronounced that 'Western Samoa took its first giant step towards industrial development by signing a 40-year agreement with Potlatch Forests to establish sawmill and veneer-slicing operations ... This new industry is to be based on tens of thousands of acres of timber that to date have done little for the economic growth of this fledgling nation.' (Between 1977 and 1990 Samoa would lose one-third of its native rainforests, one of the fastest rates of deforestation on earth. In 2002 the Samoan government admitted that it had sold its country's chief natural resource too cheap and too fast, and that a 'crisis' of tree stumps and job losses beckoned.)

But if the timber firms were looking away from the Northwest, they planned to clean up before they left. In the frenzied atmosphere of junk bonds, hostile takeovers and asset-stripping in early 1980s corporate America, leaving your company's prize assets sticking out of the ground started to look like an unacceptable risk, and many of the timber firms abandoned any pretence that they were 'managing' their huge private holdings and concentrated on stripping them bare. At the vanguard were two beneficiaries of the Checkerboard, whose properties lay in the Nez Perce and Salish lands around Lolo and the Bitterroots – and whose handiwork you can still see from the Lolo Trail. Plum Creek, despite its folksy name, was actually a spin-off from the Northern Pacific Railroad Company, while Champion had bought their checkerboard squares in the early 1970s. In the 1980s, both companies needed immediate cash more than they needed a sustainable yield, and they started 'liquidating' their forests. Bulldozers were sent forth like Panzer divisions to haul in the logs, dig roads and flatten terraces, streams were crushed and filled, any slightly less profitable trees were buried and burned in the rush to haul out the good stuff. Some of the harvesting was so mindless it's unlikely that tree cover will ever return to the land, unless there's another fertilizing volcanic blow-out to revive the soil. Between 1984 and 1991 Plum Creek hauled out timber from the Checkerboard at more than twice the rate it could ever grow back, even by their hugely optimistic estimates of growth speeds. Champion probably cut harder, and these companies weren't alone. Across the Northwest, liquidation shattered ecosystems and stored up trouble – at this rate, there would soon be a regional timber shortage, and yet more jobs lost … unless, of course, the public forests picked up the slack once again.

Initially, the Forest Service did their damnedest, offering up public timber harvests in the realm of lunacy to keep the sawmills spinning – the cut in the Bitterroot Mountains' public forests was now running at up to ten times the sustainable rate. But the appalling health of the woodlands of the Northwest was becoming undeniable, and the public clamour for restraint unignorable.

In 1912, a Nez Perce elder visiting the Wallowa Mountains of his childhood would still have recognized the open, park-like, giant pine forests surviving on more than 70 per cent of his people's original territory. By 1991, just 10 per cent of the mountains still looked that way – the remainder was coated with the shrubbery of recovering clearcuts or with the dense fir forests that had replaced the felled ponderosa giants. Regimented, monocultural tree farms dominated the private landholdings, with untouched 'old-growth' forest only remaining in isolated patches; today, nationally, less than 5 per cent of America's ancient forests have escaped the axe. Where adult trees once towered, adolescents now huddled – the average age of the trees in the Northwestern forests has fallen from over three hundred years old to, at best, fifty. The newcomers were sickly youths, prone to drought, disease and parasitic epidemics that turned whole hillsides brown, and in their cluttered state, thick with undergrowth after decades of official fire suppression (if trees are crops, you don't let them burn) the woods went up like an oily rag at the slightest spark, and the overfuelled fires no longer just cleared the natural clutter, they incinerated everything in sight.

The logging had also decimated watersheds and salmon runs, silting up and exposing streams, eroding soil and causing ruinous flooding. In one priceless touch, logging around Pierce City had turned the north fork of the Clearwater River from a rippling Nez Perce fishing ground into an annual flood risk, forcing the government to act: they simply plugged the valley with one of the largest dams on earth, drowning the homelands and cutting off the salmon – problem solved. Terrestrial species – notably bear, elk and a tiny owl with a big future – had also suffered in the transition of thousands of squares miles of land from thriving forests to dubiously productive farms.

With the evidence of their own eyes, and armed with the growing alternative concept of the public forests as a shared national responsibility, rather than just the land the government couldn't give away, the concerned citizens of the Northwest demanded, and finally got, a new direction.

Between 1980 and 1984 the area of Idaho's national forests declared off-limits to timber harvesting increased by over two million acres, while three-quarters of a million acres of Oregon's forests were similarly shut off; in 1987 a full moratorium was declared on public lands harvesting on the exhausted, flattened woods at the end of the Lolo Trail, a trend which was followed wherever enlightened public foresters could wrestle power from the old-school, hard-cutting bureaucrats; then, in 1990, after three failed attempts, campaigners got the notorious Northern Spotted owl listed as an endangered American species, legally compelling the Forest Service to protect the habitat of this plain little bird – a habitat which just happened to be, exclusively, unlogged, old-growth Northwestern forests. Pelted with lawsuits, the public foresters' assault on their estates now finally stalled – between the late 1980s and 1993, for example, the public forests around the Wallowa Valley dropped their annual timber-harvesting levels by some 96 per cent.

All this left the concerned citizens of the sawmill communities febrile with despair. The timber companies forgot their mechanizations, their downsizings and their relocations and blamed every job shed in the last thirty years on the 'damn environmentalists' (in fact, the squeeze on public timber probably favoured the large corporations, who still had some private holdings to fall back on, while their smaller competitors went to the wall). Cavalcades of logging trucks formed blockades and processions in protest at the ecologists' spiteful, tree-hugging disruption of a hallowed way of life, Northern Spotted owls were hanged, burned in effigy and suggested for countless chilli recipes, ranting local politicians chose to cling to the myth of generous public lands tree-farming, rather than explain the reality of a giant ecological experiment in tatters – but all to no avail. As the local sawmills closed one by one, those blue-collar jobs fled from Wallowa, Enterprise, Joseph, Pierce and scores of similar towns across the Northwest, and as the working families moved to the distant suburbs, the schools shrank and the stores closed, leaving timberland, in the words of one contemporary local observer, 'Stuck between a past it can't recreate and a future it can't imagine.' For most of the towns, the future was either terminal decline or, more likely, a new existence based on holiday homes and retirees, pushing property prices further out of the reach of those working families who remained. As mentioned earlier, Wallowa County lost a third of its school-age children in a decade, while Pierce, Idaho, fared slightly worse.

The end of the great raid on the public forests was probably, ultimately, to the Northwest's economic benefit. The rescue and preservation of what remained of the wilderness created a powerful lure for affluent 'lifestyle refugees' from the rest of the country, and, of course, for those arriving battalions of the retired – whose ailments, courtesy of America's private healthcare industry, soon came to represent the region's most valuable natural resource. But for the people and communities who thought they encapsulated the mountainous Northwest, the transition was a disaster, as much psychological as fiscal. In 1985, just as President Reagan was contemplating putting another swathe of the forests around the Wallowa Valley under wilderness protection, the *Wallowa County Chieftain* expressed a typical timber country howl of confusion and betrayal in its editorial column, drawn from the file marked 'unintended irony':

> We fail to see the sense or fairness in asking a population to change its entire direction after more than 100 years. Wallowa County has been a lumber orientated area almost since its very beginning. Are we now to ask those engaged in this livelihood to move on in order to make way for those who would like to take it over as some sort of wilderness Shangri-La?
>
> What gives these people the right to demand, 'Move along, you have something I want, and it's better suited to what I want than for what you are using it for'?

Eerie familiarity was also on offer as the Nez Perce emerged from the Lolo Trail, and straight into another Western tale of settlement, 'improvement' and displacement. The trail's last leg was a gentle stroll along the banks of Lolo Creek (its path now overlooked by the Checkerboard) which then fed into the capacious Bitterroot Valley, a long, straight basin of pasture and pine that crept gently up to wooded wilderness on either side. This was part of the ancestral homeland of the Salish, or Flathead, people, perhaps the Nez Perce's closest allies – Nez Perce hunters would often camp within Salish villages for protracted visits of months, even years, the two tribes entrusted one another with horses to ensure fresh mounts after the Lolo crossing, and there was also the considerable matter of offering a mutually beneficial escape from the perils of inter-breeding.

With its topographic air of seclusion and protection, the Bitter-root homeland was immediately reminiscent of the Wallowa Valley, and the Salish lived a similar seasonal lifestyle, based on reliable trout migrations, deer and elk herds, root gathering and occasional forays east to buffalo country. And the similarities didn't end with the geography. Following early incursions from first Lewis and Clark and then the ubiquitous missionaries, the typical enticements of settlement – irrigation from the dawdling Bitterroot River, plentiful forage and the green shoots of a timber industry – had been drawing Europeans here for a generation, and the Salish had paid the usual price. Isaac Stevens had negotiated with the Salish during his 1855 Treaty Tour, and had guaranteed them much of the Bitterroot Valley as a reservation. But the discovery of gold and silver in the Montana hills had changed everything, and a boom began – with Missoula, a town at the open end of the Bitterroot, serving as the mercantile hub. Missoula was founded in 1864, grew slowly to one hundred inhabi-tants by the late 1860s – then boomed to 2500 souls by the early 1870s. Dominated by a handful of entrepreneurs who monopolized the sawmills, trading stores, bars and newspapers, Missoula rapidly became a gateway for Eastern investors to get their hands on Western resources. And once the speculators had spotted the Bitterroot, the next move was inevitable: in 1872 an ambitious Secretary of the

Interior, James A. Garfield, returned to instigate a renegotiation with the Salish.

The Salish were asked to moved north out of the main basin of the Bitterroot, to land bordering Flathead Lake, but their head chief, Charlot, refused to sign away his homeland, so Garfield forged the treaty, fraudulently passing off a malleable junior chief as the head of the tribe. Such initiative would eventually secure Garfield the presidency of the United States, but the Salish were left clinging to squatters' rights, remaining camped in the Bitterroot until compelled or persuaded to leave. In the summer of 1877 they were still in residence, a situation that was, in fact, the source of very little local tension. Influenced perhaps by such a beatific setting, the Bitterroot Valley was characterized by an atmosphere of calm neighbourliness between the rural settlers, the Salish and the frequently visiting Nez Perce, hence Chief Looking Glass's confidence that his refugees could pass along the basin in peace.

Sadly, such pragmatism was scarce in the rest of western Montana, and the Nez Perce's martial adventures in Idaho had been followed in great detail by the local citizens, with fear building to mania as it became clear that the caravan was heading over Lolo. 'They will spare neither life nor property that comes within their reach,' wailed the *Helena Weekly Independent*. 'We ought to know that they will come here horse-stealing, marauding and killing,' shuddered the *Weekly Missoulian*, adding deceitfully, 'and we ought to be convinced that they will be joined by a number of our own Indians.' Just as back in Lewiston, the local press, in the employ of the local moneymen, were sensing that the Nez Perce crisis might foretell a lucrative land grab, if the Salish could also be branded renegades: 'There is a marked absence of young bucks among the scattered bands of Indians about the county,' muttered the *Missoulian*.

The settlers were also caught up in the nationwide cult of celebrity now swirling around the oblivious Joseph, who was endlessly referred to as the Nez Perce's battlefield general and strategic genius.

The Deer Lodge *New North West* reflected the widespread anti-hero worship for this fictional war chief, who was heavily laden with the Native stereotypes of the day, most notably his cunning, his nobility, his wilful savagery and his inescapable doom, opining that, 'While we hope to see his band annihilated, we cannot forbear giving the Nez Perce's chief credit for his achievements', adding magnanimously that the warriors under Joseph's command 'have shown a heroism worthy of a better cause'. The *San Francisco Examiner* was not alone in taking time to tantalize its female readers with their glowing pen portraits: 'He is now in the full vigor of manhood – about 40 years of age and the model of a warrior chief – well-formed, of bold bearing, dignified demeanour, and every inch a leader.'

As news reached these townships on 23 July that the Nez Perce were emerging from the Lolo Mountains, a panic of barricades, nightwatchmen, rumours and home guards swept the countryside. The territorial governor of Montana, Benjamin F. Potts, fuelled the fire: just as the Nez Perce had been preparing to cross Lolo, Potts had wired the federal government demanding authority to raise his own private army of Montanans, but he had been courteously knocked back. Now, with the bands on his side of the mountains, Potts went his own delirious way, declaring himself Commander in Chief of Montana, proclaiming that the territory had been 'invaded by hostile Indians from Idaho' and calling for five hundred fighting men to join him. The call was answered, with men signing up at town-hall meetings near and far, swearing an oath of personal allegiance to Potts – and, in a sign of the esteem the army was now held in, pledging never to take orders from a United States officer. In the nearby mining town of Butte, just west of the Bitterroot, a young entrepreneurial adventurer named W. A. Clark persuaded ninety-six miners to volunteer for action, and gave himself the rank of major; another young hotshot in Butte, a friend of Clark's called Marcus Daly, soon placed himself in charge of ambulances and fundraising. He would eventually raise enough money to purchase the unfamiliar supply list of four gallons of brandy, two of whiskey, fifty yards of muslin, two cases of surgical supplies, and one case each of strawberries, peaches, oysters and sardines.

But before Governor Potts' personal army could gather in force, the Nez Perce made their next move – chipping away further at the reputation of the Regular Army as they went. A small military presence had been stationed in the Bitterroot since early June – after Potts and his friends in the press had bleated about a possible Salish uprising – and on 25 July their experienced commander, Captain Charles Rawn, led around thirty soldiers and fifty volunteers up Lolo Creek, to head off the Nez Perce. When they reached a suitably narrow spot in the valley, Rawn ordered his men to start felling trees for a barricade: 'My intentions were to compel the Indians to surrender their arms and ammunition, and to dispute their passage, by force of arms, into the Bitter Root Valley.'

The Nez Perce, desperate not to revive the armed conflict they had just fled, made camp two miles upstream of Rawn. The next day Joseph, White Bird and Looking Glass visited the army barricades under a white flag, and cheerfully ribbed the captain over the state of his defences, suggesting they might serve better as a cattle yard than a fort. The men congenially agreed to another parley on the 27th.

That meeting, on an open patch of meadow between the camps, proved to be a squib. Rawn (who now had a force of some two hundred, swelled by Governor Potts and the beginnings of his volunteer army, plus some twenty loyal Salish, wearing white turbans to distinguish themselves in battle), demanded unequivocal surrender, while Looking Glass declared there was no need – his people simply wanted to pass through the Bitterroot in peace, and would do no harm if left alone. In stalemate, the two sides agreed to meet once more the next morning. Both camps then spent the night in rancorous debate – the Nez Perce were deciding whether to mount a dawn attack, while Rawn's volunteers were picturing one, and questioning why on earth they would subject themselves to almost certain massacre at the hands of people who were only asking for peaceful passage. By dawn, Rawn had lost perhaps three-quarters of his volunteers – those drawn from the Bitterroot countryside, many of whom knew and liked the Nez Perce, were particularly keen to head home – and he had no more than eighty fighting men left. Governor Potts had also remembered pressing matters elsewhere.

Then, before sunrise, the Nez Perce made their play – one that no one in Rawn's diminishing fort had predicted. The entire caravan, some seven hundred men, women and children and three thousand horses, pointed themselves straight up a steepling gorge in the valley's northern flank, and climbed above and away from the barricades. It was a scrabbling, crumbling, exhausting climb, but by the time the caravan emerged onto open ground near the ridgeline, with the warriors placed between the non-combatants and the fort, they were distant figures, looping high and wide past the opposing force. A few desultory shots were exchanged, but the mood inside Rawn's fort was far from militant – awe at the Nez Perce's daring and outdoorsmanship mingled with relief at a fight avoided and grudging acceptance at being conclusively outmanoeuvred, as yet more volunteers drifted home. As the Nez Perce clambered down a steep gully to return to the valley floor and enter the Bitterroot Basin, Rawn made a half-hearted effort at pursuit, but the dust cloud just kept moving away, and the captain (who, according to some reports, had responded to the overnight diminishment of his fortifications with the immoderate fortification of his canteen) gloomily resolved that a charge with his few remaining men wasn't a cause worth dying for. He headed back to Missoula to concentrate on damage limitation – firing off telegrams to his superiors to barricade his reputation against a spring tide of derision.

Their disdainful bypass of 'Fort Fizzle', as Rawn's effort was soon labelled, left the Nez Perce with no military opponents in their sight or their thoughts. Further down the trail, as the valley opened out into the Great Basin, the Indians encountered a group of Bitterroot volunteers. Smiling and waving, Looking Glass approached and encouraged the men to go home and spread the good news – the caravan would do their families no harm, and would be gone from the Bitterroot in little more than a week. The volunteers accepted his pledge gratefully (though not entirely without suspicion) and promised to report it widely – it seemed that the chief's contention that peace lay east of the Lolo Trail was proving true. Yellow Wolf reflected the relief and optimism of the Nez Perce refugees as they slowly entered the Bitterroot: 'The white people were friendly. No more fighting! We had left General Howard and his war in Idaho.'

CHAPTER SEVEN

TO THE BIG HOLE

'The White man does not understand the Indian for the reason that he does not understand America. He is too far removed from its formative processes. The roots of the tree of his life have not yet grasped the rock and soil. The white man is still troubled with primitive fears; he still has in his consciousness the perils of this frontier continent, some of its vastnesses not yet having yielded to his questing footsteps and inquiring eyes. He shudders still with the memory of the loss of his forefathers upon its scorching deserts and forbidding mountain-tops. The man from Europe is still a foreigner and an alien. And he still hates the man who questioned his path across the continent. But in the Indian the spirit of the land is still vested; it will be until other men are able to divine and meet its rhythm. Men must be born and reborn to belong. Their bodies must be born of the dust of their forefather's bones'

CHIEF LUTHER STANDING BEAR, 1933

'Some day, this country's gonna be a fine, good place to be.
Maybe it needs our bones in the ground before that time can come'
The Searchers, directed by JOHN FORD, 1956

'JOSEPH EXECUTED ONE of those brilliant and unexpected movements that gave him such prestige in Idaho. He is an enigma.' One

185

can sometimes sympathize with the newspaper editors and early historians who reduced the story of the Nez Perce flight to a single charismatic chief and his master plan of regional rebellion. The instantly digestible image of Joseph as the unchallenged leader of the Nez Perce caravan would prove hard to shake off – as recently as 1994, Dee Brown, whose *Bury My Heart at Wounded Knee* was pivotal in fusing Native American history to the American liberal consciousness in the early 1970s, was still referring to Joseph as a 'master strategist' who kept the refugees alive with 'a succession of masterful moves' using 'his uncanny knowledge of the geography of this vast area'. As the editor of the *Shinbone Star* famously put it, 'This is the West, Sir. When the legend becomes fact, print the legend.'

The available histories of the first night's camp after the Fort Fizzle manoeuvre suffice to put this legend to rest; here, one of the most fateful councils of the Nez Perce chiefs took place, a debate that perhaps did more than any other to settle the fate of their search for peace and freedom. And according to one report, Joseph spoke not a word, while another records this perfunctory contribution: 'I have no words. You know the country, I do not.'

The council which Joseph felt unqualified to address was called to discuss disconcerting intelligence brought by three hunters (two Nez Perce and a Yakama) recently arrived from the north. They reported rumours that the Crow were a people under duress, besieged by settlers, ranchers and buffalo hunters, and that their loyalty to the Nez Perce could no longer be counted upon. The hunters offered an alternative course: instead of Looking Glass's plan to head south along the Bitterroot Basin, then loop north-west onto the Crow plains, why not point *north* up the Bitterroot and make a straight run towards the Old Woman Country (as Queen Victoria's Canada was known)? White Bird and Toohoolhoolzote were swayed, but the pugnacious Looking Glass held firm – the main Salish Reservation blocked the route north, he argued, and those ancient allies had demonstrated at Fort Fizzle that their sympathies now lay with the army. Game was also short to the north, the chief claimed, but on the buffalo plains the Nez Perce hunters could feed the caravan with ease – and with his diplomacy towards the whites, and his discipline of the young warriors, passage east could surely be made in peace. Confident and persuasive, and with the territorial knowledge of Five Wounds and Rainbow at his back, Looking Glass won the day. The next morning the Nez Perce packed their horses and began a slow march south along the battened-down Bitterroot. Looking Glass rode among the young fighters bellowing his commands – there were to be no raids on the settlers' homes, no horses stolen, no shots fired at the white men unless they fired first. A languid pace was purposefully set, to ensure that the people of the Bitterroot understood that this was a peaceful village on the move, not a rebel army on manoeuvres.

Meanwhile, Montana was bubbling over with panic, awe and bluster. At first, Rawn was castigated in every saloon, barber shop and opinion column for his perceived cowardice and ineptitude, but relief that the captain hadn't needlessly stirred up trouble soon took over. The worst was still widely expected, though – the day after Fort Fizzle, Missoula was reportedly a ghost town, with its citizens cowering in their homes, while out on the open valley floor many settlers hastened together in makeshift timber and sod forts. In one incident, a potent blend of fear and whiskey led to a herd of cattle being gunned down for faintly resembling a Nez Perce cavalry charge.

The Fort Fizzle affair also added to the national sensation growing around this defiant journey – with many newspaper readers, particularly in the self-consciously humanitarian East, beginning to cheer for the 'plucky Indians' – and, like so many moments in history, the Nez Perce flight was now working the alchemy that turns fantasies into memories. In the bars and jail cells of backwoods Wyoming an alcoholic bullwhacker, whiskey peddler and part-time prostitute by the name of Martha Jane Canary was telling anyone who'd listen that she'd just finished serving as an army scout for one

Captain Egan, fighting in the 'Nursey-Pursey Indian outbreak' ...

> We were ambushed about a mile and a half from our destination.
> When fired upon Captain Egan was shot. I was riding in advance and
> on hearing the firing turned in my saddle and saw the Captain reeling
> in his saddle as though about to fall. I turned my horse and galloped
> back with all haste to his side and got there in time to catch him
> as he was falling. I lifted him onto my horse in front of me and
> succeeded in getting him safely to the fort. Captain Egan, on recov-
> ering, laughingly said: 'I name you Calamity Jane, the heroine of the
> plains.'*

Not all the deceit was harmless, though. The *Missoulian* was in the
business of rank fabrication: 'The Nez Perces have been committing
degradations ever since they left Lolo,' it reported, offering a litany of
fictional horse thefts and ransackings conducted within hours of the
Fort Fizzle incident. The agenda wasn't exactly hidden – the newspapers and their owners fancied a fight: 'They must be conquered,
and a condition of their surrender must be that they are to return to
their reservation and never more go on a buffalo hunt. Our security
demands this.'

Governor Potts also stuck to the script, redoubling his calls for
volunteers and his pleas to the federal government to fund his great
adventure, claiming the honour of Montana was at stake: 'The Indian
murderers must not pass unmolested.' In Butte, William Clark
answered his fresh call, and a fearsome-sounding army of some 150
miners, mostly Cornishmen, now set out to pursue the Nez Perce –

---

* Canary, of course, never got near the 'Nursey-Purseys'. Her name was probably conferred
thanks to her capacity to start a brawl in an empty room, or possibly in reference to her
reputedly impressive collection of venereal complaints. She was also never an army scout, but
was a renowned female boxer and was said to have the foulest language in the West. When she
died, in 1903, her funeral was the best attended in the history of Deadwood City. The
description of the event by Canary's first serious biographer, Roberta Beed Sollid, gives hope
to us all: 'People seemed willing to forget her sordid life and remember her sunny disposition.'

only to turn back when the government finally slapped down the increasingly Napoleonic Potts.

All this posturing paid off in the long term, however. On 7 August, President Hayes issued a general order banning the sale of arms and ammunition to any Indians, a decision Potts executed with unseemly vigour. The Salish people suffered a crop failure that autumn which, thanks to Potts' constraint of their hunting weapons, and of their movements, rapidly turned into a famine. Ultimately, in 1889, the enfeebled remnants of the Salish occupation of the Bitterroot were forced to capitulate before the ceaseless proclamations that they were a threat to the settlers' security, with the Nez Perce outbreak always cited as proof of monstrosities to come – as the *Missoulian* put it, 'We know intuitively that whites among Indians are in the presence of constant danger, and they know not the day nor the hour when they may see the smoking ruins of pillaged farm houses or the inhabitants fleeing in terror.' Chief Charlot signed an agreement to head north to the reservation; the Salish were escorted from their ancestral valley at gunpoint.

Another corner of the Northwest had been secured for the great enterprise of settlement – and was then used, of course, primarily for liquidation. Entire libraries could be – indeed, have been – filled with the fate of the Bitterroot and its neighbouring valleys after the Europeans took control. Perhaps more than anywhere else, the high country of Montana has come to symbolize the colonial despoliation of the West in the generations following the Indian Wars. But as the Nez Perce passed methodically down the deserted, shivering Bitterroot of the early settlement days, they encountered the beginnings of perhaps the most remarkable story traced by this landscape's scars. Two young men had been particularly keen to fight the Nez Perce, stir up trouble with the Salish and help cleanse the Northwest of its troublesome tribes. In 1877 William Clark and Marcus Daly, the amateur major and ambulance driver from nearby Butte, were just a pair of chancers making a few waves in the mining business; within two decades they would ride the natural riches of the Bitterroot over the threshold of an exclusive club designated by one US senator, with admirable honesty, as 'a hundred men who own America'.

William Clark was born in Pennsylvania, of Irish immigrant parents, in 1839. Though he trained as a schoolmaster his first and last love was always profit, and he packed up and followed the tales of Rocky Mountain gold west in the early 1860s. A natural trader and far from overburdened with human compassion, he learned fast that the real money to be made from mineral mining was in offering supplies, equipment and debt, rather than in getting your own fingernails dirty, and by the time he wandered into the raggedy silver mining camp of Butte in 1872, Clark was already a rich man. With his capital liberally invested, miners soon sprawled over the giant massif that overshadowed Butte's tents and shacks, each man looking for seams of quartz to grind and smelt into silver, with the odd lunker of gold also on offer – while the few relatively useless lines of copper ore were considered barely worth digging out. The development of the telephone and of domestic electricity would soon change Butte's priorities, as would the arrival of another Irishman.

Marcus Daly, the youngest of eleven, had left County Cavan at just fifteen, telling his family he wasn't hanging around to see if their English landlords were minded to precipitate another famine. As he never tired of retelling, he landed in New York with just fifty cents to his name. He too then drifted west on rumours of gold, and, as he joined the herd of young men following the booms and busts around California, Utah and Nevada, Daly developed a reputation as an industrious mining engineer, with an uncanny knack of striking rich seams. Money follows talent, and by the early 1870s capital investors were willing to pay handsomely for a Daly hunch – and in 1876 the Walker Brothers investment company of Salt Lake City sent the man the newspapers were calling 'the best miner in America' to inspect a property for sale in Butte. Daly declared (correctly) that the mine would offer rich silver deposits, but the intriguing shapes and outcrops of Butte's dominant mountain suggested to this geological seer that there was more to find. Once the mania of the Nez Perce adventure had passed, Daly picked up an old silver mine called the Anaconda for a song, and dug into the hill for 100 metres – where he hit the largest lode of copper ore that's ever been found. With the market for copper wire beginning to blossom, the Butte mountain was 'the richest hill on earth'.

Daly promptly closed the Anaconda and declared the mine's treasures to be 'playing out' – precipitating a minor panic, during which he secretly bought up all the claims surrounding the Anaconda on the cheap. Meanwhile, he persuaded his wealthy Eastern backers (led by George Hearst, the father of William Randolph, or 'Citizen Kane') to gamble big on the largest mineral mining endeavour in human history.

Daly planned to haul the copper ore out of the hill at an unprecedented rate, and then smelt it into metal at his own vast works. The planned site of the works was an area of riverside pasture twenty-six miles from Butte, which had once been Nez Perce and Salish gathering grounds. In 1883 it was, briefly, being settled by homesteaders – Daly had actually met and befriended one of them while riding his ambulance through the valley during the Nez Perce panic. Now Daly used his pal as the front man to buy up the pasture cheap, then drew up his plans for a giant copper-smelting works, and a whole new town to house its hundreds of workers. When it was discovered that somewhere else had the name 'Copperopolis', Daly's personal village was christened Anaconda.

By now, the Butte mountain was an explosion of activity. In 1881 over a million dollars' worth of metals was hauled out of the hill; by 1886, it was $13 million. The valley's population had quadrupled since 1877, and Butte was now the largest city in the inland West, a

The smokestacks and slag piles of Butte in its heyday.

sprawling Babel of first-generation immigrants from the mining and smelting towns of Ireland, Cornwall, Wales, Finland, China, Serbia, Italy and more, drawn by the hope of a decent living and a fresh start. A handful got rich – Butte had its own millionaires' club – but most died trying.

By the early 1890s Butte was the deadliest town in America. Safety conditions in the mines were appalling, and silicosis, or 'miner's TB' was pandemic – but the real killer was the smoke. The copper and silver smelters produced a ceaseless belch of sulphur, arsenic and soot that, on cold, windless days, blocked out the sun. Butte's streetlamps often burned for weeks on end, and visitors to the town were found rambling lost through the permanent night, prey to invisible thieves. The smoke, which settled in the valley like an ocean, killed the grass, the trees, the livestock, the cats (they licked the arsenic off their own whiskers, and perished) and the rivers – in 1891 the nearby Clark Fork River was found to contain not a single fish. And the locals died in droves, of pneumonia, typhoid; even a bad cold could kill a man in Butte. Average life expectancy was a shade under forty years. The citizens pleaded to the mine-owners but were fobbed off – William Clark famously declared that the ladyfolk of Butte relied on breathing copious arsenic, 'to give them a beautiful complexion'.

At least the smoke blocked out the view. When Marcus Daly's backers had asked how he intended to fuel the largest smelting works in history, the resourceful Irishman had directed their view to the hillsides. He'd burn the timber. Within a year of opening, Daly's smelter was burning, in today's money, over a billion dollars' worth of wood a year – and almost every other smelter in Butte ran on the same fuel. The wooded mountains around Butte and Anaconda were rapidly reduced to stumps (and rendered yet more barren by the withered, choked grass that had once grown so freely that farmers were known to lose their cows in it) and the copper barons soon turned down the river in search of more wood to burn – to the Bitterroot forests.

In 1882 Daly invested in another priceless railroad scam when the Northern Pacific gave an exclusive contract to a collection of Missoula businessmen, ostensibly to provide the railroad with the lumber it needed to build its track. The businessmen were actually bankrolled in this venture *by* the Northern Pacific Railroad, and their brief wasn't simply to chop up a few ties and buffers, but to sell thousands of tonnes of the railroad's Checkerboard wood to the copper smelters. Confused? Their competitors were – the Montana Improvement Company, as this new venture was pricelessly labelled, was also guaranteed unfairly low freight charges by the railroad, which served as their main investor, supplier, customer *and* distributor. This, remarkably, was a typical Western business arrangement.

But even this cosy contract couldn't satisfy the smelters' hunger for timber, so the Improvement Company started to steal the Bitterroot, sending their lumbermen deep into the public forests, and particularly the Salish Reservation, where they pilfered, in three years, an estimated $600,000 worth of wood. When the federal government began to gripe about this blatant criminality, Daly simply bought the 1888 election for Montana's representative to Congress, and his placeman had the dogs called off. It was a decision with multiple consequences – William Clark had been trying to buy the election for himself, and his fury at Daly's shenanigans ended their friendship and began a bitter feud for power which would taint Montana's politics with corruption and bile for generations; Daly also got a taste for king-making that he never lost, even trying to buy the presidency in 1896, bankrolling William Jennings Bryan's run on a disconcertingly familiar platform of banning the teaching of evolution and reducing any regulatory restraints on his corporate fan base; finally, Daly realized he needed a more secure timber supply, so he set forth to buy the Bitterroot for himself.

Daly began buying up thousands of acres of high forest land on the flanks of the basin, then in 1889, just as the Salish were finally submitting to the constant pressure to leave the valley floor to the homesteaders, Daly really moved in. Using a familiar trick, he deployed a frontman, James Hamilton, to buy up enough home-steading land for a sawmill and another town of workers – this time called Hamilton. It became a typical company town – most of what the millworkers earned they paid back to Daly in rents, debts and produce from the company store – but, as typified the man, its ambition was remarkable. Within three years the Daly sawmill was cutting 200,000 feet of Bitterroot lumber *a day* – much of it stolen from the public lands and none of it harvested in a sane and sustainable manner – and, within a decade of expansions and land purchases, Marcus Daly became probably the single largest producer *and* consumer of timber *and* copper in America. Two pristine valleys, the Clark Fork and the Bitterroot, had now been carved up in his name. And all, as he often cared to mention, from fifty cents.

But then the romance went out of it. William Clark and Marcus Daly had been true American pirates, mendacious and spiteful in business but often noble and generous in life. Stories abound of Daly helping out impoverished old friends, and Clark was a paternalistic sponsor of theatres and libraries in Butte, and had funded the town's most beloved space, a beautiful pleasure park known as Columbia Gardens. But the heady days of the Western entrepreneurial adventure were also just a passing phase: they would be replaced by the anonymous drudgery (but comparable mendacity) of the share price-watching, spreadsheet-wielding corporation.

In 1895 London investors (including the venerable Rothschild's group) bought almost half of Marcus Daly's company; then, in 1899, he sold out completely to the vast Boston-based Standard Oil trust, made up of such capital goliaths as William G. Rockefeller and Henry H. Rogers. In 1900, Marcus Daly fell ill and died shortly after. Reading the runes, William Clark allied himself to Standard Oil – the bean-counters were now running Butte.

Two years later, the implications of this shift revealed themselves to the farmers of the Deer Lodge Valley. First- and second-generation settlers, they had cultivated and pastured around 100 square miles of the bottomland of this high-sided gorge to the east of the Bitterroot. In January 1902, Daly's old mining enterprise, now rebranded as the Amalgamated Copper Company, opened the largest copper-smelting works in history on a hillside above Anaconda. It included more than fifty furnaces, and four 200-foot-tall smokestacks. Within a few months of the smelter being fired up, the animals in the Deer Lodge Valley started dying. The farmers piled thousands of carcasses in the corners of their fields, watched the survivors waste and weaken, clearly unfit for sale, and turned their eyes to the distant smokestacks which were pumping out over 50,000 pounds of arsenic trioxide a day. The farmers consulted scientists, then lawyers, and joined battle.

In the twenty-year legal scrap to force Amalgamated to clean up or shut down the smelter, the Company, as it was universally known, ran through the full polluter's playbook. They employed scientists to spout convenient junk (one testified that the breeze at the top of the stacks was faster than a Category Five hurricane), they set their media empire – at one point the Company owned *nine* Montana newspapers – against the farmers, suggesting they were jeopardizing thousands of jobs and livelihoods. They opened their own farms to 'prove' the valley was fertile, and they made a tremendous fuss over minor improvements to the smelter to distract from the ongoing despoliation of Deer Lodge. Ultimately, they simply outlasted the farmers, dragging out the litigation for years. Most simply gave up and sold out to the Company. A few, though, wrote to President Theodore Roosevelt.

A remarkable man, with a conservationist streak and concern for the public interest that many later presidents who laid claim to his legacy would scarcely share, Roosevelt had a vision of American enterprise strictly governed by a caring and proactive executive. 'We should leave our national domain to our children,' he pronounced, 'increased in value and not worn out.'

Roosevelt had applied just that principle to the plunder of the public forests, empowering the Forest Service, and now he joined battle against Amalgamated, suing them for the damage the smoke was doing to the public forests. In the process, Roosevelt, a dedicated, almost obsessive outdoorsman who idealized the West and its pioneer families, hoped to clean the air for the Deer Lodge settlers.

What actually happened almost precisely mirrored the fate of the Forest Service – Roosevelt's vision of the government protecting the American landscape from corporate misuse was warped after his death into a symbiotic joint assault on the commonwealth. A commission was established to oversee Amalgamated's cleansing of their smelter, but the commissioners were slowly drawn into the Company's agenda, fearful of being used as scapegoats for job cuts, and they simply let the smoke keep pouring. Eventually, in 1925, a bought-and-paid-for senator sneaked a bill through Congress allowing Amalgamated to buy the public forests that they were polluting, swapping the woodland for part of their huge private holdings – and thus the problem was solved. If a Montanan poisoned his own land, that was his own business. Eventually, a burgeoning market for the very chemicals the stacks were spewing inspired Amalgamated to rein them in, but the smelter only really stopped killing Deer Lodge when it closed down, in 1980. Patches of the valley remain grassless and toxic to this day.

Back in Butte, the outsourcing of much of the smelter smoke to Deer Lodge had made the city a better place to live in, provided you didn't work in the mines. The clearing of the local atmosphere highlighted the health crisis below the ground – around 40 per cent of the miners suffered from silicosis, their lungs perforated by the razor-fine rock dust, and it wasn't until the 1960s that the Company started paying any disability benefit. (Then the foremen began X-raying the lungs of their workforce, firing the men who showed shadows, to keep costs down.) The local estimate of a 'good age' for a miner to reach remained around forty, because if you got sick, you died – in the 1950s Butte had the highest mortality rate in America for all types of illness. As a union leader proclaimed in 1959, 'All during the more than 75 years that the Company has been in existence and has grown into a worldwide corporation, their prosperity has been made off the backs of the Butte miners. All Butte has to show for it today are large graveyards.' (One miner got out, and started scraping an alternative living leaping his souped-up motorbike over wooden crates filled with local rattlesnakes. We have already encountered him launching the Knievel Skyrocket over Hell's Canyon on the Snake River.)

Then the mine started eating Butte. In 1955 the Company set upon a new extraction technique – open-pit mining, carving out the ore like ice cream, rather than burrowing in search of it. Their pit on the edge of town was soon disgorging 10,000 tonnes of ore a day – then, by 1962, production was round the clock, running at 320,000 tonnes a day. Five entire neighbourhoods, including three churches, had to be moved to escape the pit's growing mouth, and finally, in

The expanding jaws of the Berkeley Pit.

1973, the rim reached Columbia Gardens … and didn't stop. The crater devoured Butte's favourite place, its traditional backdrop to wedding parties, picnics, summer strolls and first kisses. As mining historian Janet L. Finn recalled, this was the last straw for many who'd grown used to the Company's relentless grasp: 'People of Butte spoke with a deep resentment of having lost a sacred place … Columbia Gardens symbolized community, a shared space of sentiment, attachment and celebration, a place where public and private memories were made on the common ground of life.'

In other words, a homeland. The Company, of course, was spared such sentiment. The pit took in the Gardens, and was 1.3 miles long, 1 mile wide and 1800 feet deep when they finally stopped digging in 1982 – at which point someone turned off the water pumps that were preventing the mine from filling up like a giant well. The pit promptly welled up, with thirty-six billion gallons of greasy, purple water pouring in from the scarred, riddled mountain, the fluid thick with acids, arsenic and metals. As an example of its toxicity, when a flock of snow geese landed on the mysterious new 'lake' they all died within a few days.

The Berkeley Pit, as it's now known, will never be rid of its lethal soup. There's too much toxic water to clean, and its current owners – as an example of the absurd reach of the modern corporation, the landlords are British Petroleum – have merely promised to stop the water from overflowing the crater, drowning Butte in poison. The lake is now a tourist draw: you can stand on a wooden platform overlooking the lifeless blackcurrant liquid while a tinny recorded voice informs you that the water will reach its 'critical level' in 2018, by which time BP have promised to open a treatment works capable of siphoning off the necessary millions of gallons a day to keep Butte safe. And completing the unwordly scene, on a hilltop high above the lake stands a sixty-foot white statue of the Virgin Mary; the locals put it there in 1985 to inspire an economic recovery in Butte, after the Company walked away in the early 1980s leaving those capacious graveyards and the largest toxic-waste problem in America by which to remember them.

But, remarkably, there's another illuminating contender for the greatest crime against the Montanan landscape wrought by Daly, Clark and their heirs, standing at the very mouth of the Bitterroot Basin. This despoliation was, unwittingly, a team effort.

Where the Blackfoot and Clark Fork rivers combine, just before they flow into the Bitterroot at the town site of Missoula, was once among the Salish people's most treasured and plentiful trout-fishing grounds – 'the place of the big bull trout'. It was also, sadly, a natural cleft into which to jam a hydroelectric dam – which is what, in 1908, William Clark did, planning to sell power to the giant lumber mills nearby and to the burgeoning city of Missoula. No effort was made to keep the ancient fish runs alive, and the Blackfoot and Clark Fork bull trout plummeted to near-extinction – but that, on this occasion, was mere detail. More significant was that, 120 miles upstream, the copper mines and smelters of Butte and Anaconda were abandoning the leftover detritus of their endeavours, worthless rock and dust known as tailings, in great piles by the Clark Fork River, to worry about later. Rainfall washed some of this spoil into the river, and then in June 1908 a flood swept down the Clark Fork so fiercely that a hole had to be blasted in Clark's new dam to stop the structure collapsing. When the high water receded the piles of tailings were magically gone from Butte's riverbanks, and no one gave a thought to where they'd fled – in fact, six million cubic yards of sediment had washed downstream, banked up against the new dam, and settled.

It wasn't until 1981 that the small sawmill town on the banks of the Milltown Dam, as it was now known, discovered highly carcinogenic levels of arsenic in its tap water. Spinach growing in local back yards was found to contain up to two thousand times the normal level of arsenic. The varied contents of the tailings – copper, zinc, lead, manganese and arsenic – were seeping into the earth around the dam and poisoning local wells. The spoil was even more deadly when unfiltered – in 1996 the river froze up, and chunks of the ice scoured sediment from the riverbed, staining the water with copper. Between two-thirds and three-quarters of the trout living downstream of the dam died.

The solution, to restore the health of the river and protect the health of the locals, seemed unavoidable, if expensive: both the dam and its detritus needed to be hauled away from the flow forever. But the legal responsibility for the mess had passed with ownership of the mines from Amalgamated Copper to a couple more entities and finally, once again, to British Petroleum – not the first or the last British enterprise to head West in search of plunder and find it had been sold mostly trouble. In resisting the pressure to clean up the dam, BP studied well from the polluter's playbook, trawling the scientific community for malleable experts who would state that arsenic was safe to drink at Milltown's levels, generously funding a 'grassroots' organization of local people who felt, unsurprisingly, that the dam and its dirt should stay untouched, and lobbying aggressively for changes to the national law that would relieve its responsibilities – a tactic which briefly worked, as President George W. Bush lowered the health standards for arsenic in drinking water soon after entering office, only to back down before a public outcry.

But times had changed since Deer Lodge, and the defenders of the Western landscape had also changed. This was explained by two popular theories, one highly romantic, the other mundane to the point of cynicism. The first vision was that the white people of the Northwest had undergone a transformation upon settling there, that the mountains and rivers had revealed their secrets and their rhythms, shared the magic that they had once conferred upon the Native Americans – the trees and the creatures, as it were, had spoken – and they had wrung the same respect and admiration from their new neighbours as from their old. In 1972 the Montana historian K. Ross Toole, one of the most impassioned chroniclers of the corporate assault on the West, proclaimed that the profound inspiration of the landscape, harnessed to the vigorous volunteerism that defined the region (Westerners still form action committees as the English form queues) would stake out the battleground where the extractors finally met their match: 'If the fight against environmental degradation can be won anywhere, it will be won here – precisely because nowhere in America is that visceral relationship with the land more powerfully felt by those who live here.' The Northwest's salvation, Toole contended, would depend on its ancient ability to enchant and beguile outlasting its modern capacity to easily, messily, enrich.

The competing theory pointed to the dusty trading town of Missoula, and what it had become. A university town now, by the 1980s the appeals of lifestyle and like-mindedness had turned Missoula into a honeypot for gentrification, an outpost for the affluent, liberal consciousness that now dominated the coastal Northwest, but was huddled close in specific enclaves in the hinterland. Farmers' markets, coffee-ground composting schemes, trout-friendly lawns, French-style patisseries, Balinese furniture shops, park 'n' ride services, bicycle paths (two months in Idaho, I'd not seen a *bicycle*), an annual 'hemp festival', a Jewish Literature festival, an Outdoor Shakespeare festival, the Celebrating Women festival – 'a gathering of drumming, movement, hot soaking, singing, stillness and organic meals'. As Missoula took this path it was as comprehensively satirized by its more prosaic neighbours in the Northwest as any comparable borough in the United Kingdom – 'Mount Muesli' in Brighton, for example, or 'The People's Republic of East Oxford' – but the citizens proved unperturbed, and indeed drew strength from a mild-mannered siege mentality, appropriating the wholly Western self-perception of a new society taking root in hostile territory. But to the considerable concern of those who were not yet ready to rethink the pioneer paradigm, the new Missoulians were both financially and psychologically severed from the struggles and defeats of the settlement era, and its heritage of *laissez-faire*, resource extraction and self-reliance. Coalescing around the local academics who drove forward three parallel disciplines – revisionist history, environmental science and respectful, often reverential Native American studies – the new Missoulian middle class, this argument contends, brought a new and jarring communitarianism and reverence for nature to the pragmatic, individualistic West. The assumptions of hard-fought progress had a new, affluent and motivated socio-economic foe (one whose affluence, its enemies often cared to mention, was indisputably built on the crimes and misdemeanours of a past it now sought to cut adrift).

The reality lies in a murky muddle between the two. One does encounter Missoulians, particularly among the dreadlocked army of out-of-state undergraduates, for whom environmentalism does seem more an issue of class allegiance than genuine affection for the Bitterroot – but then there's also certainly no shortage of local campaigners whose blue-collar backgrounds and pioneer roots suggest the mountains have cast a spell that knows no such boundaries.

Whatever the melange of causes, BP had turned up at the wrong place at the wrong point in history, and their deployment of the typical tactics of the feudal West met with a concerted resistance of billboards, bumper stickers, campaign newsletters and town hall meetings – and in 2005 they lost, and agreed to fund the removal of the dam and the disposal of the most toxic segments of the sludge. In a cheering demonstration of the political revival of the Native American tribes, the Salish people had been at the forefront of the dam removal campaign, demanding that Isaac Stevens' 1855 promise of healthy trout-fishing in their traditional places finally be upheld. As the clean-up was announced Fred Matt, the chairman of the Confederated Salish and Kootenai Tribes, spoke at the banks of the Milltown Dam, and gave thanks 'for the return of the place of the big bull trout'.

A hundred miles away, Opportunity, Montana, was a tiny, hardscrabble town in a not very scenic spot between Anaconda and Butte, precisely the kind of humble, uninspiring place a multinational polluter could still kick around a fair distance in the modern West. The refuse ponds on the outskirts of town were chosen, as they had been for many years, as the dumping grounds for someone else's trash – on this occasion, as they now formed part of BP's dolorous American property portfolio, for the sediment removed from the base of the Milltown Dam. In the drought summer of 2006, as the wind-whipped dust clouds from the arsenic-laced dumps swirled down their streets and through their back yards, the good people of Opportunity had reason to contemplate the wise words of the man who had first accumulated the dirt that they'd been chosen, without being asked, to neighbour in perpetuity. When William Clark was challenged as to whether he was concerned that some of his business practices might prove burdensome to future generations, he dismissed the thought out of hand: 'Those that succeed us, can well take care of themselves.'

The profound consolations of a homeland – of knowing, loving, belonging to a single somewhere. To find escape from the restlessness and self-obsession of the individual, to be cured of the urge to look always to the horizon, through a community of place and people that explains your part in a greater history, and gives your life meaning you would otherwise be left searching the earth for. To be allowed the tantalizing simplicity of nothing more than a place to love, a past to prove worthy of and a future to protect. It's not everyone's Paradise, a gymnastic mental leap from the modern mantras of personal freedom and self-fulfilment, but, it seems, that's what drove the Nez Perce on, footstep by footstep, camp by camp. As they began their studiously slow stroll down the wide, silent Bitterroot Basin, the jaded caravan of some seven hundred still passionately, desperately, believed that they were, eventually, heading *home*.

At least the valley itself offered familiar rites. In 1877 there were still trout massing in the Bitterroot River, and plenty of game in the dense forests. After the survival rations on the Lolo Trail, now was a time, with the going level and easy, to restock and revive. Looking Glass set the pace, often as little as twelve miles a day, but few of the white settlers took such unthreatening behaviour at face value and they remained jammed into their puny forts, leaving the valley to the Indians. At one such embattlement, the tiny dried-brick compound of Fort Owen, more than 250 women and children had been cooped up for several days by the turn of July into August, waiting for their menfolk to return from Fort Fizzle, the desperate crowd descending into panic and prayer with each false rumour that a slaughter of the innocents had begun. Sanity might have prevailed – many of the traders and storekeepers along the Bitterroot knew the tribe's leaders well, some settlers were actually holding caches of hunting equipment for them, and there was even a small Nez Perce community camped peaceably towards the head of the valley – but Looking Glass's pledge of calm clashed with the gruesome cultural images of young, angry and – most terrifying, should it happen –

drunken Indian warriors that plagued the settlers' thoughts. (Chief White Bird would later admit that they were right to be petrified – Looking Glass was barely in control of the young men, and, in White Bird's estimation, had the spark ever been lit in the Bitterroot, 'the whole country would have been fired and many a farmer would have lost his crops and home and perhaps his scalp'.) Inside Fort Owen, a storekeeper called Henry Buck who was helping guard the valley's women and children climbed the walls to watch the orderly procession of Nez Perce families trail past on the other side of the Bitterroot River. What a sight that long, slow trail must have been, a village determinedly on the move: 'Being curious enough to gain some idea of their number, took out my watch and timed their passing. It took just one hour and a quarter for all to move by, and there were no gaps in the continuous train.'

The Nez Perce's first thoughts were finally to settle where the Salish stood in all this, and they marched to the camp of Chief Charlot to ask if they could pitch their tepees nearby, a symbolic gesture of peace, if not unity. Charlot refused even to shake Looking Glass's hand, proclaiming, 'Why should I shake hands with men whose hands are bloody?', in reference to a pledge he had adopted from his father never to cut a white man's flesh – but he did then suggest a nearby pasture as a suitable place. Charlot was, clearly, desperate to remain neutral; with spying eyes all around, it's possible his refusal even to touch Looking Glass was for their benefit and to retain somehow the whites' dispensation to stay in the Bitterroot without having to fight the Nez Perce for it. According to some reports, representatives of Governor Potts had actually visited Charlot to make a specific pledge – do not side with the Nez Perce and you can stay in the Bitterroot for ever. Charlot's neutrality, in fact, would both lose the Salish an ancient tribal friendship and fail to earn the settlers' lasting gratitude, but his alternatives, with men like Potts as his neighbours, are hard to imagine.

Over the next two days the tension in the Bitterroot became, for

*Chief Charlot, who fought desperately to keep the
Bitterroot Valley for his people.*

many, unbearable. Camped next to Charlot's band, the Nez Perce
sent a group of their women into the small trading and lumber town
of Stevensville on 30 July in search of supplies. Fearful of their stores
being looted and aware that they were in something of a seller's
market, a few storekeepers emerged from the huddling masses in
Fort Owen and nervously opened up shop. The day passed peacefully
and profitably – the Nez Perce had plenty of gold coins in their
saddlebags, the wealth of generations traded for overpriced flour –
and at sunset the shopkeepers mopped their brows and emptied their

tills. At the Buck Brothers store, Henry recalled, 'We felt sure that no more would be seen of the intruders.' But the next morning, Looking Glass rode into town – with fully a hundred warriors, conducting their own shopping trip with gruff, simmering aggression. Looking Glass patrolled Main Street on horseback, bellowing at his braves to remain peaceable as they traded for food and tobacco – but then profit trumped discretion and someone started selling whiskey.

The locals desperately sought to staunch the flow, threatening to lynch the saloon barman who'd opened the bottles, and hunting down and hiding any other supplies; in one memorable encounter a local preacher declined to appeal to any divine authority while asking a storekeeper to relinquish his keg, relying instead on the persuasive powers of a loaded pistol to the head. But as the afternoon wore on the street crackled with potential violence, as the alcohol worked its usual magic on disenchanted young men. One fighter got into a row with a blacksmith's wife, his rage only controlled by a nearby Salish warrior; another threatened to kill Henry Buck, and took a whipping from Looking Glass for his bravado. The shopkeeper, with a rifle beneath his counter, was struggling to control his nerves: 'I well knew, from manoeuvres and the number of drunken Indians in sight, that it only wanted one shot to be fired, and all would be off and the crisis at hand … I had no thought of ever going through the day alive.'

Somehow, though, Looking Glass maintained control and eventually ushered the warriors back to camp. The Nez Perce village moved on south down the valley and Henry Buck went back to Fort Owen and promptly collapsed from nervous exhaustion. It had been a fruitful two days for Stevensville, though. Some historians estimate the Nez Perce had spent as much as $1000 in town, mostly on food – the local men who were accused of selling bullets to the Indians denied that charge to their graves – and the settlers had garnered plenty of information about the caravan's fighting strength and intentions, intelligence they were later not shy in sharing with the US Army.

While the caravan moved on down the valley, it also grew, as around six families from the small Nez Perce community that was based in the Bitterroot decided to join the exodus. Precisely why they fell in is debated – it's possible they too felt that peace had broken out permanently, and that the journey to buffalo country would be a safe one, but some may also have been expecting trouble and seeking protection in numbers. One of the more notable new recruits was Delaware Tom, the well-travelled son of a Nez Perce mother and a half-blood Delaware father, while another was something of a regional character – Lean Elk, also known as Poker Joe. A gregarious man and, as the name suggests, a committed gambler, Poker Joe knew the surrounding area and its white inhabitants well, and was a welcome addition to the tribal councils.

Not that Looking Glass was taking advice, as his marching pace fell to a dawdle as the Bitterroot Valley narrowed towards its finish. The idleness eventually got the better of a group of Toohoolhoolzote's warriors, who committed the first and only minor crime in the valley, stealing some food and clothes from the empty home of a farmer called Myron Lockwood. Desperate to maintain his end of a bargain that he felt certain the whites would observe, Looking Glass made the youngsters leave seven horses in Lockwood's corral as recompense.

Looking Glass had reason to be optimistic; at the last sod forts at the end of the valley the mood had been relaxed, with warriors visiting the fortifications once again gently to ridicule its defenders, pointing out that their horses could leap their walls at a canter, while some settlers emerged to sit and chat with the caravan and, it was said, sell them bullets for a dollar a shot. But White Bird was old enough and experienced enough to mistrust the jollity, and was mindful of the rumours the settlers were passing on, of fresh troops on the Nez Perce's trail, and he urged Looking Glass to accelerate towards the buffalo country. He later recalled their angry exchanges: 'By the way you are acting you seem to anticipate no danger. How do we know but that some of these days or nights we shall be attacked by the whites? We should be prepared for trouble.'

Looking Glass answered, 'That is all nonsense and bosh. Who is going to trouble us? What wrong did we do in passing through the Bitterroot settlements? I think we did very well in going through the country peaceably with a band of hostiles like we have got. We are in no hurry. We had best take the world as easily as possible. We are not fighting with the people of this country.'

Once again, Looking Glass's bluster prevailed, and as the Nez Perce headed east from the head of the Bitterroot Valley, gently uphill towards the high pass into the lush, wide, airy expanses of the Big Hole, they did so at a stroll.

'They were just women, children and old men – that's what she used to say.'

Cheryl Holden Rice sat on her garden bench, her narrow hands in constant motion as she delved into her favourite topic – a family history that stretched back to the very settlement of the Bitterroot. 'For the settlers, you see, it was just like the Native Americans – you had to know your family's history, everyone you were related to, because you didn't want to marry them!' Cheryl's great-grandmother, Martha Burton, was a young girl who had been huddled in Fort Owen as the Nez Perce caravan had passed by: 'She remembered being evacuated to the east side of the valley in 1877. She actually looked Indian herself – her mother had been killed the year before because she was a Cherokee, and this was after Little Big Horn. And she remembered that from inside Fort Owen you could see the Nez Perce walking past on the other side, and she saw all the people and the horses and the clouds of dust, and she remembered thinking, "But … they're just women and children, and old men?"'

Cheryl's ancestors had been friends to both the Nez Perce and the

Salish prior to the outbreak, and fought hard to prevent the later eviction of Charlot's band from the valley. Now, from her home high on the eastern flank of the valley, Cheryl was fighting against the latest assault on the once impregnable harmony of the Bitterroot.

'We can save this as it is,' she said, looking out over the patchwork valley, 'but see that road down there, that's now a bumper-to-bumper ribbon of lights. With all the pollution, and the dust from the construction trucks, our poor horses couldn't breathe – we had to destroy them.'

Below her, the Bitterroot was becoming a 'ruburb' – defined as where you move to after the suburbs, and then the 'ex-urbs', feel too cramped, an area that retains some of the characteristics of the countryside – few shops and a long drive to work, for example – while still being predominantly asphalt and front lawns. In the 1990s Cheryl's county had seen a 44 per cent increase in its population, and between 1992 and 1997 alone it had lost almost a quarter of its farmland to development – a significant slice when you consider the planning industry commonplace that the first 5 per cent of rural development does half the damage. This was far from unique: sprawl is the defining characteristic of the modern American geography, the urbanized nation expanding its footprint by over 300 per cent between 1950 and 1990, while the urbanized population grew by just 80 per cent, and this expanse became exponential in the 1990s, when over 3.2 million acres of rural America was paved over every year. Sprawl then went ballistic at the turn of the century: in 2004, the 'boomburg' of Phoenix, Arizona, grew outwards by 1.2 acres an hour. But the Bitterroot was getting hit particularly hard – the developers had exploited Montana's considerable surviving natural attractions and its feeble planning laws to turn farms into cookie-cutter housing estates, or 'subdivisions', or sprawling trophy ranches, heaping problems onto the valley as they went. The valley's water table had become depleted – the river was already overirrigated – and by the late 1990s the Bitterroot, once a symbol of the Big Sky State, had developed an intermittent smog problem. The tight rural community which the isolated basin had fostered was also under strain – as Cheryl put it, 'This is still a place where people still look out for each other – build a mega-subdivision for six hundred newcomers and that changes.' This might seem unwelcoming, but it wasn't unwarranted – the estates were neither built to last nor, as a brief tour of their sparse, unencumbered streets indicated, were they being occupied for life. In the most mobile country on earth – Americans move house, on average, 11.7 times in a lifetime – the West is the most mobile corner – in any year, a fifth of Westerners move on – and the rururbs are the spiritual home of the corporate-nomadic 'wherever Head Office needs me' culture. Locals had learned to expect new subdivision residents to live on Wild Rose Court, Cheyenne Trail and, of course, Chief Joseph Acres for, on average, less than five years, while most of the inhabitants of the giant trophy ranches – the rock stars, TV chat show hosts and merchant bankers – stayed for just a few months each summer. And the fact that there were precious few jobs where the houses were being built only added to the dormitory dislocation – as the classic suburbanite josh goes, 'I've seen a lot of your car recently, but not of you.'

A heroic army of Bitterroot residents had gathered to beat back this warped version of progress, in an endless guerrilla war of town hall meetings and public consultations, but victories were scarce. The developers rarely struggled to find local elected officials either cheerfully corruptible or susceptible to intimidation by lawsuit – and one new version of the colonial management of the West, closely tied to the mythology and outlook of the pioneer days, had proved particularly fruitful.

Due to a constitutional quirk, the states of the Northwest are highly susceptible to government by ballot – simply wander the streets getting enough signatures on your petition for a new law, from a smoking ban to a minimum wage increase, and it'll be put to the public in a referendum. In the early twenty-first century this apparently democratic facility was basically bought by the development industry – huge out-of-state landholders and business lobbying groups raised petitions for laws that would free them to pave over the Northwest with gay abandon. Distressingly often, these laws would then be approved by a public vote – because they were aggressively and expensively marketed as upholding the founding principles of the West: individual freedom, private property, a man's right, indeed duty, to put his patch of the continent to work. Conservationists in the Wallowa Valley, for example, desperate to prevent their farmland from turning into precisely what the Bitterroot had become, watched aghast in 2004 as the people of Oregon voted in the infamous Measure 37, which offered full government compensation to any landholder prevented from making the maximum profit from their land – the astonishing equivalent of the planning officer either approving the extension above your garage, or buying you an imaginary extension to say sorry. Such triumphs are fronted at grassroots by local good ol' boys in greasy caps and jeans, standing up for the little man against an overweening government – but are funded almost exclusively by New York-, Chicago- and Boston-based real-estate empires.

In Cheryl's county, just as I passed through, the local conservative firebrand, a preacher by the name of Dallas Erickson who'd briefly achieved national fame by getting the teaching of evolution barred from one school district in the Bitterroot, was running a ballot campaign to let ordinary, hard-working local folks build shops on their land, of whatever size they chose. His campaign, Citizens for Economic Opportunity, had raised $41,752.41 to fight this noble cause – $41,000 of which came from the Wal-Mart corporation. Erickson's ballot passed, by 8003 votes to 7489 – a fair reflection of the bitterly narrow division between the Old West free-market individualists and the conservation-minded communitarians that had come to poison the valley's civic life – and Wal-Mart started drawing up their plans.

Everyone in the Bitterroot agreed on one thing, though – that at least some growth was good, particularly compared to the atrophied communities that lay both east and west of the valley. The storefronts in Hamilton and Stevensville actually had shops behind them, the popular schools were packed with kids and the local pews were full. But the Bitterroot's old families were being steamrollered, by property inflation, the lack of steady, family-wage work and by the usual squeezes on small agriculture; in the usual indication of depletion of a working community, the county's average age had risen nine years in two decades. Meanwhile, the developers knew no restraint, and wouldn't voluntarily stop building until every ounce of marketable charm had been sapped from the valley. It was all a considerable rebuke to K. Ross Toole's hope, expressed in 1959, that the white Northwest might one day overcome its congenital inability to take any ride other than the roller-coaster: 'If there is one thing the Montanan ought to have learned, it is to beware of the boom – too much too soon.'

Everything about the current land grab, from the unreliable carpentry to the bumper-to-bumper highway (and, it would soon emerge, the frantically mis-sold mortgages), was unsustainable – and many locals, exhausted by the ceaseless meetings, pamphlets and protests, were contemplating the traditional Westerner's response to the end of a good thing: moving on. Others, though, were defiantly digging in, and a tantalizingly oblique letter to the *Ravalli County Republic* in January 2007 reassured local residents: 'There are organized efforts underway to stop Wal-Mart from setting up shop … we have the tools.

'Get involved, so that five years from now we can celebrate our achievements and pass the baton to the next generation of patriots and visionaries, which will be an absolute necessity until which time these powerful and wealthy entities finally get the message: "Stay away from our homeland", for we will protect it at all costs.'

'My brothers and sisters, I am telling you! In a dream last night I saw myself killed. I will be killed soon! I do not care. I am willing to die. But first, I will kill some soldiers. I shall not turn back from the death. We are all going to die!'

Wahlitits, the young warrior whose vengeance for his father had first sparked the fighting in Idaho, had been visited by his medicine powers in the night and now rode through the Nez Perce camp proclaiming his dream. Other tribe members were gripped with similar dark visions, the warrior Lone Bird bellowing his desire for greater haste to all and sundry: 'My shaking heart tells me trouble and death will overtake us if we make no hurry through this land! I cannot smother, I cannot hide that which I see. I must speak what is revealed to me. Let us be gone to the buffalo country!' But the apprehension passed, as the caravan finally slipped up and over the Continental Divide and slowly poured east, as the rivers now flowed on this side of the great Western spine, into the Big Hole.

The Big Hole was a rift valley to rival East Africa's, with its herds of deer, elk, antelope and buffalo scattered across a grassland fully sixty miles long and fifteen wide, the pan-flat, featureless valley floor banked by forests and barren sierra, lying beneath the crisp, elevated atmosphere. With a low point just under 7000 feet, baking summers and long, violent winters added drama to a scene that, for centuries of Native American travel and conflict, had stood for peace. With plentiful water from the rivers that scored the valley, and that copious game, the tribes of the Northwest had long understood the Big Hole to be a neutral place of pause and rest along several nomadic routes. So when the Nez Perce arrived on 7 August at their traditional site by a winding creek they took pains to set camp for a relaxing residence, forming a convivial 'V' with their lodges, and not a defensive position. The next morning a group of young warriors, inspired by yet another dream of troops and travails, volunteered to scout back towards the Bitterroot and double-check that such laxity was justified, that no force haunted their trail. But they couldn't persuade an elderly tribal member to lend them his fast horses, and Looking Glass also objected – why antagonize the whites with a war-footing, when the pact of peace still held? 'No more fighting! War is quit.'

And so for one blessed day the village concentrated on recu-peration – new lodgepoles were cut and stripped to replace those abandoned in the hurried escape from the Clearwater, the horses were grazed at leisure, a few deer and antelope fell to the hunters. With their eighty-nine tepees along the riverbank, standing proud with their new lodgepoles, the village must have made a soothing, familiar sight. 'That night,' Yellow Wolf recalled, 'the warriors paraded about camp, singing, all making a good time. It was the first since war started. Everybody with good feeling. Going to the buffalo country! … It was past midnight when we went to bed.'

CHAPTER EIGHT

SURVIVAL

'I saw many soldiers, many Indian men, and oh, so many women and children lying on the ground. I wondered if they were sleeping so. Afterwards I understood'

PAHIT PALIKT, Nez Perce

'With such sacrifices have Western trails been blazed. Alone with nature and nature's God Bugler Brooks' grave will remain for many a year... And later on, some day, the settler will come, and the district school, and the teacher will tell her little pupils the tradition of the lonely grave'

COLONEL J. W. REDINGTON, *The Story of Bugler Brooks*

THE ARMY SAT in the darkness and waited. One hundred and eighty-three men hunched along a narrow trail on the hillside above the sleeping camp, shivering but silent. The village slept on. The Nez Perce horse herd stayed calm and quiet, grazing on the hill above where the troops now sat. A few dogs seemed to sense the threat, barking into the night, but even they soon fell to silence. The night passed, in peace and bitter cold. Barely a word was spoken, as the army sat and watched the campfires fade. Just before dawn, the Nez Perce women rose to fuel the glowing embers, and returned to their

216

Colonel John Gibbon.

beds. This was the sign the aching, shuddering soldiers had been waiting for. They prepared for action.

Colonel John Gibbon was the commander of the District of Western Montana, within the Military Division of the Missouri – which meant the Nez Perce had been on his beat since they crossed the Lolo Trail. An unsentimental professional, he made no secret of his belief that there was only space in America for a single, uncontested civilization – making the Indian Wars a fight to the last. While the refugees had been negotiating Fort Fizzle and trailing down the Bitterroot, he had gathered a small infantry army from Montana's few, isolated forts, and had set off south from Missoula on 4 August. So desperate was Gibbon to end the humiliation of this travelling rebellion that he'd declined to wait for poor General Howard, still dragging his army of seven hundred over the mountains, planning instead to strike the caravan with a roughly equal fighting force, and no cavalry. Gibbon had fairly torn along the Bitterroot, marching two days to Looking Glass's one, and had picked up invaluable intelligence along the way from the settlers who'd so recently traded with the Nez Perce. One such spy made it clear that the colonel lacked the numbers to challenge the Indians' superior marksmanship, and against his initial judgement, following their questionable contribution at Fort Fizzle, Gibbon had accepted civilian volunteers. Many of the Bitterroot's men declined, saying that the Nez Perce had done them no harm, but some thirty-four signed up, drawn by the prospect of adventure, vengeance for the people of Idaho and Colonel Gibbon's promise of free horses from the hostiles' herd. Amos Buck, whose family store had done so well from the tribe, signed up, as did Myron Lockwood, dissatisfied with the band's compensation of only seven horses for a burgled shack.

Gibbon's scouts had reached the Nez Perce camp on the morning of the 8th, and had crouched in the pine trees and watched the village's hunting, fishing and merry-making on that solitary day of rest. Young White Bird, the great chief's nephew, was one of the children who had spotted the strange men in grey blankets by the light of the campfire. 'Foolishly, we said nothing to the older people about it. We ran away and then came back to our playing.'

Setting off at around eleven o'clock, Gibbon's army had tripped and stumbled some five miles through the forested night, to emerge above the undefended camp. And now they waited, while Gibbon and his officers whispered their plans for a dawn assault. Perfected by George Armstrong Custer, the sunrise raid on a dozing village had become the most consistently successful US Army response to an Indian rebellion, precisely because it was so unthinkable to the enemy; as military historian Merrill D. Beal wrote of the Nez Perce: 'Their code of ethics convinced them that no one would execute a surprise attack upon a sleeping and undefended camp.'

Gibbon's plan was simple – a shocking assault along one wide front that would shove the Nez Perce out of their village and onto the expanse that lay behind them. He would then just fold up either end of his line, corralling the band like livestock. Two of the colonel's reported orders that foggy morning have become enshrined in infamy: one volunteer later recalled that when their leader asked Gibbon what the policy was on taking prisoners, he was sharply informed that this army lacked the manpower to observe such niceties, while another remembered that the lack of concern for the women and children was made absolutely clear: 'We had orders to fire low into the tepees.'

Finally, at the first shade of dawn, Gibbon ordered a creeping, crawling advance.

The front was shuffling gradually, tentatively, forward when the elderly Wetestokayt emerged yawning from his lodge, and set off to check on the horse herd. With his poor sight, he wandered, oblivious, to within five or six yards of the troops, approaching the huddle of volunteers in a dip in the land ahead of him.

They shot him down. The attack was on, and the orders were followed well – three low volleys tore through the tepees, sending shrieks of terror and confusion through the camp, before the bellowing, screaming troops forded the river, charged into the village and began to kill.

Many Nez Perce who visit the Big Hole today say they can still hear the screaming, still feel the reverberations of what the next half-hour brought to their people. One of the first lodges the troops reached was a maternity tent – someone went inside, shot the mother and the midwife and staved in the baby's head. Nearby, the mother's two other young children cowered – and were killed. Five more children were gunned down in one lodge. The Nez Perce warriors were in chaos, many waking without their rifles nearby, others either struck down or forced from the village by the ferocious gunfire, and the troops soon held the southern end of the camp, continuing their spree with little semblance of order or tactical purpose, while a few armed Nez Perce tried desperately to resist their progress. One woman was shot in the back as she sprinted for cover, a single bullet killing her and her infant child, five more women were targeted and killed where they huddled for safety in the freezing river, trying to hide under the bank. Many more non-combatants fled to the river, some trying to hide in the water beneath blankets – but as one volunteer recalled 'we only had to notice where the blanket or buffalo hide was slightly raised, and a bullet at that spot would be sufficient for the body to float down the stream'. Troops worked in teams, some pulling over a lodge while the others poured bullets onto the exposed inhabitants. A young girl was shot out from under a woman's arms, hiding beneath the branches of a willow tree. The elderly were picked off with similar dispatch, and the winding creek soon ran red, the sandbanks clogging with bodies. Not every trooper murdered indiscriminately: some lowered their rifles at the sight of shuddering noncombatants, others, surreally, shook their hands and offered them gifts – one volunteer recalled pointing his pistol at a pair of women, who were protecting an infant: 'I began to think. Why should I shoot an Indian woman, one who had never injured me a bit in the world? I put up my gun and left. A little later in the day I heard a fellow bragging that he had killed those two women.'

The Nez Perce rally was not long in coming. White Bird scolded his warriors into a charge, armed or not, from their hiding places: 'Why are we retreating? Since the world was made, brave men fight for their women and children. Are we going to run to the mountains and let the whites kill our women and children before our eyes? It is better we should be killed fighting. Now is the time: fight!' Elsewhere, Looking Glass called on the men who had started the war, the cousins Wahlitits and Sarpsis Ilppilp, to sacrifice their lives prolonging it: 'Now is the time to show your courage and fight. You can kill right and left. I would rather see you killed than the rest of the warriors, for you commenced the war. Now go ahead and fight.'

Emboldened warriors joined the tiny number of fighters challenging the troops' progress north through the camp, while others began to snipe from the willows and high ground. Gibbon's plan had by now descended into little more than slash and burn –

Today, uncovered lodgepoles stand as memorials to the
Nez Perce encampment at Big Hole.

he'd failed to envelop the camp, and many of his troops were now
wasting their time trying to torch damp tepees – and the warriors
were able to launch a frenzied counter-attack. The fighting was
chaotic and desperate, men blasted away toe to toe, reduced at times
to clubbing one another with empty rifles – both sides suffered
terrible losses, some shot by their own side in the melee, white and
Indian bodies falling side by side in the dirt. Wahlitits was killed, and
his pregnant wife, huddling wounded next to him behind makeshift
wooden defences, took his rifle and shot her husband's killer, before
herself being gunned down. The revered war chief Rainbow also fell,
fulfilling his *wyakin*'s pledge that he could only die in a battle before
sunrise. Ollokot fought with his usual fearlessness, though his wife
had been wounded, as had Joseph's – warriors recalled seeing that
young chief desperately protecting his newborn daughter from the
bullets, and later sprinting to secure the horse herd, without which
the caravan could not escape.

221

But the Nez Perce's sacrifices bore fruit: two hours or so after launching his raid, Gibbon realized he was losing too many men trying to hold the camp, and ordered a retreat. Under merciless fire from the Nez Perce snipers, his men returned to the protection of the tree line, found a patch of level ground within the pines and started to dig in. For a while the fighting abated, with the soldiers distracted by carving trenches and avoiding sniper fire. With their enemy voluntarily pinned down, the Nez Perce were finally able to turn their thoughts to what had just happened. As the warriors headed back to the smouldering camp, the scene was unimaginable.

'It was not good to see women and children lying dead and wounded. A few soldiers and warriors lay as they had fallen – some almost together. Wounded children screaming with pain. Women and children crying, wailing for their scattered dead! The air was heavy with sorrow,' Yellow Wolf recalled. 'I would not want to hear, I would not want to see, again.'

Such was the chaos that exact casualty figures have proved elusive, but Joseph and White Bird later testified that around fifty to sixty women, children and elderly non-combatants had been killed that morning, or would soon die of their wounds. More young men would also die, but the great majority of the perhaps thirty or so genuine fighting fatalities that the Nez Perce would sustain at the Big Hole took place in those lunatic first few hours. The survivors' sobs and screams drifted on the breeze to Colonel Gibbon, entrenching a quarter of a mile away: 'Few of us will soon forget the wail of mingled grief, rage and horror which came from the camp four or five hundred yards from us when the Indians returned to it and recognized their slaughtered warriors, women and children.'

Astonishingly, another improvised strategy was wrought from the confusion. Under Joseph and White Bird's supervision, the camp would prepare to evacuate south along the Big Hole – which meant rushed, unceremonial burials for the fallen, and building travois from lodgepoles to drag the badly wounded away by horsepower.

Fighters were given time off from the front line to attend to their families and their dead, while the remaining warriors, Ollokot and Looking Glass to the fore, would prevent Gibbon's force from pursuing the limping caravan by keeping them pinned in their trenches.

One other dilemma presented itself: what to do with a volunteer soldier, a Bitterroot settler named Campbell L. Mitchell, who was found alive within the camp? As the Nez Perce debated how to treat their prisoner, the warrior Otskai took the initiative, shooting Mitchell dead. 'Are not *warriors* to be fought? Look around! These babies, these children killed! Were *they* warriors? These young girls, these young women you see dead. Were *they* warriors? These young boys, these old men! Were *they* warriors?

'*We* are the warriors! Coming on us while we slept, no arms ready, the soldiers were brave. Then, when we have only a few rifles in our hand, like cowardly coyotes they run away.

'These citizen soldiers! Good friends in Bitterroot Valley! Traded with us for our gold! Their Lolo peace treaty was a lie! Our words were good. They had two tongues. Why should we waste time saving his life?'

In the years following the Big Hole battle, Otskai's would be the only war crime the US government ever sought to prosecute.

Not that Gibbon's men weren't paying their penance. Conditions in the shallow trenches of their sparse, wooded grove were woeful and worsening – a third of the command was dead or wounded, the injured lay screaming and unattended, many of the healthy still wept with fear as the Nez Perce snipers picked them off. There was no water, no food bar the uncooked flesh of a downed horse, and ammunition was beginning to run low. When the force's one advantage, a howitzer placed high on a ridge above the camp, was lost to a Nez Perce raid, some spoke of 'another Big Horn' in the offing – the loss of the entire command – while others wrote their wills. As the siege stretched into the afternoon the killing wasn't entirely one way – Sarpsis Ilppilp, the second of the cousins who had devised that fateful first Idaho raid, died as he circled the trenches – but the Nez Perce were well in control, and able to release many of their fighters to escort the caravan south. The remainder tried to burn the troops out, setting fire to the grass around them, but it didn't take, and they were largely satisfied with simply holding Gibbon in place. As night fell, perhaps just ten fighters remained at the siege, under the command of Ollokot, who was unaware that in the distance the caravan had paused to rest, and his wife was dying of her wounds.

With no clue that such a tiny force now pinned them down, Gibbon's men shivered through the night, sending runners into the darkness to summon help and to fill canteens from the creek. Seven Bitterroot volunteers took advantage of the gloom to desert, leaving the wounded to their own devices. Early the next morning a rider burst through the trees and into the barricade –Yellow Wolf recalled that the Nez Perce let him breach their lines, to gauge the troops' response – and announced that General Howard and two hundred cavalrymen were fast approaching. Those who could gave a cheer, and the few Nez Perce still in the woods understood perfectly: 'We gave those trenched soldiers two volleys as a "Goodbye!",' Yellow Wolf recalled, 'then we mounted and rode swiftly away.' The Big Hole battle was fought: of 183 men, Gibbon had lost twenty-nine dead and forty wounded, of whom two would later die of their injuries. Of those Nez Perce used to the role of warrior, Yellow Wolf claimed, 'Only twelve real fighting men were lost in that battle. But our best were left there.' Whatever the exact tolls, at the end of one of the most brutal encounters in the Indian Wars neither side had been defeated but one side had certainly failed. For the third time, the US Army had tried to bludgeon the Nez Perce into surrender – and yet, somehow, the caravan was still on the move.

'All along the trail was crying. Mourning for many left where we thought no war would come. Old people, half-grown boys and girls, mothers, and little babies. Many only half-buried – left for wolves and coyotes. I can never forget that day.' Black Eagle, a teenager at the time, expressed just part of the cacophony of emotions swirling around the Nez Perce as they hurried on from the battlefield. It's impossible for an outsider to comprehend the effect of that morning on that people – and on their descendants, still left physically shaken by a visit to the Big Hole

The caravan echoed with weeping as the march continued, grief for the fallen – almost every family in the village had lost at least one member – compounded by the stolen opportunity to deliver the tribe's sacred burial rites to their loved ones. There was rage and bewilderment at their enemy's breach of sanity and honour, and at the betrayal by the Bitterroot volunteers, who'd accepted peace and patronage just a few days before. There was concern for the wounded, suffering dreadfully as their stretchers bounced along the rocky scrubland. The caravan moved slowly in the first few days following the battle, for the casualties' sake, but some still died along the way, while others were granted their demand to be left behind, to meet their fate at the hands of their pursuers. General Howard's scouts encountered at least two such people, waiting stoically for death, wrapped in their blankets by the wayside. (The Bannock Indian trackers who accompanied those army scouts, long-time enemies of the Nez Perce, were not shy in delivering the *coups de grâce*.)

There was also, particularly among the caravan's leaders, profound worry about what this attack meant for their continued pursuit of peace and freedom. Were there truly to be no truces along the way, no refuges, no respite? Was every single white man their enemy? Perhaps the first doubts crept in – that the government might *never* let them go home. What was certain was that Looking Glass had comprehensively misjudged the situation in the Bitterroot, and his control over the camp's movements was lost. While the agreed plan of hiding out on the Crow plains was not abandoned, responsibility for dictating the length of each day's march and the choice of campsites passed, perhaps surprisingly, to Poker Joe, the urbane gambler who had joined the camp in the Bitterroot. It was a sensible choice, as he knew both the terrain and the people between here and Crow country well, but one that also spoke of compromise – suggesting that the leaders of the main bands were in no mood to take orders from one another. There was also an element of resignation about Poker Joe's appointment. He would have little or no control over the actions of the belligerent young warriors, but after the Big Hole such restraint was a faint, diminishing hope. They would kill whom they would kill.

'It was a sublime effort and must ever stand forth as a shining mark of human achievement. The attack by this Spartan band was one requiring the highest attributes of courage – an unfaltering courage that sustained them throughout the bloody drama ... there is nothing connected with the battle of the Big Hole which any Montanan would wish to see erased from our history.' The *Missoulian* had only one regret, that Gibbon had lacked the men to finish the job: 'If there could have been enough force to have flanked the village and attacked in force along the whole line, the Indians could not have escaped annihilation.'

Montana's initial response to Big Hole had been panic, as rumours spread that Gibbon's command had been wiped out. The irrepressible Governor Potts had started accruing volunteers for a recovery mission, and Marcus Daly and William Clark had sprinted towards the battlefield in their makeshift ambulances. But as General Howard reached Gibbon on the morning of 11 August, to find the troops shattered but in reasonable spirits, the narrative was rapidly rewritten. Big Hole would be a triumph. Gibbon's superior officers set the tone, one of them declaring in a telegram, 'I beg you that you will accept for yourself, your officers and your men my heartiest congratulations for your most gallant fight and brilliant success', and the press fell into line, presenting the fight as one in the eye for the Indian renegades. The traditional civilian contempt for the US Army, all sneering officers and work-shy privates, was put to one side, and by the time Gibbon, who'd been shot in the leg, was transported to Deer Lodge, the town was in festive mood: 'Flags were flying from every flag-staff and houses were decorated with streamers and bunting,' witnessed the *New North West*. 'The Deer Lodge Brass Band discoursed sweet music; the ladies were all out upon the street, and everyone felt happy and had a "God Bless You" for the gallant old soldier.'

Another old soldier, however, received none of the reflected glory. Tired but relentless, unloved but unbowed, General Howard and his army set off from the battlefield on 13 August, two days' march behind the Nez Perce. The public assumed that after Gibbon's heroics at the Big Hole, the Christian General had little to do but mop up the remnants of a broken rebellion. As the *Missoulian* put it: 'The Nez Perce cannot travel very fast with their wounded and stock, and their being overhauled (by a force double in numbers at least) seems the inevitable result of a few days.'

On they marched now, on and ever on. Poker Joe had no doubt that all that was expected for this caravan was oblivion, and he pushed the suffering bands forward relentlessly. They rose before dawn, marched until a break for grazing and cooking at mid-morning, then pushed on again until past sunset. These long days on the trail were unavoidable, as the wounded slowed the pace of the caravan to a crawl; barely a night passed in the week after the battle in which a victim's suffering didn't end before sunrise. The laconic ramblings down the Bitterroot were a memory now, as scouts and back-markers were posted and overnight fortifications set. And there were no gullies in which to obscure the train's passage here, no ridges behind which to hide. This was the biggest of the Big Country, the cavernous valleys of the Big Hole and the great Horse Prairie offering nothing but exposure and silence, an implacable semi-desert of scrubland and dry grass, in which the Nez Perce were oppressively alone, a tiny speck on as broad a canvas as in all Creation, the dust cloud from their caravan visible more than a day's travel away. A handful of ranches had been established in these basins, and it was clear that taking their horses was a question of survival – to replenish the Nez Perce herd, but, far more importantly, to deny fresh mounts to any pursuing cavalry. Most of the ranchers had fled to gold camps in the hills long before the Indians' vanguard reached them, but on 12 August five male settlers who'd yet to evacuate their homes died in Nez Perce horse-stealing raids. The caravan was heading due south at this time, a path that took them back over the Continental Divide for a short spell, into another towering basin – the Lemhi Valley – where the tiny mining community of Junction lay in their path. Most of the inhabitants of this shack town (which the Mormons had abandoned after two years of trying to build another Jerusalem in the desert, but which had regained its pulse after a gold strike in 1866) had already fled, but a few huddled behind a flimsy log barricade. The local Shoshone Indians, in no mood to join a rebellion, served as neutral emissaries between the Nez Perce and the whites, and no shots were fired as the caravan passed. The Shoshone chief urged the refugees to get away from his reservation with all haste, pledging that they wouldn't be harassed or robbed (though a few of his young men couldn't resist such a chance for honour, and launched a moonlit horse raid). The Shoshone were left in peace as the dust cloud moved on; another shackled tribe had chosen self-preservation over justice as the great Nez Perce journey passed them by.

By now, across the plains, deserts and mountains of the West, the Indian resistance to the great project of settlement was burning away to ash, and the last few renegades, such as the non-treaty Nez Perce, were looking ever more isolated and overwhelmed. The US government's reservation policy had been, by its own unlovely standards, a great success, crippling tribes through division between those resigned to the Europeans' dominance and those repelled by it. For the former, reservation life sapped their capacity to imperil the new white empire, as corruption, famine, population collapse and the loss of their traditional means of physical and cultural subsistence actually left them threatened, not threatening, as burgeoning settler communities salivated over the Indians' remaining reserved lands. As for the rebels who refused to sign up or stay within their new enclosures, the Western Army – under the leadership of a pair of hard-bitten Civil War veterans, William Sherman and Philip Sheridan – had ultimately devised a treatment that, despite the individual inferiority of their fighting men compared to most warring bands, sullenly worked out in the end. Simply by harassing renegade villages, shoving them around the West, raiding at dawn when possible, following at a distance when not, the army made the rituals and necessities of Native life impossible; one Apache chief, surrendering after a winter of rebellion, described his village's life on the run: 'Could not go to sleep at night, because they feared to be surrounded before daybreak; they could not hunt – the noise of their guns would attract the troops; they could not cook mescal or anything, because the flame and smoke would draw down the soldiers.'

This relentless, plodding pursuit of a more nimble enemy regularly broke army commands, leaving horses and men skeletal and shivering (Sheridan preferred to harass in the dead of winter) but it also, eventually, tended to break the rebels. In 1875 the southern plains had been pacified, as the vainglorious Colonel Nelson A. Miles had hauled his frostbitten troops across the Texas Panhandle until the rebel Cheyenne, Kiowa and Comanche ran out of will, and Miles had then employed the same vigour to the pursuit of the Northern Cheyenne and Oglala Sioux into the bitter northern winter after Little Big Horn. On 6 May 1877 the peerless warrior Crazy Horse had paraded into Camp Robinson, Nebraska, with a train of a thousand Sioux, thrown his rifle to the ground and accepted reservation life. By September he would be dead, killed while facing arrest for insufficient deference to his keepers. To the north, in Canada, Sitting Bull was beginning to realize that there was not enough game to feed the four thousand Sioux who'd followed him into exile, and was contemplating his reduced options. There were a few more Indian outbreaks to come after the summer of 1877 (the Bannocks, pursuing and scalping the Nez Perce under Howard's command, would get their own measure of betrayal and belittlement the very next year) but they would be bursts more of rage than resistance. The frontier was narrowing like a noose.

On the Nez Perce marched. Poker Joe kept up the pace along the length of the Lemhi Valley and the young men kept up their horse raids. On 15 August a further five white men perished when a group of warriors encountered a foolhardy wagon train and claimed its forty mounts. In a sign of the grim mood enveloping the fighters, the wagon's whiskey barrels were then swiftly dispatched, after which a petty row degenerated into a brawl, and the respected warrior Ketalkpoosmin was mortally wounded by one of his own comrades.

Grinding on, the Nez Perce emerged from the valley and onto the northern edge of the Snake River Basin, an endless expanse of scrubby nothingness scoured by the great river and its many tributaries. In the future, those rivers would be tamed to turn this vista of dirt into the kingdom of the humble potato, but for the Nez Perce it offered little more than flat, navigable terrain, and they swung east and sped towards the relative safety of fresh mountain ridges. Rest was scarce – the scouts reported to the chiefs that an army was back on their trail, and marching hard. The travel, the wounds, the baking days and freezing nights were still taking their toll – two ailing women were left behind at a barren riverbed known as Dry Creek, unable to maintain this marathon. When the local settlers emerged from their cave hideouts after the caravan had passed, they found the pair huddled among the rocks, frozen to death.

If you stand on the banks of Dry Creek today, you can see the defining symbol of Dubois, Idaho, a few miles down the highway: the plastic sign for the truck stop and gas station advertising just about the only going concern left in town. If you linger, you'll find the small farming community's wide, airy Main Street dominated by nailed-up boards and broken windows, hotels, grocery stores and bars abandoned in what looks like a hurried, careless exodus. There are new government buildings – there are always new government buildings – but little else, except a *cantina* that has occupied an old diner, now serving chow to the Hispanic farm workers who live in the trailer parks on the edge of town, conjuring a life from their scandalous, seasonal wages.

I found an elderly couple playing with their visiting grandchildren in the town park, and asked them what had happened to their town. The grandmother offered a simple response: 'Wal-Mart. It opened about an hour down the Interstate, everything was under one roof, and that was that. The shops here closed up.' Her husband, however, took a wider view, defaulting to one of the most popular lines in the rural Northwest: 'Round here, our number one export is young people. If you can find a job, you can't raise a family on it, so our young people – well, they've just upped and left.'

One cursory effort had been made to spark Main Street Dubois back to life – cheery civic bunting had been hung from the lampposts, then, sadly, left to perish in the unforgiving elements. Through the fluttering sun-bleached shreds of cloth, you could just about discern the boosters' pleading message, perhaps reminding the departing shopkeepers and job-seekers that the soil they were leaving had been claimed, with menaces, in the expectation that an empire of virtue would plant permanent roots: 'Home, Sweet Home.'

General Howard was breaking his army. He had set off in pursuit along the Big Hole Valley with his mixed force of cavalry and infantry, under orders to overtake the Nez Perce and force their surrender – despite his own opinion, amply illustrated by now, that this was a foot race he could never win. Two days after setting out, Howard was joined by a galloping company of volunteers, under the command of the irrepressible William Clark. A cacophonous clash of egos ensued, with Clark offering unwanted tactical advice, while Howard gave the mining magnate an irrelevant scouting role, probably designed to emphasize who was in command. Disgusted, Clark turned and took his men home, where their outraged reports of Howard's dismissal of their flawless 'Indian sense' stoked the public perception that the Christian General had lost his military mojo, and was stumbling, lost.

Howard, in fact, was moving his troops just about as fast as he could – his infantry were an anchor and his cavalry didn't have the Nez Perce's resource of hundreds of spare horses, while the Indians' tactic of denying him any fresh mounts found along the way was a masterstroke. The warriors were also slaughtering and driving off livestock and game as they went, leaving the trailing army with diminishing supplies. Desperate to regain the initiative, Howard gambled – correctly – on the Nez Perce's route, predicting that they would skirt the top of the Snake flatlands and re-enter the mountains via a cleft known as the Targhee Pass. Dispatching a small force to block the pass, Howard set a course to 'cut the corner' off the Nez Perce's arcing trajectory, thus intercepting them at Dry Creek, and forcing battle. For six days he pushed his footsore and hungry men as hard as Poker Joe was driving the Nez Perce, and on 18 August the army reached Dry Creek – a day late. The Nez Perce still held a slim lead, trailing a dust cloud fifteen miles distant. The next day Howard took up the caravan's tracks – never difficult, as the Nez Perce were beating a path up to fifty metres wide wherever they went – and resumed pursuit towards Targhee Pass. He lacked two nuggets of intelligence, though: firstly, the officer he'd charged with blocking the pass, Lieutenant George Bacon, had grown bored and taken his men off to look for the Nez Perce, ultimately getting lost; secondly, with now just a day's march between them and their pursuers, the Nez Perce had begun to consider how to slow the army down. On the morning of 19 August, a young warrior reported to the chiefs that the previous night, in a dream, he had stolen the general's horses.

Of all the encounters throughout the Nez Perce's long summer, the skirmish that came to be known as the Battle of Camas Meadow is probably the occasion when the US Army most closely resembled a circus troupe. The night of the 19th had in fact begun impressively, with Howard taking great pains to fortify his overnight camp against raiders, but the Nez Perce were emboldened by their warrior's vision and the leadership of Looking Glass, Ollokot and Toohoolhoolzote, and their war party approached in silence in the moonless early morning. A few crept past the guards and began to cut the cavalry's horses away from their fence posts – but a rifle was fired in error and the alarm was sounded. Chaos ensued, as the Nez Perce kept the waking, half-dressed soldiers pinned down with rifle fire and terrifying war cries while they stampeded as many horses as they could, the thunder of hooves surrounding the pitch-black camp, then drove their plunder away over the scrubland, towards their own camp. As dawn broke, though, Yellow Wolf recalled the disappointment at a devalued prize: 'Getting more light we looked. *Eeh!* Nothing but mules – all mules!' In the darkness the raiders had only captured Howard's pack train, not his cavalry mounts. Still, a blow had been struck, and they continued home.

Back with the soldiers, all was bugles and bustle as Howard prepared his riposte. Three cavalry companies, around one hundred men, were dispatched under the command of Major George B. Sanford to recapture the mules, galloping after the receding dust cloud. The chasing pack reached a small elevation in the scrubby flatland, to see that the Nez Perce had taken a stand on a similar elevation about half a mile away. For a pointless hour, Sanford and his men dismounted and exchanged potshots with the distant

Indians, far beyond the range of their rifles – only to realize, when a trooper was shot in the buttocks, that they'd been trapped. The Nez Perce stand was a decoy, and groups of warriors had scooted around the right and left of the cavalry and were threatening to surround them. Sanford announced a retreat but not a dignified one. Many of his cavalrymen had sent their horses to a clump of trees 500 metres behind the line of fire, where they were being held in peace and safety. Now, though, panic struck the unmounted soldiers, many of whom couldn't remember where they had left their horses. Once a bugler had offered directions, the pell-mell sprint towards the steeds began, with bullets whizzing and hats flying. Harry Davis recalled that 'the race to that thicket was something never to be forgotten, for a cavalryman is not trained for a five hundred yard sprint; luck was with us, however, and no man was hit in that mad race for safety.' Sanford and his men eventually galloped back towards Howard's main force, where the general made a pertinent observation – 'But where is Norwood?' The major conceded that he didn't know: he'd mislaid around a third of his command.

Captain Randolph Norwood was not a towering military figure – he'd spent much of the past two years malingering, stretching out a sick leave to include a tour of Europe. It's unlikely that he relished the assignment Major Sanford had given his company at dawn, to form the central third of the pursuing pack, and it's certain he didn't appreciate the rapid disintegration of both his flanks in the chaotic retreat. His thirty-five or so men had borne the brunt of the Indians' fire during the madcap sprint back to the horses, and on reaching the copse Norwood realized that he'd been left behind, and faced being cut off and annihilated if he just kept on retreating. He ordered his men to gather in a shallow cauldron in the ground and build defences from the volcanic rubble that lay around them. Their feeble, two-foot-tall breastworks are still visible today on the scrappy, neglected battlefield and the four hours for which these defences

*The makeshift defences built by the stranded US Army forces at
Camas Meadows.*

were peppered must have stretched on unendurably, with Nez Perce
sharpshooters crawling among the hillocks and scrubs, pinning the
troopers down. Six of Norwood's men were wounded, two of whom
would later die of their injuries.

While Norwood's men were being whipped, Howard and Sanford
had spread their men out to sweep over the flatlands and find the
missing company, as if hunting for a wayward tee shot. Eventually, at
around nine in the morning, the lost men were located, and, as
General Howard made his customarily tardy arrival at the battlefield,
the Nez Perce departed at pace, with only two minor casualties.
Captain Norwood, by most reports, greeted his rescuers with an
unrestrained analysis of the inadvisability of leaving thirty-five men
behind in a firefight.

One further fatality, the baby-faced Private Bernard A. Brooks,
illustrated once again which career choice must have reduced

nervous nineteenth-century mothers to the greatest attacks of the vapours. The company bugler, he had been struck in the heart by one of the very first shots of the engagement.

When the warriors caught up with the main caravan, there was something of a scramble to claim the valuable beasts of burden they drove before them. The mules would be a considerable asset in the mountains that lay ahead, and the Nez Perce understood that their loss would hobble Howard, so they moved at a leisurely pace for the next few days. Pausing to fish at the windswept Henry's Lake, they then climbed the unguarded Targhee Pass and crossed back to the east of the Continental Divide, re-entering the Rockies. A few miles on they traversed a boundary that would have been profoundly curious to them, delineating a concept that was both influenced by their natural philosophy and fundamentally opposed to it. They were now in Yellowstone, the world's first National Park.

General Howard, meanwhile, did not follow them. Grinding on as far as Henry's Lake, he was forced to concede that his command was exhausted, men and mounts shattered, supplies running low, clothing and equipment wearing out. On the camp doctor's advice, Howard called a four-day rest. Not for himself, though – the general saddled up and rode the sixty miles to Virginia City, to buy wagon-loads of fresh supplies from the delirious storekeepers, and to telegraph his superiors. It wasn't an exchange of pleasantries. Howard made his thoughts plain to General Sherman, commander of the US Army, that one force chasing after the Nez Perce would never reel them in; the Indians' knowledge of the landscape, their ability to find sustenance in the wilderness and their all-important herd of horses would always keep them ahead: 'What I wish is for some eastern force, the hostiles be headed off … My command is so much worn by over-fatigue and jaded animals that I cannot push it much further.' If another army was dispatched to stand between the Nez Perce and the Crow plains, then Howard's men could stay put and recover from their ten-week march: 'I think I may stop near where I am.'

Sherman was brutal in response: 'That force of yours should pursue the Nez Perce to the death, lead where they may ... If you are tired, give the command to some young, energetic officer, and let him follow them.' Chastened, Howard came out blustering: 'You misunderstood me. I never flag. It was the command, including the most energetic young officers, that were worn out and weary ... we move in the morning and will continue till the end.' With an inkling that his career was back on the line, Howard returned to Henry's Lake to fire up his men for several more weeks on the march. Though mildly embarrassing, his telegraph exchange with Sherman was helpful to Howard – the commander realized that the Nez Perce warranted more respect than he'd given them thus far, and he ordered not one but *three* armies into position, to block every conceivable route from the Yellowstone Mountains to the Crow plains. With the national press still taking a keen interest in this race for survival, which had already lasted from late spring until the cusp of autumn, Sherman also let his officers know that only crushing victory was now acceptable:

> If the Nez Perces be captured or surrender it should be without terms. Their horses, arms and property should be taken away; many of their leaders executed preferably by sentence of a civil court for their murders in Idaho and Montana and what are left should be treated like the Modocs, sent to some other country; there should be extreme severity, else other tribes alike situated may imitate their example.

Finally, Sherman revealed a politician's instinct for sacrificing his friends in the cause of self-preservation; while sending a final encouraging telegraph to Howard, he also made plans for the general to be humiliatingly relieved of his command. Luckily for Howard, the man chosen for the job was an incompetent, Lieutenant Colonel Charles Gilbert, who set off with a cavalry company to intercept and replace the general, but never actually found him, wandering lost through the mountains until his horses were exhausted and it was time to head home. Unaware of his good fortune, the Christian General marched on into Yellowstone.

With so much manpower now mobilized to send them to their Creator, it was perhaps fitting that the Nez Perce had just entered the most unworldly corner of the Northwest, a region both feted as Heaven on Earth and demonized as 'the place where Hell bubbled up'. The Yellowstone high country was an implausibly beautiful and bewildering place, a *magnum opus* of natural creation in which fearsome mountains overlooked twisting valleys, through which rivers sometimes elegantly meandered and at other times plunged down tremulous rapids and towering falls. At a challenging altitude, the plateau wasn't, intriguingly, a carnival of fauna, but some great herds prospered on the enclosed grasslands – elk, antelope and buffalo, sustaining wolf packs and grizzly bears – while a few of the tumbling rivers were thick with trout. And to add an air of magic to the scene, steam and sulphur drifted on the breeze, simmering from countless volcanic mud pools and hot springs, and firing into the sky from roaring geysers. The first Europeans to visit the region, fur trappers and gold prospectors, were so awestruck that they were unable to restrain their imaginations, reporting that they'd seen valleys in which all the animals had been turned to stone, and others in which the creatures had shrunk to miniature. Whatever they may have seen, they didn't, mercifully, find much gold, and when a series of geographical expeditions surveyed the mountains in the late 1860s and early 1870s, they found the area largely unspoilt by exploitation. Determined that it should remain that way, the scientists lobbied Washington to confer special protection on this exceptional land-scape, and in March 1872 they triumphed when Yellowstone was declared a National Park, set apart from the development of the West 'for the benefit and enjoyment of the people'.

It was an admirable and visionary decision (in 1912 the British diplomat James Bryce declared national parklands to be the best idea America ever had, but the United Kingdom would take all of seventy years to borrow the concept) but there was an undoubted darkness at its heart. This protected, apparently unpopulated, space would be just as off-limits for Native American residence as for European settlement. This, the legislators told themselves, was no great concern – no tribes claimed ownership of the plateau, they decided, and with the exception of a few backward cavemen in the hinterland, tribal visits to the mountains were fleeting and cursory. The Indian West didn't much like Yellowstone, all concurred, and they wouldn't greatly miss it – chiefly, the commonplace asserted, because they were scared of the geysers.

This was obviously hokum. Native Americans had been living in and passing through Yellowstone for at least nine thousand years. The east of the park was part of the traditional semi-nomadic range of the Crow, while the Blackfoot and Salish were regular visitors from the north. The Shoshone made regular hunting incursions from the south and the Nez Perce had often used the mountains as a path to the buffalo plains. The region was, in fact, one of the most archae-ologically dense patches in the West, a crossroads marked by a variety of cultures – but since the advent of the horse, the Native presence in the mountains had tailed off, as the wide-open buffalo plains offered easier hunting and travel, a diminishment which led the Europeans to conclude, quite wrongly, that the steaming volcanic land was somehow taboo. One culture remained in permanent residence, though, families of high-altitude hunters, known as the Sheepeaters for their predilection for mountain mammals. Spurning horse culture, the Sheepeaters lived a harsh but fascinating backwoods life, but the creators of the National Park dismissed them as barely human and virtually extinct, and confined them to reservations beyond the new boundaries, for their own good. As for the other tribes who passed through the park, they were now trespassers, and their millennia-old hunting trips were now illegal poaching raids. Yellowstone was to be 'untouched' – and nine thousand years of history was hastily being erased.

The new park was still sparsely staffed in 1877, however, and no one challenged the Nez Perce's entry as they followed the banks of the Madison River east into the high country. They were, of course, entirely unfazed by the bubbling pools that were supposed to fill them with fear of 'evil spirits', but they did have brief difficulties route-finding – there were several clear Indian trails across the park, but these, the Nez Perce apparently surmised, might be guarded. Thankfully, a prospector by the name of John Shively was camped in their path, and he was press-ganged into helping as a guide along a more obscure route. Shively spent what must have been a remarkable week travelling with the caravan, before slipping away unharmed in the night. He also guided the Nez Perce into one of the most curious encounters on their whole journey – with some of Yellowstone's very first tourists.

Around five hundred tourists a year were visiting Yellowstone by 1877, wagon-camping, fishing and generally congratulating themselves on beating the crowds to this quasi-mythical place. But on the night of 23 August, a group of nine friends and relations from Radersburg, Montana, sharing a camp with a lone gold prospector, were in a far from bright mood – they suspected the Nez Perce were nearby and they planned to speed for home in the morning. In fact, a scouting party under Yellow Wolf's command was already watching from the shadows, debating whether to kill or capture them. The next morning Yellow Wolf and his friends burst into the camp, primed for slaughter, only to be dissuaded by a charm offensive – one of the tourists, A. J. Arnold, gamely greeted the warrior with a handshake, a gift of some flour and sugar and the offer of a cooked breakfast. 'The food made our hearts friendly,' Yellow Wolf recalled, but he also took pains to explain to Arnold that this détente wasn't a guarantee of safety, as the caravan was not a cohesive whole – while most of the people were simply, pragmatically, trying to stay alive and free, there were now plenty of young warriors committed to killing every white man they saw, until they reached their own violent end: 'They heard me say that the Indians were double minded in what they can do.' The leader of the tourist party, a blustering individual by the name of George Cowan, chose to ignore these warnings and soured the mood by slapping down Arnold's food handouts. Now less inclined to secure his new friends' survival, Yellow Wolf decided to take the captives back to the main camp where they were immediately surrounded by storm-faced young fighters. Immediate bloodshed was stalled when the chiefs learned of the capture and detailed Poker Joe to resolve the situation. Putting the tourist's two female members out of harm's way, he then arranged a trade of all the tourists' possessions and horses for some broken-down mounts and their lives. George Cowan continued to be a tiresome presence, trying to convince the other men to perish in a blaze of glory – 'I was satisfied that I would be able to get only one shot, but felt sure that I would kill at least five Indians as they were sitting so close together' – but the trade seemed to be passing off peacefully, Poker Joe even assisting two of the party in making an early escape.

Two warriors, however, galloped into the tense scene with just one thing on their minds – Cowan was shot in the leg, while another tourist, Albert Oldham, was shot in the face, the bullet passing through both cheeks. With his shrieking wife cradling him in her arms, Cowan was then shot once more, a point-blank bullet to the forehead, and left in the dirt. In the commotion, three more tourists sprinted off, and Oldham stumbled into the bushes, his face in tatters. Of the ten captives, six were now wandering lost through Yellowstone without food or shelter, one of them the hapless Cowan, while the other three, Cowan's wife and her brother and teenage sister, were still being detained.

The prisoners probably had the best of it, as they spent the next day and night being well fed and cared for, the two women taking note of the remarkable good cheer with which the refugees were facing their travails, before Poker Joe released them with fresh horses, plentiful supplies and solemn pleas to spread the word that the Nez Perce sought only peace. Meanwhile, afflicted to varying degrees by hypothermia, hysteria and starvation, the six escapees spent the next four days or so cowering in bushes by day and wandering the mountains in search of salvation by night – Oldham suffered particularly, as he could barely breathe, let alone eat, through his ruined visage – before gradually being mopped up by General Howard's scouts and guards. The general was surprisingly uncharitable in his treatment of men he probably considered foolish thrill-seekers, offering them minimal food and scant medical care, but he did at least instruct his scouts to complete the final act in this melodrama – locating and burying George Cowan.

George Cowan, however, was proving a hard man to kill. In a testament to the inadequacies of nineteenth-century ballistics as much as to the superhuman thickness of his skull, the shot fired straight between Cowan's eyebrows had merely lodged in his forehead, knocking him senseless. Two hours later he awoke, and began to stumble off for help – only to realize he was being watched by a Nez Perce back-marker, who uncharitably shot Cowan yet again, in the left flank, and rode off. Now denied the use of both his legs, Cowan dragged himself into the bushes and then spent the next three days crawling nine miles back to his wagon, in search of food. There he enjoyed an emotional reunion with his faithful gun dog, Dido, who then accompanied Cowan on a further day's crawling back into camp, for a cup of coffee – but still no food. By now delirious and caked in blood and mud, Cowan slithered on for one more day, then gave up and waited for death, Dido dozing loyally at his side. But by a considerable stroke of luck, it was here that two of Howard's scouts were delighted to find that the corpse they'd been sent to bury had

The indestructible tourist George Cowan.

not yet entirely expired, and they gave the shattered Cowan some food, lit him a fire and left him for the main command to sweep up the next day.

Unfortunately, the doughty holidaymaker's travails were not yet completely finished; as he dozed by the fire that night, the moss bed which the scouts had kindly laid down for him caught a spark, setting fire to the invalid in his sleep. Crawling through the flames to safety, Cowan seriously burned his hands and knees. Unsurprisingly, as his friends reached the camp the next morning they found the filthy, emaciated, scalded, thrice-wounded survivor 'a most pitiful looking object'. Unable to walk or ride, Cowan was thrown in the back of a supply wagon and spent the next three weeks bouncing along the trails with Howard's army, until finally being reunited with his disbelieving wife, who had been wearing the widow's black on his behalf for almost a month. It was a remarkable odyssey, and, while there are very few people upon whom one might wish such an experience, it's hard to shake the suspicion that George Cowan was

just such a man. As soon as he had revived, his true nature resurfaced: 'My desire for life returned, and it seems the spirit of revenge
took complete possession of me. I knew that I would live, and I took
a solemn vow that I would devote the rest of my days to killing
Indians, especially Nez Perces.'

One surprising revelation from the memoirs of Cowan and the
other Radersburg tourists was the lack of urgency with which
Howard's command travelled through Yellowstone. Some of the
terrain was certainly tricky, with wagons having to be lowered down
near-vertical slopes by ropes, and difficulties with the supply train
also causing delays, but there was also a fair amount of sight-seeing
going on. A. J. Arnold, who accompanied Cowan in his ambulance
wagon, complained that at one day's camp 'there would not have
been an officer or a surgeon captured by the Indians, in case of
attack, as they were all off visiting the geysers'. Howard had employed
a gnarled, heroic-looking scout named S. G. Fisher to track the Nez
Perce, with the help of some Bannock Indian recruits, but this
experienced *montagnard* soon developed suspicions that the troops
were breaking insufficient sweat: 'Am tired of trying to get soldiers
and hostiles together,' he noted in his journal, 'Uncle Sam's boys are
too slow for business.' It's not certain that such tardiness cost lives,
but lives *were* sadly lost in Yellowstone while the army picked flowers.
Soon after releasing their three remaining captives, a group of Nez
Perce scouts encountered a second camp of ten tourists, killing one
and scattering the others into the forests – then, by cruel coincidence,
one of the survivors reached a bunk-house in the north of the park
just in time to meet a second scouting party, who shot him dead.
Yellow Wolf was part of that second group, and his recollection of the
words of the warrior who took aim at that unfortunate music
teacher, as he stood framed in the doorway of a wooden shack, offer
an insight into these far from motiveless crimes. 'Chulsum Hahlap
Kanoot (Naked-footed Bull) said to me, "My two young brothers and
next younger brother were not warriors. They and a sister were killed

at Big Hole. It was just like that man did that killing of my brothers and sister. He is nothing but a killer to become a soldier sometime. We are going to kill him now. I am a man! I am going to shoot him!'"

Back with the main caravan, very little is known of the non-combatants' journey through the National Park, except a sense of the difficulties they endured – eschewing the well-beaten paths meant beating a fresh one, driving and cajoling horses through dense forest, once again tearing flesh on the branches, and once again exceeding the physical limits of a female elder, who was left for the merciless Bannock scouts. The caravan's precise route is still unclear, but the terrain made their journey a slow one, allowing the tarrying Howard, taking the low roads, to stay within a few days' march. In early September, the Nez Perce left Yellowstone Park by its north-eastern extremes. Their remarkable exodus was now into its fourth calendar month – and the nights were beginning to grow cold.

After the Nez Perce left Yellowstone the supervisors of the fledgling park, terrified of never seeing another tourist, redoubled their efforts to expunge the plateau's Native heritage. Neighbouring reservation Agents were reminded that they were being paid to keep their wards in one place, the myth of the terrifying geysers was pushed hard and wide, and conservationists joined the calls to lock the Indians out; with poaching still rampant in the park, tribal hunting visits now looked like assaults on endangered species. In 1895 a Supreme Court ruling declared that National Park protection trumped any treaty promises that supposedly enshrined Native hunting or fishing rights. The gates were closed.

Not, however, that Yellowstone would be left untouched. Mandated to organize the park for popular 'benefit and enjoyment', and initially under great pressure from the railroads to attract tourists, Yellowstone's managers spent the next eighty years essentially running a zoo, cheerfully intervening in biology for the sake of the visitor experience. Picturesque mega-fauna such as elk and bison were protected to reproduce at sterling rates, overgrazing the range and squeezing out deer, beaver, moose and other species, while the wolves and mountain lions that preyed on the nibbling herds were shot right out of the park. Exotic fish that would be fun to catch were dumped into the rivers, while suppression of natural fires kept the tourists safe and the views clear. Strangest of all was the bear policy, informally established in 1920 when a black bear known as Jesse James (undoubtedly smarter than the average) learned to sit down in front of motorcars until the passengers threw food at him. 'Please feed the bears' became unofficial policy, and watching a grizzly tear through a trash dump or letting a black bear stand at your car window became the most treasured memories of most visits. The bear population was corrupted and every time a paw swiped in anger, and a human nose or ear came off, the perpetrator would be gunned down.

Unsurprisingly, the park's ecosystem went haywire, animal populations soared then plummeted in famines and winter die-ups, native species disappeared beneath the plagues of exotics, grasslands depleted and soil eroded, as the park managers pulled frantically at their barely understood levers of ecological control, organizing great culls and hunting purges of the bloated herds, poisoning rivers and denying the bears the food they now depended on, creating dangerous and doomed 'outlaws' in the process. Yellowstone was a great holiday – and its rampant species, particularly elk and bison, were slowly helping to repopulate America with pre-Columbine life – but it was an unholy, unsustainable mess.

But in the early 1960s, just as America was changing direction so would Yellowstone. The mass realization of the damage done to the natural continent drew attention to the National Parks, and their representation of a seemingly less sullied past. In 1963 the US Secretary of the Interior, Stewart Udall, announced a near-complete reverse from the 'benefit and enjoyment' policy. Overnight, man was taken out of the loop: 'park management shall recognize and respect wilderness as a whole environment of living things whose use and enjoyment depend on their continuing interrelationship *free from man's spoliation.*' Yellowstone was no longer to be a zoo or fun park, but an inspiring glimpse of the pristine, 'as nearly as possible in the condition that prevailed when the area was first visited by the white man,' Udall's chief adviser, A. Starker Leopold, declared. He went on, 'A national park should be a vignette of primitive America.' The following year this sentiment found another, still more remarkable, legislative expression, when the US government began to set aside areas of 'wilderness' for near-absolute protection from development or habitation – the act defined America's wilderness thus: 'an area where the earth and its community of life are untrammelled by man, where man himself is a visitor who does not remain.' The wilderness law was hugely popular – US Congress got more mail in support of this piece of legislation than any other in its history – and saved tens of millions of acres of magnificent landscape from ski lifts and oil rigs, lumbermen and subdivisions – but it was also a slightly gloomy triumph. This new style of protectionism encapsulated a dark, negative reflection of old-fashioned Western optimism, in which man was now divided from the natural planet no longer as a benign overlord, but as a pollutant, to be barred and controlled, the only alien on earth.

The obvious flaw in this endeavour was revealed by Leopold's admission of the actual chances of turning parks like Yellowstone back to their 'natural state' – recreating nature required, he declared, 'a set of ecologic skills unknown in the country today'. This was not true. At least six Native American tribes lived on reservations surrounding Yellowstone at that time, in dire economic straits but still in possession of oral histories that described the skills and knowledge which had sustained nine thousand years of human involvement in Yellowstone. And those nine thousand years of impact and interrelation had, of course, rendered the park anything but untouched long before the park rangers had arrived. The Indians had hunted, fished, harvested roots, used burning, grazed horses – but these facts inconvenienced the reinvention of Yellowstone as a window into the fifth day of Creation, and they were neglected. Across the continent, the wilderness areas placed under protection had each witnessed up to twelve thousand years of man living within nature, but were now being redefined as nature without man's corrupting touch. It was a fallacy, but for a nation that saw itself as young and unfinished, inhabiting a New World, it was a potent and alluring one.

The dream of preserving somehow unstained patches of the continent persists; as recently as 2002, the environmentalist publishers Island Press produced coffee-table photography of America's National Parks, now sanitized of their millennia-long Native inhabitants, to represent a mythical Eden of 'How It Was ...' before mankind's malevolent interference began. The pictures in fact capture a past that never was, no moment in history – there was man for twelve thousand years, and before that there were mammoths. As the Western geographer Paul F. Starrs observes: 'A geographer's assessment of all landscapes as cultural – no land is realistically "natural" without counting its human residents – would find no argument almost anyplace else in the world outside the United States.'

That a thin, black streak of misanthropy runs through much of America's environmental movement can, sadly, be scarce denied – a man-sized blind spot in their affection for living creatures that creates, to mix metaphors dreadfully, a pair of Achilles' heels. Firstly, their foes can too often present them as godless curmudgeons, embracing the trees too tightly to wrap an arm around their fellow human, and secondly their relationship to Native America is often ambivalent, genuflecting towards the ancient spiritual protestations of natural harmony, but not always embracing the historical and modern Indian reality of wishing to occupy and utilize the land-

scape, rather than simply to preserve it. As one fisheries employee
told me – 'Too many environmentalists just want to count the
salmon – the Indians actually want to catch and eat some.'

But a compelling barrage of explanation for this seeming lack of
common humanity can be found at the entrance to Yellowstone,
right along the route the Nez Perce used. As you climb up to Targhee
Pass, giant trophy homes ceaselessly interrupt the forest, their
towering driveway arches bearing such saccharine mottoes as 'For the
Good Times' and 'Welcome to Our Cabin', before you reach the
banks of Hebgen Lake, a drought-stricken reservoir besieged by acre
upon acre of scrappy, scarred, recovering timber industry clearcuts.
Ten miles down the road, the tireless Yellowstone Park rangers are
trying to recreate a vision of pre-Columbine Paradise by endless
tweaks and fiddles, rules and regulations – allowing fires, reintroducing wolves, re-seeding ranges, fiercely protecting the bears and
genuinely, seriously, debating whether the introduction of llamas,
lions and elephants might best replicate the ecosystem contributions
of long-extinct American species. But here, beyond the park's protection – though, science and common sense dictate, well within its
ecological interrelationships – the usual Western alliance of bureaucratic slackness, commercial interest and personal hubris has
flattened and paved the forest. Between the start of the rethinking of
Yellowstone, in the early 1960s and the early 1980s, the national
forests surrounding the park went ahead and trebled their timber
harvests, bird life and river health be damned. The harvesting was so
brutal that this eastern border, dividing the protected park from
the timberland free-for-all, was visible from space. Now, although
the logging has been largely curtailed for the sake of the Greater
Yellowstone Ecosystem, subdivision into holiday homes is the latest
threat to a landscape where grizzlies, elk and moose are supposed to
roam. Planning regulations are so chaotic and feeble that estimates of
how much land is being carved up are hard to determine, but a 1991
study estimated that a million acres of land abutting the park had

already been developed, and some Greater Yellowstone counties have seen their residential property treble in size since then. The developers are making a killing because a nearby National Park is such a 'desirable local amenity' – and they're doing their best to kill the park in the process. There are even threats to the landscape from the very people elected to protect it – in 2003, George W. Bush's Secretary of the Interior, Gale Norton, lobbied the United Nations to remove Yellowstone National Park from its list of at risk World Heritage sites, to make it easier to permit oil and gas drilling on the edge of the plateau.

In the summer of 2006 a final, bewildering threat could be found at the nearby deadpan-titled Chief Joseph Elk Farm – a 'canned hunting' operation where rugged outdoorsmen could pay around $6000 to hand-pick a farmed stag from an enclosure, shoot it and stuff it. As I passed through the region, part of the farm's herd had just escaped, threatening to wander into the park and despoil the obsessively protected genetic integrity of the Yellowstone elk. While frantic Fish and Game employees were desperately trying to gun down the rogue beasts before they had a chance to corrupt the priceless wild bloodstock, the owner of the farm was telling anyone who'd listen that he planned to sue the interfering Feds for violating his 'bedrock inalienable right' to do exactly what he fancied on his own land: 'They took my private property ... But America will soon know that there's a mountain man out here that's not going to let the government do it.' Unsurprisingly, the negligent farmer had become a local celebrity, hero to that half of Idaho that still worshipped the pioneer spirit and loathed ecologically minded interference, and hate figure to those that had left all that behind. In an unexpected twist, the controversy reignited when his daughter strolled to victory in the 2007 Miss Idaho pageant – and then refused to be photographed with the property-thieving governor of the state. The farmer was reportedly considering a run for the governor's mansion himself in 2010.

Faced with this kind of evidence, the conclusion that the wilderness campaigners of the 1960s drew, and many of their descendants in the environmental movement still draw today, seems more understandable – that the American economy simply couldn't be trusted with the American continent. In a system where restraint was too often presented as a personal flaw and a political crime, compromise was impossible, and the only resistance was all or nothing. It was best to fight to save what they could, fence it off completely, ban every human activity bar the campfire song, and move on to their next full-bore battle with the hard-charging pioneers of progress.

The Yellowstone grey wolf is a mercilessly dedicated hunter, not an efficient killer but a relentless one, happy to brawl and scratch away at prey, more of a mugger than an assassin. One of its most illuminating tactics, though, is simply to walk its prey to death. A pack will keep a moose or elk on the move for days, working shifts to keep the beast from settling, eating or drinking, until exhaustion triumphs and the kill is easy. Battling their way out of the National Park and into the neighbouring Absaroka Mountain range, the Nez Perce must have suspected that the US Army had such a fate planned for them – endless pursuit, ceaseless movement, leading to their ultimate exhaustion and surrender.

But as the caravan tackled the ragged, crumbling Absaroka slopes, General Sherman finalized his preparations for a more dramatic, decisive end to this adventure; while the Nez Perce had been struggling through the dense Yellowstone forests, the general's four armies had converged, blocking all the refugees' likely next steps. The journey down from the frigid plateau to the bounty and friendship of the rolling Crow plains followed one of two rivers – either the Clark Fork or the Stinking Water. Both were now guarded by troops – and turning back was an impossibility, with Howard still lurking behind. Briefed on these manoeuvres, the newspapers salivated at the thought of the crushing victory to come, the Red Napoleon finally brought to heel by William Tecumseh Sherman, the military colossus of his generation. Across the Northwest, generals and colonels hovered nervously over telegraph machines, waiting for the latest intelligence. The end was in sight. The Nez Perce had nowhere to go.

CHAPTER NINE

CRESCENDO

'Our good luck consists more in the natural advantages of our country than in the scale of our genius. Those advantages are gradually disappearing'

Rocky Mountain Husbandman, 1882

'Our ideas will overcome your ideas ... We Indians will show this country how to act human. Someday this country will revise its constitution, its laws, in terms of human beings, not property'

VINE DELORIA, JR, Sioux, 1971

COLONEL SAMUEL D. STURGIS was a man in need of a victory. In the ebb and flow of popular acclaim that characterized nineteenth-century military command, his stock was at rock bottom, following a spectacular rout towards the end of the Civil War. In June 1864 Sturgis had led nearly eight thousand Union troops onto the field against a Confederate force of fewer than five thousand, at the Battle of Brice's Crossroads, and had somehow engineered a running retreat that crossed almost the whole state of Mississippi, mislaying two thousand casualties and prisoners as he went. Sturgis was demoted from brigadier general to colonel for his efforts and booted out West, where his career languished. For a vain man who liked to

Colonel Samuel D. Sturgis.

pose for photographs with his right hand resting, Bonaparte-style, within his tunic, this must have been unendurable – but now Sturgis was in command of part of Sherman's dragnet of four armies, leading around 360 members of the Seventh Cavalry to guard the Clark Fork Canyon against the oncoming Nez Perce. From the northeast corner of Yellowstone, the Indians' only other route down from the high country was to take the Stinking Water Canyon,* where another force was rushing to block them – but if the caravan did try to descend into the Clark Fork, via its narrow, precipitous scree gullies, they'd surely be trapped in a shooting gallery, picked off by Sturgis's men while General Howard blocked their retreat. The trap was set, and this ageing officer had a fifty-fifty shot at redemption.

Not surprisingly, while his men relaxed and enjoyed fishing and rock climbing, Sturgis was jittery. He couldn't stop relocating his camp, based on every incoming snippet of intelligence and rumour.

---

* Since renamed the Shoshone River.

He fretted about the lack of communication with General Howard. He sent a pair of volunteer scouts into the high country to try and locate the Nez Perce, but they didn't return. He sent further scouting parties onto the plateau, and they found the arrow-punctured bodies of the two volunteers, one of them still alive.

Then, the scouts caught a pulse-raising glimpse of glory – the Nez Perce horse herd, battling through the high country, heading south. They raced back to Sturgis and shared their conclusion – from where they'd spotted the caravan there was no possible route down into the Clark Fork: the descending gullies were just a few feet wide and barely negotiable without a rope. The Nez Perce were surely heading down to the Stinking Water, and the other army. It didn't take Sturgis long to reach a decision – his force would not also serve by standing and waiting, they would head into the hills and track the Nez Perce down. The command set off, and for two cold, rain-drenched days they sought out the Nez Perce trail, following traces of hoof prints, catching moonlit glimpses of what looked like distant sentinels. Eventually, a trail emerged, but with a curious addition: 'About noon we in the advance were surprised at discovering wheel tracks apparently leading farther into the mountains,' Trooper Goldin recalled. 'They were evidently made by a two-wheeled cart of some sort!' Shrugging off the anomaly and pushing on, the soldiers struck a clear, fresh trail, the wide footprint of the caravan leading, unexpectedly, back north towards the Clark Fork. The Nez Perce were surely close by, and Sturgis drove his men and their tiring horses on for one last surge. 'The trail was growing fresher every hour,' Goldin recalled, 'and we lost all sense of fatigue and hunger in the excitement of a prospective fight.' Within reach of a famous capture, the troopers dragged and cajoled their horses down the perilous gullies into the Clark Fork Canyon and pushed on in fervent pursuit, only to find another perturbing clue in their path – an abandoned US military horse. With realization slowly dawning, Sturgis led his men down the dripping canyon, and when General

Howard's campfires came into view he called a halt and resigned himself to another humiliation: he'd been chasing the United States Army. The Nez Perce had somehow doubled-back, vanishing into the forest as Sturgis's troops had blundered past them towards the Stinking Water, and had then climbed down into the Clark Fork, leaving the plateau via an exit that the overeager Sturgis had left wide open for them. Abandoning his guard and wandering the hills, the colonel had then taken third place in a procession out of the mountains, behind Howard's poor second, while the Nez Perce were already fifty miles north, in open country. Even by the lax linguistic standards of the US Army, Colonel Sturgis's vocabulary that evening was reportedly shocking.

The entire truth of how the Nez Perce eluded Colonel Sturgis will never be known; as with the Lolo crossing, an astonishing feat of wilderness travel seems to have been considered so unremarkable as barely to merit a mention in the protagonists' memoirs. Some newspapers surmised that they'd used magical powers to slip unnoticed past the troops, and scores of interested parties, myself included, have been left bewildered by long hikes into these rugged canyonlands, reduced to craning up at the fearful, cramped ravines down which the Nez Perce must have dragged and whipped their horses, hardly beginning to imagine the effort and courage involved. It's not at all certain that the chiefs even knew that Sturgis blocked their path; all their endeavours may have been designed just to throw the chasing Howard off their scent. Whatever the motives, an imperfect picture of their actions can be pieced together.

As they neared the edge of Yellowstone, the caravan seems to have adopted a quite sensible informal policy of counter-intelligence, succinctly expressed by Yellow Wolf – 'All white men were spies. Enemies to be killed.' Through either this bloodshed or their own incompetence, Howard and Sturgis were unable to communicate the refugees' position to one another, and only the master scout George Fisher, by now sick of babysitting the US Army, had kept on their trail.

According to Fisher's findings, the Nez Perce had clambered up to the final ridgeline of the plateau – in itself a shattering effort, up an unforgiving hillside now barely conquered by a switch-backing, radiator-burning mountain road – and pointed south towards the Stinking Water, a move Sturgis's scouts had witnessed. But after a couple of miles of heading south, they'd sold their pursuers a dummy, doubling back and hiding their tracks – 'To do this, the hostiles "milled", drove their ponies around in every direction, when, instead of going out of the basin in the direction they had been travelling and across an open plain, they turned short off to the north, passing along the steep side of the mountain through the timber for several miles.' And while the Nez Perce were concealed, traversing the high, forested shoulder of this giant mountain ridge, Sturgis had barrelled past them on lower ground, clueless. Then, somehow, the men, women and children, the elderly and the wounded, had clambered down from the high country via the near-cliff face of the Clark Fork Canyon, now left unguarded, and had shot out of its jaws and north towards the Crow plains, four armies converging on thin air behind them.

Though the acclaim for the Yellowstone plateau escape was placed, wrongly, on a single pair of shoulders, the praise itself was fully justified. To have escaped with an army of young men would have been remarkable, but to do so with five hundred non-combatants and thousands of horses in tow was almost inexplicable. When news of the manoeuvre spread through the ranks of the US Army, some soldiers began to express the view that perhaps this young Chief Joseph, and not William Tecumseh Sherman, was America's greatest living general.

There is some confusion over the few days that followed this great escape, as the Nez Perce made their way north. They were now in the

gently undulating grassland that lay between the high country and the bleak, featureless northern plains, a bucolic respite dominated by the Yellowstone River and its various tributaries. This was Crow country, guaranteed by an 1868 treaty, and some reports suggest that Looking Glass made diplomatic overtures to the local chiefs, seeking out the protective alliance that he'd long promised the caravan. General Howard, by contrast, telegraphed his fellow generals declaring that the Nez Perce, disillusioned by the attitude of the Bannocks, Salish and Shoshone, had already abandoned all hope of an alliance with the Crow, and were fleeing due north to Canada. This uncertainty was probably reflected in the camp itself – the Nez Perce, one suspects, were keeping their options open, letting the evolving situation dictate their plan. One thing was certain: decisions had to be made on the move; even if there wasn't total agreement on where they were heading, stasis was not an option. The sensible direction to take was north.

The caravan spread out considerably for a few days, seemingly enjoying this tranquil landscape. There was hunting to be done, with the possibility of encountering the great northern buffalo herd, or scattered groups of antelope and longhorn sheep – and there was always the continuing task of terrorizing the local settlers, ensuring they were too scared to ride out and share the Nez Perce's where-abouts. A few homes were burned, and two miners lost their lives.

The passengers of the 13 September Helena City stagecoach would also have a tale to tell. As they approached the Brockway ranch on the Yellowstone, the travellers – including, according to some reports, an itinerant dentist, an English gentleman cowboy and a local vaudeville performer known as Fanny Clark – were signalled to by some settlers cowering in the brush. Spotting an onrushing war party, the passengers took flight, sprinting to the scrubland just in time to avoid the young Nez Perce fighters, who ransacked the coach and then, demonstrating once again that there was always time for fun, set off on a joyride across the open country. Army scouts tracking the Nez

Perce's movements reported the unexpectedly frivolous sight of 'a big stage coach with its four horses trotting along, and on the box was an Indian driver, with nearly half a dozen other Indians squatting on the roof'. When the warriors spotted the scouts, however, they rapidly remounted their own horses and sped back towards the non-combatants. It was clear that the army was much closer than the tarrying, relaxing Nez Perce had believed.

For Samuel Sturgis had been marching hard in search of his reputation. After running into Howard at the Clark Fork, the apoplectic colonel had declared that his horses were not yet played out, and his men should attempt to chase the caravan down, while Howard adopted his usual position as johnny-come-lately. After just a few hours' rest, the men had set off before dawn and rode until midnight, then rose in darkness again and spurred their weakening horses on – until, by mid-morning, the evidence of exhaustion could no longer be ignored and Sturgis was forced to call a rest. His men lay down and passed out. Giving the order to unsaddle the horses, Sturgis seemingly gave up the chase. But barely five miles away, concealed by the folds of the land, the Nez Perce caravan was only just breaking camp to move on. When the army scouts spotted them, complete with stagecoach fun ride, it was more panic than battle stations: 'We heard a shout from the lower end of camp,' Goldin remembered. 'Looking up we saw Pawnee Tom, one of our best scouts, coming down the valley at a wild gallop, yelling "Indians! Indians!" at the top of his voice.' The cavalry saddled up in a mania and galloped at full pelt towards their quarry.

The Nez Perce were similarly shaken – they were in wide-open country, where an attack from four hundred flying cavalrymen would be disastrous. A few miles ahead, a shallow canyon led up onto the rolling tablelands, the cleft forming a rocky gorge that would make a perfectly defensible bottleneck in which to block the troops while the non-combatants sped north. But if the camp was cut off before they reached the canyon's jaws, all was lost. The race was on –

two clouds of dust tore across the empty, echoing landscape, converging on a single point.

The cavalry divided, looking to encircle the canyon entrance. The Nez Perce accelerated, urging their horses on, but they seemed to be losing the race as Sturgis's fastest chargers thundered into the canyon's jaws. But then, as ever, the fighting prowess of the individual Nez Perce made all the difference – as Yellow Wolf put it, 'We had our warrior ways.' Lone raiders on horseback and snipers who positioned themselves above the canyon floor cut the cavalry down, forcing a retreat, and the non-combatants started to file between the boulders and trees to safety.

At which point Samuel Sturgis finally established his mediocre place in history, ordering his troops to dismount and advance on foot. It was a bizarre decision – even down the narrowing canyon, a full-steam, four-hundred-horse charge would have been hard to resist – but Sturgis seems to have decided that the Nez Perce wanted an old-fashioned open-field battle, and was starting to position his men for a lengthy game of chess. In fact, the Indians wanted nothing of the sort, simply wishing to protect their women and children, but now they had a sluggish, immobile opponent to hold off, which they did with ease. Sturgis may well have been nervous about a death-or-glory cavalry charge into an unknown valley – his son had died in just such an endeavour at Little Big Horn the year before – but his men certainly weren't: some reports claim a few troopers were in tears as they tried to dissuade the colonel from calling the dismount. Whatever his motives, the outcome was that a few Nez Perce warriors held off the pedestrian soldiers in the gorge all afternoon, while their caravan drove on until darkness, out of harm's way. The Nez Perce, who lost no fighters at Canyon Creek, while Sturgis lost three, barely afforded the whole incident the status of a battle – but one truly shattering revelation dominated their thoughts as they sped due north across the tablelands.

They had spotted Crow, fighting side by side with the US Army.

It should be stressed here that there was (and, indeed, is) no universal brotherhood of Native America, no cast-iron alliance against the white man. History would have been unimaginably different if that had been the case. Pragmatism, old scores or simply thirst for glory often led tribes to ally with the USA against its enemy of the day – the Nez Perce themselves had served with distinction as scouts in the Northwestern outbreaks that followed the 1855 treaty. In desperate times, protecting your own interests often needed to take precedence over suspect justice.

As soon as it had become clear the Nez Perce were heading their way, the Crow had been placed under pressure to demonstrate their allegiance to the Stars and Stripes. Army commanders had arrived at their Indian Agency on the Yellowstone River offering generous terms for scouting work – in essence, the Crow were promised they could keep everything they stole from the Nez Perce. The alternative to donating their young men to the army's cause never needed stating – if the Crow joined a rebellion, they would first pay in blood and then, inevitably, in land.

The choice, one suspects, was simple. Although in the past the Crow and Nez Perce had been allies against the Sioux, and Nez Perce families had been allowed to take up residence on the Crow buffalo plains, times were changing. The Crow chief Sacred Raven had the gift of visions, and as a young man he'd been visited by a white spectre, bearing advice: 'I come from the land of the rising sun, where many, many white men live. They are coming and will in time take possession of your land. At that time you will be a great chief of your tribe. Do not oppose these but deal with them wisely and all will turn out all right.' As the Crow's tribal history was replete with grudges against their Native neighbours, this seemed like good advice, and the bands had accepted a reservation treaty, an inevitable rewrite reducing the reservation by over three-quarters, and the curtailment of their semi-nomadic lifestyle, all without rebellion – and in 1876 they'd served as scouts in Custer's campaign against their plains rivals. A devastating smallpox pandemic in the 1840s had also torn the fighting heart out of the nation – reducing their numbers from around eight thousand to perhaps as low as one thousand. Although the Crow no doubt felt sympathy for the Nez Perce, by 1877 they were clearly in no shape to join a bloody war of resistance, and they took the army's coin.

For the Nez Perce, though, the betrayal was unforgivable. Yellow Wolf craned from a hilltop to identify the unfamiliar pursuers: 'I rode closer. *Eeh!* Crows! A new tribe fighting Chief Joseph. Many snows the Crows had been our friends. But now, like the Bitterroot Salish, turned enemies. My heart was just like fire … They were fighting against their best friends!'

For the Nez Perce chiefs the diminishing possibility of holding out on the buffalo plains until Idaho calmed down had now disappeared entirely: their only sanctuary lay beyond the United States, in the Old Woman Country. And they had to head north fast, for they now faced a worthy adversary. While Sturgis patched up his wounded and started a limping pursuit, the Crow warriors sped on ahead of him, catching the Nez Perce and attacking them where it would hurt most – harassing the non-combatants and the horse herd. At least three Nez Perce died fending off these raids, which lasted for two days, and some of the herd was stolen, but the caravan pushed on, Poker Joe returning to his exhausting schedule of dawn-to-dusk marches, the fatigue now exacerbated by the damp autumn nights.

Gradually, though, the Crow fell back and the Nez Perce were left alone on the great, bewildering emptiness of the northern plains, a becalmed, draining, seemingly limitless grassland. This elemental place, at the mercy of an intemperate sky, was, in 1877, the last great unconquered space in the new America, a sort of geographical bogeyman of wild creatures and haughty, lawless tribes that few white men had ever seen and even fewer had settled in. Pushing on west to Oregon, California and the Rocky Mountain mines, the great wave of settlers that had been the bane of the Nez Perce had left the

The northern plains rolling away from Canyon Creek.

treeless, wind-scorched northern plains until last, and had not yet summoned the courage to arrive here. Now unconcerned by spying eyes, the Nez Perce caravan could rush on through these empty rolls of land, beneath the ceaseless slate clouds, sprinting north, the onset of winter a new opponent to race.

Surely, though, as they reached the Musselshell River, they noticed the first small changes in the ecosystem they'd previously visited for hunts, celebrations and wars. And here, before them, was the most significant explanation for the Crow's refusal to rebel – and why there would never again be a great plains uprising, not from the Cheyenne, the Sioux, the Arapaho or Plains Cree, the Assiniboine or any of the thirty or more tribes whose independent way of life was drifting away or had already passed, just as the Nez Perce were marching past, in several million puffs of smoke. This very year, another of Sacred Raven's visions was beginning to come true on the northern plains, perhaps the greatest change of all those wrought upon the ancient West, and the most damaging to the cause of Indian independence. In his dream, Sacred Raven had seen the great herds of the North American bison disappear from the plains, to be replaced by countless battalions of the white man's 'horse buffalo', an excessively romantic description for the humble cow.

The drizzle was swirling listlessly around Pioneer Park, on the edge of Billings, Montana, not so much rainfall as the inside of a murky cloud. One might charitably surmise that the teenagers milling around the trees with a comparable lack of purpose were drawing their blank, disdainful mood from the weather, but the teachers who were half-heartedly imploring them to gather closer to the temporary, scaffolded stage at the centre of the park suggested that the students' ennui was slightly more endemic. On the escarpment above the park, lost in the day's cold soup, lay the graves of the two miners killed in 1877 while the Nez Perce had passed through here. Today, the guest speakers fought the breeze to be heard through the damp, back-feeding PA system. This was Montana American Indian Heritage Day, a state-sponsored effort to remind the local young people of the cultural wealth that lay beyond their city limits, in the past and present of the great northern plains. For whatever reason, this batch didn't particularly want to know.

The Crow spokesman, Burton Pretty on Top, welcomed us to the festival, maintaining his statesmanlike poise beneath a black Stetson as a few of the teenagers were corralled into joining the opening friendship dance by a handful of increasingly embarrassed and furious locals – the teachers, as if seeking to fulfil their own stereotype, had largely given up. A towering Native American college basketball star was brought to the stage to give a speech on healthy living, and captured the mood astutely – 'I remember when I was at school I didn't really listen to motivational speakers either – and, to be honest, I'm struggling for motivation a little myself up here.' Then an elder known as Henry 'Sarge' Old Horn was invited to give a short talk on the unreported Native American influence on the Founding Fathers – to which just three non-Indians, myself included, sat and listened.

Standing with faintly intimidating poise at the side of the stage, Janine Pease Pretty on Top appeared to have seen all this before. One of the event's organizers, she was a long-standing heroine of Crow culture and intellect – the first woman from the tribe to earn a doctorate, she was head of the blossoming Little Big Horn College, churning out an ever-growing number of Indian graduates. 'We often organize cultural events to which people come from thousands of miles away, as far away as Russia, and they even come back the following year – but we might not get a single visitor from next door,' she told me, appearing quite unconcerned.

Such confidence may not be misplaced. What was now happening in the old Crow country – and something was certainly afoot – might not yet have been on the radar of the white culture that dominated the land today, but it soon enough would be: 'We're now the second fastest-growing ethnic group in the state, behind only the Hispanics,' the professor smiled. 'We're gaining strength.' Just then, as if to prove her point, a crew-cut barrel of a man came marching over the lawn towards us, minions in tow, looking for hands to shake. John Tester, Democratic candidate for that autumn's senatorial election, currently stuck in a statistical tie and in no mood to ignore a burgeoning constituency, was paying a flying visit to the festival. Teenagers might not recognize the green shoots of change – but pollsters do.

In the years after the Nez Perce had fled their lands, the Crow had been rewarded for their loyalty with no fewer than three enforced reductions of their reservation, as they were driven into the eastern corner of their holdings by the discovery of lucrative coal deposits to the west, and by the ceaseless demands for fresh land by the new kings of the northern plains, the cattle ranchers. Confined to reservation life and sorely mistreated by the white bureaucrats in charge, the Crow were then subjected to an astonishingly spiteful assault on the remnants of their identity – in a war against their horses.

The Crow's veneration for horse culture was perhaps even greater than the Nez Perce's, as a result of the coincidence of the tribe reaching the northern plains in their own historical movements at around the same time that the creature perfectly suited to war and hunting on the great steppes made its return. By the 1870s, personal wealth – and generosity – was measured predominantly in stock, and the Crow used their reservation lands predominantly as breeding and grazing grounds. But, sadly, so did the arriving cattlemen, and they manoeuvred their political puppets towards restraining the Crow herds, deceitfully classifying them as 'wild'. In 1923 the government put a bounty on Crow horses – and over forty thousand were gunned down in a few years, sackfuls of their ears exchanged for federal cash. The horses all but disappeared from the plains – and, denied their defining career, pastime and passion, the Crow had been driven to their nadir.

But not to extinction. Around the time of the horse war, the population of the Crow began to recover, climbing gradually, until by the turn of the twenty-first century they were approaching the same level as before the 1840s' smallpox disaster – around seven thousand. And the growth was continuing – the US Census had mapped out that Montana's total Native American population was set to bloom by 74 per cent between 1995 and 2025, eventually clearing ninety thousand souls. Gaining strength indeed.

And as the Crow had revived so they had gradually loosened the grip of the bureaucrats from their affairs, allowing a steady, determined cultural recovery. It became best expressed in the famous Crow Fair, the giant annual Native American and Canadian gathering, up to forty thousand Indians collaborating in song, dance and sport on the Crow Reservation. Later in the day in Pioneer Park, I chatted with Sarge Old Horn. He was almost disbelieving of the change he had witnessed in post-war Crow country: 'The Fair, when it started, it wasn't what it is today – it was pitiful. Nothing was organized, you didn't know when anything was going to start, people just turned up and then dispersed. Now it's such a huge success – and all of these people suddenly want to be Crow. They're all trying to out-Crow the real Crows. But it's like the Masons, it's like the Elks – hey, it's like the Ku Klux Klan – you have to learn the ways, the beliefs, and then you have to be accepted into the group. You can't just play a drum.'

The irony of a man who'd just been comprehensively ignored by several hundred young people expressing his displeasure at being excessively admired and imitated is an important one. It seems that while many of the people whose ancestors settled on the old Crow land are still largely indifferent to their neighbours' recent revival, the tribe is plagued from further afield by relentless wannabe affection and affectation. Crow ceremonies such as the Sun Dance and their Spirit Quest have been appropriated as 'spiritual cleansing' rituals by nearby luxury spas, run by dubious white 'medicine women', sacred carved pipes have resurfaced as pothead paraphernalia and Crow Fair now generously hosts everyone from German scout groups to Japanese coach tours. But such attention is little more than a diversion and an irritant to the Crow themselves, much more interested in maintaining the steady but incomplete progress exemplified in the proudest moments of the Fair – the parades of the tribe's horses. After a momentous effort over the past two generations, the Crow are back breeding, riding and racing their most treasured possessions, to be found grazing on the northern grasslands. They have a small number of ancient companionship, too, from a carefully protected herd of the other beast that defined the short heyday of the plains Indian – and the creature whose story the Nez Perce passed over next.

The herd was in residence as the Nez Perce reached the Musselshell River, a tantalizing glimpse of the respite towards which Looking Glass had been trying to lead the caravan since July. Here, along the clear, fast-flowing river, under the benign watch of the cottonwood trees in their autumn foliage, were berries ready for harvest, and buffalo and antelope to hunt at leisure. There would have been nowhere better to sustain the village until the rage of the US Army had died down.

But such a détente was clearly out of the question now, and Poker Joe pushed the pace still further, fording the Musselshell and driving through the wind-whipped Judith Gap, a wide saddle of plains country between two great mountainous outcrops. It appears likely that the caravan divided to try and maximize the hunting as they passed; suspecting the Nez Perce might eventually travel this way, an army detachment had been sent out in August to burn the grass here, and remove the herds, but enough game remained to help stave off the encroaching threat of starvation. But the caravan's health was deteriorating nonetheless, hunger and exhaustion, old age and injuries all worsened by the enfeebling cold. Like so many of the planet's oceanic landscapes, the northern plains feel, instinctively, as if they've settled at sea level – but Judith Gap, a local low point between towering hills, actually sits higher than the sub-arctic plateau of Scotland's Cairngorm Mountains. Such elevation brings an uncompromising, all-or-nothing climate, and by late September the bitter nights were being joined by consistently miserable days. One further challenge had also arisen – the Crow had enjoyed some success in their horse-stealing raids, and the Nez Perce now had fewer fresh mounts. The horses were the engines of the flight, and broken stock would mean slowing to a pedestrian crawl. Poker Joe had to strike an uncertain balance between riding too hard and travelling too slow.

In fact, the threat of pursuit had all but passed, for the plains had already broken Samuel Sturgis. As his men stumbled into the

Musselshell, still several days behind the Nez Perce, the colonel was forced to concede that they could chase no further, and he called a halt. Ecstatic, his shattered troopers, who'd been eating horsemeat for days, scattered to enjoy the fruit crop, the chance of a bath and the hunting opportunities that lay all around them. When General Howard rode into the luxuriating camp almost a week later, he and Sturgis shared another rueful failure, and devised a fresh strategy.

Howard had long suspected that he would never overrun the Nez Perce, and, with less than two weeks' travel to the Canadian border, there was no denying it. The only hope was somehow to slow the caravan down, and buy time – giving Sherman the chance to manoeuvre one last army into the Nez Perce's path before they crossed over the line. Howard decided to do this by easing off the chase himself, guessing the Nez Perce would relish the chance to loiter north, rather than continue their charge. The caravan had in fact christened Howard 'General the Day after Tomorrow', in recognition of the consistency with which they'd kept his troops a steady two days' riding away, and the general's last gamble was that stretching that lead would hold no attraction to the chiefs. He and Sturgis combined forces and set off north – at sightseeing pace.

For their broken-down troops, who, realistically, were in no shape for a forced chase (leading some historians to suggest that Howard and Sturgis fabricated their slow-down strategy *after* the event, to confect the appearance of control), this was a golden opportunity – to see the last great unsettled space, and, much more important, to partake in its greatest pleasure, buffalo meat. They passed by great black herds numbering hundreds of thousands almost every day of their gentle march, and had the time to fill their bellies from what, at the time, seemed like a limitless natural larder. One scout named Cruikshank recalled, 'As we entered the Judith Basin I helped to kill several buffalo for the army,' before adding ruefully, 'I killed many of these animals on the plains, but this was my last buffalo hunt.' For at precisely the same time as the Nez Perce and their pursuers were crossing the northern plains, another ragtag collection of outsiders were making their first, tentative visit to this corner of the continent – the men who made their living from buffalo hides.

It's unwise to dwell too long on the fate of the North American buffalo – the most routinely revisited episode in the continent's ecological history is also its least comprehensible, the hardest to believe without seeing. Pound for pound, the buffalo (in fact two interwoven species, *Bison bison*, mainly on the plains, and *Bison athabascae*, mostly in the woods) was quite simply the greatest animal ever to walk the earth. More biomass was dedicated to generating this creature's hunched shoulders, tapered feet and obnoxious disposition than any other creation in the planet's known history. Perhaps sixty million beasts utterly dominated the ecosystem of the continent's central grassland, cropping and fertilizing the flora, sustaining the predators and, for a brief period, supporting an explosion in human cultures. Tiny nomadic bands of plains Indians had followed the herds on foot for millennia before the horse returned to America, but the arrival of equestrian culture coincided with a litany of Native westward migrations – caused, to a considerable degree, by white activities in the East – and by the eighteenth century there were up to thirty distinct cultures living, hunting and fighting on the plains. Itinerant, colourful, more than faintly macho, these cultures, such as the Sioux, Cheyenne and Blackfoot, were the model for the 'Red Indian' stereotype of a thousand cinematic raiding parties and smoke signals, a considerable irony considering their very brief and recent heyday. And at the centre of these young civilizations was the buffalo, the primary source of meat, shelter and countless other needs, from bone-carved tools to intestinal gourds. Herds determined a village's movements and locations, while hunting provided identity and stature for young men and the ceaseless intertribal wars of the Great Plains era were often sparked by conflicts over killing fields. As you would expect, this close bond with a ubiquitous natural presence almost always acquired a spiritual element, with some tribes' belief systems conceiving of humans and buffalo as almost interchangeable, while others acquired creation stories in which this astonishing natural bounty sprang from underground caves, almost as a gift from earth to man. Rituals of song and dance were used to request, prepare for and celebrate good hunting.

Thanks to what would soon follow, another discourteous historical squabble has opened up over just how reverential this relationship truly was – in the excessive, *Dances with Wolves*-style deification of plains culture, Indians are portrayed kneeling in tearful prayer over each fallen buffalo brother, and proceeding mindfully to put everything but the snort to good use, while the gainsayers point to anecdotal and archaeological evidence of Natives' wanton hunting and wasteful butchering to undermine such suggestions of innate respect and care. While the disparate plainsmen may have lacked the physical capacity to wipe out the buffalo, the sceptics suggest, there were no spiritual or social barriers to such destruction – with the guns and numbers, they would have cleared the grasslands themselves.

Based as it is on defining an imaginary history – the one in which the Europeans reach North America, realize it's already taken and go home – this quarrel will never be concluded to universal satisfaction: for by the time the plainsmen caught on that the buffalo was disappearing, they had already lost the power to apply their stated philosophies of sacred interdependence, to demonstrate if their reverence was genuine or disingenuous. Once again the chance truly to live their values was stolen.

The first white arrivals on the plains were less complex – they saw the buffalo as nothing more than free profit, literally easy meat. From the 1820s hunters began to nibble away at the great herds, collecting their winter coats as robes and trading the questionable delicacy of pickled buffalo tongue. As the operations expanded, particularly in the southern plains of modern Nebraska, Kansas and Texas, young Indian men who'd been severed from their traditions by reservation life and the unscrupulous provision of whiskey served as foot soldiers to burgeoning trading operations, which by the mid-1860s were shipping east a quarter of a million furs in a good year. The railroads added additional pressure, hiring men such as William 'Buffalo Bill' Cody to shoot buffalo to feed their workers, and dividing the plains into a northern and southern herd with their iron road.

Then, in 1871, the tanning technique for turning buffalo hides into leather was finalized and the frenzy began. Now that buffalo could be cheaply converted to saddles, belts and boots, particularly for the lucrative market of the British Army, tens of thousands of hunters, skinners and traders poured onto the plains. For the next three years the annual slaughter on the southern plains ran into the millions, with the waste beyond control – it's estimated that ten buffalo died for every one skin that ever made boots. This the Indians had never seen before – as the Sioux leader Red Cloud lamented, 'Where the Indian killed one buffalo, the hide and tongue hunters killed fifty.' Unsurprisingly, in 1874 it was buffalo hunters who sparked off the last Indian rebellion on the southern plains, when seven hundred Comanche and Cheyenne warriors attacked a hunting camp, setting off the Red River War. By the spring of 1875, though, Nelson A. Miles had broken the impoverished rebels and pacified the southern plains forever. An ecosystem and a culture were passing in unison.

Much has been made of America's military and political leaders wishing for precisely that unhappy coincidence, most notoriously in Western commander Philip Sheridan's exhortation to let the hunters wipe out 'the Indian's commissary' – 'For the sake of a lasting peace, let them kill, skin and sell until the buffalo is exterminated. Then your prairies can be covered with speckled cattle and the festive cowboy.' The government certainly offered little resistance to the great kill, and smatterings of help – army posts reportedly gave free bullets to the hunters – but while Sheridan's malodorous sentiments were no doubt sincere, it's wrong to think that the government planned or managed the great kill. In the late nineteenth-century

West, the government no more controlled the economy than the weather – the hunters were an unstoppable, millennial plague. By 1877, the vast southern herd was all but destroyed, and the hunters turned their attention north.

Here, the joint reign of the buffalo and the plainsman had proved more durable. Throughout the 1860s and early 1870s, white encroachment on these great grasslands had been feeble and isolated, terrorized by the great Sioux and Cheyenne fighting nations. In 1868 Red Cloud had negotiated the only treaty ever signed on Native terms, the puny US military presence having to concede that his Powder River lands were closed to passage and settlement – but, tellingly, such closure was qualified: 'so long as the buffalo may range thereon in such numbers as to justify the chase.'

With the plains still unsafe for all but the hardiest white hunters, Red Cloud could never have foreseen that clause becoming active. Indeed, by 1870 the scattered, petrified northern plains pioneers had been reduced to organizing gold prospecting expeditions in the hope of starting a rush, which would in turn precipitate a deadlock-breaking conflict. As the early twentieth-century grassland historian Ernest Staples Osgood put it, 'the people of Montana and Wyoming rather welcomed an Indian War', illustrating his point with a local newspaper editorial which huffed that without a flashpoint of some sort 'the tedious process of Indian extinction must go on for years'.

The people of Montana and Wyoming got their wish: in 1874 an expedition under Custer's command found gold in the Black Hills of Dakota, the sacred centre of the Sioux universe, and the rush began. The war that followed would be best remembered for Custer's fall at Little Big Horn, but it was the military reprisals that followed that battle which decided the fate of the northern plains. With the renegade bands either crushed, forced to surrender or driven to Canada, most of the grasslands were open at last – and in the fateful summer of 1877 the buffalo hunters began to arrive in force. Initially, problems with distribution limited their assault on the northern herd, but then in 1880 the Northern Pacific Railroad reached Montana, and the killing, skinning and shipping could begin in earnest. By 1882 the railroad was carrying 200,000 buffalo hides east in a year. Three years later, in 1885, it wasn't carrying any. The liquidation of the buffalo was over – there were perhaps six hundred specimens left standing on the entire continent. The central fifth of America was covered in so many carcasses that the next mercantile mania was harvesting the bones for fertilizer.

But the northern plains did not fall silent – commerce abhors a vacuum almost as much as nature, and the dense, nutritious grasses that had sustained the buffalo were put to immediate use. Cattle were driven in north from Texas and east from Oregon, to graze on the unclaimed, unsettled land, setting off one of the most dramatic and revealing episodes in the history of the landscapes the Nez Perce passed over.

For at the very time the Nez Perce were crossing the Musselshell and heading north, yet another visitor was exploring the grasslands that surrounded them. The Scottish journalist James Macdonald was under orders to report back to the bankers, investors and entrepreneurs of Edinburgh – then a gilded hub of imperial adventure – on the business opportunities offered by the romantic pursuit of cattle-ranching in the American Northwest. His report, *Food from the Far West*, piqued the capitalists' interest, and, as the buffalo receded, the British arrived. The giddy historical interlude known as 'The Beef Bonanza' was on.

Within ten years of Macdonald's report at least thirty-three British companies were launched to invest in Western cattle ranching, scattering up to $45 million in capital across the plains. Young gentlemen, usually the wayward junior sons of the landed gentry, sought backing from every esteemed family and bank in the land (with confident pledges of 25 per cent annual returns) then boarded an Atlantic crossing, put on a Stetson and purchased hundreds of Texas, Kansas and Oregon cattle and released them onto the northern plains to fatten on the open range. A cattle-ranching operation in Montana or Wyoming rapidly became the latest fashionable accessory in high society. The land along the Musselshell that the Nez Perce passed through fell into the hands of the 25th Baron Grey de Ruthyn – a title which, fittingly, bestowed the duty to carry the royal spurs at British coronations – as polite dinner-party conversation extolled the cattleman's stirring, outdoor lifestyle (it became a commonplace that ranching was the ideal cure for consumption).

The Americans showed few scruples when it came to separating the high-rolling arrivals from their money. Non-existent 'paper' cattle were routinely sold to guileless investors, along with 'grazing rights' to land that nobody owned. Everybody also stole cattle from the ignorant foreigners, including the cowboys and managers under their employ, who simply left the cows on the 'book count' while selling them off – when the British sent inspectors out onto the range to count their cows, they often found that more than half their herd was imaginary. In one famous, though hotly disputed, incident, a Wyoming rancher claimed that he'd sold the same herd of cattle several times over to a British aristocrat by driving the steers round and round a hill and counting them afresh each time.

If the boom is big enough, however, stupidity is no barrier to profit, and investments – and cattle – kept pouring onto the plains. At the end of the 1870s there had hardly been a single beef cow on the rangelands of east and central Montana; by 1883 there were over 600,000 munching away, in place of the now obliterated buffalo. The frenzy was joined by Boston, New York and Chicago moneymen and in less than a decade more than a thousand cattle-ranching opera-tions opened up on the northern and central plains. A grassland ecosystem covering an area the size of France, Spain and Germany combined was practically wiped off the continent, replaced by whatever flora could survive the trampling, close-cropping herds.

Initially, the Beef Bonanza was fuelled by a remarkable gift of history – free grass. Neither the government nor settlers had established control over the northern plains, so the cattlemen just doled them out on a first-come, first-graze basis, fattening their stock for nothing. As Ernest Staples Osgood put it, 'It was all so simple. The United States furnished the grass; the East, the capital; and the western stockman, the experience.' But as the open range grew ever more crowded with steers, the cattlemen realized that their investments needed the security of private property – and thus began yet another bewildering Western land grab.

The ranchers got their hands on grass any way they could, deploying tens of thousands of tonnes of the latest invention, barbed wire, and exploiting the feeble land laws designed to deal with wagon-rolling families, not merchant empires. The total quantity of fraudulently acquired property will never be known, but the US government estimated that the ranchers made off with between 4.4 and 7.3 million acres of America. The Cattle Kings, as they were now known, had acquired vast empires – the Dundee-based Matador Land and Cattle Company, for example, now controlled 1.5 million acres, running clear from Texas to Canada – and their many vocal detractors, who'd seen through the ranchers' pioneer, wilderness-taming rhetoric, and denounced them as the monopolistic enemies of the small-fry settler, seemed powerless to stop them.

But then, in 1886, came the reckoning. It was a dry summer on the plains, adding to the pressure caused by overstocking. In addition, the government had finally found the gumption to put the brakes on public land theft, even, unexpectedly, kicking the ranchers out of some of the Native reservations they had all but annexed. Finally, the ranchers were getting a taste of their own monopolistic medicine – their purchasers, in the meat processing industry, had congealed into a cartel, colluding to drive down the buying price and shut out the competition. By 1886, just four companies controlled 86 per cent of the beef output of the booming meat-packing metropolis of Chicago, and held regular, barely secret meetings to fix prices and set demand levels.

As trading conditions worsened, the Cattle Kings, of whatever origin, reverted to Western corporate type. First they squeezed their employees, making the miserable, insecure existence of their 'cowboys' yet more unrewarding, with salary cuts, food rationing and lay-offs. With considerable irony, the very first cowboy bestseller, *A Texas Cow Boy*, was reaching a million sales that very year, beginning the glamorization that made one of the West's most arduous careers by far its most feted and desired. Secondly, they squeezed the little man, signing anti-competitive pacts with the railroads and meatpackers that undermined small family ranchers, whose land and water they also pilfered. (Intriguingly, fewer of the small operations folded than the bald economics would have suggested – in fact, it was a curious quirk that many cattlemen, unlike, say, the corporate miners or lumbermen, kept on the exhausting cattle drives and roundups longer than was financially necessary or prudent. There was, it seemed, something different about ranching.)

Finally – and typically – the Cattle Kings overplayed their hand, filling every available acre of grassland with cattle, so that by the autumn of 1886 skinny, underfed steers dominated the overburdened plains. Not all of them would have survived even a mild winter. But as autumn began to turn, an unfamiliar bird visited the treetops of Montana – the ethereal white Arctic owl. On seeing this, the Indian elders are said to have wrapped their blankets tight around them and proclaimed with a shudder that a winter of winters was coming.

They were right. The blizzards raged for ten weeks, as the temperature reached minus 43 degrees C, freezing families to death in their homes, killing hundreds of cowboys as they desperately fought to save the starving herds. In a brutal twist, when the first thaw came it was followed by another freeze, creating a sheet of ice that the steers desperately pawed away at to reach grass, cutting their feet and muzzles to shreds. Herds were reduced to invading town centres and devouring the municipal shrubbery.

When, finally, the chinook arrived in the spring of 1887, melting the snow, the thawing scene was so awful that some veteran ranchers declared they'd never ride the range again. Perhaps 900,000 carcasses littered the plains – the snows had drifted so high that cows' corpses were often found dangling from trees.

It was the end of the Cattle Kings. Mortgaged to the hilt and missing up to 70 per cent of their assets, the speculative ranchers retreated to London, Edinburgh and New York to nurse their losses or declare their bankruptcies. Owning a ranch fell from European fashion as rapidly as it had risen, and the plains were largely left to Americans. The era of feeding cattle on free grass had passed, and observers predicted that another herd was set to disappear from the grasslands forever: 'Range husbandry is over, is ruined,' declared the *Rocky Mountain Husbandman*, 'destroyed, it may have been by the insatiable greed of its followers.'

But ranching never went away. Out of the spotlight of an international capital boom, the domestic Western stockmen steadily became more professional, more organized, more cautious and more militant, and ever more committed to gaining the security of guaranteed land and water – but their industry never stopped being a precarious and often arduous one, prey to the vicissitudes of the weather and the brutalities of the meat-packing cartels.

And yet, there was never a shortage of volunteers to give this tricky trade a try. Ranching was, and *is*, different – in ways that, one might cautiously surmise, the homeless and homesick Nez Perce caravan could well have recognized.

Mike Smith cut an unexpected figure as he strolled into the bright Formica of the Buffalo Trail Café, sing-songing his good mornings to every customer; the dust-worn boots, mangled toothpick and ragged hat marked him out as a cattleman, but he was closer to five foot than six, carried barely a spare ounce on him and squinted benignly at the world through scratched, wire-rimmed spectacles. As we piled into his battered pick-up and set out alongside the Musselshell towards his ranch, however, Mike's pedigree became clear enough: 'My mom's side were homesteaders from Slovakia, and my dad's side were Irish miners. My dad had a ranch north of here, up around Cow Island, right where the Nez Perce passed through.' Mike's own ranch lay near the town of Shawmut, close to where the Nez Perce must have crossed the Musselshell (the exact spot is unknown) and where Baron de Ruthyn had played at being a cowboy, and as we cruised the arrow-straight road past the golden cottonwood trees he told the story of the land after the Indians and then the Cattle Kings had passed by. 'First homesteaders came out here, farming people, and they, well, they basically starved to death – this ain't farming country – then it was sheep out here, but it got hard to find herders, and sheep are susceptible to predators. So, today it's mostly cattle.'

Fording the Musselshell, we bounced and rattled onto Mike's land, running out into the caramel, sun-baked prairie, the horizon drifting away to a crystal-blue haze. 'We don't have mountains or forests out here, but it's still kind of beautiful,' he murmured. As we toured the ranch, Mike checked on the state of his drinking wells, the various patches of forage he'd be rotating his munching herd over during the year, and, most of all, the health and plumpness of his cows, strolling the empty landscape in search of anything worth chewing, drinking or sheltering beneath. 'Dang, I'm proud of my cows this year,' he grinned. 'You look out across here, and it looks barren, but there's plenty to eat, and they're just thriving.'

Mike's pride extended, in fact, to all of his four thousand acres; as we bounced over his land, each feature brought a fresh, affectionate recollection – the gully where he and his kids bagged a mule deer one winter, the prairie-dog town that was rotavating his soil for free, a few flashes of neighbourly amusement at the travails and errors of adjoining farmers, and, most of all, a humble awareness of the enviably benign, spacious, healthful upbringing he'd been able to give his children. 'They ride, they rodeo most weekends all summer, they can help out on the farm. Now they're getting older, they're pretty busy, they don't do as much with their mom and dad, and that's kind of sad, but that's life.

'I still like to come out here by myself, though, even when I don't have a reason to. I just get on a horse and come out here on my own – just to look around.'

The textbooks call it 'ranch fundamentalism'. The economists who coined the phrase, Arthur Smith and William Martin, offered a dry definition for a very human faith: 'the attitude that being a cattle rancher leads to a higher state of total well-being than an alternative method of making a living and way of life could provide.' In essence, ranchers think they've found the best way to live in America. Fresh air, hard work, cultural identity, clean upbringings, good neighbours and a truly luxurious quantity of space, all add to the belief that the cattleman's life, however tiring and uncertain it may be, is a blessed existence. But nothing contributes more than the land itself, and the ties that bind to it. Another economist, Paul F. Starr, offered a more lyrical, and more familiar, description of the emotional value of 'family land' to ranchers: 'the idea that the struggles of one's parents and grandparents to prosper on the land meant something, and one's children and grandchildren should be able to continue the tradition, on land already steeped in tradition.' The rancher's land, he contends, serves as 'a repository of past experiences, social significance, and the individual values of their distinctive culture'.

Since it began, ranching has been an anomaly in the white Western economy, an enterprise that its protagonists have persisted with long after their ledgers told them to give up. Between 1945 and 1980, 58 per cent of America's arable farmers got out of the business, but only 14 per cent of ranchers sold out. The majority of family ranches now rely on second and third jobs to stay afloat – Mike and his wife worked for the Post Office, the government farm inspectors and the local radio station to make ends meet – and if you count family labour as a cost the majority of ranches in the West actually run at a loss. Setting aside the giant corporate operations, most ranchers are, essentially, more consumers than producers, buying a lifestyle they love with their time and savings. Paul F. Starr again observed that, 'In quiet moments I have heard ranchers claim that they continue in ranching mostly because it lets them see what they want to: a land and its parts, country that they know like few, if any, others.'

Here then, for the first time on the Nez Perce's trail, their ancient values of permanence, continuity and love for the land seemed to have found successful new converts, somehow holding off the harsh clamourings of profit and progress in favour of a good, human life. As the historian Wallace Stegner noted, 'Ranching is one of the few western occupations that have been renewable and have produced a continuing way of life.'

What seems to mark ranching out, versus logging, mining, fur-trapping, fishing and to a certain extent farming, is the freedom to make that choice. The working lumbermen of Wallowa and the miners of Butte would have carried on their hard but proud lives, tied to a homeland they'd grown to love, but the corporate account-ants ran the show, overheated the pot, exhausted the resources and pulled the plug. But once the Cattle Kings had retreated, the largely self-employed family ranchers could choose to continue their new love affair with the West for as long as they could keep their heads above water, demonstrating the very desire for ancestral roots, a sense of place and a sustainable, cyclical life that this landscape had inspired in its Native inhabitants for millennia. And that inspiration has not passed. Travelling over Mike's land, it was impossible not to be seduced into a daydream, and to reach the conclusion that thousands have drawn before – if you ever moved out West, ranching is the life you'd choose.

And that, the ranchers' enemies will tell you, is how they catch you; transfixed by the romance of the lifestyle, you don't notice the state of the land. Mike's ranch may have had its own beauty, especially to him, but some would question if its nibbled grass, pumped wells and patches of exposed, cracked mud showed a picture of ecological health. In the consistently intemperate debate on how to occupy the West, nothing generates more ferocious contempt than the dumb cow – for nothing can match its impact.

Around 40 per cent of the area of the eleven Western states is grazed by cows, and over four hundred million acres – a fifth of the entire contiguous USA – is estimated to be in a parlous ecological condition because of their shuffling hooves, multiple stomachs and prodigious rear ends. Where buffalo once wandered, cows stand still, eating the grass to death; where buffalo once visited watering sites, cows camp there for weeks, ruining riverbanks and clogging streams; where buffalo once jousted with predators, cows fall hapless prey, forcing the ranchers to take murderous defensive measures. And to magnify the hoof print still further, cows need more feed than the range alone can supply, leading to yet more of the West's land – and, more importantly, its precious water – being dedicated to growing their fortifying alfalfa, grain and hay. Most agonizing of all for their detractors, more than twenty thousand ranchers (Mike not included) have the right to release their burdensome beasts onto over three hundred million acres of the public domain, thanks to a hoary old subsidy from the days of the Great Depression, which makes the 'Welfare Rancher' the most despised federal supplicant of them all. The American government charges ranchers less to fatten their cows on public land than it costs, on average, to sustain a domestic cat.

Overall, it's not hard to portray an industry with an astonishing ecological footprint – two-fifths of the West's land, and perhaps the same proportion of its water, doing little more than keeping a mythical, state-subsidized lifestyle alive: ranching accounts for barely one per cent of the income of 'cowboy states' such as Montana and Wyoming, and it doesn't even serve as America's meat trolley – ninetenths of the country's cows actually come from mundane, unromantic but much more productive farms outside the Western range. Ranchers might love the West, their enemies contend, but they still don't belong in it.

Inevitably, it all comes down to water. 'Water is everything,' Mike declares, as we tuck into lunch back at the Buffalo Trail Café. 'When it's hot like it is today, a cow and a calf will drink perhaps twenty-five, thirty gallons between them in one day – and there's an old joke that back in the Bible, when it rained for forty days and forty nights, this county only got an inch and a half!'

There's the rub: Wheatland County only gets around twelve inches of rain a year – as a comparison, west-central England, a typical genetic homeland for most of Montana's cattle, gets three or four times that. And once cut off from their damp, lush heritage, the West's cows need more land to spread across, more dry, harsh grass to eat, more hay to tide them over, and more time drinking at the well or riverbank. Mike estimates that a cow and a calf need thirty-five acres of land to thrive in Wheatland County – the absolutely greenest, most organic, lowest-impact hobby farm in Herefordshire wouldn't need more than four acres for the pair – while in the parched rangeland of Nevada there are some ranches that need over six hundred acres to keep a single cow going for a year. Estimates of how much water it takes to make a decent Western steak vary considerably, but the mid-range figure is around 2–3,000 gallons per pound of meat. It's charged that the harder the ranchers try to tame this wild, arid space, the more resources they use and damage they do; many propose that they should simply give up and let the land return to its prior state of empty grasslands, wandering herds and a scarce, fleeting human presence.

The truth of the situation is that, as Mike puts it, 'There are good ranchers and there are bad ones', on a spectrum from careful stewardship to reckless exploitation. But the arduous reality that drives the debate – of dry air, tough grass, cold winters and short growing seasons – is the same for everyone. And for those reasons the

An abandoned farmstead, a common sight in Wheatland County.

evidence steadily mounts that the cow haters may well get their wish: though the ranchers and their neighbours might have strapped themselves onto the back of the great beast of the northern plains, vowing never to be shaken loose, slowly, inexorably, the monster has still been brushing them off.

Wheatland County had seen a diminishing population in every US Census it's ever taken part in, since 1920. There were once more than five thousand people living here – now there were fewer than two thousand, in a cavernous 1200 square miles of prairie, dotted with empty, sun-bleached homes and collapsing farm buildings. According to the accepted definition, Wheatland wasn't actually settled any more, it was The Frontier once again, untamed land, with fewer than two people per square mile – emptier than the Siberian steppe.

The town of Shawmut itself had retreated into little more than a ramshackle couple of streets, cropping up at the roadside for no obvious reason (when the railroad came through, they simply opened a town every fifteen miles, and hoped they'd stick). On the wrong side of the tracks, beneath the cottonwood trees, wooden shops sat empty, twisted by the wind, while at the end of the shady, unkempt streets the large brick schoolhouse towered over the small weather-worn cluster of houses and trailers like a folly mansion. Shawmut School, Mike told me, where his son was in sixth grade, now had a roll-call of just seven children.

There had been a drought for the past eight years now, the county missing even its stingy rainfall average, heaping pressure onto the ranchers and nearby wheat farmers – 'You see, this is unseasonable,' Mike muttered, squinting out at the glaring late September sunshine, 'it should be cold already. And I'm telling you, it's stressful.' With yields falling and the range suffering, not least from wild fires, the long, dry spell was encouraging everyone in Wheatland to concede defeat and cash in on their only asset: the family land.

'Now we've got movie stars and computer magnates buying up the land, because they all want to own a ranch. This ranch out here, some Californian bought it for a fortune, ten thousand acres – and he's had no livestock on it in seven years! He's just sitting on a rock, looking at it!

'The land's worth a lot – but if I did sell, what would I do? I'm fifty years old, I'm not a prime candidate to retrain in proficiency in computers, am I?

'I don't know – the best thing I could probably do is sell up and split the money between my kids. But that don't seem the right answer at all.'

For now, at least, Mike was planning to stick it out, keep doing what he loved, in a place he felt he belonged, driven on by the West's most renewable natural resource – optimism.

'Anyway, it'll rain here soon enough … It always has.'

At the same time of year, but at a gloomier point on the climatic curve, the Nez Perce faced cold Canadian winds as they dropped down from the saddle of Judith Gap and into the sheltered flatlands of the Judith Basin. At least now they were on familiar ground, particularly for the hunters – this was the heart of buffalo country, crossed with trails and campgrounds well known to tribes from all points on the compass. With its relatively placid climate and consistent game, the basin was a fiercely fought-over territory, with the Crow and the Blackfoot most regularly at odds for hunting and bragging rights, but the Nez Perce also harboured memories of raids and campaigns over this land. Some of the caravan's men made time for a brief excursion to a popular stopping-off point from their past expeditions – the notorious Reed & Bowles trading post.

Major Alonzo S. Reed and J. J. Bowles were old-fashioned scoundrels, making a disreputable living as far away from authority as an American could be in the autumn of 1877. Reed had once been a gentleman and a scholar, became a prize-fighter and a hired goon for corrupt Montanan politicians, then settled into life as a drunk, while Bowles was an uneducated and, it's claimed, consistently unwashed former mule-skinner. This unlikely partnership had opened their isolated trading post for hunters, travellers and troops in 1874. Most of their income was derived from flagrantly ignoring the law against serving whiskey to Indians – there were rarely any troops posted at the nearby Camp Lewis, so the pair were more than a hundred miles from justice in all directions – and they lubricated hunting parties with a noxious homebrew reputedly made from ethanol, tobacco and red pepper. Presumably out of fear of the hangovers such a concoction induced, drinking sessions at the post often lasted for several days and regularly ended in violence, which Reed tended either to start or finish – the two men were said to have kept a private graveyard behind the store for the many customers the major had shot dead.

The pair were natural survivors, cannily cultivating friendships with both rival bands and the troops that chased them, and the visiting Nez Perce were cheerfully greeted, placated and served. The effects of the whiskey were felt around twelve miles north-west of the post, where a Crow hunting camp stood. The Nez Perce, with both revenge and starvation on their minds, raided and scattered the camp, stealing the Crow's drying buffalo meat and some horses. It's a tribute to the flexible allegiances of Messrs Reed and Bowles that the first thing the Crow did once they'd recovered from the raid was head back to the trading post for a drink and a sympathetic ear.

Another chance for the Nez Perce to replenish their fading rations would soon present itself as they drove on at pace across another blank swathe of prairie, in the shadow of the Snowy Mountains, to reach the Missouri Breaks. Running across the grassland like a ragged tear, the breaks are badlands, rutted, eroded mounds of rock that follow the path of the wide Missouri River. On a dry day, they're dusty, crumbling and arduously undulating, and on a wet day they're almost impassable, as the dust coagulates into an adhesive, hard-setting mud known locally as 'gumbo', which clings tenaciously to feet, hooves and wheels. Following a creek down through this sapping terrain, the Nez Perce reached the banks of the Missouri on 23 September, at a shallow crossing point known as Cow Island.

Here they were in luck – Cow Island was used as a drop-off point by paddle steamers, bringing supplies to isolated military posts and townships, and at the time of the Nez Perce's arrival several tonnes of food and cooking equipment were sitting on the island, awaiting collection, under the guard of just sixteen men, cowering in hastily dug trenches. The Nez Perce got their non-combatants across the river and safely distant, then approached the men and asked for food. Somewhat unwisely, the leader of the defending force, Sergeant William Moelchert, offered the seven hundred tired and hungry travellers one side of bacon and half a sack of biscuits: unsurprisingly, the firing opened up soon afterwards, and, while the guards were occupied, Nez Perce women visited the stockpile after nightfall

The Missouri Breaks badlands, tumbling down to the riverbank.

and helped themselves to whatever food and utensils they wanted. Once they were satisfied, a few of the caravan's rowdier young warriors started what must have been a remarkable fire, lighting a giant pile of bacon sides, while the band retreated into the darkness. Two of the guards had been wounded in the Cow Island skirmish, while the Nez Perce suffered a single injury, but the food must have served as a significant fillip to their ever-resilient morale.

Another stroke of fortune emerged the following day, when the village's advance riders overtook a sluggish, oxen-drawn train of supply wagons; three of the wagon-drivers died as the Nez Perce plundered for desperately needed provisions. As they were stripping the carts, however, the warriors were warned of a fresh threat – a dispatch of around thirty soldiers that had come to the aid of the smouldering Cow Island camp had followed the caravan's trail, and were now sniping at their rearguard. A few sharp shots turned the troops back for home, also killing a civilian volunteer.

With this last assault seen off, fresh supplies secured and no sign of Sturgis or General the Day after Tomorrow for nearly two weeks, the situation must have seemed mildly improved to the exhausted Nez Perce, now less than a hundred miles from the Canadian border. But Poker Joe, mindful of the American military's encircling reach, and the communicative power of their telegraph, was in no mood to slow down. He pointed the caravan towards the wide, barren pass between two islands of elevation in the grassland – to the Nez Perce's east lay the angular, elegant Little Rocky Mountains, to their west the hunched, round-shouldered Bear Paws – and he drove them on beneath the sagging, laden late autumn sky. The caravan crossed into the great northern reservation, a huge swathe of emptiness beneath the Canadian border, pledged as a hunting ground to the Blackfoot, Gros Ventre and Assiniboine buffalo peoples during Isaac Stevens' 1855 treaty frenzy. As the Nez Perce passed over the silent, blank grassland, an exodus which, by now, had lasted 1600 miles, was nearing an end.

Across the prairie that rolls away towards Canada, a new feature of the landscape emerges, the perfect coda to the story of this land: pristine white schools, lying silent in the sun, their playgrounds rattling and rusting in the breeze. It's called zeroing out – schools losing their very last child. The buildings look well cared for, only recently abandoned, much like the empty farmhouses close by them, with their tins of coffee still on the shelves and the new farm equipment left lying in the grass for the debt collector. The strangest, saddest sight of all, though, are the graveyards without towns, the hilltop cenotaphs with no living settlement beneath them, ancestors buried in the hope that they would mark out a heritage, find commemoration in a way of life – that didn't last. Blaine County is another steadily emptying corner of the plains. Immigrants had poured onto this land once the railroads finally reached it, in the

A 'zeroed-out' school, closed down when the last child left.

early twentieth century, had exhausted the soil with their farming efforts, starved to death and receded like a wave. Now, just like Wheatland, it was frontier again, its population slipping back year by year. Some locals liked it that way, sensing that somehow, in the genetics of the West, the only alternative to steady decline would be unsustainable success. As one told me: 'People want to do a Bitterroots on me? Move out of the cities, come up here, build their subdivisions? Not a chance!' But most faced their community's fate with regret and anger, talking of high schools that could no longer raise a cheerleader, Main Streets crumbling into false fronts, epic, gas-guzzling drives to the nearest cinema or hardware store. Order a coffee in a foreign accent in north-central Montana and it's never long before someone's telling you what it used to be like round here.

Blaine and Wheatland are not alone. The grand mission of settlement is in recession across great swathes of the West, particularly on the plains, too harsh and dry for the dreamed-for civilization of yeoman farmers, too flat and dull to draw the lifestyle émigrés replacing the settlers in the mountains. Around 150 counties, fully a quarter of the United States' area, are technically unsettled once again, and the hollowing out is gathering pace – almost two-thirds of rural America has lost population since the turn of the twenty-first century. And the most dramatic disappearance is the most disheartening, among those citizens that country communities depend on for their purpose and meaning – the number of children in rural America fell by over one-third between 1950 and 2000, at a time when the child population of the whole nation rose by a third. And many of those still determined to give their children the spacious, healthy upbringing that the pioneers sought do so in considerable hardship – a quarter of the children in rural Montana grow up below the poverty line. Those parents who can afford to, leave – and the silence of those empty schools spreads ever further over the plains.

On the edge of the prairie, on a gathering slope towards the Little Rockies, though, stood Hays, a small, sprawling community of family homes and cluttered yards, sheltering from the wind against the low slopes of the Little Rockies. Hays lay within the Fort Belknap Native American Reservation, yet another creation of a renegotiated treaty. Once the buffalo hunters had arrived here almost immediately after the Nez Perce, the local tribes were immediately impoverished, and forced to 'come in' to full Agency life, living off unreliable federal rations, their desperate efforts at farming undercut by starvation and tuberculosis. In 1835 there had been around 10,000 Gros Ventre people – by 1884 there were around 1500. In 1888 the broken nations had agreed to give up the bulk of the great northern reservation, over seventeen million acres – which the local ranchers had been drooling over for a decade – and moved onto three far smaller enclaves. Now, though, this reservation town's architecture of social housing and community services stood in stark contrast to the privatized decay of the nearby white towns. Another difference was immediately audible – the shrieks and screams of a nursery school at break time. I popped in to the Ramona King Head Start Center to ask how many kids were enrolled in this bright, bustling pre-school. The answer was thirty-seven, in a town of 1500 souls and growing. Across the whole reservation, the Native Gros Ventre and Assiniboine population was rising at around 15 per cent each decade; in 2008, if the curves stayed on course, Native Americans would outnumber the white Americans in Blaine County for the first time in a century.

No one would call the Fort Belknap Reservation a rural idyll. With few natural resources on the land they'd been left, and many miles to the nearest economic centre, unemployment sat at perhaps 60–70 per cent, with corresponding challenges in alcoholism and domestic violence just part of the difficult picture. But Hays stood in unsettling dissonance to the commonplaces of departure and decline that surrounded it. Here were people sticking it out on the plains, staying near their family, friends, the remnants of their homeland, suffering for that choice no doubt and desperate to find the path to a sustained future, right here. Meanwhile, all around them, the people for whom this land had been taken were grudgingly accepting that the economy wanted them elsewhere, and were quietly fading away. It's not perhaps too surprising that more than one advocate has suggested that the best thing to do with the great northern reservation would be simply to *give it back* – handing the tenacious Native tribes the land and resources they need to support themselves, while relieving the United States of a territory in which it seems to have largely lost interest.

Chief Looking Glass, one suspects, had been brooding ever since the Big Hole. Poker Joe's elevation to camp commander in his stead had been a public humiliation, and Looking Glass's promises of a peaceful welcome from the Crow had later been proved badly wrong, further degrading his influence. Once the caravan had crossed the Missouri, however, the chief's old bluster began to return and he started to chide Poker Joe for the relentless pace he was setting. The people were exhausted, Looking Glass proclaimed, their horses footsore and ragged, while the army was nowhere in sight. Surely the time had come to slow down, enjoy a few short days of travel – not least because the threat of a winter famine loomed if the hunters weren't given time to bag some buffalo. Finally, the night after the Nez Perce had raided the wagon train, it seems a meeting of the chiefs took place, at which Looking Glass pulled rank. As Many Wounds reported it, Looking Glass declared to Poker Joe 'that he was no chief, that he himself was chief, and that he would be the leader'. No doubt exhausted himself, and carrying a bad bullet wound to the torso from the Big Hole, Poker Joe stepped aside: 'All right, Looking Glass, you can lead. I am trying to save the people, doing my best to cross into Canada before the soldiers find us. You can take command, but I think we will be caught and killed.'

For the next three days the caravan staggered slowly north, skirting the Little Rockies and the Bear Paws before emerging onto the final sliver of open prairie before Canada. Most nights were bringing snow now, and the lack of proper shelters – the last few lodgepoles had been abandoned at the Big Hole – made for sleepless, freezing conditions. Looking Glass abandoned Poker Joe's strict regime, calling late starts and early halts to each day's travelling, to spare the horses, give the elderly some much-needed rest and to allow his buffalo hunters to ride ahead and secure supplies. On the mid-morning of 29 September, the snow was already falling as the caravan reached Snake Creek, a dawdling little stream that sliced a curving path through the shallow folds of the prairie. The low-slung hillocks circling the creek's banks offered partial shelter from the vicious wind, and the hunters had left some buffalo meat to sustain the march. Despite the early hour, Looking Glass decided to end the day's travel here, and the Nez Perce scattered the horse herd over the prairie to forage, set about building makeshift shelters from willow branches and blankets, and lit fires fuelled by the dried buffalo dung that lay all around. As had always been their practice, the village of some seven hundred weary souls camped in clusters around their chiefs, Joseph, Looking Glass, White Bird and Toohoolhoolzote, in remembrance of their territories back home – a home from which they were now 1700 miles distant. The caravan was just forty miles, one hard day's travel, from the Canadian border, and the protection of Sitting Bull's giant rebel encampment. The Nez Perce were homeless, impoverished, grieving and exhausted, but at least they would soon be safe.

That night, though, the old warrior Wottolen had a dream, of a great battle at Snake Creek: 'I saw the waters of the stream all red with blood of both Indian and soldier. Everywhere the smoke of battle hangs dark and low.' Then Wottolen's *wyakin* came to him, and ordered him to open his eyes.

'I saw falling from trees, frost-yellowed leaves; mingling with withered flowers and grass. In my own country, each snow I have seen this, and I know it is the end. Those leaves are dead. This tells of the end of fighting.

'Soon we are to be attacked for the last time.'

CHAPTER TEN

CLIMAX

'I came into this world to die. My body is only to hold a spirit life. Should my blood be sprinkled, I want no wounds from behind. Death must come fronting me'

TOOHOOLHOOLZOTE

THE RELENTLESS WIND whipped the sleet into Horace Axtell's face as he huddled beneath an increasingly damp blanket, the cold draining the colour from his ageing, fragile skin. The small group clustered near him on the hillside overlooking Snake Creek, men lined to his left, women his right, all shuffling their feet to try and combat the frozen ground. A few wives and children had been defeated by the cold and had retreated to watch from inside the steaming cabs of their pick-up trucks. Even the jovial, gregarious figure of Soy Redthunder, the long-time representative of the non-treaty Nez Perce, struggled to raise a smile against this bleak, dark day.

'Perhaps it's good that the weather's like this today,' muttered Horace. 'Perhaps it's good that we suffer a little bit, so that we can feel a little of how our ancestors suffered in this place.' He pointed to a small outcrop of exposed rock, just to the north of where the caravan had camped on 29 September 1877: 'That is where my ancestor, my great-grandfather, Timlpusmin, fell, out there at those rocks, fighting

295

alongside Toohoolhoolzote.' Shaking and visibly weakened from the cold now, Horace's thoughts drifted past this life:

'None of us are going to live forever. When you realize that, you realize that you need to know who you are, and where you come from. Then you'll know how you want your children to grow up, what kind of people you want them to be.'

And with that he rose to his feet, rang the sacred bell and began to sing in the ancient language of the Nimiipuu. And as the few white faces retreated into the background, knowing this was not their place, the Nez Perce took the time to stand against the monstrous elements and proclaim who they were, and just where they came from.

The Nez Perce's final adversary was their toughest. Colonel Nelson A. Miles was a young man of transparent ambition; he intended to reach the high country of the US Army and was content to clamber over the bodies of Indian men and women to get there. He'd fought with distinction in the Civil War, gaining the battlefield rank of major general, and was desperate to regain that status in the new national army, his greasy-pole climbing extending even to a suspect marriage to William Tecumseh Sherman's niece. He'd then seized his first chance at Indian-fighting fame in the Red River War of 1874–5, when he'd kept his men marching throughout the miserable southern plains winter, long after most of his rival commanders had retreated to barracks. Then, in 1876, he pulled strings with his favourite uncle-in-law to get a starring role in the punitive campaign following Custer's Last Stand. Miles repeated his trick of wintering at war while others succumbed to the elements, wrapping his men in buffalo robes and driving them on against Crazy Horse's fighters, often showing flashes of lunatic bravery, and he gained much of the public credit for breaking the northern plains rebels. This was no

Colonel Nelson A. Miles.

accident. Young and of humble stock, Miles had developed a much greater understanding of the relatively new phenomenon of national fame than some of his older, more patrician superiors – such as General Howard – and he'd taken to promoting widely his own triumphs and carefully denigrating his peers. A typically understated self-assessment appeared in a telegraph to his uncle demanding yet another promotion: 'I ... have fought and defeated larger and better armed bodies of hostile Indians than any other officer since the history of Indian warfare commenced, and at the same time have gained a more extended knowledge of our frontier country than any living man.' The young braggart had also become a touch obsessed with personally accepting the surrender of famous chiefs – particularly after he felt he'd been unfairly denied the honour of 'taking in' the indomitable Crazy Horse.

Through the summer of 1877 Miles had been involved in the Nez Perce campaign only at a distance, firing out patrols and memos from his barracks on the Yellowstone River as the army failed in all their efforts to corral the caravan. As the flight continued, however, he clearly became increasingly aware that a prized bounty might be heading his way. In August he let Samuel Sturgis, who was under his command, know that reputations were built in battles, not negotiations, women and children be damned: 'I would prefer that you strike the Nez Perces a severe blow if possible before sending any word to them to surrender.'

Then, on 17 September, Miles had received word from Sturgis and Howard that they'd been outwitted and were now giving up the ghost, idling north from the Musselshell in fake pursuit. Miles seized his chance and overnight prepared a force of more than five hundred men to race north-west and cut off the bands before the Canadian border – pausing only, typically, to cover his backside, letting Howard know, 'I fear your information reaches me too late for me to intercept them, but I will do the best I can.'

The ten-day forced march was arduous, tedious and, initially, misdirected, as Miles first believed he would catch the Nez Perce south of the Missouri, then had to veer north when the pace of Poker Joe's regime became clear. But this officer had ability to match his vanity; he also had battle-hardened plains fighters under his command, and he drove his men across the featureless country at a shattering speed. Then, as the troops reached the Little Rockies, they slowed to a creep, certain that the village was hidden in the folds of the prairie ahead of them. Troopers recalled being surrounded by 'hundreds of thousands' of buffalo and antelope, but Miles wouldn't permit hunting for fear of a stampede. He sent scouts in all directions, but the miserable weather ensured that neither the troops nor the Nez Perce outriders spotted one another as they wandered through the dank half-light of the encroaching winter. On the sodden evening of 29 September, when the Nez Perce caravan was hunkering down by Snake Creek, Miles's men made their shivering bivouac no more than fifteen miles away.

It was not an auspicious morning for Looking Glass to have

ordered yet another slow start. Long after a clear, crisp dawn had broken on 30 September, most of the caravan had yet to strike camp and head north and many families were still eating breakfast when two scouts arrived with the disturbing news of a nearby buffalo stampede – surely caused by approaching soldiers. Looking Glass refused to panic, however, riding through the camp slowing the rush to leave: 'Do not hurry! Go slow! Plenty, plenty time. Let children eat all wanted!'

In fact, Miles's army had been awake since two in the morning, and marching in search of the Nez Perce's trail since four, crossing the crisp grass and frozen streams in the thin dawn light. As the sun rose and the men began to thaw, the scouting reports grew ever more insistent – the village was surely nearby. Miles ordered his troops to lighten their loads and break their horses into a trot – then, when his scouts spotted the smoke from the Nez Perce campfires, he called for a gallop. Finally, over the thunder of running hooves, Miles roared the order for a full-pelt attack: 'Charge them! Damn them!'

Nearby, a lone Nez Perce rider raced towards his camp, whipping his horse to frantic speed across the open prairie. When he reached a ridge overlooking the village, he gave a blanket signal – 'Enemies right on us! Soon the attack!'

Chaos erupted immediately. Those families that had ignored Looking Glass and packed their horses in haste now scurried off north, while others rushed towards the herd to try and secure their rides to safety. Joseph raced unarmed towards the herd, bellowing, 'Horses! Horses! Save the horses!' Warriors grabbed their rifles and ran to the shallow slope protecting the village's southern edge, and waited for the charge to come into view. 'Soon,' Yellow Wolf recalled, 'from the south came a noise – a rumble like stampeding buffaloes.'

Miles had divided his careering force into two main groups, one to shatter the village, the other to drive off their horses. The group aiming for the herd arrived first, and met a cacophonous scene of defending warriors and fleeing women and children, desperately trying to mount their panicking horses. Joseph was here, placing his teenage daughter on a mount and sending her north, but, despite the manic warriors, the troops managed to drive away several hundred Nez Perce ponies. The tribe was now denied the tactic that had served it so well since June – the young fighters stalling all-comers, while the non-combatants rode to safety – and many Nez Perce who'd sprinted for their herd were forced into a terrifying foot race back to the relative safety of the village.

But they weren't yet beaten, for the main body of Miles's charge, which he'd hoped would overrun and ransack the village, was taking a hammering. Miles had ridden most of his men straight for the heart of the camp, but the charge had been stopped cold by Nez Perce gun-fire, spinning and felling the army's horses, forcing the troops to leave their dead and retreat. Other groups of soldiers became trapped in a fatal game of hide and seek with warriors negotiating the ridges and furrows of land to the east of the creek, while some who reached the Nez Perce shelters were driven back by a bloody toe-to-toe fusillade. A brutal slugging contest of a battle developed, with Miles sending his men to die in failed charges, while Nez Perce warriors were cut down trying to organize escapes to the north. By the afternoon Miles realized he was overseeing a killing field, and accepted a change of tactics. His death-or-glory style had worked against the Cheyenne, the Minneconjous and Crazy Horse's Oglalas, but not the Nez Perce – 'They fight with more desperation than any Indians I have ever met,' he declared. But without their horse herd, the tribe couldn't hope to escape, so conquest became containment. As evening approached, the army's charges were halted, and the Nez Perce were put under siege. Miles wrapped a cordon around the camp and dug in.

That night, as the snow began to fall, both sides were in dire straits. Miles had almost fifty dead and wounded men, many left freezing in no-man's-land – a few injured troopers even committed suicide where they lay, fearful that the Nez Perce would scalp them in the night. To be inside the village was far worse, though, as the shivering Nez Perce worked through the darkness, digging shelter pits for the elderly and the children, and building up fortifications for their snipers. One woman recalled the scene: 'We digged the trenches with camas hooks and butcher knives. With pans we threw out the dirt. We could not do much cooking. Dried meat ... would be handed around ... given to the children first. I was three days without food. Children cried with hunger and cold. Old people suffering in silence. Misery everywhere. Cold and dampness all around.'

The tribe also buried their dead and counted their losses. Perhaps twenty-two Nez Perce had died on 30 September but it was the calibre of the fallen that shook the village. Joseph's brother Ollokot, the charismatic role model of the young warriors, had died in the rush to secure the horse herd. Toohoolhoolzote, the irascible *montagnard* who'd defied General Howard at the final meeting of peacetime, had fallen while holding off attackers at the northern end of the village. And Poker Joe, whose continued leadership would surely have dragged the Nez Perce over the Canadian border, had died by 'friendly fire', mistaken for a Cheyenne scout working for Miles. They, and others who fell on that day, were the fighting heart of the great exodus, and their loss left Joseph, White Bird and Looking Glass with a still heavier burden of leadership.

All agreed that with the horse herd diminished, breaking the siege and fleeing north en masse was now impossible. Joseph later confirmed this – 'We could have escaped from Bear's Paw Mountain if we had left our wounded, old women and children behind. We were unwilling to do this. We had never heard of a wounded Indian recovering while in the hands of white men.' The best, perhaps last, hope lay with Sitting Bull, the renegade leader in exile just over the border, who could raise an army of a thousand Sioux warriors to annihilate Miles and escort the Nez Perce to safety. Six men were chosen to crawl through the siege lines under the cover of night and speed north to plead for his help.

As the next day dawned, though, the fighting recommenced, and the Nez Perce were trapped in their shelters by a blizzard of both bullets and driving snow. Yellow Wolf, a fearless young warrior who'd joined every battle of the exodus with uninhibited relish, finally began to lose heart:

> I felt the coming end. All for which we had suffered lost[1]
>
> Thought came of the Wallowa where I grew up. Of my own country when only Indians were there. Of tepees along the bending river. Of the blue, clear lake, wide meadows with horse and cattle herds. From the mountain forests, voices seemed calling. I felt as dreaming. Not my living self.
>
> The war deepened. Grew louder with gun reports. I raised up and looked around. Everything was against us. No hope! Only bondage or death! Something screamed in my ear. A blaze flashed before me. I felt as burning! Then with rifle I stood forth, saying to my heart, 'Here I will die, fighting for my people, and our homes!'

But although he had the Nez Perce cornered, Nelson Miles was also running short on confidence. He felt certain that Sitting Bull would accept the chance to wipe out a US command and gain fresh allies, and Miles was actually contemplating retreat, to higher ground that would prove more defensible when the Sioux inevitably arrived. He was also racing against the clock, to end the siege before General Howard made his languorous way north to the battlefield. As he outranked Miles, if Howard arrived in time he would rightfully claim the glory of accepting the surrender of Joseph, the Red Napoleon. Through the second day of the battle, 1 October, Miles made various overtures to meet with Joseph (whom he believed to be in sole command – so much for his unparalleled 'Indian sense'), and eventually a truce was agreed. The guns fell silent, and both Indians and soldiers emerged to collect their dead, while Joseph visited Miles's tent to discuss terms for a permanent end to the fighting. As ever with Joseph, the meeting was friendly; the army's camp doctor recalled, 'He is a man of splendid physique, dignified bearing, and handsome features. His usual expression was serious, but occasionally a smile would light up his face, which impressed us very favourably.' But nothing could be agreed, as Miles's fundamental demand was for the Nez Perce to hand over all their weapons, something Joseph couldn't promise; he didn't speak for the whole caravan, and, even if the Nez Perce agreed to cease their flight, they still needed rifles with which to hunt. As Joseph turned to leave the tent, Miles, impatient and impetuous, ordered the chief to be taken as a prisoner of war. According to several indignant Nez Perce memoirs, Joseph was promptly bound hand and foot, rolled up in a blanket and thrown in with the army mules. It was a treacherous breach of the battlefield truce and an unwise one, for at precisely the same time, Lieutenant Lovell Jerome was touring the Nez Perce camp under Miles's orders, ostensibly using the ceasefire to look for army dead but actually reconnoitring the village's dug-out defences. When word reached the warriors that Joseph had been imprisoned, Jerome was detained as a bargaining chip.

That night, while Joseph reportedly slept with the mules, Lieutenant Jerome was fed, watered and given blankets by the Nez Perce. He later recalled that, somehow, the Indians were still in possession of their sense of humour, joking with him, as the bitter weather swept in once more, 'If it doesn't get warmer than this, we'll have to go to fighting again.' Jerome also witnessed Nez Perce kindnesses to wounded US soldiers, and their strict observation of the truce, and was clearly more than a little affected by his time in the village, later proclaiming: 'Why, these Indians are the bravest men on this continent.' The next morning, he and Joseph were exchanged, taking time to shake hands in no-man's-land.

That day, 2 October, passed in a strange mix of a truce and a stalemate, with long periods of quiet punctuated by bursts of fire as the army probed the village's defences, and some Nez Perce families attempted to escape north. An unlikely camaraderie began to develop between the two sets of fighters, as entrenched combatants agreed short ceasefires to let one another stretch their legs, and the Nez Perce demonstrated their wit in sharp exchanges of 'sledging' across the lines. But behind the banter, conditions in the village were ever worsening, with groups of sometimes fifteen people huddling together for warmth in the damp earth shelters, their blankets brittle with cold, their food and ammunition running low. Fatigue was also turning to sleep deprivation, as Ollokot's widow recalled: 'We slept only in naps; sitting in our pits; leaning forward or back against the dirt wall. Many of the warriors stayed in their rifle pits all the time.' As was always the case, individual Nez Perce were free to choose their own path, and many did – under the cover of night, perhaps a hundred members of the caravan slipped away to take their chances on the snow-swept prairie.

Another day – 3 October – dawned and Colonel Miles was feverish with anxiety. His nemesis, in the form of either Howard or Sitting Bull, must, he knew, have been within a day's march by now, and either ignominy or obliteration beckoned. Another laggard had already reached him, though, a slow supply wagon carrying with it a heavy Napoleon cannon and two dozen shells. A man in a hurry, Miles resolved to make an early contribution to what would become a disconcerting theme in American military adventures – the use of superior technology to circumvent a straight contest between fighting men, instead delivering a morale-sapping and far from discriminate barrage from an untouchable distance. When the cannon's shells began to land in the village, mid-morning on the 3rd, shrieks of terror filled the air. Miles had placed the gun more than a mile west of the village, and dug its tail into the ground, so it was lobbing its missiles high into the air, mortar-style, before they shattered into the dug-out shelters. Lieutenant Jerome's new-found admiration for the Nez Perce didn't, sadly, prevent him from letting his commander know the exact layout of the trenches.

Women and children were buried alive as their dug-outs collapsed upon them; some were pulled gasping to safety, but a grandmother and a teenage girl suffocated in the dirt. The panic among the non-combatants dismayed and disheartened the warriors, as Yellow Wolf recalled: 'It was bad that cannon guns should be turned on the shelter pits where there were no fighters. Only women and children, old and wounded men in those pits. General Miles and his men handling the big gun surely knew no warriors were in that part of camp.' Hope sprang that afternoon, though, with the distant sight of an army moving slowly from the north – Sitting Bull? Nez Perce spirits soared while the soldiers descended into panic – but only until the snow-clouds cleared a little. The ponderous battalion was just a herd of buffalo, the snow on their shoulders faintly resembling crouching riders. The Sioux were not coming.

The six messengers sent to contact Sitting Bull had paused at an Assiniboine village and been killed. The great warrior chief in exile was still undoubtedly aware of the events to his south, though – his men made regular scouting incursions across the border, and other refugees from the battle fled in his direction. But Sitting Bull's response was far from helpful; he moved swiftly north, away from trouble. He later attempted to explain his unwillingness to help the Nez Perce as a miscommunication – when word reached him that the caravan was under siege, he claimed, the message declared that they were just south of the Missouri River, far too distant from the border to be helped (they were, in fact, just south of the *Milk* River).

A far more likely explanation is that the British had made their final, fateful contribution to this history. Sitting Bull was a headache to the Empire, his rebellious residency in Canada an irritant in their increasingly special relationship with the blossoming economy of the United States. It seems Her Majesty's Canadian authorities had politely explained to the great chief that, should he lead his warriors south to help the Nez Perce, they would take the opportunity to attack his undefended women and children, pushing the whole camp back over the border. The final tribe that the Nez Perce flight encountered was forced, as all the others along the way had been, to acquiesce to an injustice rather than face down a colonial bully. With irresistible enemies, the Nez Perce were left entirely without friends.

Sitting Bull did cause one battlefield casualty, though, and in bleak circumstances. The precise timing of Chief Looking Glass's death is debated, but the manner of his passing is not. Mistaking one of Miles's Indian scouts for a Sioux outrider, he stood up in his rocky rifle pit to beckon the liberating army forward. Framed against the Montana sky, he made an easy target for the army snipers and was felled by a single shot. He was probably the last Nez Perce warrior to die in the shadow of the Bear Paws. History has not looked kindly on Looking Glass's role in the Nez Perce flight, as his overconfidence exposed the caravan to not one, but two shattering battles, at the Big Hole and then Bear Paw; but while he shouldered much of the responsibility for the fate of the Nez Perce, he surely bore none of the blame. Without doubt, as dawn broke on 4 October, the fifth day of the battle, the dominant characters of the Nez Perce flight were now reduced to just two chiefs, Joseph and White Bird.

Throughout a miserable day of squalls and sleet, little changed on the banks of Snake Creek as both sides sought to conserve ammunition. Colonel Miles reportedly slipped into depression, petulantly resigned to Howard reaching the siege in time to claim 'his' surrender. At nightfall, the Christian General finally rode into camp with an escort of around twenty men (he'd left his main army a day's march back) and was greeted by a sullen Miles. The colonel's mood brightened immediately, though, when Howard made one of his trademark gestures of false magnanimity, declaring that he would allow the grasping young man the honour of retaining field command, and receiving the surrender. When Howard's aide, Charles E. S. Wood, privately pointed out that Howard's troops had marched 1700 miles for this surrender, and were about to be denied their due credit, Howard declared that there would be glory enough to go round, and that Miles, who'd served under him in the Civil War, would surely share it: 'I would trust him with my life.'

The embattled Nez Perce had noted Howard's arrival, and understood that this meant a second, overwhelming, army was now close at hand. Some of the general's fellow travellers also altered their situation – two treaty Nez Perce, Captain John and Old George, had been serving as army scouts since Clearwater, with the extra motivation that they both had daughters travelling in the refugee caravan. Neither man would receive a warm welcome in the besieged village – Captain John was a particularly loathed signatory to the Thief Treaty – but at least they spoke the right language. As did Arthur Chapman, a settler who had also been scouting for Howard since Idaho. Chapman's presence at the closing chapter in the Nez Perce flight was quite fitting – he'd fired the opening shot at the very first battle, setting off that hapless charge into the White Bird Canyon. With Chapman and the two Nez Perce in the army camp, the linguistic channels for the precise promises and demands of surrender were now open. As Joseph, who knew Chapman well, even considering him a friend, recalled: 'We could now talk understandingly.'

The next morning the flag of truce was raised over the army lines and the two Nez Perce scouts were sent into the village, a few feathers thrust into their hatbands to distract from their European attire. Their visit was nearly an extremely short-lived one, as several Nez Perce warriors volunteered to shoot the traitors off their approaching horses, but through nervous smiles the messengers delivered Howard and Miles's unequivocal promise – a pledge that not a single participant or witness ever denied was made. If the Nez Perce agreed to cease fighting, they would be sent back to their homeland.

At the tribal council that followed, many Nez Perce argued in favour of holding out, suggesting that it would surely be a short journey from a ceasefire to the hangman's noose for most of the martial leaders. Joseph counselled for peace, however, arguing that this was a truce with honour, not a defeat: 'I did not say "Let's quit!".'

General Miles said "Let's quit." And now General Howard says "Let's quit."' The Nez Perce women and children were suffering desperately in their crumbling, iced-up shelters, and many of those who had fled onto the drifting prairie were doubtless starving or freezing to death. For the guardian of the non-combatants, such desperate scenes had become unendurable. 'For myself I do not care. It is for them that I am going to surrender.'

Most compelling of all was *that* promise, of a return to Idaho: 'Colonel Miles had promised that we might return to our country with what stock we had left,' Joseph later insisted. 'I thought we could start again. I believed Colonel Miles, or I never would have surrendered.'

A traditional Nez Perce settlement was reached. Joseph, speaking only for the Wallowa band, would surrender, and all other families were free to join him. The other leaders, White Bird included, would not speak to Miles and would reach their own decision in time. At lunchtime on 5 October 1877, Chief Joseph rode out from the battered village, accompanied by five warriors on foot, and with his rifle resting on his lap. His forehead and arms were marked by battle scars, and his blanket was torn by bullet holes. He travelled slowly, dismounted on a windswept bluff and handed his rifle to the waiting Howard. With a smile, the general indicated that Colonel Miles would in fact be claiming the prize, but it was to his old adversary, a sparring partner in debate and battle, that Joseph turned to deliver his surrender speech. The exact words he used, as Arthur Chapman translated and Charles E. S. Wood took notes, will never be wholly agreed upon, but in every marginally different transcription that has gone to print Joseph's eloquence, compassion and dignity shine through. The astonishing flight of the Nez Perce was an ensemble performance from start to end, but at its very conclusion a star of history was born:

Tell General Howard I know his heart. What he told me before, I have it in my heart. I am tired of fighting. Our chiefs are killed. Looking

Glass is dead. Toohoolhoolzote is dead. The old men are all dead. It is the young men who say 'Yes' or 'No'. He who led the young men [Ollokot] is dead. It is cold, and we have no blankets. The little children are freezing to death. My people, some of them, have run away to the hills, and have no blankets, no food. No one knows where they are – perhaps freezing to death. I want to have time to look for my children, and see how many of them I can find. Maybe I shall find them among the dead.

Hear me, my chiefs! I am tired. My heart is sick and sad. From where the sun now stands I shall fight no more forever.

As the officers stood in awed silence, Joseph drew his blanket over his head. Scores of Nez Perce began to emerge from their rifle pits and dug-outs, each raising their hand to the sky to indicate that they too would fight no more, from where the sun now stood in a crystal winter sky. Some handed in their rifles, others had already buried them as a precaution. As dusk fell Miles ordered that fires be lit and food be served to restore the weakened Indians, and arranged for a courier to be dispatched announcing to his superiors that Chief Joseph had finally been captured. Curiously, Miles's missive, which was reproduced in newspapers nationwide, failed to mention that General Oliver Otis Howard had been present at the surrender.

Not every Nez Perce relinquished his freedom. While those who had sided with Joseph gathered their few remaining possessions from the battlefield, White Bird and some of his followers did the same, but covertly plotted a nocturnal escape. Once darkness had fallen, they slipped through the now lacklustre army guard, and headed north on foot for Canada, a sombre, shrunken caravan of some forty souls. E-Wy-Tone-My, Ollokot's widow, recalled the numb melancholy of that night:

It was lonesome, the leaving. Husband dead, friends buried or held prisoner. I felt that I was leaving all that I had but I did not cry. You

The memorial to Chief Joseph's declaration of surrender to Howard.

know how you feel when you lose kindred and friends through sickness-death. You do not care if you die. With us it was worse. Strong men, well women, and little children killed and buried. They had not done wrong to be so killed. We had only asked to be left in our homes, the homes of our ancestors. Our going was with heavy hearts, broken spirits. But we would be free. Escaping the bondage sure with the surrendering. All lost, we walked silently on into the wintry night.

White Bird, born into a lost valley that wasn't even part of the United States, but now leading the exhausted remnants of his band into uncertain exile beyond the new nation's borders, was incandescent: 'We were wanderers on the prairie. For what? For white man's greed. The white man wanted the wealth our people possessed; he got it by the destruction of our people.'

Taking into account those who'd fled at the very start of the battle and those who'd drifted away during the siege, more than two hundred Nez Perce were now at large on the prairie – but there was little to celebrate in this great escape. The early refugees were mostly on horseback, but the remainder were often walking barefoot through the snow, without blankets and with little, if anything, to eat. Of those who sought the mercy of local Indian villages, many were killed for their scant possessions – army officers had gallantly let the nearby tribes know that Nez Perce scalps would earn a bounty – but eventually the bulk limped across the border into Sitting Bull's giant tepee city, where they were fed and cared for.

The long-term fate of the escapees was mixed. Some stayed in Canada for life, and their descendants are still there today. Around eighty were recaptured, mostly as a result of their efforts to slip back to Idaho and join the reservation Nez Perce. The government adopted a vindictive policy of sweeping up and imprisoning every possible participant in the flight, even those who'd been left behind along the route to give birth or to recover from their wounds. A few Nez Perce refugees were relatively lucky and encountered officials who decided they'd suffered enough, and allowed them to fade quietly into the treaty tribe. Young Swan Necklace, who had been the junior partner in the original raid on the Salmon River settlers, returned to the reservation under the pseudonym John Minthorn, and his role in 1877 was kept secret from the local whites until after his death, over thirty years later. Several young men, the indefatigable Yellow Wolf among them, were reduced to living wild in the woods around their home-land, drawn by the consolation of familiar landscapes, but ultimately forced into surrender by starvation and harassment. Yellow Wolf, whose exemplary capacity for violence led to more than a few white fatalities during his months on the run, later looked back on his voluntary capture with pride, knowing that he'd stood up to the US Army in a dozen fights, and never lost: 'I did not surrender my rifle.'

One Canadian exile suffered a particularly poignant fate. Joseph's teenage daughter, Kapkap Ponmi, had raced off at the very start of the battle and had reached Sitting Bull safely – then recrossed the border and headed back to Idaho with a group of Nez Perce men and women in the summer of 1878. When they were arrested on the reservation, most of the group were packed off east to join Joseph in captivity, but Kapkap Ponmi was detained in Idaho. 'Sound of Running Feet' was back in her father's land, but never shared the homecoming with him, or even saw him again – she died within a few years, while Joseph was still in detention.

Chief White Bird never saw his valley again either. Settling in Canada as a leader in exile, he rebuffed all official offers to join Joseph in what he was promised was a dignified captivity, proclaiming his understandable mistrust for every word the American government uttered. But then in 1882 he was killed by a member of his own band: an ailing Nez Perce child called out White Bird's name with his dying breath, convincing his father that the chief's medicine powers were to blame for the child's passing. Of the great leaders of the exodus of 1877, there was now only one left standing.

Back on that frozen Montana battlefield, the fate that befell Chief Joseph and his fellow captives from Bear Paw would become one of the most enduring stains on the bleak history of the Western Frontier. Just under 420 Nez Perce and Palouse had surrendered, drawn from every band that had joined the flight. The group contained precious few healthy men, who had either fled or died, but was dominated by mothers and children, the elderly and the wounded. Of the more than seven hundred Indians who had been involved in the flight, a cautious estimate is that just over 120 had died in the caravan's many battles and travails, which had lasted over 1700 miles and nearly four months, concluding just forty miles from freedom. Most of the material possessions of 'the wilderness gentry of the North-West' were now scattered across Idaho and Montana – of their three thousand beloved horses, just 1100 were left, and the army promptly took those – leaving several branches of an estimable ancient culture quite ruined.

Around 180 European Americans had also died, overwhelmingly professional soldiers, felled in the six battles and numerous skirmishes in which the Nez Perce had never once been bettered in a straight fight. It's estimated that the US Army had spent over $900,000 chasing the refugees from their land.

But now, as clearly and soberly promised, they were to be sent home.

'When will the white man learn to speak the truth?' Such was Joseph's resigned response when the reality slowly emerged. Both Miles and Howard did in fact believe, on that October day, that they would be escorting the captives back to the Northwest, and probably Idaho. Howard had received orders to that very effect. But the Nez Perce needed to be kept somewhere close by for the encroaching winter, then transported west in the thaw. Two days after the surrender Miles, Joseph and the Nez Perce prisoners set off back to Miles's barracks in Fort Keogh, Montana, Howard announcing that he would return in the spring to escort the charges west. That gave the Washington machinery plenty of time to find its reverse gear.

Taking a nationally famous band of renegades back to the scene of their supposed crimes soon began to look politically unwise. The civic leaders of Idaho barely drew breath before howling with rage at the surrender terms, decrying the typical Eastern limpness towards their terrorizers. The *Lewiston Teller* declared that, following Joseph's 'treason, treachery and murder', he and his fellow captives were indeed welcome home, provided they 'be hanged till they be dead, like all other murderers'. The twin pillars of the Western Army, Sherman and Sheridan, began to exchange telegrams discussing the need to make a punitive example of Joseph, and Sherman sent a lengthy report on the Nez Perce campaign to President Hayes. It was a protracted eulogy to the endeavour and honour of the tribe: 'The Indians throughout displayed a courage and skill that elicited uni-

This photograph of Joseph was taken at Fort Keogh, just three weeks after his surrender.

versal praise. They abstained from scalping; let captive women go free; did not commit indiscriminate murder of peaceful families, which is usual, and fought with almost scientific skill.' But it ended with a kick in the teeth: 'They should never again be allowed to return to Oregon or to Lapwai.'

Nelson Miles received fresh orders. Ignoring their previous commands to him and Howard, Sherman and Sheridan let the colonel know that, in fact, there had been no surrender terms on offer to Joseph. The Nez Perce weren't to winter in Montana, but were to be dragged south and east, to Kansas. From there, in the spring thaw, they would be moved onto Indian Territory, the dusty, overcrowded cattle pen in the south-centre of the continent into which the USA had herded disparate tribes from all points on the compass – a territory which would, eventually, be transformed into the state of Oklahoma. It was a bleak, alien prospect for which not one Nez Perce would have laid down his rifle.

A surreal celebrity tour set off from Fort Keogh on 1 November 1877, as the Nez Perce prisoners were transported by foot, boat and train first to Dakota and then Kansas. At many towns along the way parades were organized, riotous crowds gathering to see the victorious Miles and the infamous Joseph, and the tirelessly charming chief was invited to dinner parties and civic drinks receptions, while the Nez Perce encampments were besieged, 'rubberneckers' wandering through their shelters in search of trinkets and trophies.

It's possible, but unlikely, that Miles didn't initially understand that Joseph was being betrayed – he certainly didn't let the chief know that he wouldn't be heading home in the spring – but a combination of his growing affection for his wards and his conscientious regard for his own image did lead him to protest the unfolding injustice. Miles pointed out the stark inconsistencies in his superiors' orders, and argued that the Nez Perce had been 'grossly wronged in years past', but he certainly didn't rebel enough to jeopardize his career. Miles saw himself as a hero of progress, and the Nez Perce campaign had been a part of that great mission. Looking back later, he appraised that any injustice had been worth the reward: 'What was at one time a vast plain, wilderness and mountain waste, has been transformed into a land of immeasurable resources, a realm rivalling in extent and resources the empire of the Caesars.'

General Howard, for his part, took a typically spurious view of the unfolding crime, declaring that Chief White Bird's flight from the Bear Paw battlefield had breached, and thus nullified, the surrender terms pledged to Joseph. Even Howard's loyal aide, Charles E. S. Wood, acknowledged that this was fiction.

The Nez Perce captives, now swelled to 431 by the round-up of fugitives, reached Fort Leavenworth, Kansas, on 27 November 1877.

There they sat out the harsh plains winter, reduced to inactivity in a desolate, unfamiliar swampland, relying on army handouts for sustenance. And then, when the spring thaw came, the Nez Perce started to die.

Unfamiliar southern diseases such as malaria and yellow fever began to claim lives as soon as the plains sun regained its ferocity, the thunderstorms broke and the mosquitoes hatched. Joseph was distraught at the suffering, begging the army to move his people away from the fetid swamp and back to the mountains: 'We had always lived in a healthy country, where the mountains were high and the water was cold and clear. Many of our people sickened and died, and we buried them in this strange land. I cannot tell how much my heart suffered for my people while at Leavenworth.'

With little urgency, US Congress debated where to move this dwindling band next, and in the high summer of 1878 they were packed into freight cars and moved to an Indian reservation in southern Kansas. (Six children died from the heat in the boxcars, and were buried in shallow graves by the rail tracks.) At the new reservation, no effort had been made to find shelter for the Nez Perce, and what medicine anyone bothered to secure for them was hawked by corrupt agents. By the autumn of 1878 the captives had lost between sixty and seventy lives to disease and trauma. At the next thaw, they were shunted on to another territory, in present-day Oklahoma, where again they were met with no provisions or care, and the dying continued – they had now lost over a hundred souls. Finally, in Oklahoma, the Nez Perce came to a standstill and were able to make the first tentative steps towards subsistence, planting some crops and tending a few cattle. But as a year passed, then two, then three, their physical bond with their distant homeland could never be repaired, and the deaths mounted. Joseph's infant daughter, born on the very first day of the exodus, passed away. Yellow Wolf, arrested in Idaho and packed off to Oklahoma, witnessed the attrition: 'All the newborn babies died, and many of the old people too. It was the climate.

Everything so different from our old homes. No mountains, no springs, no clear running rivers.' Perhaps a hundred Nez Perce children died in Oklahoma, as infant mortality ran, visiting doctors attested, at 100 per cent. This fatal homesickness was not unique to the tribe – the vast internment camp of Indian Territory was dotted with the crowded graveyards of Native peoples, who couldn't survive where they didn't belong.

In an irony he surely detested, while his people endured Joseph's star rose. The Nez Perce camp had become a tourist attraction, home of the Great Chief. Joseph was invited to meet the president, to speak before congressmen; he was pestered by journalists and his short published account of the flight of 1877 was a national sensation. The chief tolerated the flattery, however, because it brought attention for his relentless campaign to get his people home, or at least to a healthy piece of country – 'Death comes almost every day for some of my people,' he proclaimed in 1879. 'A few months more and we will be in the ground.'

Miles and Howard lobbied gently on his behalf (though not in concert – Howard never forgave Miles's deceit at Snake Creek) while the ever-honourable Charles E. S. Wood helped make the Nez Perce a fashionable *cause célèbre* among the humanitarians of the East Coast elite. But the Northwest was distinctly unimpressed. Every fawning portrayal of Joseph made him more of a hate figure among the settlers, reminded almost daily by their local press and politicians of the scandalous crimes committed in June 1877; the *Lewiston Teller*, as ever, pulled few punches, offering scant sympathy for the Nez Perce suffering in Oklahoma: 'They claim it to be unhealthy for them there. They will find it far more unhealthy here, and their diseases will be much more suddenly fatal.'

For seven years, Joseph patiently explained his people's plight and Colonel Miles's broken promise to anyone who would listen, and finally, in the fall of 1884, swamped by fourteen different petitions on the tribe's behalf, the government acted. It was decided that the following spring the Nez Perce would be moved back to Lapwai – all except Joseph, and any captives designated, either by choice or by official decree, to be loyal followers of the renegade chief and his Dreamer religion. These individuals would be pushed further north and west, onto a reservation in the high salmon valleys of Washington, known as Colville. It was a tolerable solution for all – the members of the White Bird, Looking Glass and other bands who'd surrendered along with Joseph were finally heading home, the settlers weren't being forced to accept the return of loathed 'criminals' and potentially disruptive influences, and Joseph and his people would surely survive better in Colville's northern climes.

And for the relentlessly optimistic Joseph, this move was surely only a stepping stone – from much closer to home, he could now plead, debate and beg for an ultimate return to the sacred Wallowa. Joseph, remarkably, never seemed to lose hope that the white powers whom he tirelessly harangued and charmed would one day see sense, abandoning their infuriating habits of 'talk that comes to nothing', 'broken promises', 'misrepresentations' and 'misunderstandings', choosing instead to answer his case with simple, honest principle.

> There need be no trouble. Treat all men alike. Give them all the same law. Give them all an even chance to live and grow. All men were made by the same Great Spirit Chief. They are all brothers. The earth is the mother of all people and all people should have equal rights upon it … We shall all be alike – brothers of one father and one mother, with one sky above us and one country around us, and one government for all. Then the Great Spirit Chief who rules above will smile upon this land, and will send rain to wash out the bloody spots made by brothers' hands upon the face of the earth. For this time the Indian race are waiting and praying.

Four hundred and thirty-one Nez Perce had been dragged to the southern plains, and the fugitives arrested returning from Canada swelled their numbers to perhaps close to five hundred arrivals in total. But after seven years in the 'Hot Place', where the elderly had been unable to hold onto life and the young had been born too weak to grasp it, fewer than three hundred now headed back north. Twenty-nine people, mostly widows and orphans, had been sent ahead early, but the bulk departed on 22 May 1885, eight years now since the Nez Perce had left the Wallowa.

At Walla Walla, where Joseph's father had met the hard-charging Isaac Stevens back in 1855, the bands were divided – 118 Nez Perce whom the authorities considered potentially peaceable, Christian, reservation Indians were shipped to Lewiston, while 150 Nez Perce who were deemed or self-proclaimed Dreamers and dissidents carried on to Colville. When the tattered, dishevelled 'peaceful' refugees were finally unloaded at Lewiston, the treaty Nez Perce who'd come to meet them wept for what had befallen their kin. There were also a few glum faces among the white citizens on the dockside – there had been rumours that Chief Joseph would be on board, and a reception committee had been arranged, complete with noose.

The released Nez Perce were returning to a reservation under siege. The treaty bands had largely done well in the years since the uprising, making substantial, if uneven, progress as farmers, cattlemen and traders – an Indian Bureau report in 1879 declared that the reservation was possibly the most advanced in the West, and that the cottages and schoolhouses of Kamiah 'would lead a stranger, not knowing of its inhabitance by Indians, to ask what prosperous white settlement was located here'. But greedy eyes noted that the tribe was blessed with more acreage per capita than the local settlers were entitled to, and that the Nez Perce were failing to squeeze every ounce of profit from their land. Even before the great flight had finished, in September 1877, a correspondent to the *Teller* had opined that the time could be ripe to rectify that imbalance: 'Efforts have repeatedly been made by citizens, to either force all the Nez Perce to reside upon the reservation or to curtail the boundaries of the reservation and throw open its rich lands to settlement by white citizens. These efforts so far proved abortive. The war has changed the prospect.'

Indeed it had. Local boosters began to lobby ceaselessly for the diminution or abolition of the reservation, arguing that the war had reduced the Nez Perce population to a feeble rump, incapable of cultivating the excessive lands under their control, and suggesting that territory should be seized punitively, as many more of the Natives had innocent blood on their hands than they cared to admit. One well-placed source even announced, once again, 'We are credibly informed by men who know well many of the Indians ... they do not want all the land of the reservation, and they much rather that the whites would settle upon portions of it and cultivate it.'

As the 1880s began, these vultures found themselves some potent but unlikely allies among their most committed irritants – the bleeding-heart Eastern elites. A surge of self-disgust swept through American high society as the decade opened, the thrill of following the distant Indian Wars turning into a realization that the ruination of Native America had left an almighty smudge on the New Republic's shining beacon to humanity. Helen Hunt Jackson's *A Century of Dishonor* was a publishing smash in 1881, a melodramatic litany of broken treaties and displaced, impoverished Native peoples: 'every page and every year has its dark stain.' Church leaders and capital philanthropists formed Indian Rights organizations, and a succession of faddish Native heroes (Joseph included) were feted and championed. Most influential was the annual congress of 'Friends of the Indian' at Lake Mohonk, New York, where humanitarians gathered to debate the salvation of the red man. By the mid-1880s a near-universal consensus had been formed – which harked straight back to the comforting mythologies of the Pioneer West. The only possible salvation of the Native population, nearly all agreed, was 'civilization' – they needed to be rescued from their antiquated savagery and ignorance, and imbued with the morality, independence and work ethic of true Americans, so that they might thrive in the modern nation. To do this, they had to be transformed into the paragon of American values – the doughty settler. Only one sacred moral panacea, the supposed backbone of the new nation, could now stand the Indian tall – 160 acres.

'To get the Indian out of the blanket and into trousers …' pronounced Merrill Gates, leader of the Lake Mohonk movement, 'we have found it necessary, as one of the first steps in developing a stronger personality in the Indian, to make him responsible for property.' The communal, ancestral homeland that defined most Native tribal systems needed to be replaced with individual landholdings, individual wealth, to generate the virtuous, civilization-building sentiments – Gates, a lay preacher, brazenly declared – of greed, envy and selfishness. 'We need to awaken in him wants. In his dull savagery he must be touched by the wings of the divine angel of discontent.' To create citizens from Indians, their new trousers needed a pocket: 'a pocket that aches to be filled with dollars!'

This revelation became a political movement, which became a Senate Bill, which became, in 1887, the Allotment Act. The Western boosters could scarcely believe their fortune – the interfering liberals had drafted a law declaring that each Indian would be transformed into a virtuous homesteader, allocated 160 acres of reservation land to cultivate and grow civilized upon.* Once every individual had been given his patch, the remaining tribal lands, supposedly held in common and enshrined in treaty, would now be pronounced 'surplus' and opened up to white settlement. Native America was to be driven to its nadir by its self-appointed saviours.

When a diminutive and idealistic anthropologist called Alice

---

* Unmarried adults got eighty acres, children forty. In some damp, forested parts of America these allocations were halved, in the interests of tree farming.

Fletcher arrived on the Nez Perce Reservation in 1889, to explain and execute the allotment process, she was met with incredulity and wrath. No one had asked the Nez Perce if they wanted to divide their communal lands, and several treaties had supposedly secured the reservation from plunder. Gradually, though, Fletcher made the unavoidability of this latest folly clear, and the individual tribe members travelled over their land with her, pointing out the tiny slivers they wished to call their own. In 1893, following yet another negotiation process characterized by division, corruption and deceit, enough Nez Perce men were induced to sign an agreement declaring over two-thirds of the reservation 'surplus', which the government could then buy up and release for settlement. White land-grabbers poured onto the fertile Camas Prairie and the timberland above the Clearwater, staking their claims – 380 in the first week alone. White demand for Nez Perce land was so great that more than a hundred allotments to tribal members were fraudulently 'cancelled' soon after the 1893 agreement, increasing the surplus but leaving many Nez Perce families landless. Thirteen white towns opened inside the supposed Nez Perce enclave. For many of the Native families now holding allotments, the unfamiliar predations of speculators, loan sharks and the taxman were too much to bear, and their homesteads passed rapidly into white ownership. By the time the government realized that allotment had been a disastrous idea, in the 1930s, the Nez Perce owned just 11 per cent of their own reservation.

Unsurprisingly, allotment reversed almost all the progress the reservation Nez Perce had made in the 1860s and 1870s. Tribal unity was all but shattered, disease and alcoholism tore through what was left of traditional community structures, and only a tiny handful of successful farmers and bureaucratic favourites stood distinct from an overwhelming scene of poverty, enforced idleness and exploitation.

The dogmatic faith that this harsh medicine would ultimately work, that eventually such a wrenching dislocation would 'kill the Indian and save the man', found expression in further official transgressions. Nez Perce children were torn from their families and sent to reprogramming boarding schools in Oregon and Utah, where they were given English names and pudding-basin haircuts, taught to recite the Founding Fathers and had their mouths washed out with soap for speaking their tribal language. They were also put to work as child labour and, as one might expect, the type of people who volunteered to run such schools rarely limited themselves to cultural abuse.

Back on the reservation, an official classification system rewarded abandonment of traditions and persecuted cultural continuity – fully anglicized 'Class 1' Nez Perce could open bank accounts and run credit at the local store, while traditionalist 'Class 3' Indians were declared 'incompetent' and not allowed control over their land or access to their own money, which the local Agent, rarely immune to corruption, 'managed' on their behalf.

Nationally, the allotment era broke Native America's back. Almost two-thirds of the land the original nations had been promised in their three hundred treaties passed into white hands, and federal efforts to wrench the tribes permanently from their roots were almost without exception catastrophic. As the official Nez Perce tribal history declares, it was during this era that the precipitous decline of the Native West took its final tumble: 'from nations of prosperity to reservations of despair'.

One group of Nez Perce declined to take up their allotted 160 acres. Chief Joseph and his fellow exiles were all too aware of the bitter divisions between modernizers and traditionalists back on the reservation, and preferred not to volunteer themselves into third-class status. By the late 1880s a return to Idaho held few attractions; the welcome would have been mixed at best, as resentment of the Dreamer Nez Perce was still high among both the white community and many of the Christian Nez Perce, who traced their declining fortunes back to the 1877 uprising. Taking an allotment would also have meant finally relinquishing all claims to the Wallowa.

The Dreamers were free to practise their own religion at Colville, and after a fractious start they had settled into a stable if desperately impoverished existence. Although progress towards self-sufficiency moved at almost glacial speed, as Yellow Wolf recalled, 'On the Colville we found wild game aplenty. Fish, berries and all kinds of roots.'

Gradually accepting that a return to the Wallowa was growing unlikely, the Nez Perce exiles began to invest their affections in their new homeland. They built up their horse herd, held their races once again and organized an autumn deer hunt. In winter they gathered in their lodges and the young were taught the songs and stories of the ancestors with a new urgency – this, it was understood, was no longer a matter of habit, but of cultural survival.

Joseph genially presided over these quiet accommodations with reality, his leadership over the exiles never in doubt as he approached the autumn of his life. But the chief refused to abandon hope of a homecoming, and continued to exploit his national celebrity to campaign for a return to the Wallowa. This was far from fanciful – the isolated valley was still sparsely settled – but the chief's pleas were more humoured than listened to now. He was entertained by two further presidents, in 1897 and 1903, paraded through the crowded streets of Washington with Buffalo Bill Cody during the dedication of President Grant's tomb in 1897 (declining Cody's offer of a star billing in his world-famous Wild West show), and appeared at the Pan-American Exposition – a giant profiteering circus of celebrity chieftains – at Madison Square Gardens in 1903.

But such acclaim counted for little in the corridors of power, where the Indian Wars were now considered to be finished business, and it counted for nothing among the settlers who'd claimed the Wallowa as their home. In August 1899 Joseph returned to the valley for the first time, accompanied by a government inspector investigating the feasibility of giving the Nez Perce their own corner to call home. Joseph visited his father's grave, and attended a public meeting at Enterprise, one of the bustling villages along the Wallowa River.

The room that afternoon was crowded, and initially respectful, but the mood changed when Joseph laid out his mission – Washington had promised, he proclaimed, that if he could find a section of the valley for his people to peacefully occupy, they would buy him the land at a fair price.

'The statement was very much doubted by those present,' reported the *Wallowa County Chieftain*, 'and considerable sport was made at the expense of the old gentleman when he said he wanted the land down near Wallowa at the forks of the river, where his father Old Chief Joseph is buried, the country around and south of the lake, and the Inmaha country.'

Joseph was laughed out of the hall, and the government inspector concluded that the Wallowa Valley, now irrigated, fenced and prospering, was Nez Perce country no more. 'It is enough that the white man has turned the desert into a garden that he should enjoy the profit of his enterprise.'

As old age began to claim him, Joseph continued to plead for justice. In 1904 he told a gathering of worthies in Seattle: 'I have but a few years to live and would like to die in my old home.'

Then, on 21 September 1904, the frail chief was sitting enjoying an open fire in front of his tepee, seeming older than his sixty-four onerous years, when his head slumped forward and he was gone. It's entirely fitting, for a man who'd spent all his days trapped in the Western chasm between perception and reality, that even his passing would be mythologized to the point of fiction: the doctor who attended the body pronounced, in a poetic flourish that was reported nationwide as a cast-iron diagnosis, that Chief Joseph of the Nez Perce had died 'of a broken heart'.

Chief Joseph's glowing obituaries traded in the commonplaces of the age – another remnant of America's Native past had faded away, another chapter was closed. And the whole story of the Indian West, by now almost all were agreed, had only one ending. It's difficult to conceive of how universally accepted was the truth expressed by a correspondent to the *Wallowa County Chieftain* in 1902: 'Indianism is an anachronism and must pass away.' Via extinction, or absorption, Native America was destined for simple non existence, the turn-of-the-century republic overwhelmingly concurred. The agreed 'final moment' of Indian resistance had been the massacre at Wounded Knee in the dead of winter 1890. At least 150 Sioux, who'd become entranced by the Ghost Dance movement, a millennial revival of ancient rites which promised to end and re-create the world as it had been before the white man came, were shot down by panicking soldiers of the Seventh Cavalry. For some commentators at the time, the instant oblivion handed to the Ghost Dancers seemed preferable to the gradual, and apparently irreversible, disappearance that awaited the rest of the Native continent. 'Why not annihilation?' asked an editorial on aboriginal America in the *Aberdeen Saturday Pioneer*. 'Their glory has fled, their spirit broken, their manhood effaced; better that they die than live the miserable wretches that they are.' (In one of history's less explicable quirks, the author of those words, Lyman Frank Baum, would later acquire international fame as the creator of *The Wonderful Wizard of Oz.*)

As the American century opened, the nation's poetry, essays, sculptures, paintings all subscribed to a single icon – the Vanishing Indian – and such certainty seemed to have foundation in hard fact. Fewer than a quarter of a million Native Americans now clung to a continent where they had once numbered perhaps ten million, and, though their tribal experiences were still varied, the breadth of their poverty, diminution and desolation offered little hope for revival.

There were fewer than a thousand Nez Perce left alive at the time of Joseph's death, where there had once been perhaps six thousand, and they were fragmented over four regions, in Colville, western

Canada, Lapwai and the nearby Umatilla reserve, their circumstances almost universally defined by penury, division and dependence. This once-prosperous people now clung to a feeble tenancy of less than 1 per cent of all the land they had held on the day Lewis and Clark had stumbled out of the Lolo forest. In 1906, just a single century after their ten-thousand-year-old culture had welcomed those first European visitors, a federal bureaucrat at Lapwai offered a stark assessment of what the Nimiipuu had become, and where they were undoubtedly heading: 'It will be only a few generations before the tribe is extinct.'

CHAPTER ELEVEN

'WE'RE STILL HERE'

'It's easy for people to love us for our past, for what we were. It's easy to love our history, our dances, our costumes, our songs. But it takes a special person to love us for who we are now, the people that we are today'

REBECCA MILES, Nez Perce

'The question is not how you can Americanize us, but how we can Americanize you'

Unnamed Native American man,
addressing the Bureau of Indian Affairs

AMERICA'S MANIFEST DESTINY was not yet fulfilled. So thought the ageing, sun-creased cowboy as he squinted genially across the dusty, scrubby ranchland in the Santa Ynez Mountains. Seeming to draw his strength from the luxury of space ahead of him, his thoughts turned to what hand might have conferred such a blessing: 'I've always believed that there was some plan that put this continent here, to be found by people from every corner of the world who had the courage and the love of freedom enough to uproot themselves, leave family and friends and homeland, to come here and develop a whole new breed of people called American. You look at the beauty of it. God really did shed his grace on America, as the song says.'

It didn't matter much to this particular cowboy that he hadn't inherited this corner of California from a pioneering grandfather, but had bought it with his old film royalties and stratospheric corporate speaking fees. Nor did it seem significant that his supposedly working farm actually only had twenty-two cows on it, just enough to qualify as an 'agricultural preserve' and sneak a $40,000 tax break. Ronald Reagan understood that the mythology of the West trumped the reality every time, proclaiming that it was America's stories, not its truths, which 'bind us together'. He didn't even feel the need to show loyalty to his adopted cowboy costume, doing more than any other post-war president to make the lives of small family ranchers untenable, putting the interests of his donors in the meat-packing cartel ahead of his fellow cowpokes. In every regard, Ronald Reagan had brought the language, and the hypocrisy, of Manifest Destiny back to the foreground of American life. More than a hundred years after the Nez Perce felt its full force, the Great Western Adventure was still not history.

After a generation of slow, often painful retreat from the public commonplaces of American destiny and divine progress, Ronald Reagan made his decisive contribution to the survival of the Western creed, and got the nation's wagons rolling again with astonishing confidence, born of faith. The mythical homesteader was returned to the high altar in the president's celebrated 1985 inauguration speech: 'A settler pushes west and sings a song, and the song echoes out forever and fills the unknowing air. It is the American sound. It is hopeful, big-hearted, idealistic, daring, decent, and fair. That is our heritage; that is our song. We sing it still.'

Once more there was no doubt expressed in America's divine mission – the country was routinely declared 'uniquely blessed' and 'set apart in a very special way' by its cheerleader-in-chief. The intellectual extensions of Manifest Destiny were also put back in place: in word and deed, the Reagan presidency held true to the assumption that man had been handed dominion over nature, and was duty bound to make profitable use of it. Environmental protections were weakened, oil, coal and mining companies were given licences to pollute, public lands were sold off, acid rain was studiously ignored. Such harm mattered little – harking straight back to the biblical literalism which had enthused the mid-nineteenth-century patriots, Reagan was obsessed with America's role in the impending Revelation, the catastrophic end of the world which he discussed often with his spiritual mentors. Infamously, when Reagan's fiercest ecological storm trooper, his Interior Secretary James Watt, was asked about the effect of his government's environmental butchery on future generations, he replied that the American continent's natural inheritance could be liquidated with impunity, because: 'I do not know how many future generations we can count on before the Lord returns.'

The cowboy president served his two terms, and his country began to edge back towards a more humble, less exceptional public discourse. In 1994 the Western writer and activist Barbara Rusmore felt able to pronounce that her standard of sanity was finally prevailing over the historical psychosis of the West: 'Many Americans simply will no longer accept the nineteenth-century approach to the West's resources. Manifest Destiny is dead.'

She was, sadly, a little previous. In January 2001, a whey-faced man leaned into a bitter Washington wind and delivered his inauguration address with a lopsided smirk that would, via the new phenomena of the global media, soon come to be the most universally annoying facial tick in the history of human civilization. Drawing to a close, he reviewed the story of America, one of justice, generosity and dignity. 'This story goes on. And an angel still rides in the whirlwind and directs this storm.'

It was such a strange choice of phrase – perhaps first penned in a mediocre English poem about the Battle of Blenheim – that commentators and conspiracy theorists analysed it to dust, but George

W. Bush's meaning was clear: America's divine destiny was once again back on the agenda. 'We are guided by a power larger than ourselves.'

As its overture suggested, in every relevant regard the parlous presidency that followed was little more than a feeble facsimile of the Reagan era. No more a cowboy than his role model, George Bush wore embroidered boots to his inauguration ball, built photo-op fences on his Texas trophy ranch, then gave genuine family ranchers a raw deal on behalf of his meat-packing and agri-business pay-masters. His conservation record was defined by the fundamentalist dogma of dominion and development, and although heroic resis-tance by grassroots environmentalists rendered the administration much less damaging than it intended to be, George Bush was still consistently damned by watchdogs and historians as 'the worst environmental President ever'. And his fundamentalist faith in the pointlessness of preservation was possibly even stronger than Reagan's – Bush was known to communicate via video message with the followers of the popular Texan pastor John Hagee, whose favourite apocalyptic slogan declared, 'Jesus's hand is on the doorknob!'

Such illustrative idiocies, apparently endorsed by electoral victory, are often used by outsiders to suggest that, at the start of the twenty-first century, a democratic majority of Americans still believed in the sacred tablets of Manifest Destiny – a chosen nation, occupying a gifted continent, leading the world to its divine redemption. That seems both unfair and untrue, but a much more robust accusation is made by the Native American writer John Mohawk: that although 'Rational America' was now numerically dominant, and had shaken off the old credo of the angelic, unimpeachable nation, it was still 'dangerously tolerant' of such a faith. Through intimidation and cowardice, old falsehoods, and their last few true believers, were allowed to retain their prominence in the public square.

What this meant, as Bush amply illustrated, was that the classic faux-Western elitist, invoking the folk memory of the patriotic, individualistic settler to justify the conduct of the corporate polluter, the extractor, the outsourcer and the down-sizer, and exploiting the dreams and prejudices of that settler's descendants to secure and apply elected power, was very much alive and potent as the new century dawned. This also meant that one final, gloomy continuity was still in place; judging by his administration's budget cuts, sweeping legal reversals and lack of interest in consultation, President Bush had also adopted his hero's antiquated attitude to those peoples who represented an alternative history of the West, possessed a rival collection of icons and maxims and idealized a different model for the continent's occupation. When Reagan was challenged in 1988 by a Moscow student over his unwillingness to meet with Native Americans, he replied with a monologue that could have been a hundred years old:

Let me tell you just a little something about the American Indian in our land. We have provided millions of acres of land for what are called preservations – or reservations, I should say. They, from the beginning, announced that they wanted to maintain their way of life, as they had always lived there in the desert and the plains and so forth. And we set up these reservations so they could, and have a Bureau of Indian Affairs to help take care of them. At the same time, we provide education for them – schools on the reservations. And they're free also to leave the reservations and be American citizens among the rest of us, and many do. Some still prefer, however, that way – that early way of life. And we've done everything we can to meet their demands as to how they want to live. Maybe we made a mistake. Maybe we should not have humoured them in that wanting to stay in that kind of primitive lifestyle. Maybe we should have said, no, come join us; be citizens along with the rest of us. As I say, many have; many have been very successful.

And I'm very pleased to meet with them, talk with them at any time and see what their grievances are or what they feel they might be … I don't know what their complaint might be.

Horace was chopping wood in his garage when we pulled up. He chose not to live in the Lapwai Reservation, staying instead in a bungalow on the outskirts of Lewiston. His friend Margot, a local television presenter who managed the many requests for Horace's time, reminded me that the octogenarian would only have the energy to chat for an hour or so. Axtell was in near-constant demand, his position as leader of the Nez Perce spiritual longhouse conferring responsibilities at weekly ceremonies of worship and tribal rites of passage, his knowledge of the Nimiipuu language and customs was treasured and craved, and friends, relations and visitors simply wanted access to his long-accumulated wisdom and reflection. It was (Horace would, I think, pragmatically concede) as if all were agreed that any ounce of his mind and memory that wasn't passed on before he himself passed on would be an unconscionable loss.

Margot had also told me that Horace didn't strictly respond to questions; he simply talked, and if you just listened you'd learn far more than the answer you sought. So as we settled into his snug, memento-crammed living room, Horace's crooked neck burying his face into the high collars of a padded lumberjack shirt, I did as I'd been told. I mentioned that I'd been to the Baptist church in Pierce, Idaho, the day before, where the preacher had chosen John 2: 15 as his text: 'Do not love the world or anything in the world.' And then I just listened.

'Well, I guess, our feelings are that when we're born from our mothers and fathers, we're born into another mother, who we call Mother Earth. Our mothers took care of us for the time that they were carrying us, and then when you come out you have to be fed by nature, you're nurtured by Mother Earth. So that's our strong belief, in her, she provides all things, the food that grows in the ground, the animals, birds, fish, everything is connected to her, everything is produced by her. And I guess the reason we all believe so much in nature, and the things that Mother Earth provides, is that that's our connection to our spirituality. Our spirituality is connected to all living things, to ourselves, to the animals and birds, the plants, the water that runs from the earth, the fish that grow in that water.

'So, I don't contradict anything that the ancestors figured out about how life became part of earth. I don't try to analyse every little thing that happened – just that everything was natural, and everything became natural to us.

'And before the other nationalities came to our land here, there was life, all kinds of life, different tribes, they all lived their own way. Every tribe had a different language and a different spirituality, and their own food from their own area. We had a way of telling time by the sun and the moon – there were all these different ways that we had, we weren't the animals people thought we were. We had our own spirituality, we had our own way to count. My grandmother knew a lot – how to collect the food, what food to collect at what time of year, the cycles.

'The changes now are so different. If you run out of food you go to the store and buy it – which makes it easy on some people and hard on others, because now we need the money. Before, everything was helping each other, giving and receiving. If some people ran short and you had it, you helped them – and it's still kind of like that for us, pretty much. But it doesn't seem like there's gonna be a peaceful time for Native Americans no more.

'Except in one respect – we're beginning to get educated. Some of our kids are getting more educated than some of the non-Indian people. We've got professionals, we've got lawyers, we've got doctors. Our ancestors had their own system of teaching the young people, men taught boys, women taught girls, it was all taught in the family. But we didn't have the formal education, everything was taught verbally, in *here* [Horace patted his heart] and that's still how a lot of our people receive things, heart to heart. There are two words for education in our language, what you learn from books and what you learn about your customs and your Indian ways. So I don't have anything against modern education, some of my own children are in high-paying jobs now, because they went to school – but they still come and ask me about the values of our old ways.'

Outside the window, the clanking construction of another layer of Lewiston's ex-urban sprawl was carrying on. I asked Horace what the traditional religion he observed had to say about the recent changes to the Nez Perce homeland we were sitting in – about the dams, the mines, the strip malls and the subdivisions.

'Myself, I opposed the dams, because it stops the migration of the steelhead and the salmon, coming upriver to spawn. And all that slack water that the dams create, it's not good for the fish, they get tired swimming in all that warm water, they like the fresh, cold water, it makes them stronger. But that's where the "need" for all the modern electrical appliances took over, you know?

'Now we're having lots of battles about these dams, especially now that all the young environmentalists who are helping us, they think the dams are causing the fish to become almost extinct. It's pretty close to that now. And it's one of our sacred foods, because it comes from the sacred water. The water is considered sacred, because without water, nothing lives, so it's the number one element that we use in our spirituality. But blocking off the water makes a lot of light, and of course someone realized that if you pour a lot of water onto sand, it'll make things grow. So the rivers are blocked and blocked, and they're using all the rivers, all the water – to make money.

'It don't seem right, they don't seem to understand what it does to our whole community, they don't regard how the homeland has to deal with it – because of money. Everything's connected to money now. I think most Native Americans, they see these things.'

Horace had seen more than most. He'd been born in 1924, to

Idaho Nez Perce who had adopted Christianity after the retreat of 1877, and was baptized and raised as a Presbyterian by his mother and grandmother. His grandmother hadn't wholly abandoned her Indian ways, though, and her traditidional knowledge of food gathering had kept the family alive during the Great Depression. When Horace was around eight years old, a seed of ambition had been planted in his mind – he had shared a sweat lodge with a blind old man who'd fought in the battles of 1877, and who had been friends with Horace's paternal great-grandfather, Timlpusmin. The elder told Horace of his ancestor's renowned courage, his horsemanship, his spiritual powers and his skill in Nez Perce dance and song, and of his battlefield death at Bear Paw. But there was no scope to keep that inheritance alive in 1930s Nez Perce country; the churches and the bureaucrats would have none of it: 'They banned everything. They made them burn their costumes, they forbid the dances, the beliefs, the natural medicines, everything.' Only the inherent tribal traditions, of generosity, patience, kinship and family closeness, still thrived beneath this cloud of cultural herbicide.

Horace instead made his way through the bleak landscape of the mid-twentieth-century Native American experience. He joined the army in 1943, before finishing high school, and patrolled the pulverized streets of Nagasaki and Hiroshima. On his return, alcohol and joblessness helped deliver the young man to 'a place where I had a lot of time to think': a fourteen-year sentence in Boise Penitentiary for robbery, mercifully reduced to a year for his good work teaching maths to his fellow students. Soon after, he caught a decisive break – securing a job at the Potlatch sawmill in Lewiston, where the camaraderie, the generosity and the shared crafts of the lumber workers struck a chord with this warrior's descendant: 'I was stepping into something that I think I'd been looking for. These guys were a different breed of people. To me, it felt like I was at home.'

Now with steady work and soon a steady wife, Andrea, Horace's confidence rose in tandem with the tentative cultural revival of the

Native Northwest, as his children's triumphs in the burgeoning pow-wow circuit of the 1960s and 1970s drew him back to his ancestral traditions. Eventually he resolved to grow his hair long, to master the ceremonies and songs of the traditional Nez Perce religion and lead the revival of the ancient faith on the Lapwai Reservation. Guided by spiritual leaders from up at Nespelem, where the Nez Perce faith traditions had continued unbroken since Joseph's people had arrived there in 1885, Horace began to lead the rites and rituals of his esteemed great-grandfather's ways, the ceremonies of sunrise and sunset, earth and water, salmon and sacred roots – and more and more Nez Perce joined him, either turning their backs on Christianity or taking two paths to the Creator. Now, near the end of an astonishing journey, Horace was the human epicentre of an upsurge of Nez Perce cultural and spiritual expression, of naming ceremonies, first hunts, salmon celebrations, traditional funerals, language lessons, drum circles, craft clubs and sweat lodges. His efforts were far from solitary, but his personal satisfaction was understandable: 'For a while there, they had us. But we're starting to come back. I don't dance no more, I'm too old for that – but my children do, and my grandchildren, and I've even got some great-grandchildren that are learning, they get up and dance. As our ancestors did. It's just one thing we do, so that people understand, that we still hold on to our traditions, and our culture. That we're still here.'

We're still here. It's difficult to comprehend the pleasure that simple statement must bring – for the Nez Perce had spent over half a century on the very brink of disappearance. The tribe that Horace had been born into in 1924 was, along with almost all of Native America, bouncing along the bottom, almost entirely severed from the giddy national explosion of the Roaring Twenties. Economic activity on the reservation had been practically extinguished – perhaps 2 per cent of the land the Nez Perce had received through allotment was being worked by Nez Perce hands, the remainder was being leased to white farmers. The loathed BIA, the Bureau of Indian Affairs, was in monolithic control of all aspects of reservation life, pimping the tribe's resources of timber and land to local interests, and waging its continued war against any remnants of traditional culture. The renegade legacy of the heroes of 1877 was no source of pride or commemoration, as a generation was now in the ascendancy who'd been so bullied and belittled by allotment, boarding schools and the BIA that many had come to fear and resent Indianness as a source of suffering and subjection. The Nez Perce were doing little more than surviving.

The faint beginnings of a renaissance coincided with the arrival on the national scene of a truly intriguing figure – John Collier. A social worker from south-west USA, Collier was a full-blood member of the Wannabe tribe – he'd had a miserable childhood and had grown disillusioned with the individualism and profiteering that he felt defined white America, so chose to model himself as defender and friend of the native Pueblo communities of the Southwest. As he rose to national prominence for his articulate campaigning against the government's neglect of Native America, Collier expressed views a clear generation ahead of their time. He was a multiculturalist, believing that ethnic diversity was a greater virtue than the one-culture-fits-all 'melting pot' mantra that went unchallenged in American public policy at the time, and he also declared that the moral salvation of the nation lay in elevating the ancient cultures he idolized – 'They had what the world has lost. They have it now. What the world has lost, the world must have again, lest it die.'

Such overwrought stuff got short shrift in the corridors of power, where the assumption remained that tribal arrangements were just a passing phase on the route to the melting pot – until the Great Depression offered a more damning critique of unfettered capitalism than Collier could ever pen. With *laissez-faire* out of favour, and evidence mounting of the shameful poverty on most reservations, Franklin D. Roosevelt made a rare political decision – handing the bureaucracy to an activist. Collier was appointed head of the BIA in 1930, and was given remarkably free rein.

Allotment was finally called off. Freedom of religion was enshrined on the reservations. The steady bleed of land out of tribal hands and into white ownership was staunched. The legal rights of the tribes were more vigorously enforced. Most remarkably, Collier drew up plans for Indian self-government, giving tribes the chance to draft constitutions and elect representative councils. It was a remarkable one-man revolution – but Collier's fantasy of revived, empowered tribes showcasing values that modern America couldn't ignore didn't fall into place. Many tribes were profoundly suspicious of his motives – the Nez Perce among them, whose leaders felt Collier's reverence for traditional religions smacked of an enforced step backwards, and that his model for tribal governments proposed turning their nationhood into little more than a government department. The Nez Perce had in fact drafted their own 'modern' constitution in 1927 – but their nascent government was blighted in just the same way as those tribal administrations set up by Collier's reforms: they were still little more than pets of the BIA, which was blooming into a textbook sprawling, self-serving bureaucracy, a holding tank for sub-par civil servants and senators' sons. Collier's top-down reforms were easily lost in the murky soup of the Bureau. A genuine Indian revival would have to start at its roots, within Native America itself.

The Second World War made a significant contribution to that recovery, as 25,000 Native Americans (granted citizenship of their own land in 1924) served in the Allied forces. Those who survived came home with the confidence born of comradeship, and many concluded that the continued neglect of the reservations was now a two-fold breach, of both the tribal treaties and the military covenant.

The contrast between the gleaming post-war nation and the reservations was indeed bewildering – Native American life expectancy still barely crept over forty, infant mortality rates were more than double the national average and average incomes were less than a quarter of the national level. Alcoholism was a constant attrition on family and community life, and provided white America with a fresh icon to fixate on – the Native man asleep on a pavement, brown paper bag in hand. But prejudice and stagnation alone didn't radicalize the post-war generation – the fresh threat of total disappearance did.

For the renewed confidence in the American Way during the Eisenhower boom years had turned Washington attitudes to Native America 180 degrees from John Collier's multicultural idealism, and the politicians were facing the melting pot once again. Reservations, it was felt, had the distinct odour of Communism about them, and a new policy to assimilate indigenous America into a single, free-market society was devised in 1953. The scheme was called, with insufficient regard to public relations, Termination. In essence, the government offered to buy reservations out, offering individual tribe members cash for their land and their identity – if tribes voted for Termination, their reservations and governments would cease to exist, as would any legal rights enshrined in their treaties. Overnight, they'd become simply individual Americans, holding a relatively large cheque to get them started. To add to the pressure to fragment the reservations, the American states were encouraged to meddle in tribal affairs, and tribe members were also offered cash to relocate to the city. Many thousands did, with mixed results.

For those few tribes who were bullied, browbeaten or bribed into accepting Termination, it was a disaster, as the money fizzled away to reveal broken societal bonds, abandoned federal care and a paralysing loss of identity. The famous Native critique of white American society – 'You are each a one-man tribe' – was being forced onto its authors. But for many other tribes, Termination was a catalyst, a threat so terrifying that apathy and resignation were swept aside by a revived activism. The Nez Perce tribal government, which had strengthened its constitution in 1948 but was still a feeble, unrepresentative group, suddenly found that its general meetings were standing-room only. Traditionalists who had shunned the modern tribal governments now got engaged, to argue down any advocates for Termination, and the small but growing number of Indians with legal training were shoved front and centre to battle for their communities' survival. A corner had been turned.

As the 1960s opened, the stars aligned for a remarkable, if uneven, resurrection. Across America, the Native population had finally stopped declining, and was back up to over half a million – and while this fact often worsened the burden of poverty, at least the Vanishing Indian had seemed to have vanished. A new generation of leaders and activists also sprang up, some empowered by law degrees, others influenced by the counter-culture radicalism of the era, most inspired by both of Horace's types of education, as traditional Indian spirituality and custom enjoyed a revival through developments such as the pow-wow circuit and bestselling books such as the Oglala Sioux treatise *Black Elk Speaks*. A series of demonstrations helped embed confident demands for Native American rights in the national consciousness: the protest march across the country entitled the Trail of Broken Treaties, and forced occupations of Alcatraz Island and Wounded Knee. Like all movements for change, the Native American activists disagreed with each other almost as much as with their combatants, but a coherent demand shone through: to retain their communal identities, and exercise their right to manage their own affairs and solve their own desperate problems, their way. As the newly formed National Congress of American Indians put it, 'a right to choose our own way of life'.

Not, to many minds, coincidentally, the federal governments of the 1960s and 1970s that did so much to protect what was left of the natural continent also listened most closely to the demands of its

341

indigenous peoples, and Presidents Kennedy, Johnson and Nixon each made their contribution to the liberation of Native America. The suffocating blanket of the BIA was partially lifted, as the government began to give funds directly to tribal governments to run their own childcare, schools, health services, natural resources and more. The new federal mantra was 'Indian self-determination' – and this time it truly meant something, because, unlike in the Collier era, it was the tribes driving reform forward, not the government deigning to allow it. For the most dramatic changes in Indian Country in the 1960s, 1970s and early 1980s weren't handed down by benign legislators, they were confirmed with the rap of a judge's gavel. Native America was winning its most important battles in court – and for the Nez Perce, in common with many of the tribes of the Northwest, their most important ally was an unexpected figure from their past: Isaac Stevens.

If you'd told Isaac Stevens in 1855 that the treaty he was negotiating with the tribes of the Columbia Plateau would still be legally enforceable 150 years later, he may well have responded with a laugh. Stevens himself described his treaties, in which the Nez Perce had handed over 7.5 million acres of land to create their first reservation, as 'temporary', prior to what he saw as the inevitable absorption of the Northwest's tribes into American society: 'the great end to be looked to is the gradual civilization of the Indians.' In a considerable rush, he'd cadged many of the treaties' clauses from other people's work, and got the names and numbers of several tribes badly wrong. His colleague Benjamin Shaw later described Stevens' attitude to the creation of the reservations: 'there was no thought or expectation on the part of Gov. Stevens in the capacity of superintendent of Indian affairs, or treaty commissioner, that these were to be the permanent homes of the respective tribes.' But that's not what he told the Nez Perce: 'If we make a treaty with you,' he declared, 'you can rely on all its provisions being carried out strictly.' He was also reported to have told one elder that the treaty would last 'as long as the water flows in the rivers'. And when you're handing over half your ancestral lands to allow a new country to come into being, it doesn't matter a jot, either legally or morally, that your negotiating partner is lying through his teeth.

Almost as soon as the treaty-signing process began, America's judges began to reveal the true potency of these documents – by interpreting them in the only rational, possible way: as solemn agreements between two parties who actually meant what they were saying. Treaties, American legal tradition dictates, are part of the 'supreme law of the land', binding on all aspects of the nation's government unless repealed by a specific Act of Congress. Another perfectly sane legal principle was also germane – that when a large, powerful organization fails properly to clarify an agreement with a smaller, less powerful group, any fudging, flannelling or ambiguity is settled in the junior partner's favour. For a century and more, these legal judgements did little more than clarify the transparently obvious – that the government was breaking its promises to Indian Country – but in the 1960s, as Native America regained the confidence and the capacity to hold the United States to account, it was time for a few of those promises to be honoured.

The greatest significance of the Indian treaties now lay not in any particular clause, but in the documents' very existence. Put simply, if America signs a treaty with France, it's implicitly accepting France's status, independence and freedom of action, as a nation state – in a single invaluable word, its *sovereignty*. America doesn't sign treaties with book clubs or restaurant chains, only sovereign bodies. So, as the seminal handbook of Indian law (commissioned by John Collier) states, 'Each Indian tribe begins its relationship with the Federal government as a sovereign power, recognized as such in treaty and legislation.'

There was a considerable irony here – many of the Indian Wars, including the Nez Perce's conflict, had been caused in part by the fact that the Indian signatories *were not* acting as representatives of entire and definite tribes, but were speaking only for their band or village, leaving their allies and relations free to take their own path. But to get hold of the land, Stevens and company had treated the chiefs as national governments, who were speaking with a single, binding voice. But now, in the 1960s, there *were* unquestionable tribal governments in place, either formed by the Collier reforms or by internal initiatives, and they were using that single voice to lay claim to the sovereignty enshrined in their treaties And far more often than not, the judges agreed, deciding lawsuits that established tribal control over an ever-expanding civic sphere, of criminal justice on the reservations, resource management, tax collection, employment law and, of course, gambling. The once omnipotent BIA was trimmed down to not much more than a purchasing department, funnelling funds to the blossoming tribal administrations, to run their own day-care centres, drop-in clinics, colleges and so on. Most important, and controversial, were the tribes' litany of victories over the states in which their reservations stood – local sheriffs, taxmen, foresters and wildlife managers all got put in their place, which was out of Indians' business. The treaties made it clear – the sovereign tribes dealt with the national government they'd signed with, and them alone. Congress *did* have the right to meddle in Indian affairs, and to apply federal law on the reservations, but they also had the responsibility – known as the trust doctrine – to act in the tribes' interest. It was a complex and sometimes contradictory relationship, but with a simple truth at its heart – the treaties confirmed that the tribes were independent, unique Americans.

For the Nez Perce, one tarnished guarantee did more to radicalize and revive their public dealings – and indeed those of the entire Native Northwest – than any other. They'd been promised fish.

'The exclusive right of taking fish in all the streams where running through or bordering said reservation is further secured to said Indians; as also the right of taking fish at all usual and accustomed places in common with the citizens of the Territory.' Such hazy, soporific prose does much to explain why American judges have traditionally drawn straws to avoid sitting on Indian treaty cases, but for the Nez Perce in 1855 the significance of Article 3, Paragraph 2 of their compact with Isaac Stevens was beyond doubt – all the fishing spots on the reservation were theirs alone, plus they had retained the right to take fish at any traditional spots that lay beyond the new boundaries. Stevens, one suspects, saw this as a negligible concession – surely, there would always be enough fish for everyone in the Columbia rivers?

By 1960, it seemed entirely possible that there would soon be no fish at all migrating through the Columbia system. Overharvesting, habitat ruination and dam building had all contributed to the implosion of the great salmonid migrations, and the imperilled commercial and sports fishing industries turned to the states of Idaho, Oregon and Washington for rescue. All parties swiftly agreed on the greatest threat to the survival of the ancient runs – Native American fishermen, who were using traditional means to fish at their usual, ancestral places, and refused to be controlled by state-licensing arrangements.

Official campaigns of Indian harassment, arrest and confiscation became commonplace across the Northwest in the early 1960s as states cited their new-found fervour for conservation to prevent and restrain off-reservation tribal fishing. The new generation of Native activists responded with 'fish-ins', provocative assertions of their treaty rights to harvest ancient sites, that may or may not have been helped by the presence of such celebrity well-wishers as Marlon Brando and Jane Fonda. It was a tense, spiteful time, often flaring into scuffles and armed stand-offs on riverbanks and roadsides – one congressman later compared the battle over Northwestern salmon with the conflict over segregated buses in the Deep South. Eventually, the federal government was persuaded to help settle the matter in court, joining the Nez Perce, the Yakama, the Warm Springs and the Umatilla in a joint 1968 lawsuit against the State of Oregon, ostensibly to decide the fate of fourteen Yakama members arrested for off-reservation fishing, but ultimately to determine what the tribal treaties meant in an age of scarce salmon.

They meant plenty. On 8 July 1969 Judge Robert Belloni confirmed that the tribes retained the treaty right to their 'usual and accustomed' fishing spots, and that they were equal, if not senior, partners with the states in deciding how to protect and restore the migrating runs through those areas. The states had to consult with the tribes before agreeing to any harvest restrictions, and, crucially, they were ordered to cut back on non-treaty (predominantly white) fishing first, in order to ensure the Natives got a 'fair and equitable share' of the fish, as Stevens had clearly promised. The tribes were driven still deeper into the heart of the great salmon debate by a second momentous ruling, in 1974, when Judge George Boldt clarified what 'fair and equitable' meant – the treaty tribes were entitled to fully *half* the sustainable catch passing through their traditional spots. This was perhaps ten times more fish than the states were currently allowing the tribes to take – but Isaac Stevens had promised Native fishing 'in common' with the settlers, and what else could he have meant but a fair, fifty-fifty split? Also noting that there was, in fact, no meaningful evidence that the Indians represented a conservation threat to their sacred salmon, Judge Boldt re-emphasized that the tribes had the right to be involved in, and often in charge of, efforts to ensure the fish they'd been promised didn't become extinct.

It's hard to overstate the tectonic reshuffle these decisions forced. The tribes stormed the gates of salmon recovery and regulation, rapidly acquiring armies of hundreds of scientists and fieldworkers to work with the states, the federal hatcheries and the hydropower companies to increase the numbers of salmon and steelheads surviving their compromised migrations, and to decide how many fish could be caught. As campaigning author Alvin Josephy recorded with pleasure: 'Given an opportunity, the tribes quickly proved that they were capable and committed conservationists who had always known that their own future lay in the survival of the fish.' The breathtaking clout of the treaty promises continued to emerge. Tribes could apply pressure to local and national authorities to clean up despoiled habitats that were jeopardizing their pledged catch, even on 'usual and accustomed' sites hundreds of miles beyond reservation borders – which the Nez Perce did at Hanford, the nuclear bomb-making site on the Columbia River that may well be the most polluted place in America. And, most controversial of all, they'd been handed a potent claim on the precious Western water. Stevens had implicitly conceded enough of the rivers flowing through the reservation to allow the Nez Perce to enjoy full 'use and benefit' of their land, but now there was another pledge to honour – enough water to keep the catch alive. As one federal dam engineer told me with a resigned shrug, standing at the top of the Dworshak Dam on the Clearwater River: 'The Nez Perce run this dam now. Their scientists stick their thermometers in the river, and if they think it's too hot for the fish, they pick up the phone, and we release some water downstream. They're in charge.'

For the white neighbours of the tribes this was a bewildering and infuriating turn of events. Once the states abandoned their initial response of simply ignoring the Belloni and Boldt rulings, their new harvest restrictions helped force many white fishermen out of business and rendered recreational fishers apoplectic with rage. Both judges received death threats; Boldt was hanged in effigy and slandered mercilessly. A new cultural and political industry – treaty paranoia – blossomed in the white Northwest and spread across the country, as a fresh pejorative was aimed at Native Americans: they were now labelled 'super-citizens', set apart from other Americans by their enshrined rights and freedoms, in what many saw as a profoundly un-American way. The public square in Idaho took perhaps longest to adapt to this new reality and in 1977 the Nez Perce found themselves fighting a fresh war – just a few miles upstream from where the last one had started a century earlier in White Bird Canyon.

Rapid River, a fast-flowing tributary of the Salmon, was undoubtedly a 'usual and accustomed' place for Nez Perce fishermen, who'd been hauling salmon onto the banks for thousands of years. But when the final splurge of dam-building tore the heart out of the migration, the State of Idaho simply banned all fishing at Rapid River without consulting the tribe. The stand-off that followed veered from bald terror to bleak farce – more than eighty Nez Perce were arrested for asserting their treaty rights, truckloads of heavily armed state policemen patrolled the roads alongside Rapid River, cheerless bumper stickers such as 'Save the salmon, kill an Indian' encouraged locals to fire regular potshots at tribal fishermen. The state governor displayed an impressive ignorance of treaty law by suggesting, as a compromise, that the Nez Perce be allowed to continue to 'fish', but without nets or hooks. Eventually, in 1982, a local judge imposed sanity and Idaho was forced to cooperate with the Nez Perce on preserving the Rapid River runs. It was a decisive victory for the increasingly confident tribe, but not for the salmon: at the time of writing, there remains next to no chance that the Nez Perce will ever see their ancient fishery sustainably restored, or that the white communities alongside Rapid River will ever have their livelihoods secured, without some of the four Lower Snake River dams being breached. And for that to happen, the ever more influential Columbia River tribes and their growing litany of allies from federal scientists, conservation campaigners and fishing communities will have to lead their neighbours, the descendants of the great Western settlement, over a considerable mental leap – into accepting that their presence here isn't down to destiny but to a deal that still stands. Donald Sampson, a fish biologist for the neighbouring Umatilla tribe, described the difficult dialogue perfectly.

'A farmer came in and told me how hard his grandfather worked to make a homestead three generations ago, and how things could go belly up if the Snake River dams are breached. I told him about my grandfather, who worked the same way to make a living fishing the Columbia … he was a seven-hundredth generation fisherman.'

'If you want an example of the failure of socialism, don't go to Russia. Come to America, and go to the Indian reservations.' James Watt, Ronald Reagan's caustic Interior Secretary, generated just as much offence as he intended with this ignorant barb, but for a European visitor to the Nez Perce community at Lapwai there's an intriguing ambiguity to his comment. Visited from a continent dominated for half a century by a social contract which Watt would surely have considered 'socialism', Lapwai stirs memories of home that no white town in the area evokes. Small houses, scrappy yards and battered trucks speak of hard, uncertain lives; but a gleaming public health centre, sprawling school, social homes and numerous community endeavours – the day-care centre, cultural services department, resource managers, sports facilities, employment bureau and more – testify to a committed civic effort, visibly 'European' in scale. In the year 2000 the Nez Perce's public sector accounted for around 42 per cent of the tribe's economic activity – the same proportion as in Great Britain.

Passing through the community centre, its walls plastered with the faces of young Nez Perce currently serving in the armed forces, you reach the government offices, a fiercely lit bungalow complex of quiet industry; in 2006 the government had, overall, more than nine hundred employees, growing essentially from zero in 1948. Down one corridor, a team of young lawyers work on the tribes' rolling cast of legal conflicts over water, land, employment rights and conservation. And on the morning of my visit Rebecca Miles was sitting in her corner office, the elected chairperson of the Nez Perce Tribal Executive Committee, the highest position in the tribal government.

Horace Axtell and Rebecca Miles, photographed in 2006.

If Horace Axtell embodied the spiritual revival of the Nez Perce, Rebecca personified its astonishing political resurgence.

Just thirty-three when we met, Rebecca had combined raising two children with securing her bachelor's and master's degrees, before turning down a career in academia to come home and serve her tribe. When she was chosen for the Executive Committee chair, in 2005, she was the youngest person, and the first woman, to hold the job. Unsurprisingly, her old alma mater, Washington State University, had elected her their Woman of the Year in 2006.

A watchful, cautiously charming woman, she seemed at once enthused by her elevation and a little exhausted by it: 'I've never been in a position that was so hard, that sometimes puts you in tears, but the work is the most rewarding you will ever do. The local journalists round here call us "the last true democracy". If you make a bad decision, you're always going to hear about it at our general council meetings, or the store, or you're going to get a call at home – you'll hear. Tribal government can be brutal.'

But as the pictures of her grandparents perched prominently on her desk indicated, she felt an obligation to serve, born of a troubled past.

'My grandparents, they went through the hardest time. You know, for a long time they couldn't even speak about the boarding schools, about how they were forced to denounce their own culture. My grandfather never spoke about what they did to him there – and my grandmother, just now, at the very end of her life, she's only now starting to talk about it. My grandparents gave me a good grounding, helping me to understand the war and what it did to our people, why we still have people living in different tribes. I descend from people that were in that war, that were killed. My grandfather – his grandmother survived the war and made it up into Canada, where she had his father, and then his father came back to Lapwai. So I'm as close as it gets.'

And such a focus on the past was not, she contended, a burden, but an inspiration. 'In my generation, we look back and we say, "Wow, they made some significant decisions, so that we would survive today, so what's my duty, for the next *seven generations*? What are the decisions we're making today, so that they can enjoy the same life that I have?" A lot of the time we get into disagreements with the state, or with the United States, and their focus is just so nearsighted. For them, twenty or thirty years is a lifetime, that's forever, but to us it's no time at all. We look way beyond that. There are definitely different values.'

And it's those different values which have brought the modern Nez Perce a degree of local and national fame – fame which, for those who don't share their principles, shades into notoriety. For while no community is homogeneous in its beliefs, and no government perfectly reflects that plurality, the modern Nez Perce tribe have shown time and again that they aspire to the simple credo of their most famous son – 'The earth and I are of one mind.'

'We have – and it's not something that you can even teach, it's just kind of within you – an unwritten law of the way you do things,' Rebecca insists. 'There are certain things that you just do. For example, there's no question in salmon recovery, or in any of the natural resources, innately we know that their preservation and conservation are of the utmost importance, as they're all culturally significant to us. So there's never a debate on salmon, or on our roots and berries, or the elk, or the deer, it's agreed they're the highest priority, because they're our culture. So on the environment, you don't see a debate from our table – where you'll see "healthy discussions" is on business decisions or economic expansion, but on these cultural issues, the unwritten law is there to guide us.'

A record of decisions supported the politician's rhetoric. The Nez Perce had positively exploded into the salmon and steelhead recovery campaign, developing ground-breaking hatchery systems along more natural lines, working with landholders and the Forest Service painstakingly to restore the riverside habitats that had been rendered uninhabitable by the great timber plunder and irrigation projects, and telling the state and federal powers, over and over again, that they would eventually have to choose between fewer dams or no salmon. They'd also campaigned against thoughtless sprawl in their sacred ancestral homelands, most obviously where those lands sat within Oregon's borders, and had thus been subjected to the bewildering Measure 37. The tribe had managed the timberlands within their landholdings along sane, sustainable lines, and had also secured government funding for their efforts to clean up the air and the water in their corner of Idaho. Most of all, as one Idaho Fish and Game worker explained to me, they helped their numerous partners in the West's sprawling public sector get things done in environmental rescue: 'What the Nez Perce really bring is leadership. When they start talking about the fish, and the wildlife and the water, people stop and listen, because they're talking about their way of life. They're leaders.'

One piece of leadership stands out, and one creature. The wolf belongs, naturally and culturally, in north-central Idaho – wolves were a thriving predatory presence prior to the pioneers, and the Nez Perce's Coyote stories regularly refer to their shadowy, unsociable presence in the forests. They were revered as outstanding hunters, and some stories record that they taught the Nez Perce to sing, while others suggest that if starvation ever beckoned, your final resort could be to boil the bones of a wolf's victim, and drink the broth. When the settlers arrived, their relationship with the wolves was initially an unfortunate mix of carrot and stick – filling the landscape with dull, edible cattle and sheep, while relentlessly persecuting the packs that grew fat on such benevolence – but the bullets and poison pellets won out in the end and wolves were eradicated from the Northwest by the 1930s. Their defeat in many ways symbolized the pragmatic taming of this landscape, a just war fought and won to secure families' livelihoods. And when, in the late 1980s, the US Fish and Wildlife Service began to tiptoe around the idea of reintroducing wolves into the region, the battle that commenced became almost the exemplary conservation debate. While the prospect of getting wolves back into the Rockies generated nationwide enthusiasm, as letter-writing and lobbying campaigns grasped at this chance to undo a totemic ecological crime, Idaho's ranchers, hunters and politicians simply couldn't believe what they were hearing, a laughable whimsy that rapidly, inexplicably, grew into a genuine threat. As the 1990s opened, and it became clear that the government really *was* going to use the Endangered Species Act to bring wolves home, the State of Idaho declared that it would have nothing to do with instigating such folly: 'Historically, wolves were eliminated in Idaho in recognition that an agricultural economy could not coexist with an exploding predator wolf population.' All branches of the state's government were barred from touching the restoration programme – if the Fed's wanted to release wolves into Idaho, they would have to find another local partner.

They did. In 1995 the Nez Perce became the first Native American tribe to take management control of an Endangered Species programme. Fifteen Canadian wolves were released into the Idaho wilderness – Horace Axtell was there that day, to sing and pray for them – and the Nez Perce's team of scientists began to monitor and manage their wards' homecoming. In conservation terms, the tribe and their partners across the Rockies enjoyed unparalleled success, as the wolves raced in just eight years far beyond the sustainable population minimum, of thirty breeding pairs. The restoration of a missing piece of the regional ecological jigsaw also had benign, if not always predictable, impacts: it seems likely, for example, that the elk herds became more mobile, which was good for the willow trees, which helped revive the beaver population. And there was little evidence of Armageddon on the ranches – in 2006, wolves accounted for just 1 per cent of local sheep and cattle loss. Overall, wolf restoration, and the Nez Perce's role in it, seemed to many campaigners, political leaders and ordinary Americans to be a profound statement about the national direction of travel, and the country's changing relationship with its wild places and dark past.

But there was little talk of success in the white rural communities of north-central Idaho – pictures of eviscerated cattle and shredded lambs were stuck on cafeteria walls, anecdotal proof of disappearing elk herds trumped all the statistical evidence that they were actually thriving, and an intractable myth sprang up that the modern wolves were somehow twice the size of the old ones. One spectre was dangled to particularly unsettling effect: some day soon, a wolf would surely take a baby. (In fact, there have been no recorded fatal wolf attacks in America since the start of the twentieth century, and just one in Canada.) But the gloom persisted. In one inspired reaction to the out-of-state liberals blamed for this imposition, an Idaho representative introduced a congressional bill proposing a wolf-return programme a hundred miles outside New York City – 'Eighty per cent of New Yorkers say they are in favour of wolf reintroduction,' he sniffed. Back in north-central Idaho, wolf restoration was lamented as insult and idiocy, and as a disturbing symbol of the regional influence of a revived Nez Perce tribe and its many allies. Only one image could generate more distress – the ever-expanding edifice of the Clearwater River Casino.

'Our people always gambled,' explained Rebecca Miles, her face betraying a touch of boredom at having to cover such well-worn ground. 'Historically, we have always had ways of gambling, in games and races. So it is a fit, you know, it's a modern fit. Particularly in terms of the actual fulfilment of our promises.' This is the point made again and again nationwide – that the Isaac Stevens treaty, like all the other legal treaties, made it crystal clear that tribes dealt direct with the United States government, as sovereign entities. And in the late 1970s a few enterprising tribes realized that this principle meant that the restrictions on gambling in their home states – usually opening hours, or the size of jackpots – couldn't touch them, so they went to work. It was a serendipitous discovery – Ronald Reagan was slashing domestic spending at the time, and, perhaps unsurprisingly, the cuts were disproportionately impoverishing Indian social services – so tribes across the country leapt on this desperately needed source of income. State governments went spare, sending in their sheriffs to shut down the operations (not because gambling was a sin, but because the Native set-ups threatened state lotteries and white bingo halls) but the judicial verdicts all went one way – gambling was undoubtedly sovereign territory. Lobbied from both sides to clarify the situation, Congress passed the Indian Gaming Regulatory Act in 1988, which allowed the states to participate in the establishment of tribal casinos, but broadly let the boom continue. Within fifteen years, Native America had claimed a fifth of the country's gambling market – in 2006, their revenue amounted to over $22 billion a year. Taken as a whole, Native Americans shot from the poorest minority group in America to the second richest – and a brand new stereotype was born, of the morally and culturally compromised Casino Indian, selling his sovereign rights to mob connections and Washington lobbyists for a Hummer and a rhinestone Stetson. The reality was that more of this astonishing boom was invested in social, educational, health and environmental improvements than any previous great American economic explosion, and that the voices bewailing the moral collapse of Native America were almost always those of local politicians who had no intention of closing the casinos down, but just wanted to tax them more. The benefit was also incredibly uneven; while some tribes had single properties pulling in $1 billion a year, over half of the tribes in the US hadn't even opened casinos by 2007, and many of the very poorest tribes would never see any gain, because their reservations were in isolated, sparsely populated corners of the country.

But the Nez Perce tribe, by chance, did have a large conurbation nearby, which almost perfectly matched the mediocre demographic traits of the ideal casino catchment – Lewiston.

In 1996, after experimenting with a small bingo operation in Kamiah, the Nez Perce opened the Clearwater River Casino, in a gigantic plastic tent at the nearest corner of their reservation to Lewiston. It was a hit with the locals, hauling in $10 million a year by 2000 – but the Idaho State government, with a constitutional ban on slot machines to enforce and a lucrative state lottery to protect, offered endless objections. Eventually, in 2002, the Native tribes of Idaho gathered enough signatures to force a state-wide referendum legitimizing their efforts – and the people of Idaho decided that tribal gambling was a small step to correcting a large wrong, and voted, by 58 per cent, to let the tribes run their casinos as they proposed. Feeling more secure, the Nez Perce announced plans for a full-tilt operation, with hotel, swimming pool, conference centre and a small arena to host boxing matches and fading Country and Western stars.

The new complex was completed just as this book was being finished, and I've yet to visit it, but I did spend time in the original giant plastic tent, and in several other tribal casinos across the

Northwest. They are all profoundly depressing places, not for any particular puritanical reason regarding the tribes' proud histories or cultural values, but simply because *all* mechanized gambling halls – mindless, manipulative, cynical, impoverishing – are designed to sap the soul. Watching the largely elderly and not obviously wealthy clientele of the Clearwater Casino – many bussed in on free transfers from Lewiston – blankly feeding their cash into the clanking, bleeping avenues of gaming machines, the common critique of all government-sponsored gambling springs easily to mind: it's just a way of recycling welfare cheques. One also can't help but conclude that while the local nickname of the Clearwater River Casino may not be entirely decorous, it also contains a modicum of truth: welcome to 'Chief Joseph's Revenge'.

Rebecca Miles, however, is quite unrepentant. 'Gaming is absolutely necessary. It allows us to actually *live* sovereignty, to live free.

'I've actually heard government officials say there's no way the Federal government could ever uphold their promises to all the 542 tribes they made them to, and that gaming is the *only* thing that can supplement that, and allow us to do it for ourselves. For example, in our treaty the government promised us health and education – well, even the lowest state welfare is better than our service from the government. If you look at the funding of the Indian Health Service, you can probably attribute early deaths and unnecessary deaths to that funding – and the government can't seem to fix that. So now we do it ourselves. And we can say, "You know, the government's not putting enough into education, so we're going to supplement that, and put in $200,000 so that all our students can have all their unmet needs covered to go to any college in the country." Without gaming, that wouldn't be possible.'

The impact of the casino had been nothing less than revolutionary. Unemployment on the reservation had fallen from seasonal highs of up to 75 per cent down to perhaps 10 per cent. (Previously, reservation unemployment had seemed essentially insoluble, as the modern global economy could find no place for communities where extended family ties were so tight that moving away for work was a rare and traumatic decision. The Nez Perce, for example, had been unable to fill National Parks jobs at their own historic battlefield sites in Montana, as that was too far from home.) And there'd been money to invest in the tribe's social problems – because while the tribe has seemingly escaped oblivion (membership by 2007 was over 3500, more than treble the nadir of the turn of the century) by no measure were the Nez Perce healed from what Miles calls the 'historic trauma' of the last two centuries – there was the astonishing pandemic of diabetes (Native Americans are by far the most afflicted group in the country, with an incidence reaching 10 per cent), there were the challenges of alcoholism and domestic abuse in a community shorn of its historic measures of male status, and a constant battle to engage those tribe members who felt excluded by the recent revival in traditional skills and activities, or resentful of the esteem bestowed upon such modern figureheads as Miles. But at least the casino money could be spent with care and commitment – on support for young mothers, for example, or on the cultural revival programmes that had been shown to help reverse destructive life-styles through discipline and self-respect, or on education, through schooling, tuition fees, retraining and scholarship funds.

The tribe had even pledged, following that 2002 referendum, to spend several hundred thousand casino dollars a year supporting the desperately underfunded schools in their neighbouring white communities. The local educators were ecstatic but elsewhere enmity remained. The Nez Perce faced a familiar problem in modern Indian Country, that many of their neighbours could accept Native sovereignty, or the gradual escape from Native poverty, but don't seem to enjoy seeing *both*.

'To be in poverty is not freedom. And the State of Idaho, and the residents around here, they just don't get that. There's almost this feeling that they *want* to keep us down, and pathetic, and not worthy.'

But the communities of which she spoke were themselves in profound trouble. Pierce, Grangeville and Cottonwood nearby, plus Dubois to the south, Enterprise and Wallowa back in Oregon, Darby, Opportunity, Shawmut and Judith Gap over in Montana, all the fading little towns I'd passed through on the Nez Perce's journey, their populations ageing and falling, their schools shrinking, Main Streets emptying, their family wage jobs getting cut and their land prices getting hiked by the trophy ranchers. Did Rebecca not feel any sympathy for them?

'Most of the time ... no. Because it's so ironic that, still, when we get into our battles, over water, or salmon, *our* way of life is still completely disregarded.

'It's almost like there's this American right, this privilege, of "How dare these people take away my individual rights?" We especially get that from private landowners, that thinking that was ingrained in them when they started to open up the West and settle the West, that they have a *right* to it. We hear people saying, "My granddad was the first generation out here", with a total disregard for the people, our people, that lived here then. It's almost as if we weren't human, they just needed to remove us and take over. So – I don't have a lot of sympathy ... And then ... I do. Because, for example, when you get these people coming up here from California, building luxury homes and boosting the market, the local people suffer. And I have a heart for them.

'You know, there needs to be a coming together, a unification, asking, "What do we value?" People in the Northwest, what we're known for is our beautiful country – the trees, mountains, rivers, streams. But while everyday life is going on, the Northwesterners don't seem to get that what you value about being a Northwesterner, we're losing it right from beneath us, if we don't stop and say: "What we value, we're going to protect." And we *do* value the same things – healthy rivers, beautiful mountains, clean air – but we're not connecting that with our vast development of everything.

'You really need to start thinking in the way our people think – and ask what we want to see here in a hundred years, or in two hundred years. You have to ask yourself the deeper question. And we have the power to do that, we just haven't done it yet. There is an answer.'

Chief Joseph's grave, fittingly, stands proud in a scene of despair. A small white obelisk sits in the far corner of the Nespelem cemetery on the Colville Reservation, surrounded by small bundles of gifts from Nez Perce visitors, and by less tasteful donations from foreign tourists who should never have passed through the graveyard's gates. Because, as you look out from behind the chicken-wire fence, over the dry, rutted earth surrounding the chief's memorial, its shallow undulations begin to make sense – this is a mass grave. Scores of unmarked burials recount the poverty and illness that ensnared the exiled Nez Perce during their early years in this dusty corner of Washington. Many, far too many, of the graves clearly hold infants. It's a sickening sight and it's impossible for an outsider to guess how it affects those who know that their ancestors dug these trenches.

Soy Redthunder knows. His lineage, on his father's side, 'runs right down through Joseph', and his family had stayed in Colville ever since the Wallowa band had been dropped here in 1885. With his grey ponytail pulled back tight from his aviator shades, this barrel-chested and booming civic leader cut a combative figure as he crouched over a picnic table below the towering Grand Coulee Dam – and like most of the Colville Nez Perce his thoughts were never far from the conflict that brought his ancestors here. 'Chief Joseph was sold out. That history is still drilled into us – he stayed in the Wallowa, and the bands from Lapwai, they signed the 1863 treaty, they received money, they received land, they received treaty rights, and they sold Joseph out.'

The divisions that the Reverend Henry Spalding had brought to the Nez Perce, that the treaty negotiators had exploited, and that the events of 1877 had sanctified with blood, were far from healed: 'Even today, when people talk about Nez Perce, they talk about treaty and non-treaty, Christian and non-Christian. Those are still the divides. And you can talk about reconciliation all you want – but that doesn't change the fact that the non-treaty tribes are *still* getting the shaft. We're an exiled people.'

In the early twentieth century these exiled Nez Perce, along with the other eleven Columbian tribes who'd been corralled onto the Colville Reservation, had suffered the same painful diminution as their relations back in Idaho. If anything, the band's slow acceptance of the realities of farming worsened their poverty – but at least, as Yellow Wolf had recalled, they had their salmon, a bountiful supply from the main stem of the Columbia River as it wrapped around the south and east of their lands. All of the tribes on the Colville, some of which had been occupying this land for thousands of years, were salmon people, and the rituals, status and sustenance the annual migrations brought them defined their struggle for survival.

Work on the Grand Coulee Dam started in 1933. It was, and still is, the largest concrete structure in America. Its construction required a new city of almost four thousand people, the gleaming boomtown of Grand Coulee; a 21,000-acre lake of water was backed up behind the dam, irrigating an agricultural explosion; and if any dam won the Second World War it was Grand Coulee – it powered the construction of half of America's warplanes.

It also didn't have a fish ladder in it. A 1400-mile salmon run was entirely cut off, the largest of all the ruined migrations – and, just to make certain, a second, equally impassable, dam was put in downstream in 1953: the Chief Joseph Dam.

The Colville Reservation, completely ignored during the dam building, was shattered, its greatest wellspring of wealth and Indianness sunk without a trace. The psychological price was paid in alcoholism, suicide and family breakdown.

Unsurprisingly, in the late 1950s, when the government came round selling Termination, there were plenty of takers – the offer was $40,000 a head to break up a reservation many associated with fatal decline. But a coalition of traditionalist elders and young activists pulled the reservation back from the very brink: 'They became educated, and united around fighting Termination,' Soy recalled. 'And they went to Washington and said, "We will forever be Indian people, you will not make white people out of us".' The narrow defeat of Termination was Colville's turning point, as the reservation began to gain control over its considerable timber resources, opened its small casinos and started to make slow, uneven progress against its multitudinous social problems. In 1994 the government even apologized for killing the salmon, the only way it knew how, with a cheque for $53 million. The Colville tribes would much rather have had the fish. And, Soy contended, it was those missing salmon that symbolize the divisions that still echoed from 1877: 'When the government built this dam, they didn't include the Indian people, and we lost our salmon. They shut off this resource forever. And now we're fighting to get some salmon – but we're fighting the treaty tribes!'

The root problem is that the nineteenth-century treaties have become so central to the political revival of the Northwestern tribes that any Indian not covered by the documents is left legally naked. 'The white man's law says they only deal with the treaties, and so that's the way we play the ballgame now. The Joseph band, we're trying to retain our aboriginal rights to our home in Oregon, but the treaty tribes say all of that salmon is reserved for them. So that lawsuit, United States vs Oregon [Judge Belloni's case, confirming the treaty right to fishing at traditional off-reservation spots], that should really have been called Treaty Tribes vs Non-Treaties, because *we* lost that case.'

The judges' readings are that the Wallowa Nez Perce, living in Colville, have no guaranteed right to fish, or take elk, or gather roots and berries, in their ancestral valley – but the Lapwai Nez Perce, including descendants of the signatories of the Thief Treaty, *are* rightfully allowed in there, under the 1855 'usual and accustomed places' clause. The Idaho Nez Perce government points out that the Colville Nez Perce could secure access to their homeland's resources, but only by giving up their rights on the Washington reservation that's now far more of a home to them than Lapwai, Idaho, ever was. The treaty Nez Perce have also not exactly been forthcoming in offering to share their catch. Unsurprisingly, this gets Soy's goat.

'When the Creator created the salmon, he didn't say, "I'm only doing this for the treaty tribes," he said, "I'm doing this for the Indian people!" All of these Indian people were put on these rivers to share these resources.'

The treaty, so empowering to the Idaho tribe, seems constantly to disenfranchise the Colvilles. For example, when a conservation group recently purchased some land in the Wallowas and wanted it placed back in Nez Perce hands, they gave it to Lapwai. The Colville Nez Perce, who have a perhaps understandable reputation for bearing grudges, were furious. 'You know, there's a misconception that Chief Joseph is from Lapwai, Idaho. Chief Joseph was from Wallowa, Oregon, and he came here to Colville. We have to keep reminding people of that. It seems to me to have been very good planning from someone, to pit the treaty tribes against the non-treaties in this way. That was started a hundred and fifty years ago, and it's still in effect today. And, in essence, it's still a war.'

Despite their own tribal casinos and a couple of sawmills, unemployment on Colville still ran at around 45 per cent, and there was a desperate need for housing and infrastructure investment. These absences came to the fore in 2006, when the Colville Nez Perce were involved in a defining, almost essential dilemma.

Molybdenum is a relatively unsung element – you find it in tooth enamel, sunflower seeds and pork liver, and, in very substantial quantities, in the upper half of Mount Tolman, an unspectacular forested outcrop in the heart of the Colville Reservation. It would almost have certainly stayed there, untouched, had the element's market price (it's used in steel manufacture) remained anchored at its usual $5 a pound. But in 2005, a shortage occurred, and molybdenum hit $33 a pound. Mount Tolman was suddenly worth $20 billion.

The mining corporation executives arrived and made their pitch. Even if prices stabilized, the reservation could expect to pocket perhaps $1 billion from mining Mount Tolman, plus there would be up to four hundred secure jobs for a generation. It was a significant offer to people in need – all they had to do was let the miners remove the top of the mountain and dig an open pit a thousand feet into its flanks. Some of the tribal officials with responsibility for economic growth bought into the plan, and began working to revoke the reservation's constitutional ban on mining (firms had sniffed around Tolman in the past). But – remarkably, if one looks back at the history that surrounds this land – the corporation and the politicians couldn't carve up the mountain without asking the public. A tribal referendum was called for 18 March 2006 – take the billion, or keep the hill?

Tribal elders, spiritual traditionalists and the ecologically aware combined to campaign feverishly against the mine – not only was Mount Tolman a sacred prayer site, but air quality would surely suffer as the hill was ground to dust, water pollution was a near-certainty, streams would have to be dammed and mining trucks would clog the country roads day and night. It was the classic cash-for-chaos deal – and just as at Anaconda, Butte, Opportunity and Milltown, the legacy could well have lasted for centuries.

The outcome was no landslide but the mountain was decisively saved, by 1254 votes to 847. But Soy Redthunder, who'd campaigned hard against the Tolman mine, offered this word of warning: 'From talking to people, I would say it was more the old tribe members who'd voted against the mine, and it was the young people who were more in favour of it. And that's a worry, because they'll be back – I told my own kids this, I said, "Be ready, because every generation, they're going to come back, and offer us even more money for that mountain." Next time it'll be $50 billion.'

And it would be a hard slog for the reservation to achieve economic self-reliance without the molybdenum – this was a poor, lonely corner of Washington, pouring power and water to the rest of the Northwest, but seeing little benefit itself. Once the Grand Coulee Dam was finished, the white boomtown across the river from where Soy was sitting rapidly lost its defining purpose, and three-quarters of its population. Of those families that stuck around, many, ironically, did so because the Indian kids ensured the local school was comparatively well funded. Most, however, had just upped and left.

'The people in that little town over there, they always talk about, "How come the Indians don't leave?" Well, we can't. This is our home. We can't move from here to Seattle and call that "home", because our home is here. We can't leave for San Francisco, and call that "home", because our home is here.

'And they don't understand that concept, because this was only a temporary place to them, and after they graduated from high school, this wasn't a home to them, it was just kind of a "nesting spot". And after the dam was completed, they moved on, and called someplace else "home".

'But they don't understand, that this land provides for us, it nurtures us. We just can't leave it. It's our home.'

Orofino, Idaho, feels besieged, if only by topography. Perched on the banks of the Clearwater River, it sits wedged between two forested slopes leading up and away to the high plateaus that host the Wieppe meadows to the north and the Camas Prairie to the south. Though within the boundaries of the Nez Perce Reservation, it's a very white town, just a few Mexican tree planters and restaurant staff altering the monochrome. The closed-up shops, quiets streets and clusters of uninspired teenagers are reminiscent of many other stories nearby – Orofino had been hit hard by the Potlatch Corporation's retreat from labour-intensive lumbering, and its vitality was seeping away. The town had even cut school to four days a week, to balance the municipal books. To add to the air of embattlement, today's sky was tainted with the smoke from the worst forest fire season in Idaho's history.

Around thirty of us were gathered in the Veterans of Foreign Wars Club, waiting for an elegant, grey-haired man in slacks and open-neck shirt to call us to order. Senator Larry Craig took his time to chat with the local activists and decorated veterans, before asking with polite authority if we would like to begin. Within a year of this town hall meeting, the senator would achieve international fame for probably the least interesting thing about him – his sexuality – but on this broiling day he was demonstrating his significant contribution to an enduring confidence trick: how to keep the creed of the West alive, while its believers faded compliantly away.

Senator Craig was a central-casting Western Republican – a loyal friend to the gun lobby, the corporate rancher, the hydropower firms and the timber barons, his legislative legacy included relaxing the pollution restraints on gold-mining, opening up millions of acres of roadless wilderness to the logging trucks, reining back the regulation of industrial 'battery-cow' feedlots, limiting the liability of negligent gun salesmen, and proposing a new international measure of greenhouse emissions, which divided carbon by economic output, instantly rendering America the world's most climate-friendly nation. Thick-skinned beyond measure, he had nurtured the violent antipathy of environmentalists and liberals – the *New York Times* once called him 'obnoxious' and 'repugnant' (he had, to be fair, just blocked hundreds of US Air Force promotions, to incentivize the government into spending more defence dollars in Idaho).

Here, though, you could only admire him as he warmed up the room with his folksy, antiquated rhetoric, dropping in the references to his grandkids, his ranch, his rifle, recalling every public meeting as a 'humbling experience', telling a heart-warming tale about an Iraq war veteran getting his golf handicap back down to scratch, on 'one of these phenomenal new legs they can make these days'. And as the floor was opened for questions, a conservative masterclass began, the senator piquing his audience's impotent nostalgia and their resentment of modern life, and offering them protection against a dark, confusing future. Today's first touchstone was immigration. Ever since the West was opened up, people have been declaring it full.

'Mexico is invading us,' proclaimed a long-haired gentleman in shorts and a singlet. 'They're sending their citizens across the border, they're letting them come over here, because they think the land is still theirs. California, Arizona, they think it's their land.'

Craig nodded: 'I said to our president myself, face to face, "Mr President, you should declare a National Emergency, and close the southern border." We have probably thirty-five to forty thousand illegals here in Idaho. And you know, of the one million people apprehended at the southern border last year, two hundred thousand were not Mexicans – there were Chinese, Russians, Lithuanians, so on. And I'm not about to say all of them were good guys ... The terrorists will attack us any way they can.'

Such bunker psychology was aired at length, the senator at one point shaking his head ruefully as a woman described her two-year search for a new set of pots and pans that said 'Made in America'. Occasionally, he steered the room towards an accommodation with the future – 'Just think, we're probably going to sell fifty coal-fired power plants and ten nuclear generators to China in the next five years' – but they were in no mood to embrace it. Orofino wanted to discuss what had been lost, not gained.

And where there's decline, someone's progressing. Eventually Dennis, the local chiropractor, rose to speak, a red-faced bundle of mental energy: 'I read about what's happening in Iraq, Senator, and how that country could be dividing, and falling apart, becoming separate nations – and then I look at us. And at these hundreds of tribes, pushing their issues, with their gambling and their water. And I see the same problem – nations within nations. The Nez Perce tribe round here, with their water claims, and with these wolves, they're devastating us, we're taking a huge hit here. I just believe, you know, we should rethink it all – we should all become Americans again.'

Craig stepped lightly on fractious ground: 'I didn't create this situation, or you – our grandfathers did. I'm not going to tell you to readjust your thinking. I hear you – but politically, you don't go there any more.'

Later that day, I asked the senator if that meant he didn't support the Nez Perce's tribal sovereignty. We were waiting for his second public meeting of the day to start, in the smoke-clad Camas Prairie town of Grangeville. With an unwashed journalist in his face, he modified his language: 'I accept it and therefore I support it. These things were granted by our forefathers, rightly, many years ago, and you can't change history, nor can you rewrite it.' It was a masterful misinterpretation – converting an inherent right into a generous grant, while still sounding supportive. Before I realized I'd been hoodwinked, the meeting began.

Grangeville, just a few miles up the road from Orofino, had turned out a larger, more febrile crowd. The declining timber industry was just one of the local complaints here, alongside the tribulations of local farmers, the towering price of petrol and, most of all, that fresh cultural icon of federal contempt and liberal meddling, the wolf. The room seemed ready to let off steam – clamped down, perhaps, by the silent presence of James Lawyer, the shy, grey-haired descendant of the famous Nez Perce negotiator, not here to speak, but to listen, and perhaps to restrain.

As the sun set in a rage through the smoke, the senator first soothed throbbing brows with his well-honed folksy patter, then offered a vintage salve of Western optimism – the way of life that the people of Grangeville pined so hard for was still a possibility, because the natural resources were out there, across the American continent, to make that happen. You just had to get out there and liquidate them.

First, the trees: 'We're pushing hard for more activity on our forest lands, and we're getting some back. We cannot allow the number of trees per acre that we do have, the sick, dead and dying trees, the burning forests. We have tens of thousands of acres of Idaho like that, and we need to thin and clean them.' The appalling health of the Northwest's forests wasn't due to centuries of timber plunder, but the 'California attitudes' of the environmental movement, and the judges who sided with them in protecting the National Forests – 'a tragedy for rural communities'. At least now there was a friendly face in the White House – the senator had worked with the Bush administration on the 'Healthy Forests' plan, a widely derided attempt to increase timber harvests under the cover of fire prevention, and a Corporate Westerner as president was certainly an asset. 'One thing that has improved with this administration, is that I've said to them, "Let's send in the lawyers against these environmentalists, let's beat them up a couple of times," and they have done that a little. Because we need young, healthy, vibrant forests – they make for clean air, clean water and healthy rivers.'

Craig and his president were also singing the same song on mining, particularly for energy – cheap gas and good jobs were just there for the taking: 'Is there oil out there? Yes, there's lots of oil out there, folks, and it's on our lands, perhaps sixty to eighty billion barrels. It's in Alaska, and offshore, in the Gulf of Mexico. But it's been off-limits, for environmental reasons. We thought we could conserve our way out of trouble, because of the environment, but we can't – and now America is waking up to the news that we need to get back into production.'

Surrounded by evidence that they were not emerging from their troubles – their schools were shrinking, jobs fleeing, diners closing, communities ageing – the people of Grangeville railed against their fate: 'We haven't been much of a country since 1945,' stammered a portly man in a dusty lumberjack shirt. 'We haven't been united, we haven't won anything worth winning, not since 1945.' But the senators and the corporations were not responsible for this defeat – the environmentalists, the bureaucrats and the Californians most certainly were. And, of course, at the vanguard, stood the wolves.

The senator had been well briefed and hit the panic button himself: 'Now, I understand a lot of you want to talk about wolves – and you're right to be concerned. They were dumped here, illegally, and you do not just dump a supreme predator into any environment.' The hands shot up, and the tales flowed – elk walking down Grangeville Main Street, scared out of their woods, cows fearfully abandoning their high pastures before the grass was even half cropped; a woman stood up to demonstrate that the 'new' type of wolves came up 'I'm not kidding, taller than your waist – they're huge!' Scott, a hunting guide in a padded blue work shirt, could scarcely control his emotion: 'Doggone it, we're sitting on a time bomb here! And I've had the scientists from the Nez Perce come over to my house, citing all their figures, but the fact is a wolf took one of my dogs, tore it all up – and I will never turn another dog loose.' Tears were pouring down his cheeks: 'We have to do something. I have to do something, to protect my family.'

Senator Craig, handed a shadowy, slobbering hate figure that exemplified so much that he stood against, was in no mood to deal in facts: 'This is craziness. We have an emergency here – I'll make some calls in the morning. Because I hope, I hope, we don't have to hear of a human being getting taken before we act.'

Another hunting guide, Ralph, was the last to speak, his thick, drooping moustache a symbol of the rugged traditions he clearly hoped to uphold. Rarely taking his eyes from the back of James Lawyer's head, he chose his words with care: 'I've been an outfitter here for twenty-one years – but now it's impossible for me to earn my living from these lands. I've lost three dogs to the wolves, had three horses taken down. And I've been to the tribe and they've said: "Sorry, but you live in 'Wolf Central', it's not going to change. This is the wolves' sacred land." And if I don't hunt, I might lose my hunting permit – and then I could lose my ranch.

'You know, I feel I'm being discriminated against. I'm being told I have to adapt. And we can't remove a certain organization [James Lawyer sat motionless, smiling, as if deaf] because that would be discrimination. Yet *I'm* being told to adapt.'

I caught up with Ralph after the senator had glided away (quite typically, as soon as he caught the accent, Ralph and his wife offered me, a total stranger, the spare room at their ranch for the night). He explained he was terrified that many Americans' schizophrenic attitude to the natural world could land him in legal hot soup: 'Suppose I get a hunting client up from New York City, who comes up with his wife, and they want a cougar, but instead she sees a wolf tearing one of my dogs apart, ripping out its guts – they're going to sue me!'

Ralph was no knee-jerk anti-Indian: 'I didn't want to make a fuss. I went to the tribe directly, and they appeared concerned. I asked if there was a way they could subsidize us through this, maybe my son could work for them, or I could, but there's been no answer, no financial movement – so now I'm making a fuss.

'You have to understand,' Ralph urged, his voice cracking, 'that this is the life I've aspired to ever since I was a little boy. This is all I ever wanted.'

Now he too was quietly weeping: 'I just want my way of life back. I just want it to be the way it was.'

NOTES

CHAPTER ONE

p. 3 '...*will be the coming of the human race*': an abridged and simplified version of the full myth, which appears in full in Deward E. Walker, Jr, and Daniel N. Matthews, *Nez Perce Coyote Tales*, p. 9, and Donald M. Hines, *Tales of the Nez Perce*, p. 43, and in audio recordings at the site of the monster's heart, near Kamiah, Idaho.

p. 6 '...*the wilderness gentry of the Pacific Northwest*': L. V. McWhorter, *Hear Me, My Chiefs*, p. 2.

p. 8 '...*vibrated with the songs of its fullness*': translation from Michael Oren Fitzgerald, ed., *Indian Spirit*, p. 108.

p. 8 '...*spent their time on this earth*': Horace Axtell and Margo Aragon, *A Little Bit of Wisdom: Conversations with a Nez Perce Elder*, pp. 16–17.

p. 9 '...*my blood and my dead*': Vine Deloria, Jr, *God Is Red*; Laurel, quoted ibid., p. 45.

p. 11 '...*if you only do it once a year*': in conversation with the author.

p. 14 '...*the most precious part of the state*': Henry Nash Smith, *Virgin Land: The American West as Symbol and Myth*, p. 144.

p. 16 '...*requiring but few of our supplies*': Alvin M. Josephy, Jr, *The Nez Perce Indians and the Opening of the Northwest*, p. 65.

p. 19 '...*these wandering sons of our native forests*': ibid., p. 101.

CHAPTER TWO

p. 26 '*This is where I want to live*': Grace Bartlett, *The Wallowa Country, 1867–1877*, p. 17.

p. 36 '...*and in national strength*': quoted in Nash Smith, *Virgin Land*, p. 157.

p. 36 '...*send their colonists*': quoted in Geoffrey C. Ward, *The West*, p. 59.

373

p. 37 '*...of liberty and federated government*': quoted in Stephanson, *Manifest Destiny*, p. 42.

p. 38 '*...to shed blessings round the world!*': quoted in Nash Smith, *Virgin Land*, p. 37.

p. 38 '*...to fall before the axe of industry?*': the Jubilee of the Constitution, delivered in New York, 30 April 1839, before the New York Historical Society.

p. 40 '*...to scorch and crack upon the hot prairie*': Francis Parkman, Jr, *The California and Oregon Trail.*

p. 41 '*...and men riding upon their horses*': material from Tamastslikt Cultural Institute, Pendleton, Oregon.

p. 45 '*it is from me man was made*': Tamastslikt Cultural Institute.

CHAPTER THREE

p. 51 '*too thick to flow and too thin to drink*': information from Robin Johnston of the United States Forest Service, a sparkling local historian.

p. 51 '*...it proved a sovereign remedy for the scurvy*': C. J. Brosnan, *History of the State of Idaho*, p. 104.

p. 52 '*...was waged around the campfires*': ibid., pp. 105–10.

p. 52 '*the most disagreeable hole to be imagined*': *Portland Oregonian*, 20 May 1861.

p. 53 '*...was reduced to little more than 30,000*: James Wilson, *The Earth Shall Weep*, p. 237.

p. 55 '*...formed at the land office in Lewiston*': quoted at the Nez Perce County Museum, Lewiston, Idaho.

p. 58 '*where they will not be intruded upon ...*': quoted in Alvin M. Josephy, Jr, *The Nez Perce Indians and the Opening of the Northwest*, p. 410.

p. 62 '*They were being threatened with being wiped out*': in conversation with the author.

p. 63 '*...more than three hours a week*': quoted in *The Nez Perce Tribe Treaties: Nez Perce Perspectives*, p. 43.

p. 63 *... and, in every single case, breached*: Wilson, *The Earth Shall Weep*, p. 279.

p. 64 '*It sold everything to everybody for miles around*': Robin Johnston, United States Forest Service.

p. 64 '*...than in any other locality we know of*': *Lewiston Teller*, 13 May 1877.

p. 64 '*...it will laugh you a harvest of flour*': *Idaho County Free Press*, 8 April 1887.

p. 65 '*...and ignore the authority of the United States*': *Oregonian Telegram*, 20 January 1877.

p. 66 '*...agreeably to the teachings of Smohalla*': *San Francisco Chronicle*, 27 July 1877.

p. 66 '*...these graves to any man*': quoted in 'Chief Joseph's Own Story', *North American Review* 128 (April 1879): 412–33.

p. 67 '*A man who would not love his father's grave is worse than a wild animal*': ibid.

p. 69 '*another Indian scare is about to transpire*': *Portland Oregonian*, 22 February 1873, quoted in Bartlett, *The Wallowa Country*, p. 32.

p. 70 '...*and his Band from the face of the Earth*': *Mountain Sentinel*, 31 May 1873, quoted in Bartlett, *The Wallowa Country*, p. 38.

p. 71 '...*a suitable voice for cow calling*': ibid., 29 September 1877, quoted in material from the marvellous Elgin Opera House Museum.

p. 72 '...*fish that would darken the whole stream*': quoted in Bartlett, *The Wallowa Country*, p. 27.

p. 72 '...*as to destroy the species entirely*': *Wallowa County Chieftain*, 25 June 1905.

p. 72 '...*audacity and imbecility of which leaves one gasping for breath*': Tim Flannery, *The Eternal Frontier: An Ecological History of North America and its Peoples*, p. 302.

p. 73 ...*and 30,000 bear pelts per annum*: Flannery, *The Eternal Frontier*, p. 317, and Peter Mattheissen, *Wildlife in America*, pp. 72–91.

p. 73 '...*for countless centuries were utterly destroyed*': quoted in Marc Reisner, *Cadillac Desert: The American West and its Disappearing Water*, p. 36.

p. 74 ...*so they carried on*: Michael Frome, 'Predators, Prejudices and Politics', *Field & Stream*, December 1967.

p. 75 ... *and the species all but collapsed*: Jim Lichatowich, *Salmon Without Rivers: A History of the Pacific Salmon Crisis*, pp. 81–90.

CHAPTER FOUR

p. 79 '... *his next mission was with the Indian*': Robert M. Utley and Wilcomb E. Washburn, *Indian Wars*, p. 256.

p. 80 '... *true cause of the Nez Perce division*': Major H. Clay Wood, *The Status of Young Joseph and his Band of Nez Perce Indians*.

p. 80 '... *Indian sense, experience, or knowledge*': Mrs John B. Monteith in *Lewiston Morning Tribune*, 22 January 1933.

p. 84 '... *lodged along its margin*': *Lewiston Teller*, 13 June 1889, quoted in *Lewiston Morning Tribune*, 28 May 1961.

p. 84 '... *to our fertile and healthy soil*': *Lewiston Teller*, 18 November 1876.

p. 85 '*on a fishing excursion somewhere in California*': *Lewiston Teller*, 2 December 1876.

p. 86 '... *to all things the buck commands*': ibid.

p. 88 '... *disappeared when she left*': drawn from *Lewiston Morning Tribune*, throughout July 1980; 4 April 1979; 8 December 1981; 2 June 1981; 9 July 1981; 2 June 1981; 14 December 1979.

p. 88 '... *no concern for environmental protection*': Paper Profits: Pollution Audit 1970, the Council on Economic Priorities.

p. 88 ... *Germany and Britain combined*: detailed in John Steele Gordon, *An Empire of Wealth: The Epic History of American Economic Power*.

p. 90 ... *150 years to complete*: http://www.wcei.org/apsrs/idaho/idaho-summary.html

p. 90 ... *a danger to her unborn child*: *Greenwire*, 5 February 2004, quoted in Robert F. Kennedy, Jr, *Crimes Against Nature*, p. 127.

p. 90 ... *injected straight into the continent*: Harvey Blatt, *America's Environmental Report Card: Are We Making the Grade?*, p. 24.

p. 91 '... *with which it has fettered enterprise*': 'The West Against Itself', *Harper's*, January 1947.

p. 91 '... *to make our lives better*': Rush Limbaugh, *The Way Things Ought to Be*, p. 169. (Without wishing to swell further the wages of demagoguery, this blistering rant should probably be a required text for students tackling late twentieth-century American history.)

p. 93 '*fearless sternness*': Oliver O. Howard, 'The True Story of the Wallowa Campaign', *North American Review* 128 (July 1879): 53–64.

p. 94 '... *we shall not live where He placed us*': quoted in 'Chief Joseph's Own Story', *North American Review* 128 (April 1879): 412–33.

p. 94 '... *our bodies must go back to the earth, our mother*': Yellow Wolf, *His Own Story*, p. 37.

p. 96 '... *if it did not suit them*': 'Chief Joseph's Own Story'.

p. 100 ... *reservations unsubtly erased*: David M. Wrobel, *Promised Lands: Promotion, Memory and the Creation of the American West*, p. 34.

p. 100 ... *were standard fare*: Marc Reisner, *Cadillac Desert: The American West and its Disappearing Water* (Viking Penguin, 1986).

p. 101 '... *a fresh supply of moisture*': *Idaho County Free Press*, 3 September 1886.

p. 102 '*being squeezed by history*': Patricia Nelson Limerick, *A Legacy of Conquest: The Unbroken Past of the American West* (Norton, 1987).

p. 103 ... *headed back East in defeat*: Reisner, *Cadillac Desert*, p. 107.

p. 104 ... *larger than the Nile delta*: C. J. Brosnan, *History of the State of Idaho*, p.188.

p. 104 '*get out and give us more money*': 'The West Against Itself', *Harper's*, January 1947.

p. 107 '... *suddenly and permanently broken*': Blaine Harden, *A River Lost: The Life and Death of the Columbia*, p. 12.

p. 107 ... *white towns that faced inundation*: Michael L. Lawson, *Damned Indians: The Pick–Sloan Plan and the Missouri River Sioux, 1944–1980*, pp. 27–9.

p. 108 ... *through the Columbia River every year*: Jim Lichatowich, *Salmon Without Rivers: A History of the Pacific Salmon Crisis*.

p. 109 ... *99 per cent of its historic levels*: ibid.

p. 113 ... *than nature can replenish it*: quoted in Blatt, *America's Environmental Report Card*, pp. 8–11.

p. 113 ... *to the West's farmers*: Agricultural Resources and Environmental Indicators (Washington, DC: USDA, Economic Research Indicators, 1994), quoted in Norman Myers and Jennifer Kent, *Perverse Subsidies: How Tax Dollars Can Undercut the Environment and the Economy*, p. 136.

p. 114 ... *a quarter of the world's food*: quoted in Nelson Limerick, *A Legacy of Conquest*, p. 130.

CHAPTER FIVE

p. 117 '*... why don't you kill the white man that killed your father?*': L. V. McWhorter, *Hear Me, My Chiefs*, p. 190.

p. 117 *... and disguised himself as a Chinaman*: Yellow Wolf offers this colourful image, while settler testimonies, perhaps unsurprisingly, paint a less cowardly one.

p. 119 '*No more soft pillows for the head*': Yellow Wolf, *His Own Story*, p. 42.

p. 120 '*There is no danger of that, Sir!*': John D. McDermott, *Forlorn Hope: The Battle of White Bird Canyon and the Beginning of the Nez Perce War*.

p. 121 '*...in a very peculiar way not characteristic of the coyote*': William R. Parnell, *The Nez Perce War, 1877: Battle of White Bird Canyon*, United Service, October 1889: 364–74. Included in Peter Cozzens, *Eyewitnesses to the Indian Wars, 1865–1890*, Volume 2, *The Wars for the Pacific Northwest*, pp. 344–55.

p. 122 '*isolation, boredom and monotony*': Don Rickey, Jr, *Forty Miles a Day on Beans and Hay* (University of Oklahoma Press, 1963) – a highly recommended read for both Western and military history enthusiasts, which inspired and informed this passage.

p. 122 '*she went to the soldiers*': ibid.

p. 123 *... target practice in six months*: quoted in McDermott, *Forlorn Hope*.

p. 123 '*any Indian who happens to catch sight*': ibid.

p. 125 '*Soldiers seemed poor shots*': quoted in McWhorter, *Hear Me, My Chiefs*, p. 247.

p. 125 '*..."Let the soldiers go! We have done them enough! No Indian killed!"*': Yellow Wolf, *His Own Story*, p. 51.

p. 127 '*the red skins*': The Times, 14 August 1877.

p. 127 '*...the vain hopes of these dreaming, superstitious nomads*': *Daily Bee Supplement*, 11 November 1877.

p. 128 '*...We will scalp you!*': Yellow Wolf, *His Own Story*, p. 54.

p. 128 '*... from the Agency Indians*': *Lewiston Teller*, 14 July 1877.

p. 129 '*... and be governed by an independent law*': letter from J. W. Poe, Mount Idaho, 19 July 1877.

p. 130 '*... that almost encircled his little home*': Thomas A. Sutherland, *Howard's Campaign Against the Nez Perce Indians*.

p. 131 '*... to devise ways and means to cross*': Michael McCarthy's Journal, quoted in Jerome A. Greene, *Nez Perce Summer 1877: The US Army and the Nee-me-poo Crisis*, p. 50.

p. 131 '*Does the General now think he will make short work of it?*': *Lewiston Teller*, 14 July 1877.

p. 134 '*We are going to charge the Indians*': Luther P. Wilmot, *Narratives of the Nez Perce War*.

p. 141 *'stirred up a new hornet's nest'*: Oliver O. Howard, *Nez Perce Joseph*.

p. 151 *'He and his people will be treated with justice'*: quoted in Greene, *Nez Perce Summer*, p. 100.

CHAPTER SIX

p. 156 *'we retreated to Bitterroot Valley'*: 'Chief Joseph's Own Story', *North American Review* 128 (April 1879): 412–33.

p. 157 *'... when the weather is dry'*; *Lewiston Teller*, 7 July 1877.

p. 158 *'slippery, sticky, muddy and filthy'*: Thomas A. Sutherland, *Howard's Campaign Against the Nez Perce Indians, 1877*.

p. 158 *'... "appear as holes in the ground"'*: trapper Joe Meek, ibid.

p. 158 *'we slept almost erect or standing on our heads'*: 3 August 1877, courtesy of Lolo Trail Park Service.

p. 158 *'... with the sunlight glinting through the trees'*: Edwin Mason, Letters, MSS 80, Montana Historical Society, Helena.

p. 163 ... per capita *consumption of wood increased eightfold*: John Perlin, *A Forest Journey: The Story of Wood and Civilization*, pp. 332–40.

p. 164 *'... with the total extirpation of the forest'*: Caroline Kirkland, quoted in Richard Manning, *Last Stand: Logging, Journalism and the Case for Humility*, p. 5.

p. 164 *'... and the trunks still encumbered the ground which they so recently shaded'*: Alexis de Tocqueville, *Democracy in America*, author's appendix U, Volume II.

p. 165 ... *of Germany and Austria had experienced in one thousand*: John Perlin, *A Forest Journey: The Story of Wood and Civilization*, p. 361.

p. 165 *'... leave behind stumps and unemployed workers'*: introduction in Derrick Jensen and George Draffan, *Railroads and Clearcuts: Legacy of Congress's 1864 Northern Pacific Railroad Land Grant*, p. xv.

p. 168 ... *while the translator relayed a different speech altogether*: quoted in Jensen and Draffan, *Railroads and Clearcuts*, p. 38.

p. 168 *'...whose purpose had been served ...'*: ibid.

p. 171 ... *as 'decadent' or 'overripe'*: Forest Service reports quoted in Nancy Langstrom, *Forest Dreams, Forest Nightmares: The Paradox of Old Growth in the Inland West*, p. 99.

p. 171 *'... was gone in less than a decade'*: ibid.

p. 172 ... *and just kept on climbing*: quoted in Langstrom, *Forest Dreams, Forest Nightmares*, p. 264.

p. 172 ... *than seven years*: J. H. Drielsma, *The Influence of Forest-Based Industries on Rural Communities*, Ph.D. thesis, Yale 1984; and S. R. Maguire, *Employer and Occupational Tenure*, 1993 update, *U.S. Department of Labor Monthly Labor Review* 116 (6): 45–56, both quoted in Thomas Michael Power, *Lost Landscapes and Failed Economies: The Search for a Value of Place*, p. 144.

p. 173 *'... an array of useful and interesting objects in the home'*: Wallowa Valley

Chieftain, editorial comment, 5 December 1985.

p. 173 '*... BECAUSE THE LOGGER IS A GIANT*': on display at the excellent Logging Industry Museum, Pierce, Idaho.

p. 173 *... but 20 per cent of the timber jobs were lost*: Power, *Lost Landscapes and Failed Economies*, pp. 136–8.

p. 174 '*... we'll return to New England, where the industry began*': reported by forester Gordon Robinson, quoted in Jensen and Draffan, *Railroads and Clearcuts*, p. 67.

p. 177 '*Stuck between a past it can't recreate and a future it can't imagine*': *Lewiston Tribune*, 14 October 2001.

p. 178 '*... better suited to what I want rather than for what you are using it for?*': *Wallowa Valley Chieftain*, editorial comment, 5 December 1985.

p. 180 '*... they will be joined by a number of our own Indians*': *Weekly Missoulian*, 20 July 1877.

p. 180 '*... scattered bands of Indians about the county*': ibid.

p. 181 '*have shown a heroism worthy of a better cause*': *New North West*, 27 July 1877.

p. 181 '*... and every inch a leader*': *San Francisco Examiner*, 27 July 1877.

p. 182 *... peaches, oysters and sardines*: *Butte Miner*, 14 August 1877.

p. 182 '*... into the Bitter Root Valley*': Rawn's report of 30 September 1877.

p. 184 '*We had left General Howard and his war in Idaho*': Yellow Wolf, *His Own Story*, p. 80.

CHAPTER SEVEN

p. 185 '*He is an enigma*': *Weekly Missoulian*, 3 August 1877.

p. 186 '*... his uncanny knowledge of the geography of this vast area*': Dee Brown, *The American West*, pp. 255–64.

p. 186 '*When the legend becomes fact, print the legend*': *The Man Who Shot Liberty Valance*, John Ford Productions, 1962.

p. 186 '*You know the country, I do not*': reported by Duncan MacDonald in the *Deer Lodge New North West*, 26 July 1878–28 March 1879.

p. 188 '*I name you Calamity Jane, the heroine of the plains*': *The Life and Adventures of Calamity Jane, by Herself*, 1896, quoted by Roberta Beed Sollid, *Calamity Jane*, pp. 2–4.

p. 188 '*Our security demands this*': *Weekly Missoulian*, 3 August 1877.

p. 188 '*The Indian murderers must not pass unmolested*': telegram sent 31 July 1877.

p. 189 '*...the inhabitants fleeing in terror*': *Weekly Missoulian*, 20 July 1877.

p. 190 '*a hundred men who own America*': Senator Robert M. LaFollette, quoted in C. B. Glasscock, *The War of the Copper Kings*, p. 26.

p. 193 '*to give them a beautiful complexion*': Proceedings and Debates of the Constitutional Convention, 1889 (Helena, 1921).

p. 195 *The farmers consulted scientists, then lawyers, and joined battle*: outstandingly chronicled throughout in Donald MacMillan, *Smoke Wars: Anaconda, Copper,*

Montana Air Pollution and the Courts, 1890–1920.

p. 197 *'All Butte has to show for it today are large graveyards'*: Janet L. Finn, *Tracing the Veins: Of Copper, Culture and Community from Butte to Chuquicamata*, p. 57.

p. 198 *'…made on the common ground of life'*: ibid., p. 193.

p. 200 *…discovered highly carcinogenic levels of arsenic in its tap water*: detailed by Sherry Devlin in a series of features in the *Missoulian*, 27–29 January 2002.

p. 201 *'…nowhere in America is that visceral relationship with the land more powerfully felt by those who live here'*: K. Ross Toole, *Twentieth-Century Montana: A State of Extremes.*

p. 203 *'for the return of the place of the big bull trout'*: *Missoulian*, 3 August 2005.

p. 203 *'Those that succeed us, can well take care of themselves'*: Michael Malone, *The Battle for Butte: Mining and Politics on the Northern Frontier*, p. 196.

p. 205 *'…there were no gaps in the continuous train'*: Henry Buck, 'The Story of the Nez Perce Campaign during the Summer of 1877', *Great Falls Tribune*, 24 December 1944–11 February 1945.

p. 205 *'Why should I shake hands with men whose hands are bloody?'*: reported by Duncan MacDonald in the *Deer Lodge New North West*, 26 July 1878–28 March 1879.

p. 207 *'I had no thought of ever going through the day alive'*: Henry Buck, *Great Falls Tribune*, 24 December 1944–11 February 1945.

p. 209 *'We are not fighting with the people of this country'*: Duncan MacDonald, *Deer Lodge New North West*, 26 July 1878–28 March 1879.

p. 210 *… the first 5 per cent of rural development does half the damage*: James Howard Kunstler, *The Geography of Nowhere: The Rise and Decline of America's Man-Made Landscape*, p. 265.

p. 210 *…1.2 acres an hour*: statistics drawn from Harvey Blatt, *America's Environmental Report Card*, pp. 74–5, and Dolores Hayden, *A Field Guide to Sprawl*, pp. 74–5.

p. 211 *…in any year, a fifth of Westerners move on*: www.census.gov, Mobility FAQs.

p. 212 *$41,000 of which came from the Wal-Mart corporation*: *Ravalli Republic*, Thursday 7 September 2006, Anthony Quirini.

p. 213 *'too much too soon'*: K. Ross Toole, *Montana: An Uncommon Land*, p. 242.

p. 213 *… 'for we will protect it at all costs'*: *Ravalli Republic*, Thursday 11 January 2007, Chris A. Linkenhoker.

p. 214 *'Let us be gone to the buffalo country!'*: quoted in L. V. McWhorter, *Yellow Wolf, His Own Story*, p. 80.

p. 215 *'No more fighting! War is quit'*: McWhorter, *Yellow Wolf, His Own Story*, p. 81.

CHAPTER EIGHT

p. 218 *…came back to our playing*: Young White Bird's Story, recounted in L. V. McWhorter, *Hear Me, My Chiefs*, p. 375.

p. 218 '...*a sleeping and undefended camp*': Merrill D. Beal, '*I Will Fight No More Forever': Chief Joseph and the Nez Perce War*, p. 115.

p. 219 ...*this army lacked the manpower to observe such niceties*: Eugene Lent, *Weekly Missoulian*, 17 August 1877.

p. 219 '*We had orders to fire low into the tepees*': Horace B. Mulkey, *National Tribune*, 29 August 1929.

p. 220 '...*bragging that he had killed those two women*': preceding paragraph drawn from Duncan MacDonald, *Deer Lodge New North West*, 26 July 1878–28 March 1879; John B. Catlin, 'The Battle of the Big Hole', Society of Montana Pioneers, Historians Annual Report 1927; Charles N. Loynes, 'From Fort Fizzle to the Big Hole', *Winners of the West*, March 1925; Charles A. Woodruff, 'The Battle of the Big Hole', Contributions to the Historical Society of Montana, 1910; Young White Bird's Story, recounted in L. V. McWhorter, *Hear Me, My Chiefs*, pp. 375–9; the narratives of Eelahweemah, Eloosykasit, Penahwenonmi, Owyeen, Wetatonmi, Red Elk, Pahit Palikt, Kowtolik, Samuel Tilden and Yellow Wolf, from McWhorter, *Yellow Wolf, His Own Story*, Appendix C.

p. 222 '...*I would not want to see, again*': McWhorter, *Yellow Wolf, His Own Story*.

p. 222 '...*their slaughtered warriors, women and children*': John Gibbon, 'The Battle of the Big Hole', *Harper's Weekly*, 28 December 1895.

p. 223 '*Why should we waste time saving his life?*': McWhorter, *Yellow Wolf, His Own Story*.

p. 225 '*I can never forget that day*': Black Eagle's narrative, from McWhorter, *Yellow Wolf, His Own Story*, Appendix C (10).

p. 226 '...*the Indians could not have escaped annihilation*': *Weekly Missoulian*, 17 August 1877.

p. 226 '...*congratulations for your most gallant fight and brilliant success*': telegram of General Alfred H. Terry, quoted in *Lewiston Teller*, 25 August 1877.

p. 227 '...*a "God Bless You" for the gallant old soldier*': *Deer Lodge New North West*, 21 August 1877.

p. 227 '...*seems the inevitable result of a few days*': *Weekly Missoulian*, 17 August 1877.

p. 229 '...*the flame and smoke would draw down the soldiers*': quoted in Robert M. Utley and Wilcomb E. Washburn, *Indian Wars*, p. 219.

p. 234 '...*no man was hit in that mad race for safety*': Harry J. Davis, 'An Incident in the Nez Perce Campaign', *Journal of the Military Service Institution of the United States*, May–June 1905.

p. 236 '*I think I may stop near where I am*': telegrams detailed in Report of the General of the Army, 7 November 1877, in the 1877 Report of the Secretary of War, Washington, DC.

p. 239 ...*they were scared of the geysers*: Peter Nabokov and Lawrence Loendorf, *Restoring a Presence: American Indians and Yellowstone National Park*, pp. 274–7.

p. 241 '...*as they were sitting so close together*': reminiscences in Hester D. Guie and

L. V. McWhorter, eds, *Adventures in Geyser Land*.

p. 243 *'a most pitiful looking object'*: ibid.

p. 244 *'...especially Nez Perces'*: ibid.

p. 244 *'...too slow for business'*: *Ogden Daily Pilot*, 18 October 1891, quoted in Beal, *'I Will Fight No More Forever'*, p. 79.

p. 247 *'...free from man's spoliation'*: quoted in Alston Chase, *Playing God in Yellowstone: The Destruction of America's First National Park*, pp. 32–7.

p. 248 *'How It Was ...'*: *Welfare Ranching: The Subsidized Destruction of the American West*, pp. xvi–xvii.

p. 248 *'...almost anyplace else in the world outside the United States'*: Paul F. Starrs, *Let the Cowboy Ride: Cattle Ranching in the American West*, p. 67.

p. 249 *...bird life and river health be damned*: David S. Wilcove, *The Condor's Shadow: The Loss and Recovery of Wildlife in America*, pp. 64–6.

CHAPTER NINE

p. 255 *'...a two-wheeled cart of some sort!'*: Theodore W. Goldin, 'A Pleasure Ride in Montana', *Ours, a Military Magazine*, November 1887.

p. 257 *'...through the timber for several miles'*: *Contributions to Historical Society of Montana*, 1896, vol. 2.

p. 259 *'...Indians squatting on the roof'*: Colonel J. W. Redington, correspondence with L. V. McWhorter, cited in *Hear Me, My Chiefs*, p. 457.

p. 261 *'...deal with them wisely and all will turn out all right'*: Joseph Crow, *From the Heart of the Crow Country: The Crow Indians' Own Stories*, p. 44.

p. 266 *... by 74 per cent between 1995 and 2025, eventually clearing ninety thousand souls*: www.census.gov, document PPL47.

p. 269 *'...but this was my last buffalo hunt'*: Cruikshank, quoted in Cheryl Wilfong, *Following the Nez Perce Trail*, p. 355.

p. 272 *'...the hide and tongue hunters killed fifty'*: quoted in David A. Dary, *The Buffalo Book: The Full Saga of the American Animal*, p. 68.

p. 272 *'...speckled cattle and the festive cowboy'*: Report of General Sheridan in the Annual Report of the Secretary of War, 1875.

p. 273 *'the people of Montana and Wyoming rather welcomed an Indian War'*: Ernest Staples Osgood, *The Day of the Cattleman*, p. 71.

p. 274 *...in 1885, it wasn't carrying any*: Dary, *The Buffalo Book*, p. 120.

p. 274 *...left standing on the entire continent*: Tim Flannery, *The Eternal Frontier: An Ecological History of North America and its Peoples*, p. 332.

p. 274 *...scattering up to $45 million in capital across the plains*: Lawrence M. Woods, *British Gentlemen in the Wild West: The Era of the Intensely English Cowboy*, pp. 51–65.

p. 276 *...4.4 and 7.3 million acres of America*: Osgood, *The Day of the Cattleman*, pp. 176–215.

p. 276 …*just four companies controlled 86 per cent of the beef output*: Jimmy M. Skaggs, *Prime Cut: Livestock Raising and Meatpacking in the United States, 1607–1983*, pp. 98–101.

p. 278 '*destroyed, it may have been by the insatiable greed of its followers*': Osgood, *The Day of the Cattleman*, pp. 221–2.

p. 280 *The textbooks call it 'ranch fundamentalism'*: Arthur H. Smith and William E. Martin, 'Socioeconomic Behavior of Cattle Ranchers, with Implications for Rural Community Development in the West', *American Journal of Agricultural Economics*, Vol. 54, No. 2 (May, 1972), pp. 217–25.

p. 280 '*…the individual values of their distinctive culture*': Paul F. Starrs, *Let the Cowboy Ride: Cattle Ranching in the American West*, p. 78.

p. 280 …*but only 14 per cent of ranchers sold out*: Skaggs, *Prime Cut*, p. 172.

p. 281 '*…have produced a continuing way of life*': Wallace Stegner and Page Stegner, *American Places*, p. 112.

p. 282 …*shuffling hooves, multiple stomachs and prodigious rear ends*: ibid.; and Jeremy Rifkin, *Beyond Beef: The Rise and Fall of the Cattle Culture*, p. 68.

p. 282 …*to sustain a domestic cat*: Norman Myers and Jennifer Kent, *Perverse Subsidies: How Tax Dollars Can Undercut the Environment and the Economy*, p. 50.

p. 283 …*six hundred acres to keep a single cow going for a year*: *Cornerstone*, January 2002, Vol. 9, Issue 1, Interview: Ben Colvin Stands his Ground – 'about 636 acres per cow per year'.

p. 283 …*2–3,000 gallons per pound of meat*: a comprehensive discussion of this difficult statistic is in John Robbins, '2,500 Gallons All Wet?' at www.earthsave.org

p. 286 …*made from ethanol, tobacco and red pepper*: Robert Dissly, *History of Lewistown*, p. 4.

p. 291 …*almost two-thirds of rural America has lost population since the turn of the twenty-first century*: Steve Jarding and Dave Saunders, *Foxes in the Hen House: How the Republicans Stole the South and the Heartland and What the Democrats Must Do to Run 'em Out*, p. 47.

p. 293 '*…that he would be the leader*': Many Wounds to McWhorter, 1935, detailed in McWhorter, *Hear Me, My Chiefs*.

p. 294 '*Soon we are to be attacked for the last time*': Wottolen to McWhorter, 1926. The McWhorter Papers, Helena.

CHAPTER TEN

p. 297 '*…of our frontier country than any living man*': Robert Wooster, *Nelson A. Miles and the Twilight of the Frontier Army*, p. 90.

p. 298 '*…sending any word to them to surrender*': quoted in Jerome A. Greene, *Nez Perce Summer 1877: The US Army and the Nee-me-poo Crisis*, p. 208.

p. 298 '*...I will do the best I can*': ibid., p. 249.

p. 298 '*...hundreds of thousands*': William F. Zimmer, *Frontier Soldier: An Enlisted Man's Journal, The Sioux and Nez Perce Campaigns 1877*, p. 117.

p. 299 '*Let children eat all wanted!*': reported by Yellow Wolf, McWhorter, *Hear Me, My Chiefs*, p. 133.

p. 299 '*Charge them! Damn them!*': *New York Herald*, 11 October 1877.

p. 299 '*Enemies right on us! Soon the attack!*': reported by Yellow Wolf, McWhorter, *Hear Me, My Chiefs*, p. 133.

p. 299 '*Horses! Horses! Save the horses!*': ibid., p. 144.

p. 300 '*...than any Indians I have ever met*': *New York Herald*, 8 October 1877.

p. 301 '*Cold and dampness all around*': unnamed woman to McWhorter, *Hear Me, My Chiefs*, p. 485.

p. 301 '*...recovering while in the hands of white men*': 'Chief Joseph's Own Story', *North American Review* 128 (April 1879): 412–33.

p. 303 '*...which impressed us very favourably*': Dr Henry R. Tilton, 'After the Nez Perces', *Forest and Stream and Rod and Gun*, December 1877.

p. 304 '*...bravest men on this continent*': 'Brave Jerome: A dashing lieutenant's experiences in Joseph's trenches', *New York Herald*, 30 October 1877.

p. 304 '*...in their rifle pits all the time*': Wetatonmi to McWhorter, *Hear Me, My Chiefs*, p. 486.

p. 307 '*I would trust him with my life*': C. E. S. Wood, *Chicago Tribune*, 25 October 1877.

p. 307 '*We could now talk understandingly*': 'Chief Joseph's Own Story', *North American Review* 128 (April 1879): 412–33.

p. 308 '*And now General Howard says "Let's quit"*': in McWhorter, *Yellow Wolf, His Own Story*, p. 145.

p. 308 '*...or I never would have surrendered*': 'Chief Joseph's Own Story', *North American Review* 128 (April 1879): 412–33.

p. 309 '*I shall fight no more forever*': I have chosen the transcript by C. E. S. Wood favoured by L. V. McWhorter and Alvin M. Josephy, Jr, following their logic that it seems to have had the shortest journey to publication, appearing in *Harper's Weekly* on 17 November 1877.

p. 310 '*All lost, we walked silently on into the wintry night*': Wetatonmi to McWhorter, *Hear Me, My Chiefs*, p. 511.

p. 313 *...the US Army had spent over $900,000*: £931,329.02: Report of the Deputy Quartermaster General to the Secretary of War, 18 December 1877.

p. 313 '*...learn to speak the truth?*': quoted in Chester Fee, *Chief Joseph: The Biography of a Great Indian*, p. 272.

p. 313 '*...like all other murderers*': *Lewiston Teller*, 27 October 1877.

p. 314 '*...to return to Oregon or to Lapwai*': William T. Sherman, Message for the President of the United States, AGO 3464-77, 1st and 2nd Session, 45th Congress.

p. 315 '...*the empire of the Caesars*': Nelson A. Miles, *Personal Recollections and Observations*, p. 51.

p. 316 '...*my people while at Leavenworth*': 'Chief Joseph's Own Story', *North American Review* 128 (April 1879): 412–33.

p. 317 '...*we will be in the ground*': quoted in Merrill D. Beal, '*I Will Fight No More Forever*': *Chief Joseph and the Nez Perce War*, p. 287.

p. 319 '...*the Indian race are waiting and* praying': 'Chief Joseph's Own Story', *North American Review* 128 (April 1879): 412–33.

p. 320 '*The war has changed the prospect*': *Lewiston Teller*, 15 September 1877.

p. 320 '...*would settle upon portions of it and cultivate it*': *Lewiston Teller*, 20 October 1877.

p. 320 '*every year has its dark stain*': Helen Hunt Jackson, *A Century of Dishonor*, p. 337.

p. 321 '*a pocket that aches to be filled with dollars*': Francis Paul Prucha, *Americanizing the American Indian: Writings by the Friends of the Indian, 1880–1900*, p. 334.

p. 323 '*from nations of prosperity to reservations of despair*': The Nez Perce Tribe, *Treaties: Nez Perce Perspectives by the Nez Perce Tribe*, p. 55.

p. 325 '...*and south of the lake, and the Inmaha country*': *Wallowa County Chieftain*, 11 August 1899.

p. 325 '...*he should enjoy the profit of his enterprise*': quoted in Kent Nerburn, *Chief Joseph and the Flight of the Nez Perce*, p. 393.

p. 326 '...*must pass away*': General T. J. Morgan, *Wallowa County Chieftain*, 30 October 1902.

p. 326 '...*die than live the miserable wretches that they are*': *Aberdeen Saturday Pioneer*, 20 December 1890.

p. 327 '*It will be only a few generations before the tribe is extinct*': quoted in Charles Wilkinson, *Blood Struggle: The Rise of the Modern Indian Nations*, p. 55.

CHAPTER ELEVEN

p. 329 '*God really did shed his grace on America, as the song says*': Peggy Noonan, *When Character was King: A Story of Ronald Reagan*, p. 105.

p. 329 ...*sneak a $40,000 tax break*: Lou Cannon, *President Reagan: The Role of a Lifetime*, p. 355.

p. 330 '...*we can count on before the Lord returns*': Robert F. Kennedy, Jr, *Crimes Against Nature: Standing up to Bush and the Kyoto Killers Who are Cashing in on Our World*, p. 26.

p. 330 '*Manifest Destiny is dead*': Karl Hess, Jr, and John A. Baden, *Writers on the Range: Western Writers Exploring the Changing Face of the American West*, p. 16.

p. 330 ...*a mediocre English poem about the Battle of Blenheim*: Joseph Addison, *The Campaign*, 1705.

p. 331 '*Jesus's hand is on the doorknob!*': the 'finest' encapsulation of Hagee's 'thinking' is John Hagee, *Jerusalem Countdown: A Warning to the World*.

p. 331 *'dangerously tolerant'*: *Indian Country Today*, 10 September 2004.

p. 336 *'These guys were a different breed of people. To me, it felt like I was at home'*: while all the other quotes in this section are drawn from my own time with Horace, this quote, which I felt was very important, is drawn from his excellent informal memoirs – Horace Axtell and Margo Aragon, *A Little Bit of Wisdom: Conversations with a Nez Perce Elder*, p. 170.

p. 338 *'...what the world has lost, the world must have again, lest it die'*: John Collier, *Indians of the Americas: The Long Hope*, p. 7.

p. 341 *'a right to choose our own way of life'*: detailed in Charles Wilkinson, *Blood Struggle: The Rise of the Modern Indian Nations*, p. 111.

p. 342 *'...the gradual civilization of the Indians'*: SuAnn M. Reddick and Cary C. Collins, *Medicine Creek to Fox Island: Cadastral Scams and Contested Domains*, pp. 374–97, *Oregon Historical Quarterly*, Fall 2005 Special Issue, *The Isaac Stevens and Joel Palmer Treaties, 1855–2005*, Oregon Historical Society.

p. 342 *'...be the permanent homes of the respective tribes'*: ibid.

p. 343 *'...as long as the water flows in the rivers'*: The Nez Perce Tribe, *Treaties: Nez Perce Perspectives*, and *Oregon Historical Quarterly*, above.

p. 343 *'...recognized as such in treaty and legislation'*: quoted in Wilkinson, *Blood Struggle*, p. 61.

p. 347 *'...their own future lay in the survival of the fish'*: Alvin M. Josephy, *Now That the Buffalo's Gone: A Study of Today's American Indians*, p. 210.

p. 349 *'...he was a seven-hundredth generation fisherman'*: quoted in Dan Landeen and Allen Pinkham, *Salmon and his People: Fish and Fishing in Nez Perce Culture*.

p. 354 *...in 2006, wolves accounted for less than 1 per cent of local sheep and cattle loss*: www.idahowolves.org

p. 354 *...and just one in Canada*: ibid.

p. 354 *'...in favour of wolf reintroduction'*: Martin A. Nie, *Beyond Wolves: The Politics of Wolf Recovery and Management*, p. 67.

p. 366 *...spending more defence dollars in Idaho*: 'Larry Craig's Air Force Antics', *New York Times*, 11 June 2003.

BIBLIOGRAPHY

I'VE LONG HELD the opinion that, for the vast majority of readers, bibliographies serve a purpose not far removed from the libraries in English country house hotels, which have clearly been bought by the yard – they convey a general air of bookishness, but are of little practical use. I therefore thought it might be helpful to highlight a selection of books which, looking back over my research, were the most satisfying experiences, speaking not as a professional researcher, but as an enthusiastic reader. Other works might have offered more scholarly detail, or specific guidance, but if a general reader wished to travel further into some of the issues raised in this book, here, in my view, are some of the most diverting guides.

AUTHOR'S RECOMMENDATIONS

Horace Axtell and Margo Aragon, *A Little Bit of Wisdom: Conversations with a Nez Perce Elder*, Confluence Press, 1997

Merrill D. Beal, *'I Will Fight No More Forever': Chief Joseph and the Nez Perce War*, University of Washington Press, 1963

Jerome A. Greene, *Nez Perce Summer 1877: The US Army and the Nee-me-poo Crisis*, Montana Society Historical Press, 2000

Blaine Harden, *A River Lost: The Life and Death of the Columbia*, Norton, 1996

James Howard Kunstler, The *Geography of Nowhere: The Rise and*

Decline of America's Man-Made Landscape, Touchstone, 1994

Patricia Nelson Limerick, *A Legacy of Conquest: The Unbroken Past of the American West*, Norton, 1987

Richard Manning, *Last Stand: Logging, Journalism and the Case for Humility*, Gibbs Smith, 1991

L. V. McWhorter, *Yellow Wolf, His Own Story, as told to Lucullus Virgil McWhorter*, Caxton Press, 1940

Don Rickey, Jr, *Forty Miles a Day on Beans and Hay*, University of Oklahoma Press, 1963 (life in the Frontier Army)

Anders Stephanson, *Manifest Destiny: American Expansion and the Empire of Right*, Hill and Wang, 1995

David S. Wilcove, *The Condor's Shadow: The Loss and Recovery of Wildlife in America*, Anchor Books, 1999

Cheryl Wilfong, *Following the Nez Perce Trail*, Oregon State University Press, 2006 (a traveller's guide to following the trail)

Charles Wilkinson, *Blood Struggle: The Rise of the Modern Indian Nations*, Norton, 2005

James Wilson, *The Earth Shall Weep*: *A History of Native America*, Grove Press, 1998

WIDER BIBLIOGRAPHY

Stephen E. Ambrose, *Crazy Horse and Custer: The Parallel Lives of Two American Warriors*, Doubleday, 1975

Lewis Atherton, *The Cattle Kings*, Bison Books, 1972

Rocky Barker, *Scorched Earth: How the Fires of Yellowstone Changed America*, Island Press, 2005

José Barreiro and Tim Johnson, eds, *America is Indian Country: Opinions and Perspectives from Indian Country Today*, Fulcrum Publishing, 2005

Grace Bartlett, *The Wallowa Country, 1867–1877*, Ye Galleon Press, 1984

Alice Wondrak Biel, *Do (Not) Feed the Bears: The Fitful History of Wildlife and Tourists in Yellowstone*, University Press of Kansas, 2006

Harvey Blatt, *America's Environmental Report Card: Are We Making the Grade?*, MIT Press, 2005

Cyrus Townsend Brady, LL. D, *Northwestern Fights and Fighters*, Doubleday Page & Company, 1923

C. J. Brosnan, *History of the State of Idaho*, Charles Scribner's Sons, 1918

Bruce Brown, *Mountain in the Clouds: A Search for the Wild Salmon*, Simon & Schuster, 1982

Dee Brown, *Bury My Heart at Wounded Knee: An Indian History of the American West*, Barrie & Jenkins Ltd, 1971

— *The American West*, Touchstone Press, 1995

Mark H. Brown, *The Flight of the Nez Perce: A History of the Nez Perce War*, G. P. Putnam's Sons, 1967

Mike Byrnes, ed., *The Truth About Butte, Through the Eyes of a Radical Unionist*, Old Butte Publishing, 2003

Edgar S. Cahn, *Our Brother's Keeper: The Indian in White America*, New Community Press, 1969

Lou Cannon, *President Reagan: The Role of a Lifetime*, Simon & Schuster, 1991

Alston Chase, *Playing God in Yellowstone: The Destruction of America's First National Park*, Atlantic Monthly Press, 1986

Ward Churchill, *A Little Matter of Genocide: Holocaust and Denial in the Americas, 1492 to the Present*, City Lights Books, 1997

Joseph S. Cone and Sandy Ridlington, eds, *The Northwest Salmon Crisis, A Documentary History*, Oregon State University Press, 1996

Evan S. Connell, *Son of the Morning Star: General Custer and the Battle of the Little Bighorn*, North Point Press, 1984

T. R. Cox, et al., *This Well-Wooded Land: Americans and their Forests from Colonial Times to the Present*, University of Nebraska Press, 1985

Peter Cozzens, *Eyewitnesses to the Indian Wars 1865–1890*, Vol. 2, *The Wars for the Pacific Northwest*, Stackpole Books, 2002

Joseph Crow, *From the Heart of the Crow Country: The Crow Indians' Own Stories*, University of Nebraska Press, 1992

David A. Dary, *The Buffalo Book: The Full Saga of the American Animal*, Ohio University Press, 1974

— *Cowboy Culture: A Saga of Five Centuries*, University Press of Kansas, 1981

Angie Debo, *A History of the Indians of the United States*, University of Oklahoma Press, 1970

Vine Deloria, Jr, *Custer Died For Your Sins: An Indian Manifesto*, University of Oklahoma Press, reprint 1988

— *God Is Red: A Native View of Religion*, North American Press, 1993

— *Red Earth, White Lies: Native Americans and the Myth of the Scientific Fact*, Fulcrum Publishing, 1997

Robert S. Devine, *Bush Versus the Environment*, Anchor Books, 2004

Bernard DeVoto, *The Western Paradox: A Conservation Reader*, containing his *Harper's* columns and unfinished work, Yale University Press, 2001

Jared Diamond, *Guns, Germs, and Steel: The Fates of Human Societies*, Norton, 1997

— *Collapse: How Societies Choose or Fail to Succeed*, Viking Penguin, 2005

Everett Dick, *Tales of the Frontier: From Lewis and Clarke to the Last Roundup*, University of Nebraska Press, 1963

Robert Dissly, *History of Lewistown*, News-Argus Printing, Lewistown, Montana, 2000

Richard Drinnin, *Facing West: The Metaphysics of Indian Hating & Empire Building*, University of Minnesota Press, 1980

Roger Dunsmore, *Earth's Mind: Essays in Native Literature*, University of New Mexico Press, 1997

Jimmie Durham and Simon Ortiz J. Fisher, *The American West: Curated by Richard William Hill and Jimmie Durham*, Compton Verney, 2005

Michael D. Evans, *The American Prophecies: Ancient Scriptures Reveal Our Nation's Future*, Warner Faith, 2004

Chester Fee, *Chief Joseph: The Biography of a Great Indian*, Wilson-Erickson Press, 1936

Janet L. Finn, *Tracing the Veins: Of Copper, Culture and Community from Butte to Chuquicamata*, University of California Press, 1998

Michael Oren Fitzgerald, ed., *Indian Spirit*, World Wisdom, 2003

Donald L. Fixico, *The American Indian Mind in a Linear World: American Indian Studies and Traditional Knowledge*, Routledge, 2003

Tim Flannery, *The Eternal Frontier: An Ecological History of North America and its Peoples*, Heinemann, 2001

Dan Flores, The *Natural West: Environmental History in the Great Plains and the Rocky Mountains*, University of Oklahoma Press, 2001

Jack D. Forbes, ed., *The Indian in America's Past*, Prentice-Hall Inc., 1964

Ian Frazier, *Great Plains*, Picador, 1990

Harry W. Fritz, *Montana, Land of Contrast: An Illustrated History*, American Historical Press, 2001

Michael Frome, *Chronicling the West: Thirty Years of Environmental Writing*, The Mountaineers, 1996

— *Battle for the Wilderness* (revised edition), University of Utah Press, 1997

Eve Marie Garroutte, *Real Indians: Identity and the Survival of Native America*, University of California Press, 2003

C. B. Glasscock, *The War of the Copper Kings*, 1935 (reprint 2002, Riverbend)

Michelle Goldberg, *Kingdom Coming: The Rise of Christian Nationalism*, Norton, 2006

John Steele Gordon, *An Empire of Wealth: The Epic History of American Economic Power*, HarperCollins, 2004

Hester D. Guie and L.V. McWhorter, eds, *Adventures in Geyser*

Land, Caxton Printers, Idaho, 1935

John Hagee, *Jerusalem Countdown: A Warning to the World*, Front Line, 2006

Aubrey L. Haines, *An Elusive Victory: The Battle of the Big Hole*, Falcon Publishing, 1999

Dolores Hayden, *A Field Guide to Sprawl*, Norton, 1994

Karl Hess, Jr, and John A. Baden, *Writers on the Range: Western Writers Exploring the Changing Face of the American West*, University Press of Colorado, 1998

High Country News, *Living in the Runaway West, Partisan Views from Writers on the Range*, Fulcrum Publishing, 2000

Donald M. Hines, *Tales of the Nez Perce*, Ye Galleon Press, 1999

Helen Addison Howard, *Saga of Chief Joseph*, Caxton Printers, Idaho, 1971

Oliver O. Howard, *Nez Perce Joseph*, Lee and Shepherd, 1881

Helen Hunt Jackson, *A Century of Dishonor*, Harper and Brothers, 1881

Steve Jarding and Dave 'Mudcat' Saunders, *Foxes in the Hen House: How the Republicans Stole the South and the Heartland and What the Democrats Must Do to Run 'em Out*, Touchstone Press, 2006

Derrick Jensen and George Draffan, *Railroads and Clearcuts: Legacy of Congress's 1864 Northern Pacific Railroad Land Grant*, Inland Empire Public Lands Council, 1995

— *Strangely Like War: The Global Assault on Forests*, Politics of the Living Books, 2003

Chere Jiusto, *Montana Mainstreets*, Vol. 4, *A Guide to Historic Hamilton*, Montana Historical Society Press, 2000

Alvin M. Josephy, Jr, *The Nez Perce Indians and the Opening of the Northwest*, Yale University Press, 1965

— *Now That the Buffalo's Gone: A Study of Today's American Indians*, University of Oklahoma Press, 1984

— *The Indian Heritage of America*, Houghton Mifflin, 1991

Robert F. Kennedy, Jr, *Crimes Against Nature: Standing up to Bush and the Kyoto Killers Who Are Cashing in on Our World,* Penguin, 2005

Shepard Krech III, *The Ecological Indian: Myth and History,* Norton, 2000

Nancy Langstrom, *Forest Dreams, Forest Nightmares: The Paradox of Old Growth in the Inland West,* University of Washington Press, 1995

Michael L. Lawson, *Damned Indians: The Pick–Sloan Plan and the Missouri River Sioux, 1944–1980,* University of Oklahoma, 1982

Jim Lichatowich, *Salmon Without Rivers: A History of the Pacific Salmon Crisis,* Island Press, 1999

Rush Limbaugh, *The Way Things Ought to Be,* Simon & Schuster, 1992

— *See, I Told You So,* Simon & Schuster, 1994

John MacArthur, *The Second Coming: Signs of Christ's Return and the End of the Age,* Crossway Books, 1999

Donald MacMillan, *Smoke Wars: Anaconda, Copper, Montana Air Pollution and the Courts, 1890–1920,* Montana Society Historical Press, 2000

Michael Malone, *The Battle for Butte: Mining and Politics on the Northern Frontier,* University of Washington Press, 1981

Joel W. Martin, *The Land Looks After Us: A History of Native American Religion,* Oxford University Press, 1999

Peter Mattheissen, *Wildlife in America,* Viking, 1959

John D. McDermott, *Forlorn Hope: The Battle of White Bird Canyon and the Beginning of the Nez Perce War,* Idaho State Historical Society, 1878

Bill McKibben, *The End of Nature,* Random House, 1989

T. C. McLuhan, *Touch the Earth: A Self-Portrait of Indian Existence,* Pocket Books, 1972

L. V. McWhorter, *Hear Me, My Chiefs: Nez Perce Legend & History,* Caxton Press, 1952

Laurie Mercier, *Anaconda: Labor, Community, and Culture in Montana's Smelter City,* University of Illinois Press, 2001

Candy Moulton, *Chief Joseph, Guardian of the People*, Tom Doherty Associates, 2005

Norman Myers and Jennifer Kent, *Perverse Subsidies: How Tax Dollars Can Undercut the Environment and the Economy*, Island Press, 2001

Peter Nabokov and Lawrence Loendorf, *Restoring a Presence: American Indians and Yellowstone National Park*, University of Oklahoma Press, 2004

Kent Nerburn, *Chief Joseph and the Flight of the Nez Perce*, Harper San Francisco, 2005

The Nez Perce Tribe, Treaties: Nez Perce Perspectives, The Nez Perce Tribe, 2003

Martin A. Nie, *Beyond Wolves: The Politics of Wolf Recovery and Management*, University of Minnesota Press, 2003

Peggy Noonan, *When Character was King: A Story of Ronald Reagan*, Viking, 2001

Oregon Historical Quarterly, Fall 2005 Special Issue, *The Isaac Stevens and Joel Palmer Treaties, 1855–2005*, Oregon Historical Society

Ernest Staples Osgood, *The Day of the Cattleman*, University of Chicago Press, 1929

Francis Parkman, Jr, *The California and Oregon Trail*, Putnam, 1849

John Perlin, *A Forest Journey: The Story of Wood and Civilization*, The Countryman Press, 1989

David Petersen, *Heartsblood: Hunting, Spirituality and Wildness in America*, Johnson Books, 2000

Thomas Michael Power, *Lost Landscapes and Failed Economies: The Search for a Value of Place*, Island Place, 1996

Francis Paul Prucha, *Americanizing the American Indian: Writings by the Friends of the Indian, 1880–1900*, University of Nebraska Press, 1978

Robert D. Putnam, *Bowling Alone: The Collapse and Revival of American Community*, Simon & Schuster, 2000

Marc Reisner, *Cadillac Desert: The American West and its Disappearing Water*, Viking, 1986

Kent D. Richards, *Isaac I. Stevens, Young Man in a Hurry*, Washington State University Press, 1993

Jeremy Rifkin, *Beyond Beef: The Rise and Fall of the Cattle Culture*, Dutton, 1992

Don Russell, *The Lives and Legends of Buffalo Bill*, University of Oklahoma Press, 1960

H. Minar Shoebotham, *Anaconda: Life of Marcus Daly, the Copper King*, Stackpole Publishing, 1956

Earl Shorris, *The Death of the Great Spirit: An Elegy for the American Indian*, Simon & Schuster, 1971

Jimmy M. Skaggs, *Prime Cut: Livestock Raising and Meatpacking in the United States, 1607–1983*, Texas A&M University Press, 1986

Henry Nash Smith, *Virgin Land: The American West as Symbol and Myth*, Vintage, 1950

Roberta Beed Sollid, *Calamity Jane*, Western Press, 1958

James Gustave Speth, *Red Sky at Morning: America and the Crisis of the Global Environment*, Yale University Press, 2004

Paul F. Starrs, *Let the Cowboy Ride: Cattle Ranching in the American West*, Johns Hopkins University Press, 2000

David Stiller, *Wounding the West: Montana, Mining and the Environment*, University of Nebraska Press, 2000

Cal Thomas and Ed Dobson, *Blinded by Might: Can the Religious Right Save America?*, Zondervan Publishing, 1999

Alexis de Tocqueville, *Democracy in America*, Appendix U, Volume II, 1840

Jane Tompkins, *West of Everything: The Inner Life of Westerns*, Oxford University Press, 1992

K. Ross Toole, *Montana: An Uncommon Land*, University of Oklahoma Press, 1959

— *Twentieth-Century Montana: A State of Extremes*, University of Oklahoma Press, 1972

William E. Unrau, *White Man's Wicked Water: The Alcohol Trade and Prohibition in Indian Country, 1802–1892*, University Press of Kansas, 1996

Robert M. Utley and Wilcomb E. Washburn, *Indian Wars*, American Heritage, 1977

Deward E. Walker, Jr, and Daniel N. Matthews, *Nez Perce Coyote Tales*, University of Oklahoma Press, 1998

Dave Walter, ed., *Speaking Ill of the Dead: Jerks in Montana History*, Two Dot Books, 2000

Geoffrey C. Ward, *The West*, Back Bay, 1999

Paul I. Wellman, *The Trampling Herd: The Story of the Cattle Range in America*, J. B. Lippincott, 1939

George Weurthner and Mollie Matteson, eds, *Welfare Ranching: The Subsidized Destruction of the American West*, Island Press, 2002

Lee H. Whittlesey, *Death in Yellowstone: Accidents and Foolhardiness in the First National Park*, Roberts Rinehart, 1995

Lawrence M. Woods, *British Gentlemen in the Wild West: The Era of the Intensely English Cowboy*, The Free Press, 1990

Robert Wooster, *Nelson A. Miles and the Twilight of the Frontier Army*, University of Nebraska Press, 1993

David M. Wrobel, *Promised Lands: Promotion, Memory and the Creation of the American West*, University Press of Kansas, 2002

William F. Zimmer, *Frontier Soldier: An Enlisted Man's Journal, The Sioux and Nez Perce Campaigns 1877*, Montana Historical Society Press, 1998

A NOTE ON ORIGINAL SOURCES

The following newspaper archives offered the most illuminating commentary on the issues of the day, plus first-hand testimonies and reproductions of official correspondence: *Lewiston Teller, Idaho County Free Press, Weekly Missoulian, Deer Lodge New North West, Butte Miner*. There was also relevant content in the *Portland Oregonian, Oregonian Telegram, San Francisco Chronicle, The*

Mountain Sentinel, *Walla Walla Watchman*, *Helena Weekly Independent* and *San Francisco Examiner*. The key newspapers for contemporary research, and the invaluable assistance of their journalists, were the *Wallowa County Chieftain*, *Lewiston Morning Tribune*, *Ravalli Republic*, the *Missoulian* and the *Billings Gazette*.

Two endeavours to anthologize the available first-hand accounts of the Nez Perce flight are both invaluable – Peter Cozzens' *Eyewitnesses to the Indian Wars*, Vol. 2, and Cyrus T. Brady's *Northwestern Fights and Fighters*. Of course, the primary debt of gratitude for securing Nez Perce first-hand accounts goes to Lucullus Virgil McWhorter, who transcribed the narratives of Yellow Wolf, Eelahweemah, Eloosykasit, Penahwenonmi, Owyeen, Wetatonmi, Red Elk, Pahit Palikt, Kowtolik, Samuel Tilden and others. His efforts are visible in his two works, *Yellow Wolf* and *Hear Me, My Chiefs*, and in the McWhorter Papers Collection at Washington State University Library. Further original sources of particular interest are listed below.

Harry L. Bailey, 'An Infantryman in the Nez Perce War of 1877', Lucullus McWhorter Collection, Washington State University

Henry Buck, 'The Story of the Nez Perce Campaign During the Summer of 1877', *Great Falls Tribune*, 24 December 1944–11 February 1945

John B. Catlin, 'The Battle of the Big Hole', Society of Montana Pioneers, Historians Annual Report, 1927

Harry J. Davis, 'An Incident in the Nez Perce Campaign', Journal of the Military Service Institution of the United States, May–June 1905

John Gibbon, 'The Battle of the Big Hole', *Harper's Weekly*, 28 December 1895

Theodore W. Goldin, 'A Pleasure Ride in Montana', *Ours, a Military Magazine*, November 1887

Oliver O. Howard, 'The True Story of the Wallowa Campaign', *North American Review* 128 (July 1879): 53–64

Charles N. Loynes, 'From Fort Fizzle to the Big Hole', Winners of the West, March 1925

'Brave Jerome, A dashing lieutenant's experiences in Joseph's trenches', *New York Herald*, 30 October 1877

'Chief Joseph's Own Story', *North American Review* 128 (April 1879): 412–33

Duncan MacDonald's stories in the *Deer Lodge New North West*, 26 July 1878–28 March 1879

Edwin Mason, Letters, MSS 80, Montana Historical Society, Helena MT

William R. Parnell, 'The Nez Perce War, 1877: Battle of White Bird Canyon', *United Service*, October 1889: 364–74

John P. Schorr, 'The White Bird Fight', *Winners of the West*, February 1929

Thomas A. Sutherland, *Howard's Campaign Against the Nez Perce Indians* (A. G. Walling, 1878)

Dr Henry R. Tilton, 'After the Nez Perces', *Forest and Stream and Rod and Gun*, December 1877

Melville C. Wilkinson, 'Origins of the Difficulties with the Nez Perces', *Army and Navy Journal*, 18 August 1877

Luther P. Wilmot, Narratives of the Nez Perce War, Special Collections, University of Idaho Library, Moscow

C. E. S. Wood, *Chicago Tribune*, 25 October 1877

Major H. Clay Wood, *The Status of Young Joseph and his Band of Nez Perce Indians* (Assistant Adjutant Generals' Office, Portland, 1876)

Charles A. Woodruff, 'The Battle of the Big Hole', Contributions to the Historical Society of Montana, 1910

ACKNOWLEDGEMENTS

DURING THE TIME I spent travelling the Northwest for this book, I was offered help, advice, information, and, on occasion, room and board by a litany of guardian angels, whose generosity, patience and hospitality made this endeavour possible. Within the Nez Perce tribe, government and historical community, I would particularly like to thank Horace and Andrea Axtell, and their wonderful friend Margo Aragon; Kevin Peters and his colleagues at the Nez Perce National Historical Park Museum in Spalding; Robert West at the Bear Paw Battlefield; Rebecca Miles and the Nez Perce legal team in Wallowa and Lapwai; Brian Connor and the organizing committee at Tamkaliks, and the staff and volunteers at the Wallowa Band Nez Perce Trail Interpretive Center in Wallowa, Soy Redthunder, James Lawyer, Clifford Allen, Nancy LookingGlass, Allen Slickpoo; the organizing committee of the Chief Looking Glass Days; finally, Fritz Minthorn and Clutch Johnson. If any member of the Nez Perce community is aggrieved at my retelling of their ancestral history, I can only say that I approached the story with the humility of an outsider, and claim absolutely no status as a spokesman, interpreter or advocate. As a demonstration of my ongoing commitment to the tribe's future, I have pledged to support the current development of a Nez Perce presence in the Wallowa Valley; should any reader feel inspired to do the same, details can be found at www.wallownez perce.org.

It's also a worthy tradition that writers who tackle the history of the Nez Perce retreat acknowledge their debt to the men whose efforts to capture the memories of the participants laid the foundation for all future scholarship: L. V. McWhorter and in particular Alvin M. Josephy, a man whose tireless revelation of injustice sets a towering standard.

The staff of numerous libraries, historical societies and museums were also a great help in sourcing original documents and tracking down local descendants – particularly in Oregon, in the Pioneer Museum, Elgin, the Tamastslikt Cultural Institute, Pendleton, the Oregon Trail Museum, Baker City, and the Historical Society, Joseph; in Idaho, in the Timber Industry Museum, Pierce, the Lewis-Clark State College and the Nez Perce County Museum, Lewiston, the White Bird Library, the Wolf Education and Research Center, the Grangeville library and archives, Idaho Falls archives; in Montana, the Butte Municipal Archives, the Museum of Mining, the University of Montana in Missoula, Montana State University in Billings, the Rocky Mountain Elk Foundation, the Fort Missoula Museum, the Big Hole National Battlefield, the Montana State Historical Society, Helena, the Daly Mansion, the Lolo Trail Center, the Ravalli County Museum, Hamilton, Montana State University-Northern in Havre, and the Lewistown Local Historical Society.

Personal interviewees, guides, advisers and conversers also deserve special mention. Local newspaper journalists were unfailingly helpful and tolerant, allowing me to plunder their contacts books, clippings files and anecdotes – particularly Cory Wicks at the *Wallowa County Chieftain*, Jim Fisher and Bill Hall at the *Lewiston Morning Tribune* (and their many sparring partners at the Yo Espresso coffee shack), Perry Backus at the *Missoulian* and Jim Gransbery at the *Billings Gazette*. I'm also indebted to Jeff Sayre, Senator Larry Craig's Regional Director, the senator himself, Gary Lane of Wapiti River

Guides, the organizers of the Pierce 1860 Days, Liam and Millie in Joseph, John Lenahan, Al Marshall, Almon Randall, Ace Burton, Jim Miller and family, Stewart Brandborg, Larry 'The Mushroom Guy' Evans, Bob Scott, Shirley Smith, Henry 'Sarge' Old Horn, Mike Smith, Luke, Ely and John of Harlowton, Bob Lee and the inspirational Matt Koehler and Jeanette Russell. I'm painfully aware that there is so much more expertise that I didn't have the chance to tap, but look forward to having any errors within this text pointed out – errors which are, of course, entirely my own. I'd also finally like to acknowledge the rural Northwest's most reliable sources of local knowledge, contacts and family histories – its diner waitresses; and to take the opportunity to remind Britons that our international reputation as poor tippers is a stain we'd do well to eradicate.

I'd also like to thank Vicky Tebbs, Christine Walker and William Drew for allowing me to learn to write on the pages of their publications, my editor at HarperCollins, Richard Johnson, for his effortless calm, and the painstaking work of Richard Collins as line editor. My agent, Kevin Conroy Scott, made all this possible – and due to his impressively quixotic career I also owe a debt to his colleagues at Conville & Walsh, AP Watt and now his own shop, Tibor Jones.

Finally, I'd like to credit the family and friends who've patiently asked me the same polite question for the past two years – the book is coming along fine, thanks – and one woman in particular who lost patience and shouted at me, three years ago, that maybe I should stop whingeing and just write that damn idea I'd always talked about. To Harriet, all my love and an acknowledgement that you were, as usual, quite right.

INDEX